FOOD
Preparation
and Theory

FOOD
Preparation and Theory

Eva Medved

Kent State University

Prentice-Hall, Inc. Englewood Cliffs, New Jersey 07632

Library of Congress Cataloging in Publication Data

MEDVED, EVA.
   Food: preparation and theory.

   Bibliography: p.
   Includes index.
   1. Food—Analysis. 2. Cookery. I. Title.
TX535.M44 1986   641   84-26426
ISBN 0-13-323064-3

Editorial/production supervision
  and interior design: Dee Amir Josephson
Cover design: Lundgren Graphics Ltd.
Cover photo: USDA
Manufacturing buyer: Harry Baisley

Printed in the United States of America

10 9 8 7 6 5 4 3 2 1

ISBN 0-13-323064-3   01

Prentice-Hall International (UK) Limited, *London*
Prentice-Hall of Australia Pty. Limited, *Sydney*
Editora Prentice-Hall do Brasil, Ltda., *Rio de Janeiro*
Prentice-Hall Canada Inc., *Toronto*
Prentice-Hall Hispanoamericana, S.A., *Mexico*
Prentice-Hall of India Private Limited, *New Delhi*
Prentice-Hall of Japan, Inc., *Tokyo*
Prentice-Hall of Southeast Asia Pte. Ltd., *Singapore*
Whitehall Books Limited, *Wellington, New Zealand*

CONTENTS

PREFACE

Food: Preparation and Theory offers a comprehensive presentation of basic principles and techniques involved in food preparation and was designed for beginning college classes in food study. The overall objective is to promote an understanding of the factors that influence foods and the changes which occur in foods during preparation. Concepts are presented as accurately and completely as present knowledge permits, yet concisely. Students will gain a basic understanding of why foods respond as they do in preparation and processing.

An overview of content, key words, and goals introduce each chapter. A summary, self-study guide, and suggested readings conclude each chapter. The first chapter gives recognition to the beginning of cookery, offers an introduction to food study, and views food preparation as a science and an art. Food safety, food preparation essentials, and food assessment are addressed in individual chapters. The components of food, their specific nature and behavior during preparation, and microwave cookery are presented in the chapters to follow.

A mastery of the principles and techniques of food preparation presented allows production of nutritious, palatable and aesthetically pleasing foods; and promotes individual and professional advantages.

FOOD
Preparation
and Theory

1

FOOD STUDY

OBJECTIVES

When you complete this chapter, you will be able to

1. Identify and begin to apply the objectives of food preparation.
2. Explain how palatability of foods is maintained.
3. List factors that influence nutrient retention during food preparation.
4. Give examples of ways to include variety in meals.
5. Explain how food preparation contributes to food safety.
6. Discuss the influence of food preparation on digestibility of food.
7. Explain the difference between food preparation as an art and as a science, and give examples.
8. Explain how traditional foods can be integrated with new food products and give examples.

The cooking of food began at least four hundred thousand years ago. Evidence comes from an ancient cave near Peking, China, where remnants of charred bones were discovered. Cooking is the oldest and most common method of processing food. By accident or design, primitive hunters learned to tend a fire and use it to roast meat. Although roasting meat before an open fire was a crude method of cooking, it was still a great technical innovation. Roasting softened the meat, improved its flavor, and slowed the rate of spoilage. By the beginning of recorded history, cooking had been adapted to a variety of foods, and the foundation had been laid for the basic cookery techniques of today.

(New York Public Library Picture Collection)

Although some of our methods of food preparation originated thousands of years ago, the understanding of exactly what the cooking process does to food is relatively new. We now know that chemical effects of cooking vary from food to food—boiling a potato and boiling meat cause different reactions.

Foods are mixtures of complex chemical molecules, and like all other chemical substances they can be involved in a variety of reactions, some of which influence their chemical and/or physical character. Many techniques used in food preparation induce significant changes in food. The study of food is concerned with the relation and nature of specific food components and the behavior of those components during food preparation. Many factors and principles related to food preparation have been identified, but there is still much to be learned.

FOOD-PREPARATION OBJECTIVES

The wide variety of food-preparation techniques are applied to foods available in numerous forms. Even though the number and forms of food continue to change, the basic objectives of food preparation remain virtually constant and include: (1) palatability, (2) variety, (3) safety, (4) digestibility, and (5) nutrient retention.

Palatability

The flavor, texture, size and shape, color, temperature, and arrangement of food contribute appetite appeal. The degree to which these characteristics are maintained or altered can be controlled by the preparation techniques employed.

The flavor of food may be maintained, diminished, or enhanced. The original flavor is maintained best when the cooking time is short and no seasonings are incorporated. Often, however, variations building upon the original flavor are desired, and seasonings and a variety of other ingredients may be added as enhancements; blending of these flavors is achieved by using an extended cooking period.

The textures of food can be maintained or altered beneficially by selecting appropriate preparation techniques and performing them well. Not only does cooking modify the texture of most foods, but it may alter size and shape.

Cooking techniques can maintain or change the original food color. Generally, dry-heat methods promote browning, as in baked products and meats, whereas moist-heat methods tend to maintain or diminish the characteristic food color. The effect of preparation techniques on color is especially apparent in fruit and vegetable products. Regardless of the method used, overcooked foods develop less desirable flavor, texture, and shape than foods cooked to the fork-tender stage.

Variety

Variety is one of the keys to successful meals, and the use of more than one cookery method results in menus with eye and palate appeal. For instance, the crispness of raw fruits and vegetables complements the soft texture of simmered fruits or boiled vegetables; crisp fried chicken contrasts pleasingly with the smoothness of a stuffed baked potato. Similarly, variety in shape, size, and color is fundamental to achieving maximum appeal.

Safety

Techniques of food preparation contribute to the safety of foods. The health and personal habits of those handling food are important aspects of food safety. Storage conditions, especially temperatures, need to be controlled carefully to minimize growth of microorganisms. Safety is enhanced through the use of proper procedures to ensure that the temperature reached in most foods during preparation is sufficiently elevated to destroy harmful microorganisms, thus preventing foodborne illness. Special care must be taken during the handling of food to avoid cross-contamination between raw and cooked foods.

Digestibility

The cooking process may be used to improve the digestibility of some foods. The structure of foods such as fruits, vegetables, and cereal products is softened during cooking, facilitating digestive action. During cooking, gentle heat may effect changes in proteins that enhance their digestibility.

Nutrient Retention

Nutrient retention should be of primary concern when foods are prepared. The method of preparation, quantity of water, and duration of cooking all influence it. Food preparation that increases the area of cut surfaces promotes loss of water-soluble nutrients and those susceptible to oxidation. Large quantities of water can leach out water-soluble nutrients. Prolonged heating or very high temperature may also increase nutrient losses.

A SCIENCE AND AN ART

Food preparation is both science and art. The **science** of food is concerned with the specific components of food, their interaction, and the influence of temperature, light, and air on palatability. The **art** of food preparation gives recognition to the aesthetic and cultural aspects of food.

Artistic talents with foods can be expressed through pleasing color combinations and variety in size and shape. Seasonings and food combinations may be used to accent flavor, and a combination of textures adds interest. Outstanding food-preparation and service skills can be developed so that one becomes an artist with food.

Cultural patterns of food are very near and dear to the hearts of all of us. Culture influences food choices, food combinations, service, and food traditions. Each culture gives its own unique value to food, its use, and its service.

The science of food.

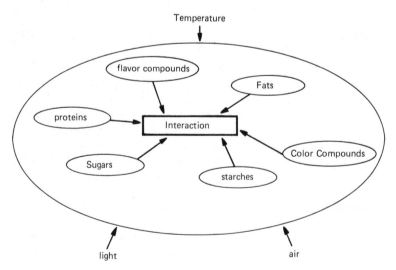

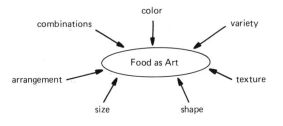

Food as art.

CHALLENGE

Research in food science and **technology** has resulted in improvement of traditional foods and creation of many new food items, adding interest to food preparation and meal planning. This growing variety, however, contributes to the consumer's decision-making dilemma. The challenge is to develop food-selection and preparation patterns that are nutritionally, aesthetically, culturally, economically, and personally satisfying and to fit these patterns to time available, preparation skill, and preparation equipment available.

SUMMARY

Even with the ever increasing variety of foods available, the basic objectives of food preparation continue to include palatability, variety, safety, digestibility, and nutrient retention. Food preparation as a science concerns the components of food, their interaction, and the influence of added ingredients. The art of food preparation recognizes the cultural, aesthetic, and creative aspects of food. The challenge is to develop patterns of food preparation that meet individual or family needs and expectations.

All foods are mixtures of chemical compounds and undergo various chemical reactions during their preparation for consumption. The components of food, their specific nature, and their behavior during preparation will be discussed in the chapters to follow.

SELF-STUDY GUIDE

1. List five objectives of food preparation and discuss each briefly.
2. How is the palatability of food maintained during preparation?
3. List three factors that influence nutrient retention during cooking and discuss each briefly.
4. Give examples of ways to incorporate variety into meals.
5. List four techniques of food preparation that contribute to food safety.
6. How does cooking influence digestibility of foods?

7. When is food preparation classed as an art; as a science? Give two examples for each.
8. Identify three factors to consider when new food products are integrated with traditional foods. Give two examples.

SUGGESTED READINGS

AHEA. *Handbook of food preparation.* 8th ed. Washington, D.C.: American Home Economics Association, 1980.

AURAND, L. W., and WOOD, A. E. *Food chemistry.* Westport, Conn.: Avi Publishing Company, 1973.

BIRCH, G., and PARKER, K. *Food and health: science and technology.* Philadelphia: International Ideas, 1980.

CHARLEY, H. *Food science.* 2nd ed. New York: John Wiley and Sons, 1982.

GUETHRIE, R. K. *Food sanitation.* 2nd ed. Westport, Conn.: Avi Publishing Company, 1980.

JARVIS, W. T. Food quackery is dangerous business. *Nutrition News,* February/March 1980.

JOHNSON, O. C. Nutritional quality in formulated foods. *Journal of the American Oil Chemists' Society* 49:215, 1972.

RITCHIE, CARSON. *Food in civilization.* New York: Beaufort Books, 1981.

ROBERTS, H. R. *Food safety.* New York: John Wiley and Sons, 1981.

SEBRELL, JR., W. H.; HAGGERTY, J.; and the editors of *Life. Food and nutrition.* New York: Time, Inc., 1967.

SIPE, M. and SAX, I. *Food style: The art of presenting food beautifully.* Chap. 2, "Food Styling." New York: Crown Publishers, 1982.

TODHUNTER, E. N. Food is more than nutrients. *Food and Nutrition News.* National Live Stock and Meat Board 43, no. 607, 1982.

U.S. DEPARTMENT OF AGRICULTURE. *Agriculture USA.* Washington, D.C.: Government Printing Office, 1979.

————. *Conserving the nutritive values in foods.* Home and Garden Bulletin no. 90. Washington, D.C.: Government Printing Office, 1980.

————. *Food.* Home and Garden Bulletin no. 228. Washington, D.C.: Government Printing Office, 1980.

————. Nationwide food consumption survey results. *Family Economic Review.* Washington, D.C.: Government Printing Office, spring 1980.

————. and U.S. DEPARTMENT OF HEALTH, EDUCATION AND WELFARE. *Nutrition and your health: Dietary guidelines for Americans.* Washington, D.C.: Government Printing Office, 1980.

————. *Your money's worth in foods.* Home and Garden Bulletin no. 183. Washington, D.C.: Government Printing Office, 1979.

————. *What's to eat? the 1979 yearbook of agriculture.* Washington, D.C.: Government Printing Office, 1979.

WASON, B. *Cooks, gluttons and gourmets: A history of cookery.* Garden City, N.Y.: Doubleday, 1962.

2

FOOD SAFETY

OBJECTIVES

When you complete this chapter, you will be able to

1. List and discuss the causes of foodborne illness.

2. Explain how food poisoning and infection can be controlled.

3. Identify foods susceptible to growth and spread of botulism, salmonella, staph and strep bacteria, and the parasite trichinella.

4. Explain and practice desirable personal habits during food preparation.

5. Identify and explain the microbiological aspects of food preparation.

6. List and discuss the factors involved in maintaining food safety.

Food safety emphasizes the reduction of risk—the elimination insofar as possible of hazards to the soundness and wholesomeness of food. Primitive humans ate the food that could be found and gambled on its safety. Today's food is carefully monitored at every step on its way to the consumer. Federal, state, and local governments and the food industry scrutinize the progress of food from farms to consumers. This scrutinizing activity provides for the United States a food supply with an excellent safety record.

Our habits and practices with food also contribute to its safety, from the time of purchase through its storage, preparation, service, and cleanup. Sanitary food handling prevents unnecessary spoilage and promotes safety. This chapter is

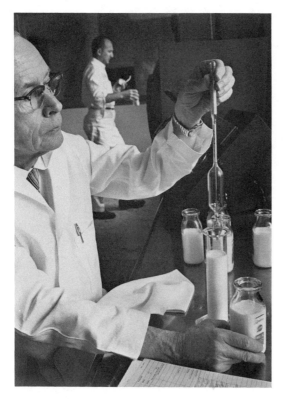

Testing milk (Joe Munroe, Photo Researchers, Inc.)

concerned with the control of foodborne illnesses and other hazards associated with food.

FOOD HAZARDS

Hazards associated with food include natural **toxins, foodborne illness,** and substances incidentally introduced as food moves from the farm to the table. The hazards of foodborne illness and natural toxins can be minimized, with the help of the food industry and government. Both industry and government strive to maintain the nutritional and overall eating quality of foods and to eliminate or reduce the hazards.

NATURAL TOXINS IN FOODS

Although poisonous varieties of mushrooms are a well-known example of toxic plants, natural toxicants in food tend to be unfamiliar to many. Some foods of plant and animal origin contain natural toxins that produce discomfort and death.

Inspecting prunes (Ray Ellis, Photo Researcher, Inc.)

Allergens present in chocolate, cow's milk, eggs, wheat, and assorted other foods have caused severe symptoms in numbers of persons and may require dietary modification. One such allergen is *oxalic acid,* a component of beet tops, rhubarb greens, and spinach. In large quantities these greens may be responsible for oxalic acid poisoning in some individuals. Carrots, celery, and nutmeg contain *myristicin* a potentially fatal hallucinogen. *Solanine* is a toxin normally present in trace amounts in white potato. Potatoes exposed to light may develop a green color in the skin or directly under the skin. In addition to chlorophyll, this green tissue may contain more than the trace amounts of solanine and should be removed before the potato is cooked. Some seafoods may contain a poisonous *alkaloid.* Cheese is a rich source of *tryamine,* a pressor amine that tends to raise blood pressure.

Poisoning from natural toxins in food is rare. When foods containing toxins are consumed in appropriate amounts as a part of a varied diet, our metabolic mechanisms can handle them. Many foods contain small amounts of components that can be toxic if eaten in excess, but these potential toxins, in amounts usually eaten, have not been shown to be toxic.

FOODBORNE ILLNESS

Foods can cause illness when they contain disease-producing agents, either microorganisms or toxins. The major classes of foodborne illness are botulism, perfringens, salmonella, and staphylococcus infections. These illnesses are due to infection or intoxication, which result from **microbial** activity. **Food infection** occurs when foods contaminated with infectious microorganisms are eaten. **Food intoxication** occurs when foods eaten contain toxins produced by microorganisms.

Bacterial contamination of food continues to be a much greater problem than chemical contamination and accounts for a majority of foodborne illnesses. Disease caused by bacteria or a virus may be contracted from contaminated food. Some persons who do not contract the disease themselves can be carriers of the disease organism. During preparation and handling of food, these human **carriers** may contaminate the food. For this reason, health examinations are required of individuals working with foods in restaurants, hospitals, and other public facilities.

Bacteria are responsible for a high proportion of foodborne illness. How rapidly bacteria will multiply in food depends upon the presence of conditions favorable for their growth. Bacteria can exist in a dormant state on dry foods. Such foods, however, lack the moisture required for bacterial growth and are unlikely to cause foodborne illness because only a small number of bacteria are present. All bacteria require nutrients, moisture, and favorable temperature for growth. Most harmful bacteria in food thrive at room and body temperature while their growth is inhibited at lower temperatures of the refrigerator and freezer.

Each bacterium has an optimum temperature and moisture level for maximum growth. Some bacteria will thrive at refrigerator temperature, others at a temperature as low as 15° F (−9° C). Even small differences in food-storage temperatures may encourage the growth of different microorganisms that cause various changes in the food.

Bacteria have specific requirements for oxygen or air, acidity or alkalinity. Bacteria that require air are classed as aerobic; those that grow better in the absence of air are known as anaerobic. Some bacteria may thrive in either aerobic or anerobic conditions. Some bacteria also grow best in low-acid foods, others in neutral or acid foods.

Botulism

Botulism poisoning tends to be rare, but it can be fatal. Clostridium botulinum is a spore-forming bacterium that is very resistant to heat and produces a deadly toxin, a protein in nature. Small doses of the toxin cause illness by paralyzing respiratory muscles, which may result in death.

The bacterium itself is not harmful since it does not multiply or produce its toxin in the digestive tracts of humans. The botulism organism does multiply and produce a toxin in anaerobic (without oxygen) situations, for instance, under the surface of foods and in sealed containers. The absence of free air makes canned and vacuum-packed foods ideal media for growth of this organism. Clostridium botulinum is intolerant of acid. It is active in low-acid food over a wide range of temperatures.

Most cases of botulism result from improperly processed home-canned foods. Signs of botulism appear twelve to thirty-six hours after contaminated food has been eaten. Symptoms include speech difficulty, double vision, inability to swallow, and progressive paralysis of respiratory system.

Commercially canned foods are rarely responsible for botulism, since they are processed at higher temperatures than are normally achieved during home canning. Home canners should process all low-acid foods such as vegetables (except high-acid tomatoes), meat, and poultry in a pressure canner at the appropriate pressure level for the recommended time.

Questions have arisen about the danger of botulism in the new low-acid varieties of tomatoes. Research shows risk of botulism is slight when firm, ripe tomatoes free from spoilage are used, and when the recommended processing time for boiling-water baths or pressure canners is observed.

Botulism contamination does not cause a change in the color or appearance of food. The USDA Food Safety and Inspection Service stresses the following precautions in using all home-canned vegetables, meat, and poultry: Bring the food to a rolling boil; then cover the pan and continue boiling for at least ten minutes before tasting. The toxin produced by clostridium botulism, but not the organism, can be destroyed by boiling the food as indicated.

Perfringens Infection

Perfringens infections cause discomfort but are rarely fatal. Symptoms include diarrhea and abdominal cramps and appear four to twenty-two hours after ingestion of contaminated foods. Clostridium perfringens is found in food, soil, sewage, and dust and in the intestinal tracts of warm-blooded animals and humans. It produces a substance toxic to the gastrointestinal tract. The bacteria may survive during cooking of food and grow when conditions are favorable. The spores produced vary greatly in their resistance to heat. The main foods associated with Perfringens infection are meats, poultry, and gravies. This illness often strikes large groups of people who have eaten in a particular restaurant, at a picnic, or at some other quantity-food operation. Usually precooked meats have been held for long periods at improper temperatures on warming equipment or steam tables.

Perfringens infections and illness are avoided by (1) cooking meat properly and maintaining temperatures above 140° F (60° C) during holding and serving; (2) refrigerating meat and meat products prepared in advance of serving and keeping it cold; (3) not allowing meat to stand for long periods for slicing as needed; (4) refrigerating sliced meats and cold cuts at 40° F (4° C) or below and serving them cold; (5) keeping slicers, knives, and cutting boards meticulously clean.

Salmonella

Salmonella-caused infections bring discomfort and distress but are rarely fatal. The sources of salmonellae are varied and include household pets and other domesticated animals and human carriers. The organism is commonly found in raw meats, poultry, eggs, fish, and dairy foods and in products made from them.

Salmonella can contaminate food during production, handling, or storage. Extreme care must be exercised to avoid cross contamination by maintaining slicers, knives, and cutting boards meticulously clean. The bacteria grow rapidly at room temperature but do not produce toxins or spores. They do not grow rapidly in the refrigerator, and they are destroyed by pasteurization temperatures. Eggs are pasteurized before freezing or drying to destroy any salmonella present.

Protein-containing foods provide a favorable medium for growth of salmonella. Contaminated food may smell, taste, and look normal. When the food is eaten, the salmonella organisms multiply and cause irritation in the gastrointestinal tract, producing nausea, vomiting, abdominal cramps and pain, diarrhea, and fever. Symptoms usually appear within twenty-four hours after eating contaminated food, and recovery takes two to four days.

Salmonella contamination can be prevented by (1) avoiding excess handling of food; (2) thoroughly cooking food or reheating leftovers; and (3) maintaining food at temperatures below 40° F (5° C) or above 140° F (60° C).

Staphylococcus Poisoning

A severe case of staphylococcus poisoning can be extremely unpleasant but is rarely fatal. Symptoms usually occur twenty-four to forty-eight hours after eating contaminated food and include diarrhea, vomiting, and abdominal pain. The bacteria themselves may be ingested with no illness as long as toxin is not produced. As staphylococcus bacteria multiply, they produce a toxin that resists destruction by boiling, baking, or other common cooking procedures. Controlled high temperatures for a specified time are necessary to destroy the toxin. When food containing staphylococcus toxin is ingested, food intoxication or food poisoning occurs. Staphylococcus poisoning is relatively common.

Staphylococcus organisms are found in the respiratory tract and on the skin of humans and animals. Skin eruptions and infected wounds are abundant sources of the bacteria. The bacteria may enter the food during handling or from contact with a contaminated surface. Foods exposed to a great deal of handling in preparation are especially susceptible to contamination.

This poisoning is relatively easily controlled by strict rules of personal hygiene (hand washing). Food handling should be avoided when nose, throat, or skin infections exist. Foods not consumed should be cooled immediately to 40° F (4° C) or cooler unless they are kept hot 140° F (60° C). The organisms grow well at room temperature. Their toxin is heat resistant, is not destroyed when foods are heated, and may be present even after boiling for an hour.

Staphylococcus bacteria grow in a wide variety of food, often on foods high in protein: meats, poultry, and egg products; in salads containing tuna, chicken, ham, egg, potato, or macaroni; in sandwich fillings; and in cream-filled pastries and pies. Staphylococcus bacteria grow best in foods kept at 70 to 97° F (21 to 36° C); the toxin is produced in significant amounts in the temperature range of 64 to 115° F (18 to 46° C).

Streptococcus Infection

Streptococci bacteria are widespread and cause illness only when present in large numbers. They do not produce spores or toxins and are easily destroyed by boiling. Protein foods should be heated thoroughly to destroy the bacteria. Refrigeration inhibits their growth, and sanitary handling practices should prevent recontamination.

Molds

Molds use a variety of substances for food. They usually require oxygen, a temperature of 68 to 95° F (20 to 35° C), moisture, and a pH ranging from 2.0 to 8.5 for growth. Some molds grow at refrigerator temperatures, but boiling temperatures readily destroy molds and their spores. The spores spread easily through the air and, under favorable conditions, grow on sweet foods, meats, cured meats, cheese, milk, fresh fruit and vegetables, breads, and cereal products. They produce a fuzzy appearance on foods and may be of various colors—blue, gray, green, orange, or white.

Molds growing on raw cereal grains and nut meats may produce toxins that cause illness and death in animals. Some molds produce mycotoxins, which are now recognized as a health hazard, for example, aflatoxin, the toxin produced by aspargillus flavus. Some molds, on the other hand, are useful in food production. For example, they contribute a characteristic flavor to some cheeses during ripening (Camembert, blue, Roquefort) and are used commercially to produce enzymes such as amylases for bread making.

Parasites

Although parasites are widespread in foods in some areas of the world, in the United States trichinella spiralis, a roundworm found in pork, is by far the most common one. It is transmitted through raw or undercooked pork. The worm can mature and reproduce in the human intestinal tract during the first stage of infection. It then migrates to various other areas of the body and forms cysts within the muscles. The disease is characterized by fever, chills, profuse sweating, muscular pain, and edema around the eyes, and the heart muscle may be affected. Those infected with the organism can be treated in the early stage, and death rarely occurs. Other parasites may be contracted in undercooked beef, pork, and fish.

A temperature above 140° F (60° C) destroys trichinella, and for reasons of safety it is recommended that pork be cooked to an internal temperature of 170° F (77° C). Microwave-oven users are cautioned to cook pork to a uniform 170° F (77° C) to destroy any microorganisms that might be present. They are first urged to check the manufacturer's directions for suggested cooking time. Microwaved pork should be rotated during cooking and allowed to rest (wrapped in foil) for five to fifteen minutes *after* cooking to ensure more uniform heat distribution. After the pork sits, check the temperature with a meat thermometer at various places to be sure all areas of the meat—in the center and around bone—have reached 170° F (77° C). If any area has not reached that temperature, remove the foil and return the meat to the oven for further cooking.

Trichinae also are sensitive to cold temperatures. A storage temperature of 50° F (10° C) for thirty days or 10° F (− 12° C) for twenty days will make the food safe for consumption. Special curing methods used to dry and smoke sausages and ham will also eliminate trichinae.

Other parasites that can cause illness enter the body in impure water or foods prepared under poor conditions of sanitation. Shigella is transmitted through water, milk, or food contaminated by humans. Bacillus cereus is found in soil, vegetables, and many raw or processed foods. It grows in moist, cooked protein foods that are inadequately refrigerated. A thorough cleansing of fruit and vegetables and hands can minimize the ingestion of parasites other than trichinae.

DESIRABLE MICROBIAL ACTIVITY

Some microbial activity is desirable in food preparation, such as mold activity in cheese production, leavening of bread by yeast, and the action of acetic acid bacteria in the production of pickled foods and vinegar. In this last instance yeast first converts sugar to ethyl alcohol, and then acetic acid bacteria convert ethyl alcohol into acetic acid (vinegar), which acts as a pickling agent. Some yeasts ferment glucose and are useful in carbon dioxide production for leavening bread. Bacteria convert sugar in cabbage to lactic acid. Pickles and olives are also products of lactic acid fermentation. The characteristic flavor of cheese is contributed by lactic acid bacteria in the first step in cheese production, followed by the use of special strains of mold or bacteria to develop the desired flavor. These bacteria or molds yield different-flavored products. The red color of **cured** meats is due to bacterial reduction of nitrates to nitrites in the brine. Thus many microorganisms are useful in food preparation; but many others cause undesirable and harmful actions, and their activity must be controlled to avoid food spoilage and illness.

FOOD SAFEGUARDS

Regular attention directed to refrigeration practices, cookery practices, **sanitation** practices, including personal habits, is the safeguard that controls foodborne illnesses. The handling of food in the home must be as careful as during its production. High standards of cleanliness must be maintained by all persons in contact with food and in the use of equipment, along with adequate refrigeration and cooking.

Refrigeration Practices

Proper refrigeration retards growth and prevents the buildup of undesirable microorganisms. All perishable foods, such as milk and milk products, eggs, meat, poultry, fish, and shellfish or any dish that contains these foods require refrigeration. Prepared foods such as cream pies, custards, and potato and meat or fish salads must also be refrigerated.

Handling prior to refrigeration determines the bacterial load of food. Only clean foods are refrigerated. Fresh fruits (except berries) and vegetables should be washed thoroughly to remove soil. The condition of the food at the time of refrigeration influences the safe storage period.

Temperatures ranging from 50 to 140° F (10 to 60° C) favor bacterial growth. Rapid bacterial growth occurs from 60 to 120° F (16 to 49° C). Foods should be refrigerated before they reach the temperature zone of rapid bacterial growth even though they are hot. Figure 2–1 lists a temperature guide to food safety. Cooked food to be stored should be lowered quickly to the safe storage

Figure 2–1   Food-safety temperature guide. (Adapted from *Keeping Food Safe to Eat,* Home and Garden Bulletin no. 162, U.S. Department of Agriculture, 1978.)

°C	(°F)	
121	(250)	Canning temperatures for low-acid vegetables, meat, and poultry in pressure canner.
116	(240)	
		Canning temperatures for fruits, tomatoes, and pickles in water bath canner.
100	(212)	
		Cooking temperatures destroy most bacteria. Time required to kill bacteria decreases as temperature is increased.
74	(165)	
		Warming temperatures prevent growth but allow survival of some bacteria.
60	(140)	
		Some bacterial growth may occur. Many bacteria survive.
49	(120)	
		DANGER ZONE. Temperatures in this zone allow rapid growth of bacteria and production of toxins by some bacteria.
16	(60)	
		Some growth of food poisoning bacteria may occur.
5	(40)	
		Cold temperatures permit slow growth of some bacteria that cause spoilage.
0	(32)	
		Freezing temperatures stop growth of bacteria, but may allow bacteria to survive.
−18	(0)	

temperatures of 32 to 38° F (0 to 3° C). A large mass of food should be divided into small portions and into shallow rather than deep containers for rapid cooling. Allowing food to cool to room temperature before refrigeration is not a recommended practice.

The efficiency of the refrigerator is increased when doors are opened as seldom and as briefly as possible and when foods are placed properly within. Special compartments are usually provided for meat, fresh fruit, and vegetable storage. The meat and milk are kept in the coldest part, and the fresh fruits and vegetables in the warmest.

Cartons and paper bags tend to take up space and to increase the amount of refrigeration required to keep the food safe. Meats generally are wrapped loosely in waxed paper before being placed in the coldest part but may be stored in the original self-serve package for a short period. Cooked meats are covered tightly to retain moisture, and fish is wrapped tightly to keep in odor. Meats and fish to be stored longer than twenty-four hours should be rewrapped for freezer storage.

When vegetables and fruits are not stored in the special high-humidity compartment, they should be placed on the lower shelf in plastic bags. Cooked vegetables and fruits and all other cooked foods should be covered during refrigerator storage to avoid dehydration and transfer of flavor and aroma. Although foods keep well in the refrigerator, bacteria are not destroyed; therefore, it is best to use perishable foods within a reasonable period of time.

Freezing temporarily stops multiplication of bacteria in food. When the food is thawed, microorganisms begin to multiply again. Foods that have thawed may be safely refrozen if they still contain ice crystals or if they are still cold— about 40° F (5° C)—and have not been held longer than one or two days at re-

(Grand Union)

frigerator temperature after thawing. Thawed ice cream and thawed meats with an off-color or off-flavor should not be refrozen. Although thawed food may be refrozen safely when temperature and time are carefully observed, the quality will be reduced.

Cookery Practices

Heat offers one of the most effective means for protecting food from microorganisms. In order to destroy all harmful organisms it must penetrate the entire area of the food. The speed of heat penetration is determined by the composition of the food. Heat penetrates porous foods quickly and compact foods slowly.

The low cooking temperatures generally recommended for meat and poultry products in the interest of palatability and loss from shrinkage may not in a given time permit the internal temperature to reach the point of sterilization. All food products, and especially ground meat and poultry, should be sufficiently heated to achieve adequate cooking. Extreme heat is required to kill bacteria that could cause poisoning; therefore a relatively high heat is also required when preparing such foods as milk, milk products, eggs, fish, and shellfish.

Cooked foods should be served as soon as possible. A prolonged holding of foods at room temperature is to be avoided. When it is necessary to warm-hold foods the temperature should remain at 140° F (60° C) or above to prevent bacterial growth. Cold foods should be kept below 40° F (5° C). When food is prepared in advance to serve later, refrigerate it promptly and reheat at serving time.

Automatic-Oven Cookery. Food held in preset automatic ovens for time-delayed cookery may increase in bacterial count. Ground-meat products held for a prolonged period may have a dangerous increase in bacteria. The hazard of excessive bacterial buildup in time-delayed cooking can be minimized somewhat with the use of frozen products, which will defrost slowly until the designated time for cooking. When an automatic oven is used, make sure food is not held in the 60–125° F zone (figure 2–1) for more than two to three hours prior to cooking.

Sanitation Practices

Sanitation practices must be applied to all aspects of food handling and preparation to control foodborne illness. Personal habits, the work area, utensils, other equipment, and the cleaning schedule should contribute to the control and prevention of food illnesses as well as disease in general. Unless strict sanitation is maintained in all aspects of food handling, the safe food becomes contaminated as soon as it reaches the food-preparation area. When sanitation practices become automatic for everyone involved, the chances of foodborne illness are greatly reduced.

Personal Habits.   Individuals preparing food for others should be in good health; their hair should be clean and confined in a net; the hands, fingernails, and clothing clean. Food and dishes are always handled with clean hands; the hands are kept away from the surfaces on which food is placed; and all flatware is carried only by the handles. Whenever possible, utensils should be used rather than hands.

Food is never tasted with the stirring or cooking spoon. Instead a small amount of food is transferred from the cooking spoon to the tasting spoon. Fingers are never licked. Dish towels and dish cloths are used only for dishes and are never draped over the shoulder. The hands are kept away from hair and face during food preparation. Hands are washed thoroughly after the use of a disposable tissue or after handling other nonfood items.

Surfaces.   Food should be kept and handled on clean surfaces. Dust, food particles, and grease collect in corners and creases and provide a space for bacterial growth and other food-spoilage organisms. All dirty surfaces can contaminate food.

Utensils.   The used dishes are cleansed of food particles with a rubber scraper and rinsed. When a dishwasher is used the water temperature should be 120 to 140° F (49 to 60° C). Hand washing necessitates a temperature somewhat lower than 120° F (49° C); therefore the dishes should be scalded with boiling water. All dishes and utensils must be washed thoroughly in hot water with adequate detergent and then sterilized.

The recommended sequence for hand washing dishes begins with glassware followed by flatware, then china—with greasy dishes done after the nongreasy ones—and last, kitchen utensils. Many of the preparation utensils may be washed and returned to their storage places while foods are cooking. The water is changed as often as necessary for properly washed dishes and utensils. All clean, dry utensils and dishes are stored in clean cupboards.

Equipment.   The surface cooking area and oven should be washed clean of all grease, food, and residue from cooking vapors. Careful control of temperature or heat settings during cooking avoids boilovers. The range is cleaned each time it is used.

The refrigerator is cleaned thoroughly inside with cool water containing baking or washing soda, rinsed, and dried. Any food spillage or leakage should be cleaned up immediately. The refrigerator should be kept clean and dry. All portable appliances should be cleaned after each use and properly stored. The manufacturer's directions for their use and care should be followed.

Supplies.   Dish towels and cloths should be kept clean and sanitized with bleach. Counters and chopping boards used for preparation of raw meats should be washed thoroughly before they are used for other foods. Chopping boards should be nonporous rather than wood. Cleaning products, pesticides, and other nonfood items should be stored in cupboards apart from those used for food storage. The windows should be screened to keep out insects.

Cleaning Schedule.   Sanitation is maintained and promoted with a regular cleaning schedule. In the food-preparation area, the schedule would include cleaning and upkeep of storage and preparation areas as well as appliances, walls, and floors. The counter tops, insides of cupboards, and walls and floors should be free of dust and debris, which attract bacteria as well as insects and rodents.

SUMMARY

Federal, state, and local governments carefully monitor food production to ensure a safe food supply. Personal habits with food from the time of purchase through its storage, preparation, and service contribute to its safety. Food free of contamination can only be prepared from clean foods by scrupulously clean individuals, with clean equipment, in a clean kitchen. Microorganisms and their toxins are the primary causes of foodborne illness. Careful attention to cookery, refrigeration, and sanitation practices prevent foodborne illness.

Underprocessed home-canned meats and vegetables may contain a toxin causing botulism unless they are boiled rapidly for twenty minutes before the food is tasted or consumed. Salmonella are found most frequently in foods of animal origin. Thorough washing of raw foods and all utensils, food-preparation areas, and hands prevents the spread of microorganisms. Pork products must be cooked well done to destroy trichinella should it be present. Microbial activity is desirable in preparation of cheese, yeast bread, and pickled products.

SELF-STUDY GUIDE

1. Define foodborne illness and list two causes.
2. Explain how food poisoning can be controlled.
3. Identify foods that are susceptible to growth and spread of botulism organisms, salmonella, staph and strep bacteria, and trichinella. List two examples for each.
4. Discuss desirable personal habits during food preparation. List four examples.
5. Discuss microbiological aspects of food preparation. Give two examples.
6. Identify four factors involved in food safety and explain the contribution of each.

SUGGESTED READINGS

BLAND, J.   Is it safe to eat? *World Health,* p. 22, April 1982.

BLOMBERG, B.   How safe is the food we eat? *World Health,* p. 16, October 1980.

CHRISTENSEN, D.   Are you careful about food sanitation in your home? *Life Health* 95:28, 1980.

CLYDESDALE, F. (ED).   Food Science and Nutrition: Current issues and answers p. 93. Englewood Cliffs, N.J.: Prentice-Hall, 1979.

FOSTER, E. M.   Foodborne hazards of microbial origin. *Federation Proceedings* 37:2577, 1978.

GENERAL SERVICES ADMINISTRATION.   When your

freezer quits. In *Highlights of New Federal Publications*, GSA no. 1707. Washington, D.C.: General Service Administration, 1980.

GLICK, R.   Getting it all: Preserving food nutrients. *Essence* x:55, February 1980.

GREEN, J.   FDA's new code: A clean sweep for food stores. *Consumer* xvi:12, October 1982.

GUTHRIE, R. K.   *Food Sanitation.* 2nd ed. Westport, Conn.: Avi Publishing Company, 1980.

Mold problems are analyzed by independent laboratory services. *Food Engineering* 53:107, June 1981.

MUNRO, I. C., and CHARBONNEAU, S. M.   Environmental contaminants. *Federation Proceedings* 37:2582, 1978.

OCKERMAN, H. W., and STEC, J.   Total plate and coliform counts for fast food service sandwiches. *Journal of Food Science* 45:262, March/April 1980.

PARK, K. Y., and BULLERMAN, L.   Increased aflatoxin production by aspergillus parasiticus under conditions of cycling temperatures. *Journal of Food Science* 46:1147, July/August 1981.

SHELEF, L. A., et al.   Sensitivity of some common foodborne bacteria to the spices sage, rosemary, and allspice. *Journal of Food Science* 45:1042, July/August 1980.

SHEPHERD, M. J.   Trace contamination of foods by migration from plastic packaging—a review. *Food Chemistry* viii:129, 1982.

SPLITTSTOESER, D. F., et al.   Detection and incidence of geotrichum candidum in frozen vegetables. *Journal of Food Science* 45:511, May/June 1980.

SVEUM, W. H., and KRAFT, A. A.   Recovery of salmonellae from foods using a combined enrichment technique. *Journal of Food Science* 46:94, January/February 1981.

U.S. DEPARTMENT OF AGRICULTURE.   Consumer response system food safety questions. USDA News Feature Service. Washington, D.C.: Department of Agriculture, May 13, 1982.

——.   *Controlling household pests.* Home and Garden Bulletin no. 96. Washington, D.C.: Government Printing Office, 1976.

——.   *Food safety for the family.* Food Safety and Quality Service. Washington, D.C.: Government Printing Office, 1977.

——.   *Keeping foods safe to eat.* Home and Garden Bulletin no. 162. Washington, D.C.: Government Printing Office, 1978.

U.S. DEPARTMENT OF HEALTH, EDUCATION AND WELFARE.   *We want you to know about foodborne illness.* DHEW publication no. (FDA) 74–2044. Washington, D.C.: Government Printing Office, 1974.

WODICKA, V.   FDA's view of food safety. *FDA Consumer,* October 1973.

3

FOOD COMPONENTS

OBJECTIVES

When you complete this chapter, you will be able to

1. List components that make up food and give examples.
2. List the six major nutrient groups and identify the members or classifications included within each group.
3. Define: polysaccharide, dextrin, glycogen, cellulose, lipid, unsaturated fatty acid, triglyceride, polypeptide, hydrolysis, coagulation, organic.
4. Give examples of the physical and the chemical nature of food.
5. Identify the roles of starches, protein, and fats in food preparation.
6. Identify differences and similarities among the various carbohydrates present in food.
7. Discuss the difference between vitamins and minerals; between protein and lipid.

Visual observations reveal that foods are composed of various tissues and structures. Even foods that appear to be the same throughout show differences in structure when viewed through a microscope. Foods are composed of many different chemical molecules arranged in various patterns. The nature of food is diverse and complex, and it is both chemical and physical.

When foods are subjected to processing and preparation procedures, changes occur in their chemical composition and in their physical nature. For example, color, flavor, and nutrient components dissolve in the cooking liquid, and fat in meat melts and remains in the drippings surrounding the meat. The chemical molecules present and their arrangement influence the changes that occur during the preparation of food.

COMPONENT UNITS

Although no two foods are exactly alike structurally, all foods share a combination of component units generally classified into six nutrient categories: carbohydrates, lipids, proteins, minerals, vitamins, and water. In addition to the nutrient categories, foods contain color and flavor components as well as enzymes. The major components of foods include the carbohydrates, lipids, proteins, and water. The other components (minerals, vitamins, pigments, flavor components, and enzymes) are present in small but important amounts. Each food has its own unique combination of component units. It is the combination of components that determines the nature of the food and the changes foods undergo during preparation.

Chemical Nature

The chemical nature of food refers to its ability to be changed or transformed through chemical reactions. Chemical changes result in the formation of new chemical compounds. In some instances the change in structure of the compound is slight; in others the change is dramatic. A number of foods undergo chemical changes during preparation. Carmelization of sugar, browning of meats, and dextrinization of starch are examples of chemical changes that occur as a result of heating foods.

PHYSICAL NATURE

The physical nature refers to the characteristics of color, odor, taste, flavor, texture, and form; in short, the factors that generally stimulate sensory responses. Water as a fluid or a component of food may be transformed from a liquid to a solid or to a vapor, but its chemical nature remains unaltered. Sugar undergoes physical changes when it is added to water to make a true solution or when it precipitates from a supersaturated solution to form the structure of crystalline candy. A physical change occurs when a solid fat is heated to form a liquid. Control of physical changes is an important aspect of food preparation.

CARBOHYDRATES

The term *carbohydrate* refers to a group of structurally similar compounds composed of sugar or saccharide molecules. All carbohydrates are composed of carbon, hydrogen, and oxygen and contain the same ratio of hydrogen to oxygen as occurs in water. Dietary carbohydrates range from relatively small, simple molecules (monosaccharides and disaccharides) to large, complex molecules (polysaccharides).

Carbohydrates are identified by the number of saccharide units in their structure. Monosaccharides are the simplest carbohydrate molecules. Dietary monosaccharides include glucose, fructose, and galactose. These compounds serve as the basic units or building blocks of disaccharides, which contain two units, and polysaccharides, which contain many units. The components and sources of common carbohydrates are shown in Table 3-1.

Monosaccharides

Glucose.   Glucose, or dextrose, is the most prevalent monosaccharide. It is found in fruits, vegetables, honey, corn syrup, and molasses. Glucose is a structural unit of all common dietary disaccharides and the exclusive unit in polysaccharides.

Fructose.   Fructose, or levulose, is the sweetest of all sugars and is found in honey, molasses, fruits, and vegetables.

Galactose.   Galactose does not occur in the free form in foods but is produced when lactose or milk sugar is digested, or when milk products are fermented.

Table 3-1   Selected Carbohydrates: Components and Food Sources

Carbohydrates	Monosaccharide Components	Food Sources
Monosaccharides		
Glucose	—	Fruits, vegetables, honey
Fructose	—	Fruits, vegetables, honey
Galactose	—	Not present in free form
Disaccharides		
Sucrose	Glucose and fructose	Table sugar (white, brown)
Maltose	Glucose and glucose	Malted cereal grains
Lactose	Glucose and galactose	Milk
Polysaccharides		
Dextrins	Glucose	Formed from starch by action of acid, heat, enzyme
Starch	Glucose	Cereals, breads, crackers, tubers, legumes
Cellulose	Glucose	Whole grains, fruits, vegetables
Pectic substances (proto-pectin, pectin, pectic acid)	Galactose derivative (galacturonic acid)	Jams, jellies, fruits, some prepared foods
Glycogen	Glucose	Not usually found in foods. Formed in living animal cells as energy source.

Yogurt and unaged cheeses may contain some lactose. Low-calorie sweet products, such as cocoa mixes, may contain free galactose by enzymatic treatment.

Disaccharides

Sucrose. Sucrose is the most common dietary disaccharide. It is composed of one moleule of glucose and one molecule of fructose, linked together through the aldehyde $(C = O)$ group of glucose and the ketone group $(C = O)$ group of fructose. Both white and brown sugars are composed of sucrose, although brown sugar contains another component (molasses), which causes the difference in color.

Sucrose is extracted from sugar cane or the sugar beet. Sucrose in the crystalline form is table sugar and is the chief sweetener in food preparation.

Maltose. Maltose, or malt sugar, is found in malted milk and cereal. Maltose consists of two glucose molecules joined together. Maltose is formed when starch, a polysaccharide, is hydrolyzed, or broken down to simpler substances.

Lactose. Lactose (milk sugar) is found only in milk and milk products. A molecule of glucose unites with a molecule of galactose to form lactose.

Polysaccharides

Starch. Starch is the most abundant dietary carbohydrate. It is composed of many alpha-linked glucose units, which form either the amylose (straight-chain arrangement) or amylopectin (complicated, branched-chain arrangement) fractions of starch. Starches are not soluble in water, but when boiled with water they hydrate to form pastes or gels. Legumes, cereal grains, and tubers are rich sources of starch.

Dextrins. Dextrins are short glucose chains formed from starch by the action of acids, dry heat, or enzymes (amylases). They are formed in the preparation of foods and in the digestion of starch. Dextrins have less thickening power than starch.

Cellulose. Cellulose is a structural component of plants made of beta-linked glucose units. This linkage makes cellulose unique among the polysaccharides. Since humans lack the enzyme capable of breaking beta linkages, cellulose primarily functions as a dietary source of fiber. Hemicelluloses are mixtures of polysaccharides that are made of various monosaccharides. Along with cellulose, they are concentrated in cell walls and fill important structural roles in plant tissues.

Cellulose serves as fiber and promotes motility of the food mass in the gastrointestinal tract. Food-preparation techniques have little influence on cellulose other than the softening of structure. Whole-grain products, fresh fruits, and vegetables are important sources of cellulose.

Pectin.   Pectin and other pectic substances are classed as polysaccharides of the galactose derivative, galacturonic acid. Pectin forms a gel when combined with the proper amount of sugar and acid. It is used as a thickening agent in jams, jellies, and some prepared foods.

Glycogen.   Glycogen is a branched polysaccharide made entirely of glucose molecules. Sometimes it is called animal starch since that is the only form in which carbohydrates are stored in animals. Glycogen is found in food only as a constituent of some meats and is not used as an individual ingredient in food preparation. Glycogen normally disappears from meat during the aging process.

CARBOHYDRATES IN FOOD PREPARATION

Carbohydrates can be converted into other compounds during food preparation. Disaccharides, dextrins, and starch can be hydrolyzed into simple sugars. For example, this property is used in candy making to aid in preparing candies with a smooth texture or liquid centers. Sugars can be transformed into alcohol by some yeast and bacteria. This process is known as fermentation and is used in bread making to produce carbon dioxide for leavening.

The starch granule is insoluble in cold water, but in simmering water the granule can undergo a physical change by binding water and swelling to cause thickening (gelatinization). As they swell, the granules lose some starch (amylose) into the water; upon cooling, the amylose can establish a network that traps the granules, and a gel results (gelation).

PROTEIN

Proteins are large, complicated molecules composed of carbon, hydrogen, oxygen, and nitrogen. They are made of chains of amino acids.

Amino Acids

All amino acids have an amino group ($-NH_2$) and an acid group ($-\overset{\displaystyle O}{\overset{\displaystyle \|}{C}} - OH$). The remainder of the molecule differs for the various amino acids.

In a general formula for amino acids, the R represents a side chain of variable structure. The R groups identify specific

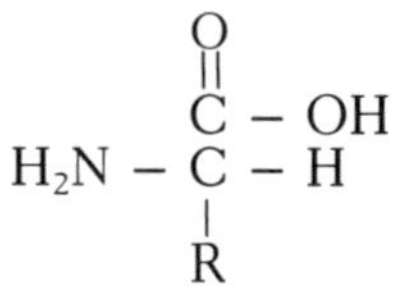

$$
\begin{array}{c}
\quad\quad\ \ \overset{\displaystyle O}{\overset{\displaystyle \|}{C}} - OH \\
H_2N - C - H \\
\quad\ \ \ | \\
\quad\ \ \ R
\end{array}
$$

amino acids and are responsible for the characteristics of a protein. Some of the R groups contain sulfur or short carbon chains, some have additional acid or amino groups, and others contain cyclic structures. Amino acids join through peptide linkages to form proteins. A peptide linkage forms when one amino acid joins through its amino group to the acid group of the adjacent amino acid (see Figure 3-1). That is to say, amino acids join together through their amino and acid groups to form proteins.

The nutritional value of proteins depends upon the particular ratios of amino acids they contain. Eight amino acids are considered essential for adults and nine for children because they cannot be produced in adequate amounts in body cells. The biological value of a protein depends upon the presence of adequate amounts of these essential amino acids. It decreases when one or more of the essential amino acids is not present in appropriate amounts. This type of protein cannot support optimal growth.

Protein in Foods

Proteins are found in abundance in animal tissues, milk, eggs, and legumes. Each kind of protein contains a unique combination of amino acids, and most foods contain a mixture of different types of proteins. The proteins in food are responsible for a number of changes that occur when foods are cooked such as coagulation, browning, and hydration.

Protein as it exists in plant and animal tissue is identified as native protein. The structure of native protein can be modified by agitation, air, acids, freezing, high pressure, and salts to yield a **denatured protein.**

During denaturation the protein molecule unfolds to some degree but yet retains all of the peptide linkages in its molecule. The degree of denaturation may be limited or extensive. The unfolded portion of the molecule may recombine in

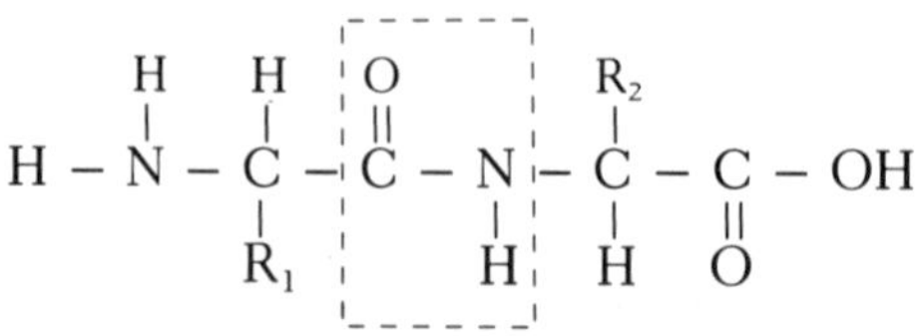

Figure 3-1 Peptide bond.

$$
H - \underset{\underset{R_1}{|}}{\overset{\overset{H}{|}}{N}} - \underset{\underset{R_1}{|}}{\overset{\overset{H}{|}}{C}} - \overset{\overset{O}{\|}}{C} - \underset{\underset{H}{|}}{\overset{}{N}} - \underset{\underset{H}{|}}{\overset{\overset{R_2}{|}}{C}} - \overset{\overset{}{}}{\underset{\underset{O}{\|}}{C}} - OH
$$

different ways to form a new molecular shape, and protein molecules may bond together to form a continuous network. Heat, acid, and agitation are most often responsible for protein denaturation during food preparation.

Protein in Food Preparation

Coagulation. The conversion of a protein from a fluid to a solid state is know as **coagulation.** Egg proteins, for example coagulate when heat is applied. The process of coagulation involves an unfolding or rearrangement of the native protein molecules and then an aggregation or clumping of the molecules to form a precipitate or gel.

Browning Reaction. Protein and sugar may interact at high temperature, resulting in a browning reaction (**Maillard**). This browning and the accompanying characteristic flavor and aroma are desirable in baked products, meats, and food with a crust.

Hydration. Proteins vary in their ability to bind water, or **hydrate.** The hydration ability of wheat protein in flour enables the protein to combine with water to form gluten. Gluten is the unique protein complex formed by mixing wheat flour and water. It is essential to the structure of most baked products of high quality.

Amphoteric. Amino acids tend to be unique in that they can act either as bases or acids. The amino group acts as a base (has a positive charge), and the carboxyl group acts as an acid (has a negative charge). Since both of these groups are present on the same amino acid, they are said to be **amphoteric.** Because of the amphoteric nature of amino acids, and therefore of protein, proteins may combine with either bases or acids to resist change in acidity and act as natural buffers.

Precipitate. When a protein exhibits neither a positive nor negative charge, it is said to be at its **isoelectric** point. Protein at the isoelectric point is unstable and will **precipitate.** This can be observed when milk sours. The isoelectric point of a protein is reached by altering the acidity of the food to the appropriate pH. Each type of protein has its own specific pH at which the isoelectric point occurs.

Precipitation of protein can also be facilitated with the addition of salts. The salts ionize in solution and help to neutralize the charges on the surface of the proteins. Without repulsive surface charges the protein molecules can approach each other readily and form aggregates.

Hydrolysis. This term refers to the breakdown of a protein molecule into a smaller molecule by the addition of a molecule of water. **Hydrolysis** increases the solubility of a protein and reduces its thickening power. Heat, acid, or enzymes (meat tenderizer) applied in cookery can initiate some protein hydrolysis, resulting in a tenderizing influence.

LIPIDS

Lipids are components of plant and animal tissues. The lipids **(fats)** of primary interest in food are classed as neutral fats. Although they are composed of the same three elements (carbon, hydrogen, oxygen) as carbohydrates, the proportion of hydrogen to oxygen is quite different. Fats have more carbon and hydrogen but much less oxygen than do carbohydrates.

Each molecule of a neutral fat consists of glycerol (an alcohol) and one to three fatty acids, respectively referred to as monoglycerides, diglycerides, and triglycerides. Glycerol is composed of three carbon atoms and three hydroxyl groups (OH). Fatty acids consist of chains of carbon atoms with an **organic** acid (carboxyl group) at the end of the molecule. Fatty acids are joined to glycerol by **ester** linkages, that is, the hydroxyl (OH) of glycerol joins with the organic acid

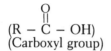

at the end of the fatty acid.

Fatty Acids.　The fatty acids may be saturated with hydrogen, or they may be monounsaturated or **polyunsaturated** (containing one or more carbon-carbon double bonds). The fatty acids with all the hydrogen they can hold have no double bonds between carbon atoms and are known as **saturated fatty acids.** Other fatty acids have some double bonds between carbons because hydrogen is missing, and they are known as unsaturated fatty acids. Examples of saturated fatty acids in food include butyric (4 carbon) in butter and stearic (18 carbon) in beef fat. Oleic acid is an eighteen-carbon unsaturated fatty acid with one double bond. Fatty acids with more than one double bond are known as polyunsaturated and include linoleic with two double bonds, linoleic with three double bonds. Oils from corn, cottonseed, soybeans, safflower, and sunflower, and special margarines are good sources of unsaturated fatty acids. The length of the carbon chain, the degree of saturation, and the configuration (cis or trans at the double bond) of the fatty acids determine their physical nature.

Fats in Food.　The fats in foods are mixtures of triglycerides containing both saturated and unsaturated fatty acids with some mono- and diglycerides. Fats from plant sources are oils; their fluid character is due to an abundance of polyunsaturated fatty acids. Animal fats are higher in saturated fatty acids than are the oils from plants, and consequently they are solids at room temperature.

Fats in Food Preparation

Fats serve a number of functions in food preparation. They contribute and carry flavor, serve as a tenderizing agent in flour products, act as a medium for heat transfer when foods are fried, and are the chief ingredient in salad dressings and mayonnaise. The properties, processing, and uses of fats are discussed in chapter 9, "Lipids: Fats and Oils."

WATER

Water is an essential constituent of all foods. Fresh fruits and vegetables have a high water content, and breads have a low water content. Lettuce contains about 95 percent water, crackers have about 3 percent water, and most foods have an intermediate water content. A molecule of water consists of two hydrogen atoms and one of oxygen. In food preparation, water acts as a solvent, or dispersing agent, for components in food and serves as a medium for applying heat when food is cooked. Water is a universal cleansing agent for food and food-preparation utensils.

The ability of water to change in form or state is used in food preparation, for example, when vegetables are steamed and frozen dessert prepared. Water changes in states or forms from a liquid to a solid (ice), and from a liquid to a gas (vapor). As it changes to a gas or from a solid to a liquid, it absorbs some heat from its surroundings and thus exerts a cooling effect. Conversely, as steam condenses to water or water freezes to form ice, heat is given up. These changes in the state of water are physical and do not require an overall change in temperature. Boiling water and steam have the same temperature of 212° F (100° C) as do ice and the water formed by melting ice (32° F, 0° C).

VITAMINS

Vitamins are organic compounds needed in very small amounts for growth and maintenance of health. They occur in foods of both plant and animal origin. They are classified as water soluble or fat soluble. In order to minimize loss of water-soluble vitamins, B complex and C (ascorbic acid), in cooking only small quantities of water should be used and vegetables and fruits cooked until they are just fork tender. Ascorbic acid, especially, is easily destroyed by heat and oxygen. Synthetic vitamins may be added to enrich or supplement breads, cereals, fruit drinks, milk products, and margarine. Since the body cannot distinguish between natural and synthetic vitamins, both are equally nutritious.

MINERALS

Minerals are inorganic components essential for regulation of body metabolic processes and structure. Macrominerals, such as calcium, phosphorus, and magnesium, are required in relatively large amounts; those required in very small amounts, such as zinc, copper, and iodine, are known as trace minerals. They are found in varying amounts in foods of both plant and animal origin and leave an ash when foods are burned. Most minerals are water soluble, tightly bound in organic complexes, and can be retained when foods are cooked in a small quantity of water and when any remaining liquid is served with the vegetable.

OTHER COMPONENTS

Foods also contain flavor compounds, pigments, and enzymes. Enzymes are organic catalysts (proteins) produced by living cells, and can be inactivated or destroyed by heat. They are found in foods of both animal and plant origin and are responsible for some of the changes in the flavor, color, and texture of foods.

SUMMARY

The physical and chemical aspects of food are complex and diverse. Carbohydrates, lipids, proteins, and water are major components of food; vitamins, minerals, color and flavor components, and enzymes are present in small but important amounts. Each food has its own unique combination of components that determine its nature. The physical nature of food is defined by its color, flavor, texture, fluidity, and form. The chemical nature of food is defined by the structural composition of a food and the chemical changes it can undergo.

SELF-STUDY GUIDE

1. What two factors contribute to the diversity and complexity of food?
2. Describe the physical and chemical nature of food.
3. What are two contributions of mono- and disaccharides to foods?
4. What role do starches and proteins serve in food preparation? Give two examples for each.
5. Identify the differences or similarities in mono-, di-, and polysaccharides; in cellulose and glycogen; in protein and lipids.
6. Indicate three differences between vitamins and minerals.
7. What three components other than the six essential nutrients make up foods?

SUGGESTED READINGS

ADAMS, C. *Nutritive value of american foods in common units.* Agriculture Handbook no. 456. Agricultural Research Service. Washington, D.C.: Government Printing Office, 1980.

BENNION, M. *The science of food.* New York: Harper & Row, Publishers, 1985.

CHANDLER, C., and MARSTON, R. *Fat in the U.S. diet.* Consumer and Food Economics Institute. USDA. *Nutrition Program News,* May/August 1976.

CHARLEY, H. *Food Science.* 2nd ed. New York: John Wiley and Sons, 1982.

HANSEN, R. G. An index of food quality. *Nutrition Reviews* 31:1, 1973.

MARSH, A. C. *Composition of foods: soups, sauces, and gravies: Raw-processed-prepared.* Agriculture Handbook 8-6, Science and Education Administration. Washington, D.C.: Government Printing Office, 1980.

MONDAY, N. *Experimental food chemistry.* Westport, Conn.: Avi Publishing Company, 1980.

RICHARDSON, M., et al. *Composition of foods: Sausages and luncheon meats: Raw-Processed-Prepared.* Agriculture Handbook no. 817. Science and Education Administration. Washington, D.C.: Government Printing Office, 1980.

SANDERSON, G. R. Polysaccharides in foods. *Food Technology* 35:50, July 1981.

SOLMAN, K. G., et al. Foods. *Analytical Chemistry* 53:242, 1981.

Sugar, how sweet it is—and isn't. *FDA Consumer,* p. 21, February.

Sugars and nutritive sweeteners in processed foods. A scientific status summary by the Institute of Food Technologists, expert panel on food safety and nutrition. *Food Technology,* p. 101, May 1979.

U.S. DEPARTMENT OF AGRICULTURE. *Composition of foods: Breakfast cereals—raw, processed, prepared.* Agriculture Handbook no. 8-8. Human Nutrition Information Service. Washington, D.C.: Government Printing Office, 1982.

———. *Food.* Home and Garden Bulletin no. 228. Washington, D.C.: Government Printing Office, 1980.

———. *Composition of foods: Fruits and fruit juices—raw, processed, prepared.* Agriculture Handbook no. 8-9. Human Nutrition Information Service. Washington, D.C.: Government Printing Office, 1982.

———. *Nutritive value of foods.* Home and Garden Bulletin no. 72. Science and Education Administration. Washington, D.C.: Government Printing Office, 1981.

———. *Composition of food: Pork products—raw, processed, prepared.* Agriculture Handbook no. 8-10. Human Nutrition Information Service, Washington, D.C.: Government Printing Office, 1983.

VAN SOEST, P. J. What is fiber? *Professional Nutritionist,* p. 7, fall 1978.

4

FOOD-PREPARATION ESSENTIALS

OBJECTIVES

When you complete this chapter, you will be able to

1. Measure accurately all ingredients used in recipes and instruct others in measurement procedures.

2. List metric units and symbols used in cookery and compare with U.S. customary measures.

3. Convert degrees Celsius to Fahrenheit and degrees F to C.

4. Discuss the influence and use of heat in cookery and give examples of heat-induced physical and chemical changes in food.

5. Explain how boiling temperature of water is elevated and decreased.

6. Contrast intermediate, boiling, frying, and cold/freezing temperatures and give examples of their use in cookery.

7. Discuss the influence of temperature on microorganisms.

8. Discuss the uses and influences of water in cookery.

9. Define solution and give examples of uses in cookery.

10. Discuss colloids and give food examples. Compare colloids with solutions.

11. Explain the pH scale and discuss the role or influence of acidity in food preparation and give examples.

12. Define enzymes, describe their role, and discuss their involvement with food.

13. Give examples of microbial action in food preparation.

Precise measures, accurate measuring techniques, and appropriate methods for combining ingredients are essential for the consistent production of quality products. All dry and liquid ingredients require special measuring techniques to obtain an exact volume or a precise measure. Recipes are developed using standard measures and techniques, and for home use, ingredients are given in volume measures—cups, tablespoons, and teaspoons.

This chapter presents the essentials of food preparation and includes the following topics: techniques of measurement, customary and metric units, and functions of water, colloids, temperatures, enzymes, pH, and microbial action in food preparation.

MEASUREMENT

Customary

Customary, or conventional, measuring equipment includes the glass and graduated measuring cups and measuring spoons. Conventional measures are based on the standard quart in which one cup holds ¼ of a quart, or 8 fluid ounces, or 236.5 milliliters. Each cup contains 16 tablespoons so that 2 tablespoons equal one fluid ounce. The glass cup is subdivided to indicate fractional measures of ⅓ and ⅔, and ¼, ½, and ¾. A set of four individual measuring cups to accommodate fractional quantities includes measures for 1, ½, ¼, and ⅓ cup. Measuring spoons are used to measure quantities less than ¼ cup. One tablespoon is equivalent to three teaspoons. Measuring spoon sets include a tablespoon, a teaspoon, a ½ teaspoon, and a ¼ teaspoon.

Accurate measurements are made quickly with measuring cups and spoons and are therefore preferred to weight measurement for home food preparation. On the other hand, commercial production and food development and research require greater precision than home preparation; therefore, measurement by weight is used.

Metric—SI (International System of Units)

In the International System of Units the symbols are identical in all languages, but unit names may be spelled differently. Base units and symbols are presented in Table 4-1. At the present time, on a voluntary basis, some attention

Table 4-1 Metric Prefixes, Units, Symbols

Prefixes and Symbol			Basic Unit for Weight Gram (g)	Basic Unit for Volume Liter (l)	Basic Unit for Length Meter (m)
milli	(m)	0.001	milligram (mg)	milliliter (ml)	millimeter (mm)
centi	(c)	0.01	centigram (cg)	centiliter (cl)	centimeter (cm)
deci	(d)	0.1	decigram (dg)	deciliter (dl)	decimeter (dm)
deka	(da)	10	dekagram (dag)	dekaliter (dal)	dekameter (dam)
hecto	(h)	100	hectogram (hg)	hectoliter (hl)	hectometer (hm)
kilo	(k)	1000	kilogram (kg)	kiloliter (kl)	kilometer (km)

is being given to the metric or SI system. In the SI system volume measures are based on the liter. The metric measure of 250 ml (milliliter) is about equal to 1 cup, 125 ml to ½ cup. The 15 ml measure has a volume of 1 tablespoon and the 5 ml of 1 teaspoon.

Up to now, the chief use for metric measurements in food preparation has been in research where it is preferred because of its precision. Four metric units—the gram for weight, liter for volume, meter for length, and degrees Celsius for temperature—are generally used in food preparation. The metric system is based on multiples of ten, which are identified by prefixes added to the basic unit. The prefixes that would be used most often in the home are *milli, centi, deci,* and *kilo.* Some of the common equivalent and conversion factors are listed in Table 4–2.

To simplify the transition from U.S. customary measures to metric measures, some manufacturers of measuring equipment have developed a metric measuring cup. One side of the cup is marked in liters and milliliters. The metric cup is based on the liter (4 metric cups equal 1 liter); the customary cup is based on the quart (4 cups to a quart). The metric cup contains about one tablespoon more than the customary cup. The difference in position on the customary and metric cups is very little, but all of the ingredients within the same recipe should be measured with one type of measure rather than mixing customary and metric measures.

Degrees Celsius is the metric unit for temperature measurement. Figure

Table 4–2 Some Metric Conversion Factors and Equivalents

Conversions

English to metric	quarts	× 0.946 = liters
	ounces (avdp)	× 28.35 = grams
	pounds (avdp)	× 0.454 = kilograms
Metric to English	liters	× 1.056 = quarts
	grams	× 0.035 = ounces (avdp)
	kilograms	× 2.204 = pounds (avdp)

Equivalents

weight	1 ounce	= 28.35 grams (28 grams)
	1 pound	= 453.6 grams or 0.45 kilogram
	1 kilogram	= 2.2 pounds
liquid	1 liter	= 1.06 quarts
	1 quart	= 946.4 milliliters (946 milliliters)
	1 cup	= 236.6 milliliters (237 milliliters)
	1 tablespoon	= 14.8 milliliters (15 milliliters)
	1 teaspoon	= 4.9 milliliters (5 milliliters)
length	1 inch	= 2.5 centimeters

Adapted from the *AHEA Handbook for Metric Usage* (Washington, D.C.: American Home Economics Association, 1977), pp 6-7, 27-28. Used by permission.

4–1 compares Celsius and Fahrenheit temperature readings. The following formulas are used to interconvert Fahrenheit and Celsius temperatures:

°Celsius = (° F − 32) × 5/9
°Fahrenheit = (° C × 9/5) + 32

Measurement Techniques

Precise measurement of ingredients requires the use of accurate measuring equipment and correct techniques for handling each ingredient. Liquids are measured in a standard glass measuring cup while dry ingredients are measured

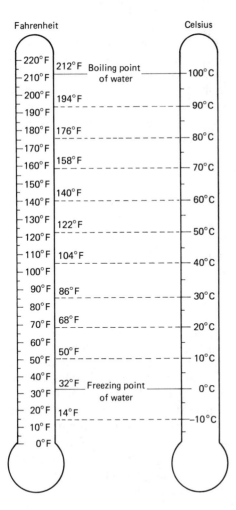

Figure 4-1
Fahrenheit and Celsius temperature comparisons.

in graduated measuring cups, which can be leveled off. Generally, dry ingredients are lightly spooned into the cup to overflowing and then leveled with a straight-edge spatula.

Flour. Because flour packs during storage many recipes call for sifted flour. A measured cup of unsifted flour weighs more than a measured cup of sifted flour. The additional flour included in each cup of measured unsifted flour could destroy the balance among ingredients and result in a low-quality product. In measuring flour never tap the cup while filling or leveling off. Tapping will pack the flour and cause more to be used than required.

An alternate method is to sift the flour directly into the cup until it just overflows. The excess is removed with a straight-edge spatula. A cup of flour measured in this way may weigh less than a cup of sifted-spooned flour.

Several years ago an instant, or agglomerated, flour was developed. Somewhat coarse, it is made from regular flour brought into contact with steam so that the flour particles adhere; it is then dried. Another instantized flour is made of cracked endosperm and is too coarse to be classed as regular flour. These flours pour easily. They are stirred in the container and spooned into the cup for measurement. They should be used with recipes developed for these special flours.

Whole-grain flour and meal are coarse and are not sifted prior to measuring. Instead they are stirred and then lightly spooned into the measuring cup.

Sugar. Sugars—granulated, powered, and brown—pack in storage. Granulated sugar should be stirred and then spooned lightly into the cup to overflowing and leveled with a spatula. Powdered sugar packs more solidly than granulated sugar and should be sifted before measuring. Brown sugar is not sifted because of its sticky nature; instead it is lightly packed into the graduated cup and leveled. The measured brown sugar will retain the shape of the cup when removed. Lumpy brown sugar should be broken up with a rolling pin or forced through a sieve before measuring. It can also be steamed in the top of a double boiler until the moisture returns and it can be handled easily. Brown sugar should be tightly sealed and stored in the refrigerator to avoid moisture loss and hardening. Free-flowing brown sugar is poured or spooned into a measuring cup and made level. A cup of free-flowing brown sugar weighs one-fourth less than a cup of regular brown sugar.

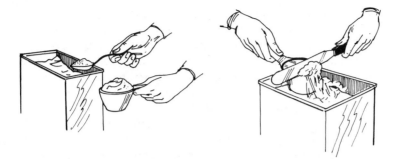

Shortening. Solid fat at room temperature traps less air when packed and is easier to measure than cold fat, which is very firm. Solid fats and shortenings are packed into a graduated cup measure and leveled with a spatula. A flexible scraper facilitates the transfer of fat from the measuring container.

Butter and margarine are usually packaged in individual quarter-pound sticks, or prints, (four sticks per pound; one pound equals two cups) and is sold in one-pound units. Each stick equals one-half cup and can be used without measuring, when the recipe calls for one-half cup of butter or margarine. Usually the wrapper on each stick is marked with tablespoon and fractional cup measures. When precise measurements of fat are not essential, a cut is made through the wrapper at the desired measure. A cup of whipped butter or margarine weighs only two-thirds as much as the regular product. Butter and margarine contain 20 percent water and should not be substituted on a one-to-one basis for shortening.

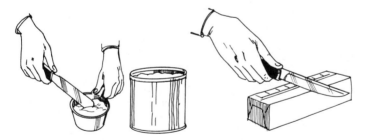

Liquids. All liquids as well as melted shortening, oil, and syrups are measured in a standard glass measuring cup placed on a level surface. Fill the glass measure to the desired level and then bend or stoop to read the measure at eye level. The bottom of the meniscus (curved surface of the liquid) should be level with the desired measure on the cup. Use a flexible scraper to remove all of the viscous liquid from the measure.

Eggs. Most recipes call for a specific number of eggs, but some call for a cup measure. Recipes are developed to use medium-sized eggs. When a recipe specifies a cup measurement for eggs, that amount should be used. When only half an egg is required, the egg is first beaten to mix the yolk and white, and then divided using spoon measures. Half of a medium egg measures about two tablespoons.

Spoon Measures. Ingredients such as baking powder, soda, salt, spices, extracts, and other seasonings are specified in spoon measures. Stir all dry ingredients to lighten them and then fill desired spoon measure to overflowing and level with a straight-edge spatula. Solid shortening or brown sugar are packed into the spoon measure and then leveled with a spatula. Spoon measures of liquids are made by carefully pouring the liquid into the desired measure.

TEMPERATURE

Food-preparation temperatures range from those used for baking or frying (325° F to about 450° F or 163° C to about 232° C) to boiling (around 212° F or 100° C) to freezing (about 32° F or 0° C).

Heat is applied to food by conduction (heat flows from one material to another), convection (heated air or liquid currents), and radiation (heat waves). The application of heat to foods can improve both palatability and sanitation.

Temperature is an important factor in determining the state of matter. Changes in temperature alone transform water from a liquid to a gas or a solid state. Temperature is an important component in cookery as well as in the transformation of matter.

Temperature can affect both the chemical and the physical nature of food. A chemical change results in a new product or combination of products. Caramelization, browning, and dextrinization are examples of chemical changes induced by heat. The physical form of the food may be changed by temperatures ranging from melting and boiling to freezing points. Gelatinization is a physical change effected by heat.

Intermediate Temperatures

Lukewarm designates a temperature of 104° F (40° C), which feels barely warm to the touch. Additional heat elevates the temperature to scalding (149° F or 65° C), at which point large bubbles appear on the bottom of the pan. With continued heating, water reaches the simmering temperature range of 180 to 210° F (82 to 99° C), which can be recognized by large bubbles that rise slowly and burst before reaching the surface.

Boiling Temperature

The point at which vapor pressure (upward pressure) of the liquid exceeds atmospheric pressure is known as the boiling point. At the boiling point some of the water changes into a vapor. The temperature of rapidly boiling liquid and of one boiling slowly is the same (212° F or 100° C). Increasing the heat input will speed evaporation but will not raise the temperature.

When water is the cooking medium, the temperature for cooking will be limited to the temperature of the boiling water. The temperature of boiling water can be elevated by increasing the pressure above atmospheric pressure, as occurs in a pressure cooker. Conversely, the temperature of boiling is lowered in a vacuum or partial vacuum because atmospheric pressure is reduced. When water is boiled in the mountains, atmospheric pressure is naturally lower. Consequently, the boiling temperature is lower, and foods must be cooked longer at high altitudes than at lower ones.

Particles that dissolve in water (sugar, salt) lower the vapor pressure and in this way raise the boiling temperature of the mixture. The point of boil is elevated progressively as the quantity of dissolved solute is increased. Substances (such as salt) that ionize when in solution contribute more particles than substances that retain their molecular form in solution. It is the number of dissolved particles that increase the point of boil rather than the size of the molecules.

Frying Temperatures

Some techniques of food preparation use fat or oil as the cooking medium, although water is the most common medium for cooking. Because of their low vapor pressure, fats do not boil and can attain a much higher temperature than that of boiling water. Temperatures for deep-fat frying range from about 350° F

(177° C) for doughnuts to 385° F (196° C) for french-fried potatoes. The higher temperatures attained by fats permit food to cook more quickly than in boiling water. Because of the high temperature pans in which foods are fried become extremely hot and must be handled carefully to avoid serious burns. They should not be transferred directly from the range to kitchen counters unless the counter is of stainless steel. Most kitchen counters can be severely damaged by the intense heat.

Cold/Freezing Temperatures

Some foods—gelatin or frozen salads and desserts—require cold or freezing temperatures in their preparation. As water becomes colder, it reaches the freezing temperature (32° F or 0° C) and becomes a solid. The freezing point of water can be altered with the addition of sugar or other substance that goes into solution or that ionizes, such as salt. The freezing point becomes lower as the number of dissolved particles increase.

Storage Temperatures

Storage temperatures influence food quality and safety. Refrigerator temperature retards the growth of microorganisms and permits short-term food storage. A temperature of 140° F (60° C) also discourages bacterial growth and can be used to retain the serving temperature of foods. Low temperature settings on ovens permit food to be held at this temperature. However, temperatures ranging between 40° F (4° C) and 140° F (60° C) favor rapid growth of microorganisms. It is important to lower quickly the temperature of cooked foods that are to be refrigerated to about 38° F (3° C), which is below the danger zone favoring bacterial growth. Large quantities of cooked food should be divided into small portions for rapid cooling. A useful cooling technique is to place a bowl of hot food—particularly liquid—into a sinkful of ice water. Frozen foods should be stored at temperatures well below 32° F (0° C) (store best at 10 to −10° F; −12 to −24° C) to maintain eating quality. Dried foods lack the moisture content to favor microbial growth and may be stored at room temperature.

WATER

Water is not only an essential constituent of food, but also serves important functions in food preparation. One of its functions is as a solvent. Water is the most commonly used solvent in cookery. It will dissolve a greater variety of substances than any other solvent. A number of flavor, color, and nutrient components of food are water soluble. The rate at which these components dissolve in water influences the palatability, color, and nutrient value of the food. Water-soluble nutrients can be lost when foods are prepared in excessive quantities of water.

Water serves as a dispersing medium for food components. Particles of starch and protein are dispersed throughout the liquid medium (water) of foods. In food preparation, particles of starch or flour are dispersed in water to permit the formation of a smooth starch gel.

Water is the medium in which chemical changes occur. Leavening agents such as soda and acid ingredients react in water to form carbon dioxide for leavening of flour products.

Water may be classified either as hard or soft, depending upon the mineral components present. Hard water contains salts, which form insoluble precipitates such as calcium, iron, and magnesium. Sulfate (SO_4) and chloride (Cl) salts give water a permanent hardness, while the bicarbonate salts (HCO_3) are responsible for a temporary hardness. Calcium and magnesium bicarbonates are changed to insoluble salts when water is boiled. These insoluble salts precipitate to form deposits in pots.

Hard water causes cloudiness in tea and coffee, a slightly yellow color in boiled white vegetables, and prolonged cooking time for some vegetables owing to reaction of pectic substances with the salts in hard water. Soft water is generally free of insoluble salts and is preferred for food preparation. However, hard water is considered beneficial from a health standpoint.

SOLUTIONS

Solutions are homogeneous, that is, uniform throughout. Particles do not separate or settle out in a true solution. The solubilizing ability of water permits the formation of solutions used in food preparation. The water (**solvent**) and the dissolved substance (**solute**) form syrups or brines. True solutions may contain solutes that ionize, such as salt; they also may contain small molecules capable of being dissolved. Sugar is the most commonly used solute of this type in food preparation. A solute may be dilute, concentrated, saturated, or supersaturated. A dilute solution contains a small amount of solute, whereas a concentrated solution contains a relatively large amount. A solution may be concentrated by boiling—as, for instance, sugar and water are boiled in candy making—and then supersaturated by undisturbed cooling.

COLLOIDS

Particles too large to dissolve but that remain dispersed form **colloidal** systems. Colloidal particles are electrically charged. Some carry a positive (plus) charge, others a negative charge (minus). Like charges repel each other, and that is why colloidal particles remain dispersed. Some foods exist in a colloidal state. Milk proteins, for example, are dispersed in a colloidal form. Colloid refers to a state of matter,

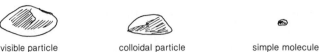

visible particle   colloidal particle   simple molecule

Particle size: Colloidal particle size lies between that of visible particle and simple molecules and they are larger than water molecules in which they are dispersed. Colloidal particles form foams, gases, gels, emulsions, solids, and liquids.

not a kind of matter. Protein, gelatin, starch, and fat may be called colloids. Colloids diffuse slowly in water, clog filters, and are not crystalline.

From the three states of matter (gas, liquid, solid) eight classes or combinations of colloidal systems can be formed. Sols, gels, foams, and emulsions are colloidal systems important in food preparation.

When a mixture of flour and water is heated, the granules swell and remain dispersed rather than precipitating. That is an example of a sol. Similarly, gelatin can be dispersed in hot water to form a sol. These are examples of a solid in a liquid colloidal dispersion. When they are chilled, the solid will entrap the liquid to form a gel, a situation just the reverse of the sol. Gels also can be formed with egg or flour proteins in the preparation of custards, puddings, or batters.

The dispersion of immiscible liquids, one liquid in the other, is known as an emulsion. Mayonnaise and margarine are examples of emulsions. Foams are colloidal dispersions in which gas is dispersed through a liquid, as is true in an egg-white foam.

pH AND FOOD ACIDITY

The properties of a number of different foods are affected by their acidity. The acid or alkaline nature of compounds is indicated on a **pH** scale. The pH scale was developed as a convenience for expressing the hydrogen ion concentration in solution. The pH scale ranges from 1 to 14. Neutral solutions have a pH value of 7; basic solutions have a pH value greater than 7; and acidic solutions have a pH value less than 7 (pH $= -\log [H^+]$).

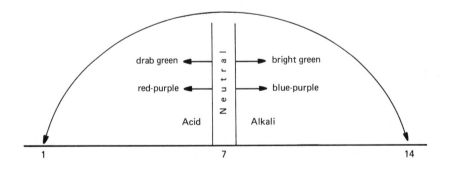

Acid

Acids are compounds that usually have a sour taste and cause blue litmus paper to turn red. They contain one or more hydrogen ions per molecule. Strong acids provide more hydrogen ions than weak acids. Most of the acids in food are classed as weak organic acids and are composed of hydrogen, carbon, and oxygen. For example, tartaric acid is found in grapes and is a constituent in some baking powders. Citric acid is found in citrus fruits and malic acid in apples and a variety of other fruits and vegetables. Oxalic acid is in rhubarb, and acetic acid gives vinegar its characteristic flavor.

Acids from tissues of green vegetables gradually begin to change the bright green of chlorophyll to the drab olive green of pheophytin. Cream of tartar causes an acidic pH in angel food cake, which has the effect of maintaining a white color in the baked product and also contributes to its volume and tenderness. Fruit juices for jelly making must contain sufficient acid so that a gel can be formed when they are cooked with added sugar. Since most vegetables are only slightly acidic, they must be processed for canning at temperatures higher than that of boiling water in order to destroy the heat-resistant bacterial spores.

Base

The alkaline nature of a base is generally derived from the presence of hydroxyl ions (OH^-). Any substance that accepts or acquires H^+ (protons) is known as a base. Soluble bases form solutions that cause red litmus to turn blue. Bases react with acids. The metallic ions of the base and the hydrogen ion of the acid exchange places to form a neutral salt and water.

In cookery baking soda is the ingredient most often used to produce the desired degree of alkalinity. The pigments in chocolate change in color with the pH of the medium in which they are dispersed. The color of chocolate cake ranges from a yellowish brown at a pH of 5 to a reddish brown at about pH 7.5. An alkaline pH may protect the green color of chlorophyll, but it will contribute to a mushy texture. Since an alkaline pH accelerates the breakdown of cellulose, ascorbic acid, and thiamin, the use of soda is discouraged in vegetable cookery. A base dulls colors except green and also imparts a bitter taste.

Salt

A compound made of any positive ion other than hydrogen and any negative ion other than hydroxide is known as a salt. For example, a salt is formed when baking soda (sodium bicarbonate) reacts in a solution with cream of tartar to yield potassium sodium tartrate (a salt), along with water and carbon dioxide.

When baking soda reacts with the acid component in baking powders to produce carbon dioxide for leavening, one or more salts will form.

ENZYMES

Enzymes are proteins produced by living cells (animal and plant), which act as catalysts to promote chemical reactions in living tissues. Because they are proteins, all enzymes are subject to denaturation (change in structure) by heat, cold, mechanical agitation, or acidity. Enzymes are effective in very low concentrations and function at optimum temperatures and pH to catalyze specific reactions. They remain unchanged while catalyzing reactions that range from the digestion of foods in animal systems to complex metabolic activity in both plant and animal systems.

Enzymes are often named by adding the suffix *-ase* to the name of the material (substrate) they act on. They are classified according to the type of reaction they catalyze. For example, lipases break up complex fats into simple ones by the addition of water. Oxidoreductases catalyze oxidation and reduction reactions and are important in food processes.

Active enzymes remain in plant and animal tissues used for food and must be controlled during processing and preparation of many food products in order to maintain quality. Enzymes make possible the improvement of traditional food products and the development of new products. Rennin is the enzyme used to clot milk in cheese making. Amylases in flour hydrolyze starch to maltose and some dextrins. Yeast enzymes break down maltose to glucose in bread dough.

Enzymes promote the ripening of fruits by changing starch to sugar and softening fruit tissues. Enzyme action is also responsible for some of the browning of cut surfaces of fresh fruits. Vegetables are blanched before they are frozen to destroy enzymes that promote texture and flavor changes during frozen storage.

Pectic substances present in fruits and vegetables are useful in jelly making but interfere with juice extraction and give a hazy appearance to some processed fruit juices (apple, grape). Therefore pectinases are added during processing to break down the pectin and thus produce a clear juice.

Meats are tenderized by the enzymes papain (from papaya), bromelin (from pineapple), and ficin (from figs). Papain hydrolyzes (breaks down) muscle fibers to smaller peptides. Bromelin and ficin degrade fibrous connective-tissue proteins and thus tenderize meat. Tenderizing occurs when meat proteins are denatured by heat during cooking. The enzyme promotes the partial breakdown of the meat protein before the proteins of the enzymes are denatured by heat.

Invertase (or sucrase) is an enzyme used in the candy industry to help control sugar crystallization. Invertase is added to the cherry centers before they are chocolate coated. During storage, invertase hydrolyzes some of the sucrose in the fondant center to form glucose and fructose (invert sugar). These monosaccharides are more soluble and inhibit crystal formation and promote softening of the chocolate-coated centers.

MICROBIAL ACTION

Even though foods were safe to eat when purchased, improper storage, insufficient cooking, and unsanitary food handling allow microorganisms in food to increase to dangerous levels. Although the action of some microorganisms is desirable in food preparation to develop characteristic flavors and textures in food products (see Chapter 2), the protection of food against undesirable microbiological action remains a major problem. Food spoilage as well as illness can be avoided by controlling conditions favorable to microorganism growth.

SUMMARY

Food preparation involves measurement, temperature, water, solutions, colloids, pH, enzymes, and microbial action. Standard measuring equipment and measuring techniques are essential for accurate measurements, which result in consistently high-quality products. Water is an essential constituent of food and serves as a solvent, a dispersing medium, and a medium for heat transfer in food preparation. Temperature affects the physical and chemical nature of food. Food preparation and storage involve a range of temperatures from about 450° F (232° C) to below freezing. Food spoilage and illness can be minimized by conditions unfavorable to growth of microorganisms.

SELF-STUDY GUIDE

1. Describe the procedures for measuring flour, sugar, shortening, liquids.
2. How are spoon measures of dry ingredients made? of liquid ingredients?
3. Contrast the metric measure used in food preparation with customary measures.
4. Identify the metric units and symbols used in food measurement.
5. How are Fahrenheit temperatures converted to Celsius?
6. How does hard water differ from soft water? What undesirable results in food preparation are due to the use of hard water?
7. What are the uses of water in food preparation? List three examples.
8. Compare the characteristics of solutions and colloids.
9. Discuss the influence of different temperatures on foods.
10. List three factors or substances that influence the boiling temperature of water.
11. Which techniques of food preparation require intermediate temperatures? freezing temperatures? Give two examples for each.
12. Compare the temperature of boiling water with temperatures used for frying food. Why does this difference in temperature exist?
13. Discuss the influence of temperature on the growth of microorganisms.
14. Which techniques of food preparation utilize microorganisms to achieve desirable results? Give three examples.
15. Identify solution and colloidal systems involved in food preparation, and give four examples.

SUGGESTED READINGS

AHEA *handbook of food preparation*. Washington, D.C.: American Home Economics Association, 1980.

AHEA *handbook for metric usage*. Washington, D.C.: American Home Economics Association, 1977.

BENNION, M. *Introductory foods*. New York: Macmillan Co., 1985.

————. *The science of food*. New York: Harper and Row, Publishers, 1980.

CHARLEY, H. *Food science*. 2nd ed. New York: John Wiley and Sons, 1982.

FREEDLAND-GRAVES, J., and PECKHAM, G. *Foundations of food preparation*. New York: Macmillan Co., 1979.

FULTON, L.; MATTHEWS, E.; and DAVIS, C. *Average weight of a measured cup of various foods*. Home Economics Research Report no. 41. Washington, D.C.: Department of Agriculture, 1977.

HOLMBERG, R. *Meal management today*. Belmont, Calif.: Wadsworth Publishing, 1983.

KENDALL, P. *High altitude food preparation*. Fort Collins: Colorado State University, 1979.

MATTHEWS, R. H., and BATCHELDER, O. M. Sifted vs. unsifted flour: Weight variations and results of some baking tests. *Journal of Home Economics* 55:123, 1963.

MILLER, B. S., and TRIMBO, H. B. Use of metric measures in food preparation. *Journal of Home Economics* 64:20, 1972.

NOLAN, D. *Metric cooking: 115 easy recipes*. South Holland, Ill.: Goodhart-Wilcox, 1981.

SLEEPER, A. *Concise metric conversion table*. Garden City, N. Y.: Dolphin Books, 1980.

TRAUB, L., and ODLAND, D. *Convenience foods and home-prepared foods*. Agricultural Economic Report no. 9. Washington, D.C.: Government Printing Office, 1979.

U.S. DEPARTMENT OF AGRICULTURE. *Food*. Home and Garden Bulletin no. 228, Washington, D.C.: Government Printing Office, 1980.

————. *Money-saving main dishes*. Home and Garden Bulletin no. 43. Washington, D.C.: Government Printing Office, 1979.

WASON, B. Cooks, gluttons and gourmets: A history of cooking. Garden City, N.Y.: Doubleday, 1962.

5

FOOD ASSESSMENT: SENSORY AND OBJECTIVE

OBJECTIVES

When you complete this chapter, you will be able to

1. Identify quality characteristics of food and suggest sensory and objective methods of evaluation

2. Define the following in terms of their use in food-quality evaluation:

objective	physical	rank order
subjective	rheology	paired-comparison
assessment	testing panel	test
sample	consumer panel	triangle test
sensory	scoring scales	duo-trio test

3. Explain the basis for selection of appropriate assessment methods.

4. Describe the preparation of samples for sensory evaluation.

5. Explain procedures for quality evaluation of food.

6. Discuss the relationship of data provided by physical, chemical, and sensory methods.

The preparation of quality products is an objective of cookery. Careful **assessment** of food products contributes to the knowledge and understanding of food preparation and places emphasis on quality. The general appearance of a food product offers the first clue to quality. Quality refers to the degree of perfection present and involves characteristics such as aroma, flavor, color, texture, and shape/size of foods. These characteristics contribute to the acceptance or rejection of foods.

The study of food involves the application of appropriate preparation principles to specific foods and also a systematic evaluation of the prepared product to determine the quality standards met. Evaluation requires both a knowledge of which characteristics to observe and a system that differentiates among degrees of quality. It results in information about characteristics that make a product acceptable and reveals a product's weaknesses. **Sensory** factors and general acceptability are measured. Once an individual has learned to apply the assessment process to a standard product, this ability can be used consistently to detect slight differences among products and identify those of high quality.

SENSORY CHARACTERISTICS

Sensory methods are used to evaluate food quality—smell, taste, sight, feel, and hearing. The aroma, taste, color, and mouth feel determine the acceptability of foods. As soon as food is placed in the mouth, the central nervous system receives signals from the taste, smell, touch, and temperature receptors.

Aroma

The aroma emitted by a food is an indication of its quality and wholesomeness. Only volatile components elicit odor sensations from the sense of smell. These volatile components are transmitted in the air passing into the nose to a small olfactory lobe within the nasal passage. Odors are perceived when the cilia (terminal ends of the olfactory organ) transmit electrical impulses via nerves to the brain for interpretation. Short, quick inhalations aid in detecting odors.

Chemical components such as amines, imines, and esters confer odor on compounds. Common classifications of odors include acid, burned, caprylic or goaty, ethereal, fragrant, fruity, mint, musty, nutty, putrid, rancid, resinous, and spicy.

Mechanisms that elicit odor sensations are not well understood. Adaptation and fatigue are problems in odor testing. Odors tend to stop being perceived after only a few observations, and recovery from fatigue on the part of the observer occurs slowly. Although odor-testing devices like the gas-liquid chromatograph have been devised, the simple act of sniffing remains the most popular method.

Taste/Flavor

Flavor represents a combination of sensations including taste, smell, and touch. Temperature influences the volatility of compounds that elicit aroma and odor. Hot and cold sensations contribute to the overall flavor of food. Depending on the food, both high and low temperatures can elicit less response from taste receptors and decrease taste sensitivity. This varying sensitivity to taste at different temperatures promotes the service of certain foods at low temperatures (most salads, fresh fruits, and vegetables) and others at hot temperatures (soups, many beverages, and casseroles).

The sensation of flavor contributes pleasure to eating. The four basic tastes are classified as bitter, salt, sour, and sweet. Receptors, or taste buds, are not equally sensitive to all taste stimuli. Salt and sweet flavors are best perceived at the tip of the tongue, sour along the edges, and bitter at the back. Some taste cells may respond to more than one taste stimulus. The sour sensation is associated with hydrogen ions, and salt sensation with ions of salts (commonly sodium chloride), and the sweet sensation to organic compounds such as aldehydes, alcohols, some amino acids, and glycerol. A bitter sensation is associated with caffeine, nicotine, quinine, magnesium salts (epsom salts), and some synthetic sweeteners.

Taste buds consist of groups of cells some of which are supporting cells and others taste cells. A substance must be dissolved in saliva and come in contact with the microvilli to promote a taste sensation. Foods usually contain varying concentrations of two or more individual tastes. The interaction of tastes and odors complicate the sensory evaluation of food flavors.

Color

Color contributes an aesthetic quality to food and is associated with the degree of ripeness, flavorfulness, and wholesomeness. Objects absorb part of the radiation that makes up white light and reflect the remainder. White light is made up of a wide spectrum of wave lengths and can be separated into the colors of the rainbow when it passes through a prism. The eye, along with the brain, is able to distinguish among the wave lengths that constitute white light. Foods appear colored because the light they reflect contains only part of the wave lengths from the visible portion of the spectrum. White objects reflect all rays while black objects absorb all rays of light.

Texture

The characteristic known as texture represents a wide range of properties attributed to foods by structural and tactile components. The tactile characteristics of food relate to its size, shape, form, and feel to the tongue and mouth. A texture profile evaluates the mechanical, geometric, fat, and moisture properties of food. Mechanical properties include adhesiveness, chewiness, cohesiveness, fracturability, gumminess, hardness and viscosity (Szczesniak 1977). Because specific terms are not available to describe texture, a variety of descriptive terms such as velvety, creamy, grainy, coarse, and chewy are used.

Texture varies with the nature of the food product. For example, the texture of cream soups and cornstarch puddings is referred to as consistency. The size of gas cells and thickness of cell walls in baked products determine their texture. Texture of food can elicit a variety of sensations and contribute to its tactile sensation, mouth feel (softness, hardness, crispness, stickiness, elasticity, and astringency) and can affect the flavor of food.

ASSESSMENT

Assessment involves systematic procedures to determine if the characteristics of the product meet established standards of quality. It is much more complex than a visual observation of the food product. Individual quality characteristics are dependent on the nature and type of food product and are responsible for the overall appearance of the product. Food products are assessed in terms of their individual characteristics, which usually include appearance, shape, color, flavor, texture, and tenderness. Other factors include aroma, consistency, flakiness, juiciness, moistness, volume, and overall eating quality.

The various techniques and procedures used to assess food products include sensory, physical, and chemical methods. Tests based on sensory assessment are subjective and may reflect personal bias. Tests that utilize special instruments or devices are objective and reflect the skill of the operator. The information desired determines the type of test used. The student may wish to know how the prepared food compares with the standard or "perfect" product; the food manufacturer may wish to know how specific ingredients or preparation methods influence the product.

Food Testing

Sensory assessment seeks to identify quality differences and to determine which products are preferred or found most acceptable by consumers. The quality testing is done by professional panels; consumer testing determines the preferred product. Commercial applications of food research may also require consumer testing.

Food-Testing Panel

Sensory evaluations of food quality are made whenever food is consumed. The senses of smell, taste, sight, feel, and hearing are used to assess the character and quality of food. A testing panel is composed of selected individuals capable of evaluating specific attributes of foods. Judges or food-testing panels are assembled to identify the sensory differences or preferences among food **samples.** They are asked to indicate differences among foods according to the selected scoring or testing method. Members of testing panels for research purposes should be the most able judges available for the entire period of the experiment, should not dislike the food to be tested, and should be in good health. Their task is to detect differences or similarities among food samples, rank or score samples for specific characteristics, and consistently assign similar values or ranks to comparable food samples.

Panel members may be trained for specific testing purposes and should have a common understanding of terminology and procedures used for food testing. Increasing the number of panel members usually decreases experimental error and improves reliability of the results. Sensory evaluations and preference judgments should be made individually by each panelist to avoid being influenced by others. Distractions and any opportunity for collaboration among the judges should be prevented.

Consumer Panels

Consumer panelists may be asked to record their reactions or judgments on a numerical hedonic scale (often a nine-point scale) ranging from "like extremely" to "dislike extremely." They seek to identify which products or characteristics consumers prefer and will accept.

Food Samples

All food samples in a series should be placed in identical white containers and should be identified by a code that does not suggest first or last to judges. Geometric shapes, colors, randomly selected letters, symbols, or three-digit numbers may be used. The code and order of presentation may be altered when a series of samples is to be evaluated more than once. Only a limited number of samples can be judged efficiently during one session. More bland than strong-flavored samples can be evaluated in one session. Simple scoring systems facilitate evaluation of more samples during one session than complex scoring systems do.

SENSORY ASSESSMENT

Sensory assessments measure, analyze, and interpret reactions to characteristics perceived by the senses of taste, touch, and hearing (Prell 1976). Sensory methods for determining quality are similar for most foods. They determine the magnitude of detectable differences among foods. Regardless of the method used, comparison with standards of known composition (such as standard product) aid in interpretation of the magnitude of difference. Common sensory testing methods include scoring scales, rank order, triangle test, duo-trio test, and paired-comparison tests.

Scoring Scales

Scoring scales may be used when a large number of samples are evaluated and when differences are easily detectable. The numerical scale should be spaced so that differences in the scores reflect detectable differences in the characteristics being scored. The judges should be in agreement regarding the perfection standard for the characteristic so that the entire scoring scale may be used.

Numerical scales are often used to score the quality characteristics of a product. Descriptive terms such as brittle, flaky, velvety may accompany the assigned numerical score and thus provide a common interpretation for score assignments. Numerical scales range from three points to more than nine. An odd number of points permits the midpoint of the scale to represent a neutral point and contains an equal number of points on both the high and low side of the scale. The high numbers usually identify good quality; the low numbers, poor quality. The assessment sheets or cards list the quality characteristics to be evaluated and the scoring scale. Visual characteristics (color, size/shape) are usually scored first.

Rank Order

Rank order may be used when several samples are evaluated. Samples may be ranked from highest to lowest in order by the intensity of the characteristic, such as flavor, tenderness, color, or appearance.

Triangle Test

The triangle test determines the existence of a detectable difference between two products. Three samples, two of which are the same, are presented. The judge selects the sample that differs from the other two and may be asked to indicate the basis for the selection.

Duo-Trio Test

The duo-trio test presents a known control sample and two coded samples, one of which is a duplicate of the control. The problem is to identify the coded unknown.

Paired-Comparison Test

The paired-comparison test is used to determine detectable differences between two samples. Judges are asked to identify the difference in the two samples.

CHEMICAL AND PHYSICAL ASSESSMENT

Chemical and physical assessments elucidate the reasons for differences identified by sensory testing. Since physical and chemical methods are not dependent upon human judgment or preference, they are usually more readily reproducible, less costly, and less time consuming than sensory tests. It is difficult, however, to devise physical and chemical tests that measure sensory qualities in a manner similar to that of the human senses.

The data provided by physical and chemical methods must show a high correlation with sensory data to be regarded as an accurate test for the specific

Refractometer (Hershey Foods Corporation)

Penetrometer (Precision)

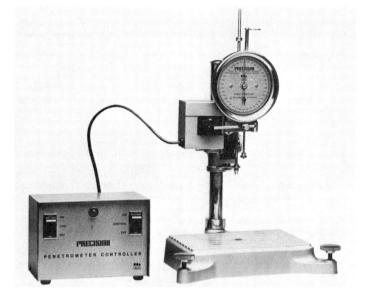

quality characteristic. Data from these tests are reported in established units of measure such as pH for degree of tartness or grams of force needed to break pastry, indicating the degree of tenderness. A variety of instruments measure food texture. A compressimeter uses a plunger to measure the resistance of a food sample to being compressed. A shear press measures the force required to cut through the food.

Chemical Methods

Chemical methods are used to determine the nutritive value of foods before and after cooking and to determine the constituents that affect the palatability and quality of food.

Structural and Physical Methods

The structure and the **physical** arrangement of food components can be determined with microscopic examination of foods such as cake batter, mayonnaise, and whipped cream. Plant and animal tissue can be prepared for histologic examination (Humason 1972). Three-dimensional images of material structures including foods can be viewed with electron microscopy (Cheng and Parish 1976). Physical properties of foods such as gel strength, length, temperature, color, volume, and liquid drainage are assessed with special instruments or simple devices (Szczesniak 1977).

Objective measurements of texture tend to be complex because it is difficult to simulate the action of the mouth and tongue in assessing foods. As indicated, textural qualities include mechanical properties (such as hardness, viscosity, chewiness) and geometrical characteristics (such as size, shape). A number of special instruments measure textural qualities of specific foods: the penetrometer measures the depth of penetration of a cone into a food; a shear device measures the force necessary to cut a food sample of specific size; the tenderometer (multiple-probed instrument) measures the maximum force required to penetrate a food sample (Campion, Crouse, and Dikeman 1975); and a tensile testing device measures the force required to pull a sample apart.

Rheologic Measure. **Rheologic** instruments measure the flow or deformity of solids and liquids (Hansen 1972). The flow of foods (such as cake batters, sauces, puddings) is easily measured with a line-spread test. The food is placed into a hollow cylinder and allowed to spread for a specified time. Consistency is reported in the distance spread in a designated time. A consistometer measures the distance that a semisolid, such as a sauce, spreads. Viscosity relates to the resistance of food to flow and can be measured with a viscosimeter that measures the rate of rotation of a cylinder with a constant force through a food mixture.

The rate of flow of juice is measured with a jelemeter and can be used to determine pectin content of fruit juice.

Rheology also concerns elasticity and gel strength of solids (pectin, gelatin, custards, for example). Solids do not flow but can be deformed by force. The firmness of these products is indicated by the extent to which they retain their height (percent sag) when removed from the container or by resistance to penetration. A simply calculated percent-of-sag test measures the height of a gel before and after unmolding. The difference in height is expressed as a percentage of the height before unmolding.

Press-Fluid Measure. Press-fluid instruments mechanically remove fluids from food samples. The moisture expressed from vegetables may be used as an index of maturity or succulence. Fluid expressed from meats indicates water-binding capacity. Moisture content of foods also serves as an indicator of quality.

Density Measure. Density indicates the amount of air incorporated into a product and can be determined by dividing the weight of the food in the container by the volume of the container. Low specific gravity indicates that a large amount of air is present.

RESEARCH

Research seeks answers to questions and solutions to problems. Research involves collecting, recording, and interpreting data and reporting results. Sensory and objective tests, such as those discussed, are used to collect data in food research, and collected data are organized into a format suitable for analysis. Appropriate descriptive and/or inferential statistics are used to put the data into meaningful and usable form.

Descriptive statistics are used to describe quantitatively characteristics of the sample from which data have been collected. Those statistics include frequency distribution; percents and percentiles; measures of central tendency (mean, median, mode); measures of dispersion (range, mean deviation, standard deviation); rank order; and correlation coefficient.

Inferential statistics provide a basis for making predictions, estimations, and inferences and include "t" test, chi square, analysis of variance, and the F test. The level of significance identifies the possibility that something happened as a result of the variable studied rather than by chance. The significance level for most research is usually identified as the .05 or the .01 level. At the .05 level of significance, the results are due to the variable under study 95 percent of the time and only 5 percent of the time by chance, and at the .01 level, 99 percent of the time to the variable studies and only once by chance.

SUMMARY

Food quality concerns the characteristics of aroma, flavor, color, texture, and shape/ size. The senses of smell, taste, sight, feel, and hearing are used to assess the quality of food. Sensory and objective tests identify quality differences and determine product preferences. Panel members use sensory evaluation to determine food quality. Sensory testing methods include scoring scales, rank order, triangle test, duo-trio test, and paired-comparison test. Objective testing methods include chemical, structural, and physical tests.

SELF-STUDY GUIDE

1. Identify five individual characteristics of food that can be assessed to determine its quality and acceptance.
2. Discuss the basis for selection of food-testing methods.
3. Discuss the differences/similarities between food-testing panels and consumer panels.
4. Discuss the preparation of food samples for assessment.
5. Discuss the common sensory tests used to determine differences among foods.
6. Identify/compare the ways in which subjective assessment differs from objective assessment. Give two examples.

SUGGESTED READINGS

AMERINE, M. A.; PANGBORN, R. M.; and ROESSLER, E. B. *Principles of sensory evaluation of food.* New York: Academic Press, 1965.

AOAC. *Official methods of analysis.* 12th ed. Washington, D.C.: Association of Official Analytical Chemists, 1975.

BODRERO, K. L., et al. Evaluation of the flavor volatiles contribution to the aroma of beef by surface response methodology. *Journal of Food Science* 46:26, January/February 1981.

BOURNE, M. C.; MOYER, J. C.; and HAND, D. B. Measure of food texture by a universal testing machine. *Food Technology* 20:522, 1966.

BREENE, W. M. Problems in instrumental analysis of texture in foods. *Journal of Texture Studies* 6:53, 1975.

CAMPION, D. R.; CROUSE, J. D.; and DIKEMAN, M. E. A research note—the Armour tenderometer as predictor of cooked meat tenderness. *Journal of Food Science* 40:886, 1975.

CHENG, C. S., and PARRISH, JR., F. C. Scanning electron microscopy of bovine muscle: effect of heating on ultrastructure. *Journal of Food Science* 41:1449, 1976.

CLYDESDALE, F. M. Instrumental techniques for color measurement of foods. *Food Technology* 30:52, 1976.

CROSBY, G. New sweeteners. CRC critical reviews in *Food Science and Technology* 7:293, 1976.

DASTOLI, F. R. The chemistry of taste. *New Scientist* 37:465, 1968.

DEMAN, J. M.; RASPER, P. W.; RASPER, V. F.; and STANLEY, D. W. *Rheology and texture in food quality.* Westport, Conn.: Avi Publishing Company, 1976.

FINKOWSKI, J. W.; and PELEG, M. Some rheological characteristics of soy extrudates in tension. *Journal of Food Science* 56:207, January/February, 1981.

FINNEY, JR., E. E. Elementary concepts of rheology relevant to food texture studies. *Food Technology* 26:68, 1972.

———; BEN GERA, I.; and MASSIE, D. R. An objective evaluation of changes in firmness of ripening bananas using a sonic technique. *Journal of Food Science* 32:643, 1967.

FRANCIS, F. J., and CLYDESDALE, F. M., *Food colorimetry: theory and application.* Westport, Conn.: Avi Publishing Company, 1975.

GREGORY, R. L. *Eye and brain, the Psychology of seeing.* World University Library. New York: McGraw-Hill Book Company, 1966.

GYASIC, S., et al.   Elastic and viscoelastic Poisson's ratio determination for selected citrus fruits. *American Society of Agricultural Engineering Transaction* 24:747, May/June 1981.

HANSEN, L. J.   Development of the Armour tenderometer for tenderness evaluation of beef carcasses. *Journal of Texture Studies* 3:146, 1972.

HARDY, S. L.; BRENNAND, C. P.; and WYSE, B. W. Fructose: Comparison with sucrose as sweetener in four products. *Journal of American Dietetic Association* 74:41, 1979.

HUMASON, G. L.   *Animal tissue techniques.* 3rd ed. San Francisco: W. H. Freeman Company, 1972.

INGLETT, G. E.   Sweetness in perspective. *Cereal Science Today* 19:258, 1974.

LARMOND, E.   Laboratory methods for sensory evaluation of food. Ottawa, Ont.: Canada Department of Agriculture, 1977.

———.   Physical requirements for sensory testing. *Food Technology* 27:28, 1973.

MACKINNEY, G., and LITTLE, A. C.   *Color of foods.* Westport, Conn.: Avi Publishing Company, 1962.

MANNHEIM, N. C., and BUKAL, A.   An instrument for evaluating firmness of grapefruit segments. *Food Technology* 22:331, 1968.

MARTIN, S. L.   Selection and training of sensory judges. *Food Technology* 2:22, 1973.

MATZ, A. A.   *Food Texture.* Westport, Conn.: Avi Publishing Company, 1962.

MELOAN, C., and POMERANZ, Y.   *Food analysis laboratory experiments.* 2nd ed. Westport, Conn.: Avi Publishing Company, 1980.

MIN, D. B.   Correlation of sensory evaluation instrumental gas chromatographic analysis of edible oils. *Journal of Food Science* 46:1453, September/October, 1981.

NEWELL, G. J.   New procedure for comparing methods in food science. *Journal of Food Science* 46:978, May/June 1981.

OCKERMAN, H. W., et al.   Design and evaluation of a modified shear head for the Warner-Bratzler shear to evaluate tenderness of cooked ground beef patties. *Journal of Food Science* 46:1948, November/December, 1981.

POMERANZ, Y.   Scanning electron microscopy in food science and technology. *Advances in Food Research* 22:205, 1976.

PRELL, P. A.   Preparation of reports and manuscripts which include sensory evaluation data. *Food Technology* 30:40, 1976.

ROWLAND, L. M., et al.   Physical and sensory properties of chicken patties made with varying proportions of white and dark spent fowl muscle. *Journal of Food Science* 46:834, May/June, 1981.

SATHE, S. K., et al.   Effect of addition of great northern bean flour and protein concentrates on rheological properties of dough and baking quality of bread. *Cereal Chemistry* 58:97, March/April 1981.

SHUEY, W. C.   Practical instruments for rheological measurements of wheat products. *Cereal Chemistry* 52:42, 1975.

SZCZESNIAK, A. S.   A overview of recent advances in food texture research. *Food Technology* 31:71, 1977.

TERADA, M., et al.   Rheological properties of dough made from flour exposed to gaseous ammonia. *Cereal Chemistry* 58:101, March/April 1981.

TOPPING, A. J.   Recording laboratory penetrometer for fruit. *Journal of Agricultural Engineering Research* 26:179, March 1981.

TSAI, T. C., and OCKERMAN, H. W.   Water binding measurement of meat. *Journal of Food Science* 46:697, May/June 1981.

VICKERS, A., and BOURNE, M. C.   A psychoaccoustical theory of crispness. *Journal of Food Science* 41:1158, 1976.

YAMAGUCHI, S.; YOSHIKAWA, T.; IKEDA, A.; and NINOMIYA, T.   Studies on the taste of some sweet substances. Part I. Measurement of the relative sweetness. Agricultural and Biological Chemistry 34:181, 1970.

6

CEREALS

OBJECTIVES

When you complete this chapter, you will be able to

1. Identify grains used as food, give examples of their uses, and list products derived from grains other than breakfast cereals.
2. List the major components of grains and their nutrient contribution.
3. Compare the nutritional quality of enriched and whole-grain cereals, and identify the contribution of grains to well-balanced diets.
4. Define: enriched, restored, converted, and re-fined cereals; pasta, processing, gelatinization.
5. Describe the cookery procedure for cereal,

pasta, and rice and describe the well-prepared product.
6. List the factors to consider when selecting cereal products.
7. Discuss the processing of cereals and explain the difference between cereals that need to be cooked and instant cereal.
8. Explain how the quality of cereal products is retained during home storage.
9. List and discuss the factors that influence the time required to cook cereals.

Cereals originated from wild grasses that may have been brought under cultivation as early as 7000 B.C. Cereal grains are the dried seeds of cultivated grasses and include barley, corn, millet, oats, rice, rye, and wheat. The cultivation of wheat spread along with the development of civilization making wheat the most widely grown of all food plants. Cereals have a high yield per acre, can be stored for long periods, and are palatable and nutritious. In most parts of the world at least one cereal grain can be grown, providing food for humans as well as animals. The grain best adapted to the soil and climate of a particular area became the preferred cereal of that area. Wheat is the preferred cereal in the United States, while rice is preferred in Japan and some regions of China.

Cereals were first cooked by parching the whole grain. Later they were ground between stones to form a coarse meal, which was made into porridge by boiling in water or into a heavy, unleavened bread. In addition to serving as a source of food, cereals are valued for their industrial uses. Wheat and rye are milled into flour, which can be used to make bread and a variety of baked products such as crackers, cakes, and pastries. The germ portion of corn is pressed to yield oil. Corn oil, cornstarch, corn syrup, and corn meal become ingredients used in the preparation of foods.

This chapter is concerned with the various cereal grains used as food, their structure, composition, processing, and preparation.

STRUCTURE AND COMPOSITION

All cereals consist of three distinct portions: the bran, germ, and endosperm. The bran refers to the outer layers that surround the grain and protect the developing kernel. These bran layers are made mainly of cellulose and hemicellulose, which are indigestible and give bulk to the diet. Bran also contains vitamins (thiamin, niacin, riboflavin), minerals, and some protein. Bran makes up about 5 percent of the entire grain. The bran is separated from the remainder of the grain by a layer of cells—the aleurone (Figure 6-1).

The endosperm forms the central and largest portion (about 85 percent) of the entire grain and is the storage area for starch granules embedded in a protein matrix or core. The endosperm contains most of the starch and protein in the grain but very small amounts of minerals, vitamins, and cellulose.

The germ is the smallest portion of the grain and is located at one end of the grain. It is the portion from which the new grain develops. The germ is a rich source of unsaturated fat, minerals (chiefly iron), and vitamins (thiamin, niacin, riboflavin) and also contains some protein and sugar (chiefly sucrose). Because unsaturated fats are unstable, the germ is often removed during milling to prevent many cereal products from becoming rancid. The shelf life of cereals and flours is greatly increased by removal of the germ.

NUTRITIONAL QUALITY

The nutritional quality of cereal products is dependent upon the portions of the grain used (Table 6-1). All cereals are composed chiefly of starch, a polysaccharide, and are less expensive sources of energy. After cereals are ground, small quantities of dextrin may be found. The carbohydrate content of cereal products ranges from

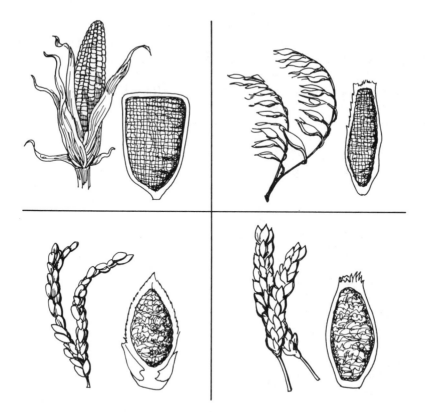

Figure 6-1 Cross-sectional diagrams of cereal grains. Source: Cereal Institute, Inc.

70 to 80 percent, with somewhat lesser amounts in refined cereals than in whole grains.

The increased interest in the probable need for more fiber in the diet to promote motility in the intestine has focused attention on whole-grain cereals. However, cereals are not a good source of fiber if the bran is not retained in the food product.

The protein and fat (more abundant in whole grain than in refined cereals) also make a contribution to the total caloric value of the cereal. Cereals are not high in protein, but their protein content is of importance when cereals provide the basis of the diet, as is true in most developing countries. The protein of cereals is classified as incomplete. The protein content of cereals is about 1 percent for rice, 8 to 9 percent for corn, 9 to 14 percent for oats, 10–12 percent for wheat. Cereal proteins are well utilized when they are supplemented with complete proteins of meat, milk, eggs or with legumes. Although legumes do not contain complete proteins, they provide some of the amino acids missing in cereals. Lysine and tryptophan are the essential amino acids lacking in cereal proteins. These amino acids are best provided by the complete protein of animal products.

Table 6–1 Nutrient Content of Selected Cereal Products

Product	Measure	Kcal	Protein g	Iron mg	Thiamin mg	Riboflavin mg	Niacin mg
Corn (hominy) grits degermed, enriched, cooked	1 cup	125	3	7	.10	.07	1.0
Cornmeal,							
whole-ground, dry	1 cup	435	11	3.9	.10	.13	2.4
degermed-enriched, dry	1 cup	500	11	4.0	.61	.36	4.8
degermed, unenriched, dry	1 cup	500	11	1.5	.19	.07	1.4
Corn flakes, plain	1 cup	100	2	.4	.11	.02	.5
Farina, quick cooking, enriched, cooked	1 cup	105	3	.7	.12	.11	1.8
Macaroni, cooked							
enriched	1 cup	155	5	1.3	.20	.11	1.5
unenriched	1 cup	155	5	.6	.01	.01	.4
Noodles, cooked							
enriched	1 cup	200	7	1.4	.22	.13	1.9
unenriched	1 cup	200	7	1.0	.05	.03	.6
Oats, rolled, cooked	1 cup	130	5	1.4	.19	.05	.2
Rice, white							
enriched, cooked	1 cup	225	4	1.8	.23	.02	2.1
enriched, instant, ready to serve	1 cup	180	4	1.3	.21	—	1.7
parboiled, cooked	1 cup	185	4	1.4	.19	—	2.1
Rice, puffed, added nutrients	1 cup	60	1	.3	.07	.01	.7
Wheat flours							
whole wheat, hard	1 cup	400	16	4.8	.66	.14	5.2
all-purpose, enriched, sifted	1 cup	420	12	3.3	.51	.30	4.0
self-rising, enriched	1 cup	350	7	.5	.03	.03	.7
Wheat, puffed, enriched	1 cup	55	2	.6	.08	.03	1.2
Wheat, shredded, plain	1 biscuit	90	2	.9	.06	.03	1.1
Wheat, flakes, enriched	1 cup	105	3	1.3	.19	.04	1.5

From *Nutritive Value of American Foods in Common Units*, Agriculture Handbook 456 (Washington, D.C.: Agricultural Research Service, Department of Agriculture, 1975); and *Composition of Foods (Breakfast Cereals, Raw, Processed, Prepared)*, Agriculture Handbook no. 8–8 (Washington, D.C.: Human Nutrition Information Service, Department of Agriculture, 1982).

The germ portion of grains is their principal source of fat, which includes oleic and linoleic fatty acids, and lecithin, a phospholipid. Compared with other foods, however, cereals are low in fat, containing about 1 percent for refined cereals and about 2 percent for whole grain.

Minerals and vitamins are present in a high concentration in the bran, with somewhat lesser amounts in the germ and endosperm. Whole-grain products are good sources of thiamin and niacin, fair sources of riboflavin, and good sources of iron. Cereals lack vitamins A, D, and ascorbic acid. Yellow corn is the only cereal containing carotenes, which can be converted in the body to vitamin A. Refined cereals are of limited value in providing vitamins and minerals unless they are enriched, and even after enrichment they do not usually provide all the nutrients in the original whole grain.

ENRICHED CEREALS

The nutritional value of refined cereals is improved by **enrichment.** If cereals are enriched, federal law requires that iron, thiamin, riboflavin, and niacin be added. The addition of calcium and vitamin D is optional for most products, but self-rising cornmeal and self-rising flour must be enriched with calcium if these products are being enriched. The enrichment of corn products is especially desirable in the areas where corn is the staple cereal, since whole corn is lower in some vitamins and minerals than whole wheat.

When the cereal is labeled enriched, thiamin, riboflavin, niacin, and iron (and also calcium and vitamin D, if added) must be present between the minimum and maximum levels specified by federal regulations. The Food and Drug Administration has established federal standards for enrichment of white bread and flour, cornmeal, grits, macaroni products, and rice (Table 6–2), which must be met if a product is to be labeled enriched, but this law leaves enrichment as an optional

Table 6-2   Enrichment Nutrient Standards per Pound of Corn Meal, Farina (Wheat), Rice, and Macaroni Products.

Nutrient	Corn Meal	Farina (wheat)	Rice	Macaroni Products
Thiamin	2.0– 3.0 mg	2.0– 2.5 mg	2.0– 4.0 mg	4.0– 5.0 mg
Riboflavin	1.2– 1.8 mg	1.2– 1.5 mg	1.2– 2.4 mg	1.7– 2.2 mg
Niacin	16.0–24.0 mg	16.0–20.0 mg	16.0–32.0 mg	27.0–34.0 mg
Iron	13.0–26.0 mg	13.0 mg	13.0–26.0 mg	13.0–16.5 mg
Optional:				
calcium	500–750 mg	500 mg	500–1000 mg	500–625 mg
vitamin D	250–1000 IU	250 IU	250–1000 IU	250–1000 IU
	(2.5–10 mcg)	(2.5 mcg)	(2.5–10 mcg)	(2.5–10 mcg)

One IU vitamin D = 0.025 mcg vitamin D.

United States Food and Drug Administration, Federal Register 137.260, Federal Register 137.305, Federal Register 137.350, and Federal Register, 139.115, 1983.

procedure. Some states have adopted legislation requiring enrichment of all refined cereal products marketed within their boundaries.

The nutritive value of rice that is to be polished can be enhanced by parboiling the rice before it is milled. This process draws some of the nutrients from
the bran layers into the endosperm. Then when the rice is milled, the nutrients
are retained at useful levels in the endosperm. This rice is identified as **converted**
or parboiled rice. Its appearance is almost identical to polished rice, although parboiled rice has a very slight yellow color due to its riboflavin content.

Polished rice may also be enriched by impregnating the surface of the rice
with enrichment nutrients and coating it with a water-resistant substance. Another
method coats the rice with enrichment nutrients that are not resistant to rinsing.
This rice is identified with a label specifying that the rice should not be rinsed
before cooking or drained after cooking in order to retain vitamins. Unless polished
rice is labeled enriched, neither of these enrichment applications has been applied.

Breakfast cereals labeled as enriched must follow federal standards for the
addition of iron, thiamin, riboflavin, and niacin. A number of ready-to-eat cereals
may contain added nutrients such as calcium, ascorbic acid, or protein. These
additions may be included with the enrichment nutrients. Some of these additions
may partially restore milling losses and may identify the product as "restored."
The package label is a good guide to the nutrient values of these products. Many
cereal products display a nutrition information panel that lists the nutrient values
as percentages of the U.S. RDA per serving.

SELECTION

Cereals can contribute generous amounts of nutrients to the diet when attention
is given to selection. It is important to select all cereal products from among the
whole-grain, enriched, restored, or parboiled/converted products because of their
higher nutrient values compared to refined, nonenriched products (Tables 6–1 and
6–3).

Cereal grains may be marketed as uncooked, partially cooked (quick cooking), and ready to eat. Generally, uncooked cereals cost less than ready-to-eat cereals. The cost of cereals should be compared on the basis of cost per ounce and
cost per serving. Most ready-to-eat cereals are relatively bulky, requiring larger
packages than uncooked cereals, which are compact and packaged in a smaller box
for the same weight of the cereal. Large packages do not necessarily yield more
servings than small packages.

Some cereals are available in more than one package size and should be
compared in terms of cost per serving. Cereals in large packages tend to cost less
per serving than those in small packages, but wise shoppers will compare economy
of various package sizes since this generalization is not always true. Sugar coating,
special flavorings, and added dried fruit and nuts increase the cost per serving of
the cereal. Information in Table 6–4 aids in determining amounts of cereal or **pasta**
products to buy.

Table 6-3 Sample Nutrition Information Panel.

NUTRITION INFORMATION PER SERVING		
Serving size (Servings per package)	1 ounce (1¼ cups) (Vary with package size)	
	1 OUNCE CHEERIOS	CHEERIOS PLUS ½ CUP VITAMIN D MILK
Calories	110	190
Protein, grams	4	8
Carbohydrate, grams	20	26
Fat, grams	2	6
Sodium, Milligrams	330	390
PERCENTAGE OF U.S. RECOMMENDED DAILY ALLOWANCES (U.S. RDA)		
Protein	6	15
Vitamin A	25	30
Vitamin C	25	25
Thiamin	25	30
Riboflavin	25	35
Niacin	25	25
Calcium	4	20
Iron	25	25
Vitamin D	10	25
Vitamin B-6	25	30
Vitamin B-12	25	35
Phosphorus	10	20
Magnesium	10	15
Zinc	6	8
Copper	6	6

Ingredients: Whole oat flour, wheat starch, salt, sugar, calcium carbonate, trisodium phosphate, sodium ascorbate (vitamin C), niacin (B vitamin), iron (a mineral nutrient), vitamin A palmitate, pyridoxine hydrochloride (vitamin B-6), riboflavin (vitamin B-2), thiamin mononitrate (vitamin B-1), vitamin B-12 and vitamin D.

CARBOHYDRATE INFORMATION		
Starch and related carbohydrates, grams	17	17
Sucrose and other sugars, grams	1	7
Dietary fiber, grams	2	2
Total carbohydrate, grams	20	26

Published courtesy of General Mills, Inc.

Table 6-4 Cups per market units purchased of selected cereal and pasta products.

	MARKET UNIT	CUPS PER MARKET UNIT	
Cereal Products			
Ready to eat:			
Bran flakes	16 oz		13¼
Bran flakes/raisins	20 oz		10
Corn flakes	12 oz		11¾
Puffed rice	7 oz		15¼
Puffed wheat	6 oz		14¼
Shredded wheat	10 oz		8
To be Cooked:			
Farina, quick cooking	13½ oz	uncooked	2
		cooked	12½
Oats, rolled			
quick	18 oz	uncooked	7
		cooked	12½
regular	18 oz	uncooked	6¾
		cooked	12
Rice			
long grain	16 oz	uncooked	2¼
		cooked	8¾
short grain	16 oz	uncooked	2¼
		cooked	8⅞
precooked	14 oz	uncooked	6¼
		simmered	9½
Brown rice, long grain	16 oz	uncooked	2½
		cooked	10
Bulgar	16 oz	uncooked	3¼
		cooked	10
Cornmeal, degerminated	24 oz	uncooked	4½
		cooked	19
Hominy, canned	29 oz	heated, drained	3⅜
Pasta Products			
Macaroni, elbow	16 oz	uncooked	3½
		cooked	10
Noodles, medium width	16 oz	uncooked	8⅞
		cooked	12
narrow width	16 oz	uncooked	10
		cooked	12¼
Spaghetti	16 oz	cooked	7¼

Adapted from USDA, Science and Education Administration, *Buying Food,* Home Economics Research Report no. 42 (Washington, D.C.: Government Printing Office, 1978).

PROCESSING

The **processing** of cereals originated in the United States and developed into a major enterprise. Grain is sold by the farmer directly from the field to operators of large elevators, where the grain is cleaned and stored. The grain is then sold to operators of elevators located near food-processing centers, directly to the food processor, or to brokers who supply the needs of the processors. The purchased grains then enter the manufacturing chain.

The bran and germ of wheat are separated from the endosperm as the kernels pass between rollers operated at high speed. Heat from the rollers melts the fat in the germ, and the germ and bran come off in flakes. A combination of sifting and air currents separate the flakes from the endosperm which is heavier. The endosperm continues to subdivide as it passes between rollers set closer and closer together. The subdivided material is sifted after each passage through the rollers.

Processing may be as simple as cutting the kernel of grain into smaller particles to facilitate cooking. Hulling, milling, and polishing are techniques to subdivide the grains into the desired particles or fractions. The variety of processed cereal products is extended by shredding, flaking, extruding, rolling, and granulating. Any number of these techniques may be applied in the fabrication of ready-to-eat cereals.

Cereal products come to the consumer in many different forms. Products made of wheat, corn, oats, and rice are most common. It is convenient to classify cereal into two general categories: hot (need to be cooked), and ready to eat (require no additional cooking).

Hot Cereals

Grains utilized in hot cereals may be the whole grain, or they may be ground, cracked, or rolled. Ground or rolled grain is divided into small fragments, which cook more quickly than the whole grain and may be marketed as quick cooking. Other quick-cooking cereals may be treated with a salt, disodium phosphate (Na_2HPO_4), making the cereal more alkaline and causing it to soften quickly, thus reducing the time of cooking.

Instant cereals are precooked to gelatinize starch and thus eliminate the need for further cooking. Instant cereal requires only the addition of boiling water for rehydration. The texture and flavor may be somewhat different from that of the cooked cereal counterpart.

Ready-to-Eat Cereal

Ready-to-eat cereals may be made of one grain or a mixture of grains and seasonings, such as salt, sugar, and malt. The prepared cereal mixture is usually

Various forms of ready-to-eat cereal (Laimute Druskis)

toasted and also may be shredded, granulated, puffed, or flaked. Sometimes a sugar coating is applied.

Shredded cereal is prepared from a cooked mixture of flour and seasonings, forced through a shredding mechine, and formed into a loose biscuit to be toasted. Flakes are prepared from a seasoned and cooked thick cereal paste, which is shaped into flakes and toasted.

When a grain is heated under pressure and the pressure is released quickly, the steam present in the grain causes the cell walls to puff out, resulting in a puffed cereal grain eight times its original size. This is a permanent increase in size, so servings of puffed cereals (corn, rice, wheat) are large in volume in comparison with their weight.

USES OF CEREAL GRAINS

Cereals are used in a number of ways. Wheat is considered the staple American cereal even though corn is native to this country.

Wheat

Wheat is probably the most versatile grain. It is used as cereal and as flour to form the basis of a variety of products. As a breakfast cereal, wheat may be served hot, for instance, cream of wheat or farina, and ready to eat, such as shredded, puffed, or flaked wheat. Wheat cereal is used as an ingredient in casseroles and baked products. Durum, a special variety of hard wheat, is the basis of pastas and noodles. Wheat is milled into flour suitable for bread or general baking; it is also used in starch production.

Bulgar. Bulgar is either soft or hard wheat parboiled and dried. Some of the bran layers remain, and the wheat is usually cracked. Bulgar requires a longer cooking time than refined cereals. Its texture and flavor are similar to wild rice.

(b) Close up of corn kernels (USDA Photo)

(a) Corn (USDA Photo)

(c) Wheat (USDA Photo)

(d) Close up of wheat (USDA Photo)

Barley

Pearled barley is a popular soup ingredient. The hulls and bran are removed from the whole grain to yield pearl barley. Barley flour is used in breakfast cereals and baby foods. Malt is derived from sprouting barley and is valued for its flavor.

Buckwheat

Buckwheat is the fruit of an herbaceous plant rather than of a grass, as are cereals. Buckwheat flour is used in griddle cakes, alone or with other flours, and is noted for its nutlike flavor.

Corn

Corn is a native grain of America and our third most widely produced grain. Young ears of sweet corn are used as a vegetable and mature ears of field corn are made into ready-to-eat and hot cereals, hominy (intact corn endosperm) and grits (broken pieces of endosperm), cornmeal and starch, and oil. Cornstarch is obtained from the endosperm by a wet-milling technique, and oil is extracted from the germ. Cornstarch is subjected to enzyme or acid hydrolysis to yield corn syrup, a mixture of dextrins, maltose, and glucose. Corn is also used for animal feed and industrial purposes.

Oats

Oats are chiefly used for oatmeal, which is made by rolling, grinding, or cutting. The outer hull is removed, but most of the bran and germ remain, making oats a good source of B vitamins and iron. Oat protein is regarded as the best of the cereal proteins.

Rice

Rice is eaten as a boiled grain, sometimes enhanced with available seasonings, and as a ready-to-eat cereal. Rice starch and flour are produced but are not often used in cooking. The whole grain with only the husk removed is brown rice. The bran and germ are removed from polished rice. There are many varieties of rice. The long-grain kernels tend to separate, remaining light and fluffy when cooked, while short-grain rice tends to cling together. Wild rice, the seed of an aquatic grass, is not a true rice. The kernels are long, narrow, and dark in color and have a distinctive flavor. It is served as an accompaniment to meat, poultry, or game or as a stuffing.

(b) Close up of grains of rice (USDA Photo)

(a) Rice (USDA Photo)

(c) Oats (USDA Photo)

(d) Close up of oats (USDA Photo)

Rye

Rye flour is available as white, medium, and dark. Rye flour is blended with wheat flour to produce a lighter loaf of bread. A very limited amount of rye is used in breakfast cereal.

Triticale

Triticale is a new cereal, a hybrid of wheat and rye. It contains more lysine and protein than wheat. Triticale flour makes acceptable breads and noodles.

STORAGE OF CEREAL PRODUCTS

Refined cereals and cereal products store well; whole-grain cereals may become rancid during prolonged storage. Cereals should be kept in closed containers in a cool, dry cupboard away from strong-smelling foods. Refrigerator or freezer storage prolongs the shelf life of refined cereals and is even more useful for long-term storage of whole-grain cereals. Tightly covered metal, glass, or plastic containers are ideal for long-term storage. The crispness and flavor quality of cereal products are maintained by refolding the inner liner of the package, when present, and keeping the package closed. Crispness can be restored to cereals that have absorbed moisture by heating them in a shallow pan in a 350° F (177° C) oven for a few minutes. Table 6–5 gives the approximate time cereals and pastas will maintain their quality when properly stored.

Table 6-5 Cereal and Pasta Home-Storage Guide

FOOD	MAXIMUM STORAGE TIME (FOR BEST QUALITY)
Breakfast cereals	2–3 months
Bulgar	6 months
Cornmeal, degerminated	4–6 months
Hominy grits, degerminated	4–6 months
Rice	
white, parboiled, or precooked	1 year
brown, wild	6 months
Pasta (except egg noodles)	1 year
Noodles, egg	6 months

Adapted from USDA, Science and Education Administration, *Cereals and Pasta in Family Meals,* Home and Garden Bulletin no. 150. (Washington, D.C.: Government Printing Office, 1979).

PREPARATION TECHNIQUES

Cereals are cooked to improve digestibility, palatability, and appearance. Heat and moisture soften cellulose and gelatinize the starch of the endosperm. Cereal cookery is essentially starch cookery.

Gelatinization

The term *gelatinization* refers to the changes that occur when starches are heated with water. Starch occurs in granules that do not dissolve in water. In the presence of water and heat, starch granules take in water and swell gradually, and the starch sol becomes clear (translucent) and thick as the temperature approaches the boiling point.

The same general cookery techniques and guides are applied to most cereals. However, the proportion of water to cereal and the cooking time vary with specific cereals. Therefore, it is recommended that the cooking directions on individual cereal packages be followed for best results.

Cooking time depends upon particle size. Fine and flaked cereal require less cooking time than coarse cereals or whole kernels. Cooking time is also determined by the processing treatment. The precooked, enzyme, or disodium phosphate-treated cereals cook in a short time. The flavor of cereal is improved when cereals are held over low, direct heat five to ten minutes or over boiling water for ten to fifteen minutes after gelatinization.

The proportion of water to cereal depends upon particle size and the ability of the particles to absorb water. Flaked cereals usually require twice their volume of water; coarse-cracked cereal, four times; and fine cereals, five or six times their volume.

Prevention of Lumps

One objective of cereal cookery is to avoid lumping. Following are three techniques for combining cereal with water without lumping. The techniques are related to particle size.

Whole or Flaked Cereal.   The whole or flaked cereal is added slowly to rapidly boiling water, while stirring. The cereal is stirred sufficiently to prevent lumps but not overstirred because too much stirring causes rupturing of starch granules.

Fine Cereal.   Fine cereal is moistened with some of the measured cold water to separate the granules. The remainder of the water is heated to a boil, and the moistened cereal is slowly poured into the boiling water while stirring.

All Cereals.   Fine and coarse cereals may be added slowly, while stirring, to hot water before a boil is reached. Whichever technique is used, once the cereal and water have been combined, cooking is continued over moderate heat, with gentle stirring to prevent sticking and lumping, until a boil is reached. Then cooking is continued on low heat until the cellulose is soft, the cereal thickened, and the raw starch flavor gone. If desired, cereals requiring a prolonged cooking period may be completed over boiling water. The formation of a skin due to surface drying of cooked cereal is prevented by tightly covering the cereal until it is served.

Well-Cooked Cereal.   A well-prepared cereal is free of lumps and has a pleasing, mild flavor. It should not be of a pasty consistency; pieces of cereal should be distinct and separate. Overstirring leads to the disruption of starch granules and a pasty or sticky texture.

Rice

The objective of rice cookery is to retain the shape of the kernel while at the same time tenderizing it. The amount of water and cooking time will vary with the kind of rice. The package directions are good guides for cooking specific kinds of rice. Generally, the amount of water rice requires is two to two and one-fourth times its volume. This amount of water is absorbed during cooking. In this way the water-soluble nutrients are retained rather than discarded with the excess water. If the rice is not soft when a grain is rubbed between the fingers, or if it begins to stick, a little more water is added to complete gelatinization of the starch.

Polished rice requires about twenty minutes to cook, and brown rice (because of the layers of bran) takes about forty minutes. Both brown and wild rice may be soaked in boiling water to soften the bran (about an hour) and shorten cooking time. When the soaked wild rice is drained and cooked in additional boiling water, the flavor becomes mild, and some loss of B vitamins in the soaking water occurs. Minute rice, since its starch needs only to be rehydrated rather than gelatinized, requires a much shorter cooking time than regular rice but greatly reduced yields of product.

Effect of Alkaline pH.   White rice and refined cereals contain flavonoid compounds, which develop a yellowish color in alkaline water. These pigments remain white when a small amount of acid is present in the cooking water.

Pastas

Pastas are made from stiff doughs prepared from water and semolina, a coarse flour ground from durum wheat. Pastas include spaghetti, macroni, and noodles. Spaghetti and macaroni doughs are extruded through discs that yield the

(National Pasta Association)

desired shapes. Spaghetti is a rod form, vermicelli a tiny rod, and macaroni a hollow tube; numerous other small shapes, such as shells and alphabets, are also available. Noodles are flat strips made with durum flour and 5 percent egg solids or yolk. Pasta products are often enriched with B vitamins and iron. Some new pasta-type products contain corn and soy and spinach along with wheat, or whole wheat which further enhance their nutrient content.

Package directions are good guides for the preparation of pastas. Generally one-half pound of pasta is cooked in six cups of water with one teaspoon each of salt and oil. The oil is used to reduce sticking and foaming. Pastas may also be cooked in minimum water—twice as much water as pasta product. A utensil with a tight-fitting lid is used and the heat reduced to low when the water boils. With this method the nutrients are retained rather than discarded with the excess water.

SUMMARY

Cereals are the dried seeds of cultivated grasses and commonly include barley, buckwheat, corn, oats, rice, rye, and wheat. They are chiefly composed of starch and contribute incomplete proteins, which are well utilized when supplemented with the proteins of milk, meat, eggs, and legumes. Minerals and vitamins are present in a high concentration in the bran and germ, with somewhat lesser amounts in the endosperm. Breakfast cereals and flour represent two major uses of cereals. Cereals are cooked to improve digestibility and gelatinize starch.

SELF-STUDY GUIDE

1. Describe the structure and composition of cereal grains. Identify the nutritional contribution of the major portions of the grain. Compare the nutritional value of enriched cereals with whole-grain products.
2. What four factors should be considered in the selection of cereal products?
3. How are cereals stored to protect their quality?
4. Discuss the processing of grains.
5. What are the common uses of cereals and grains in meals? Give four examples.
6. Explain what occurs when cereals are cooked.
7. How is lumping prevented in cooked cereals? Give three examples.
8. Describe well-prepared cooked cereal products including rice and pasta.

SUGGESTED READINGS

ALLEN, K. G.; and LLEVAY, L. M.   Copper and zinc in selected breakfast cereals. *Nutrition Reports International* 22(3):389, 1980.

AHEA.   *Handbook of food preparation.* 8th ed. Washington, D.C.: American Home Economics Association, 1980.

ANALYSIS OF CEREALS.   *Food Engineering.* 52:79, August 1980.

ANDERSON, R. H.; MAXWELL, D. L.; MULLEY, A. E.; and FRITSCH, C. W.   Effects of processing and storage on micronutrients in breakfast cereals. *Food Technology* 30(5):110, 1976.

BAKER, D.; and HOLDEN, J. M.   Fiber in breakfast cereals. *Journal of Food Science* 46:396, March/April 1981.

BRANDBURY, J. J.; COLLINS, J. G.; PYLIOTIS, N. A.   Methods of separation of the major histological components of rice and characterization of their proteins by amino acid analysis. *Cereal Chemistry* 57:133, 1980.

CEREAL INSTITUTE.   *Breakfast cereals and nutritional fortification.* Schaumber, Ill.: Cereal Institute Inc., 1979.

CEREALS.   *Food Engineering.* 53:104, August 1981.

CHRISTIANSON, D. D.; KHOO, U.; NIELSEN, H. C.; and WALL, J. S.   Influence of opaque-2 and floury-2 genes on formation of proteins in particulates of corn endosperm. *Plant Physiology* 53:851, 1974.

DAVIS, K. R., et al.   Evaluation of the nutrient composition of wheat. I. Lipid constituents. *Cereal Chemistry* 57(3):178, 1980.

DUBOIS, D. K., and HOOVER, W. J.   Soya protein products in cereal grain foods. *Journal of the American Oil Chemists' Society* 58:343, March 1981.

Flaked, whole grain cereals aimed at consumers' nutritious desires. *Food Engineering* 58:37, September 1981.

HENSLEY, G. W., HONLIHAN, E. J.   Caloric value of fiber-containing cereal fractions and breakfast cereals. *Journal of Food Science* 45:372, 1980.

HERNANDEZ, M., et al.   Nutritional evaluation of cereal-cheese-whey mixtures. *Journal of Food Science* 47:81, January/February 1982.

INGLETT, G. E., and MUNK, LARS.   *Cereals for food and beverages: Recent progress in cereal chemistry and technology.* New York: Academic Press, 1980.

LI, B. W., and SCHUHMANN, P. J.   Gas chromatographic analysis of sugars in granola cereals. *Journal of Food Science* 46:425, March/April 1981.

LOCKHART, R., et al.   Caloric value of fiber-containing cereal fractions and breakfast cereals. *Journal of Food Science* 45:372, March/April, 1980.

LORENZ, K., et al.   Proso millets: Milling characteristics, proximate composition, nutritive value of flours. *Cereal Chemistry* 57:16, 1980.

MONGEAU, R., and BRASSARD, R.   Determination of neutral detergent fiber in breakfast cereals: Pentose, hemicellulose, cellulose and lignin content. *Journal of Food Science* 47:550, March/April 1982.

POMERANZ, Y., ed.   *Advances in cereal chemistry and technology.* St. Paul, Minn.: American Association of Cereal Chemists, 1976.

RHODES, A. P., and GILL, A. A.   Fractionation and amino acid analysis of the salt-soluble protein fractions of normal and high lysine barleys. *Journal of the Science of Food and Agriculture* 31:467, 1980.

SHARIFF, G., et al.   Further studies on the nutritional evaluation of wheat, triticale, and rice grains using the red flour beetle. *Cereal Chemistry* 58(2):86, 1981.

Studies show cereals don't increase caries. *Food Engineering* 52:65. November 1980.

TABEKHIA, M. M., et al.   Crude protein and amino acid composition of three California rice varieties. *Nutrition Reports International* 23:805, May 1981.

U.S. DEPARTMENT OF AGRICULTURE. *Cereals and pastas in family meals.* Home and Garden Bulletin no. 150. Washington, D.C.: Government Printing Office, June 1979.

VANDERSLICE, J. T., et al. Vitamin B-6 in ready-to-eat cereals: Analysis by high performance liquid chromatography. *Journal of Food Science* 46:943, May/June 1981.

VARRIANO-MARSTON, E., and HOSENEY, R. C. Note on mineral content and location in pearl millet. *Cereal Chemistry* 57:150. 1980.

WANG, H. L., and HESSELTINE, C. W. Use of microbial cultures: Legume and cereal products. *Food Technology* 35:79, January 1981.

WOODBURY, W. Biochemical genetics and its potential for cereal improvement. *Bakers Digest* 46(5):20, 1972.

7

STARCH AND FLOUR

OBJECTIVES

When you complete this chapter, you will be able to

1. Describe the structure and composition of starch and identify food sources.
2. Explain what occurs when starch gelatinizes and dextrinizes.
3. Discuss the primary function of starch in cookery, and the application of starch-cookery principles to gravies, sauces, and puddings.
4. Identify and discuss the factors that influence starch gelatinization.
5. Discuss syneresis, retrograde, gel, and sol and give examples.
6. Identify types of flour available and list recommended uses.
7. Discuss gluten formation and function.
8. Explain formation of starch lumps in cooked products.
9. Explain the preference of wheat flour for bread making.

Starch and flour are derived from the endosperm of grain. Since prehistoric times, the inner kernel (endosperm) of grains has been separated from the outer layers of bran. Primitive methods used hollow stones to pound grain to a coarse powder. Later, air and water power turned heavy millstones to fragment the grain. Refinements in the process led to roller milling. Continued improvements in milling machinery led to the complex modern milling process.

Throughout history starch has been obtained from many cereal grains and root vegetables. A commercial process to extract starch from cereals was developed in the 1940s. Corn then became the best available source of starch. Other commercial starches include wheat, tapioca, potato, arrowroot, and grain sorghum. Both dry-milling and wet-milling (grain soaked or steeped to soften) procedures are used to separate starch granules from the protein fraction of the grain. A high-speed centrifuge separates out the starch; which is heavier than the protein.

This chapter is concerned with (1) the structure, types, functions, and cookery principles of starch and their application in food preparation; (2) flour milling, grades and types of flour, and gluten formation and function.

STARCH

Starch, a polysaccharide, is the main form in which plants store their energy. Starch is deposited as granules in the seeds, roots, and tubers of plants. Starch granules are laid down in small bodies called plastids found in the cytoplasm of plant cells. The size and shape of granules differ in different starches, according to their source. Most starches are a mixture of two fragments—**amylose** and **amylopectin**. The relative proportion of these fragments in starch influence the way starch performs in cookery. Starch is a common thickening agent in food preparation and an important structural component of flour and baked products.

All starches may be hydrolyzed to the intermediates of dextrin, maltose, and ultimately to glucose, and thus are an important source of energy for humans. Starch has many industrial uses. It is used to produce syrups and sugars. It can be physically and chemically modified to perform in a specific way in a variety of prepared food products such as casserole mixes, puddings, pie fillings, and sauces. Pregelatinized starches produce a thickened product without reheating. Acid-modified starches have a decreased viscosity on heating but form a strong gel when cooled. They are used in a variety of confections and fillings for bakery products. Cross-linked starches are less fragile and resistant to rupture during cooking. Stabilized starches produce a clear, nonstringy paste and maintain viscosity during cooking, cooling, and cold storage. All of these modified starches serve as low-cost stabilizers and thickeners in a variety of fabricated food products.

Structure

Glucose, a hexose (six-carbon sugar), is the structural unit of starch. In solution, glucose molecules exist in the aldehyde and ring (pyranose) structure. It is only the orientation of the hydroxyl group on carbon one that differs in the ring structures of alpha-D-glucose and beta-D-glucose. Alpha-D-glucose has the hydroxyl on carbon one oriented in the same direction as the hydroxyl on carbon four, while beta-D-glucose has the hydroxyl on both carbons one and four oriented in the opposite direction. Starch molecules are made of alpha-D-glucose, while cellulose is made of beta-D-glucose (Figure 7–1).

Maltose, an intermediate in starch hydrolysis, consists of two alpha-D-glucose linked through carbon one of the first molecule to carbon four of the

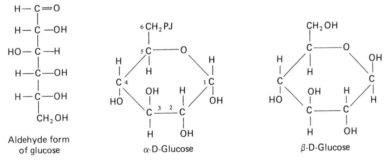

Figure 7-1 Glucose.

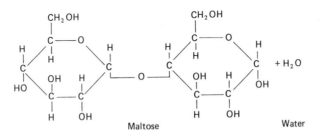

Figure 7-2 Maltose.

second molecule with a release of one molecule of water (Figure 7–2). Several molecules of glucose joined in the same fashion as maltose yield **dextrin,** another intermediate in starch hydrolysis.

The number of glucose molecules in starch range from as few as four hundred to several thousand. Starch granules are laid down in an organized pattern and form two distinct fractions, amylose and amylopectin.

Amylose. Amylose is a long, straight-chain molecule of many glucose units joined through the 1,4-linkage as in maltose. Amylose in solution forms flexible coils. Amylose is responsible for the gel-forming property of starches.

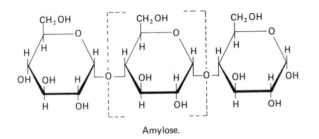

Amylose.

Figure 7-3 Amylose.

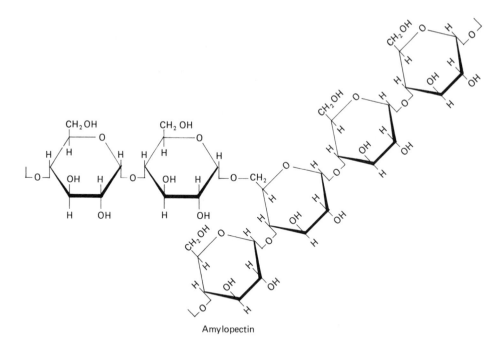

Amylopectin

Figure 7-4   Amylopectin.

Amylopectin.   Amylopectin is a highly branched molecule. Relatively short chains of alpha-D-glucose are linked through carbons one and four. These chains are joined in a branching structure through carbon one of the branch and carbon six of the glucose unit to which the branch is attached. Amylopectin molecules are larger, more bushy, and more compact than amylose. Amylopectin contributes to the thickening that occurs when starch is gelatinized, but it lacks the gel-forming ability of amylose.

When starch molecules complex with iodine, a color change occurs making possible the classic test for starch. Iodine occupies the space within the center of the helix. The color of the iodine-starch complex becomes blue when the helix is long and red when it is short.

Starch Granules

Starch granules can be seen under the ordinary microscope. The size and shape of the granules are characteristic for the specific plant. Rice granules are the smallest and potato granules the largest.

Starch granules subjected to the action of acid or enzymes indicate that starch molecules within a granule are not deposited uniformly. Starch granules are believed to be arranged in concentric rings deposited in a radial position. Positions

Magnified potato granules (E. G. Grave, Photo Researchers, Inc.)

of each ring are thought to be in a very ordered crystalline state that is linked to amorphous areas in which starch molecules are deposited in a less orderly manner. This arrangement of starch molecules within granules may be responsible for the functional properties of starch in cookery.

Most starches are a mixture of approximately 20 percent amylose and 80 percent amylopectin. Through plant breeding special varieties of rice, corn, and barley have been developed. Starch from these varieties contains only amylopectin, and these products are called waxy starch. When cooked with water, waxy starches form a smooth paste but do not gel because of the absence of amylose. They are excellent thickeners for fruit pies or other applications when gelling is not desired. Plant geneticists have also developed varieties of cereals in which the starch formed is about 80 percent amylose and 20 percent amylopectin (the reverse of the usual ratio). These high-amylose starches can be made into edible thin films and are used to protect some candies, raisins, and a few other foods during marketing.

Types of Starch

Starches used in food preparation are categorized by their plant origin. Cereal starches include corn, rice, and wheat; root starches include potato and tapioca (cassava root). These starches are similar in their general characteristics, but they do differ sufficiently to justify specialized usage.

Cereal Starches. Cereal starches produce gels and sols, will gel in moderate concentrations and have a nonpasty mouth feel. The starch in wheat yields an adequately clear paste of good viscosity, but it is accompanied by wheat proteins, which contribute opaqueness. The lack of clarity is not of concern when flour is used to thicken milk-containing products, which are opaque regardless of the type of starch used. Flour has only half the thickening power of corn-starch. Browned flour has less thickening power than unbrowned flour because some of the starch is converted to dextrins. Cornstarch is used to thicken fruit-pie fillings and sauces made without milk because the finished products will be translucent and **viscous.**

Root Starches.   Tapioca and potato starches contain less amylose and form less rigid, clearer gels than cereal starches. Root starches reach maximum viscosity at a lower temperature (203° F, 95° C) than cereal starches, which must be heated to the boiling point. Tapioca has about the same thickening power as cornstarch but does not yield a gel.

Modified Starches.   Chemical modification eliminates undesirable characteristics and extends the usefulness of starches. Cross-bonded waxy starches and tapioca do not develop stringy characteristics, and they resist thinning when stirred. Starches can be modified to control gelling and **syneresis** on standing by forming esters or ethers with some hydroxyl groups on the starch. Modified starches retain viscosity during cooking and cooling and resist syneresis and gelling when stored. Precooked, pregelatinized starches require only rehydration to produce a thickened mixture. They are used in instant puddings and convenience foods.

Functional Nature

The arrangement of starch molecules within granules may account for the functional properties of starch. Starches function primarily as thickening agents contributing viscosity and/or gel characteristics to products. To make them function as thickening agents starches are cooked during food preparation or during their production. The application of heat to starch brings about several changes. A temporary suspension is formed when starch is combined with cold liquid. When heat is applied to the starch-water mixture, the water begins to penetrate the granules and causes them to swell and soften. Starch granules vary in size and do not all swell at the same rate.

STARCH-COOKERY PRINCIPLES

Gelatinization and **dextrinization** are heat-induced changes in starch. Starch contributes maximum thickness when granules are freely dispersed in sufficient water and heated to gelatinize the starch completely.

Gelatinization

Although an acceptable precise definition is not available, *gelatinization* is the term given to the process that takes place when starch is heated in the presence of water. Both heat and water are required if gelatinization is to occur. Water penetrates starch molecules when the kinetic energy (energy associated with motion) of water molecules in contact with starch becomes sufficiently great to overcome the attraction between the hydrogen-bonded starch molecules on the granule. Water first penetrates the less dense area of the starch and then the crystalline areas as the temperature rises.

The temperature at which starches thicken water varies with the kind of starch. As the temperature increases, the milky suspension becomes translucent, the swelling starch grains lose their birefringence (luminous Maltese-cross appearance under polarized light), and begin to thicken the liquid. As heating continues, additional thickening occurs. Some of the short linear molecules (amylose) diffuse out of the swollen granules into the surrounding liquid.

The final increase in thickness may be due to an exudate (oozed-out material) from the swollen grains. The starch grains become less dense and remain suspended in the liquid assisted by the exudate, which contributes to the thickening. It appears that gelatinization of starch occurs in steps:

1. Begins with swelling of the starch grain.
2. Continues swelling as heat is applied and translucency increases.
3. Completes swelling with continued heat and release of exudate.

Factors Affecting Viscosity

A number of factors influence the viscosity of starch products including (1) the kind and concentration of starch and its dispersion, (2) the temperature to which it is cooked, and (3) the addition of sugar and acid.

Starch Concentration.   Starch is the ingredient responsible for the thickening of most cooked mixtures. Viscosity increases as the proportion of starch to liquid is increased. The thickening ability among the starches varies. Root starches have less thickening power than cereal starches. The firmness of the gel is also related to the type of starch. Cornstarch produces a firmer gel than wheat or rice starch. The proportion of starch required is influenced by the viscosity and gel firmness it promotes. Generally, one tablespoon of flour is equivalent to one-half tablespoon of cornstarch, rice starch, potato starch, or arrowroot starch and to one tablespoon of quick-cooking tapioca.

Dispersion of Starch.   A complete dispersion of starch is essential for maximum thickening and for a product free of starch lumps. When starch granules clump together, only the outside granules imbibe water and swell; the inner granules remain dry and do not gelatinize. Considerable lumping would have the effect of reducing the quantity of starch undergoing gelatinization and thus also reducing thickening or viscosity.

A complete dispersion can be achieved by (1) blending starch granules with other dry ingredients, (2) blending starch with melted or liquid fat before liquid is added, or (3) thoroughly blending starch with cold liquid and stirring the starch-water mixture just before it is slowly stirred into the hot liquid. One or more of these techniques may be used in the preparation of a food. For example, flour is blended into melted fat and then combined with liquid in the preparation of white or cream sauces; the flour may be blended with cold liquid and then stirred into hot drippings to make gravy; the starch may be blended with other dry ingredients (sugar, salt, cocoa) and then with cold milk to prepare a chocolate pudding.

Temperature. Viscosity is influenced greatly by the final temperature to which the starch is permitted to rise. Gelatinization begins at temperatures below boiling, but gelatinization of most starches is not completed until the paste is heated very close to the boiling point. Undercooked starch mixtures remain thin. Starch mixtures must be cooked beyond the temperature at which thickening begins to obtain a firm gel. For maximum thickening and to avoid a raw starch flavor, cornstarch or flour mixtures are heated to a boil, and tapioca to a high simmer. Maximum gelatinization of tapioca occurs below the boiling point, and further heating results in thinning.

Sugar. Sugar tenderizes a starch gel and can weaken the rigidity of the gel structure. When too much sugar is used, gelation may be prevented. Not only is gel structure weakened by sugar, but also pastes will be less viscous and more translucent. Sugar is hygroscopic (has a high affinity for water) and therefore presumably competes with starch for the liquid, thus restricting the amount of water available for hydration of the starch.

Acid. Acids cooked with starch reduce the thickening ability of the starch. Acids hydrolyze or cleave starch molecules into shorter, more soluble molecules possessing less thickening power. In order to avoid the hydrolysis of starch and achieve maximum thickening, acids such as lemon or other fruit juices are added after the starch mixture is gelatinized.

Gelation

The formation of a gel is referred to as gelation. Gels are colloidal systems that hold their shape and do not flow. A cornstarch pudding is a familiar example of a starch gel.

During gelatinization amylose molecules are leached into the liquid surrounding the granule. The kinetic energy decreases as the paste cools and the amylose molecules are no longer kept apart. The amylose molecules rebond to each other and to the outer edges of the starch granules to form a network. Amylose molecules tend to link together through hydrogen bonding. The cross bonding occurs at random intervals, and a gel structure forms. Very weak bonds may form between some branches of the bushy amylopectin molecule, but they do not yield a gel. Only starches that contain amylose form a rigid gel since amylose is primarily responsible for gel formation. Waxy starches contain very little amylose and therefore do not form gels.

Retrogradation

Starch gel formation is a gradual process as the paste cools. Additional bonds are formed between the straight-chain amylose molecules as the starch-thickened mixture stands after gelation. Starch gels will very slowly undergo a textural change during storage. Some of the amylose molecules aggregate (recrystallize) in an organized manner. **Retrogradation** refers to this increased association of amylose molecules as a starch gel stands. The amylopectin molecules show little tendency to retrograde. The gel network shrinks as the amylose molecules squeeze together and release water form the network.

Syneresis

The release of liquid from a gel is known as syneresis. When the starch network is allowed to stand for a period of time or is cut or disturbed, a separation of liquid may be noted. This is some of the liquid that was trapped by the amylose network until that network was disturbed and was then released.

Dextrinization

When starch is subjected to dry heat, it becomes brown and darkens with continued heating. A change is effected in the starch molecule, causing it to fragment and form shorter-chained molecules identified as dextrins. Dextrins have less thickening power and are more soluble than starch. The longer and more intense periods of heating result in a progressive breakdown of the starch molecule. The change in the size (length) of the molecules is known as dextrinization. Dextrins vary in size and are smaller than starch but larger than sugar molecules. Dextrinization contributes to the browning of toast and baked products. Dextrins also contribute a very pleasing flavor to foods.

APPLICATION OF STARCH COOKERY

Starch cookery techniques are applied in the preparation of foods ranging from soup to main dishes and desserts. Starch-thickened white sauces and gravies are used frequently. White sauces are the basis for the preparation of cream soup,

Table 7-1 Proportion of Ingredients for Cream Sauces

Type of Sauce	Flour (Tbsp)	Fat (Tbsp)	Milk (C)	Salt (tsp)	Uses
Thin	1	1	1	¼	Cream soups
Medium	2	2	1	¼	Creamed dishes
Thick	3	3	1	¼	Soufflés
Very thick	4	4	1	¼	Croquettes
Brown sauce	1–2[a]	1–2	1[b]	¼	Meat sauces or gravy

[a]Measure is for browned flour, which is prepared by heating the measured flour alone in a frying pan (while stirring constantly with a wooden spoon) until the flour is a medium brown color.
[b]Meat or vegetable stock may be substituted for milk.

creamed meats and vegetables, croquettes, and soufflés. Cornstarch puddings serve as a relatively light dessert or as a base for preparation of other desserts.

Flour and starch-thickened products (gravies, sauces, puddings) can be prepared with different degrees of thickness or viscosity. The proportion of flour per cup of liquid is increased if a thicker product is desired. The fat increases at the same rate as the flour to facilitate the dispersion of the flour in melted or liquid fat. The proportions for starch-thickened sauces and their uses are shown in Table 7–1.

White Sauces

White sauce is often referred to as cream sauce because it may have the consistency and appearance of cream. The viscosity of white sauce ranges from thin to very thick. The use of the white sauce determines the appropriate viscosity.

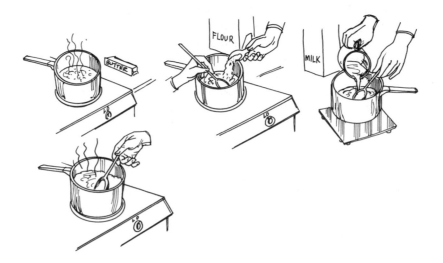

Thin white sauce is used for cream soups; medium white sauce is a general-purpose sauce and is often used for casseroles, creamed foods, and gravies; the thick sauce is used in making soufflés; and the very thick sauce functions as a binding agent in croquettes.

The basic method for preparing white sauce involves the melting of solid fat and blending in of the flour to form a smooth mixture. The fat-flour mixture is heated until it bubbles, and then it is removed from the heat while the cold milk is slowly added and blended into the fat-flour mixture. While being heated to a boil, the sauce is stirred constantly to achieve a thickened sauce without the formation of lumps. Stirring prevents accumulation of gelatinized starch on the bottom and sides of the pan, areas that are hotter than the interior of the sauce.

A well-prepared white sauce is free of lumps, shows no evidence of fat separation, has a pleasing flavor, and is of an appropriate consistency for its intended use.

Gravies

Drippings may be obtained from roasted or fried meats or from the liquid in which meats are braised. Meat drippings give flavor and color to gravy. The technique for gravy preparation is determined by the source of drippings—whether the drippings came from meat cooked by dry heat or meat cooked by moist heat.

Dry-Heat Meat Drippings. Drippings from dry-heat cookery can be blended directly with flour. The fat remaining from fried or roasted meat is removed from the pan. The appropriate amount of fat is measured (two tablespoons of fat for each cup of gravy) and returned to the pan in which the meat was cooked. An appropriate amount of flour (two tablespoons of flour per cup of gravy) is stirred into the measured fat until the mixture is smooth. A mixture called a **roux** forms when the blended dry flour and fat mixture are heated. The measured cold liquid (one cup for each cup of gravy) is added slowly to the roux and blended to maintain a smooth mixture. The gravy is stirred constantly until it reaches the boiling point.

Moist-Heat Meat Drippings. Because flour cannot be added directly to hot liquid without lumping the flour is first dispersed in cold liquid. This is easily done when a small amount of water is placed into a container with a tight-fitting lid, the measured flour placed on top of the water, the container covered and then shaken vigorously. The resulting smooth mixture is added slowly to the measured braised-meat liquid with constant stirring and heated to boiling. The constant stirring prevents lump formation in gravy. A well-made gravy has a pleasing flavor, is free of surface fat, and is free of lumps.

Cornstarch Pudding

Cornstarch puddings may appear as simple or elegant desserts. Cornstarch can be dispersed by blending it with sugar and other dry ingredients and then mixing in a small amount of cold milk or other liquid and thoroughly blending in the remainder of the liquid. Continuous gentle stirring is required during heating to avoid lumps in the pudding and to avoid damage to the starch granules. Attention must be directed toward stirring all around the edges and completely across the bottom of the pan so the entire pudding will gelatinize at the same rate. Overstirred or vigorously stirred puddings may become gummy and heavy.

Puddings of the desired firmness are best achieved with accurate measurements, a thorough starch dispersion, and complete gelatinization of starch through adequate cooking. Puddings are cooked sufficiently when the broad side of the spoon drawn through the pudding leaves a distinct trail or path. Undercooked puddings are of a thin consistency.

Flavorings and extracts are added after the pudding is removed from the heat. Extracts are very volatile, and much of their flavor would dissipate if added earlier. The pudding is cooled in a covered container to avoid scum formation. A well-prepared pudding has a smooth, light, soft texture and a pleasing flavor.

Commercial pudding mixes are available in several flavors; some require cooking, and others are instant. Pudding mixes requiring cooking yield a product similar to one prepared from ingredients. Instant puddings contain pregelatinized starch and require only rapid beating into cold liquid to form a soft gel. Instant puddings tend to be slightly granular and less flavorful than a cooked pudding.

FLOUR

Wheats are identified as white or red, according to the color of the kernel surface, as soft or hard, and as spring or winter. Some red wheat planted in the fall is known as winter wheat. Climate conditions of an area determine whether hard red wheat is planted in the fall or spring. The difference between hard and soft wheat is the greater continuity of the protein matrix and the tighter bonding of starch granules within the protein matrix of hard wheat. The protein matrix of soft wheat lacks continuity. Soft wheat flour feels smooth; hard wheat flour feels grainy.

Milling

The process of milling separates the endosperm from the bran and germ and reduces the endosperm to fine particles. Primitive milling methods utilized hollow stones to pulverize the grain. The modern milling process is a very complex operation: After the wheat is cleaned and conditioned, it is sent through the first set of break rolls. The break rolls are driven at different speeds and the grain subdivided by a scissorslike action. The resulting fragmented grain (first break) is sifted through a series of sieves. The coarsest fraction moves to the second break rolls; intermediate coarse particles move to the middlings purifier; the finest particles move to smooth reduction rolls for further fragmentation. Coarse particles usually flow through four or five break processes. Each set of break rollers has progres-

(Courtesy the Pillsbury Company)

sively finer corrugations, and each break process is followed by a sifting and purification process.

The wheat fragments are gradually reduced to granular particles called middlings. The middlings pass over a vibrating screen while air currents lift off most of the light particles of bran. Purified middlings of various sizes sift to the bottom. Coarse, flattened particles that do not go through the sifter are known as trailings. Purified middlings of small size go through reduction rolls, which further reduce endosperm particles. The bran and germ particles are flattened and separate easily from the pulverized endosperm.

Air classification is used to separate flour particles into uniform groups. A column of air whirling in a cyclone separator causes heavy particles to move toward the wall and then fall while smaller particles are pulled to the center, lifted up by air currents, and separated out. The particles of flour are separated according to size and weight. Since heavier particles of flour contain more protein, air classification permits the blending of flour streams according to desired protein content. This technique permits formulation of flours with 5 to 20 percent protein content from the same kind of wheat. The various fractions of flour differ greatly in composition and baking quality. The rolling and sifting processes during milling of wheat yield several streams of flour from which various grades and types of flour are made.

Bleaching/Maturing Agents

Freshly milled, unbleached flour is yellow in color due to yellowish pigments (carotenoid xanthophylls) present. When flour is stored for several months, the color becomes lighter, and baking qualities improve. A similar effect can be produced quickly by the addition of bleaching and maturing agents. The Food and Drug Administration permits the addition of specific bleaching and maturing agents to flour. Flour so treated must be labeled as bleached. Benzoyl peroxide, a bleaching agent, may be used. Chlorine dioxide, chlorine, and acetone peroxides may be added, and they act as both bleaching and maturing agents. Azodicarbonamide may be added to flour as a maturing agent but does not react until the flour is made into dough.

The maturing of flour apparently occurs through complex reactions, which may involve oxidation of flour proteins. Disulfide bonds (-S-S-) in the glutenin molecule may give elasticity to dough and enable it to resist expansion. Sulfhydryl groups (-SH) may weaken dough by disrupting disulfide bonds (Nielsen, Beckwith, and Wall 1968). It appears that sulfhydryl groups decrease as flour matures and may be responsible for the changes in rheological properties of the dough—decreased extensibility and increased resistance to extension. Matured flour yields a bread of higher volume and finer texture than freshly milled flour.

Enrichment

Enrichment is part of the milling process and adds thiamin, niacin, riboflavin, and iron to refined flours at the level specified by the Food and Drug Administration (Table 7–2). The addition of calcium and vitamin D is optional. Many states require that all white flour sold must be enriched. Most all-purpose flours on the consumer market are enriched and are so labeled. Although enriched flour contains adequate amounts of the added B vitamins and iron, it is not nutritionally equivalent to whole-grain flour, which contains vitamins and minerals not replaced by enrichment. Nevertheless, enriched flour and flour products contribute im-

Table 7–2 Enrichment Nutrient Standards Per Pound of White Flour.

Nutrient	Milligram/pound
Thiamin	2.9
Niacin	24.0
Riboflavin	1.8
Iron	13.0–16.5
Optional	
Calcium	960.0

United States Food and Drug Administration, Federal Register 137.350, 1983.

portant quantities of readily available nutrients to the diet. The selection of a wide variety of foods will contribute the nutrients not provided by enrichment.

Grades of Flour

Flour is graded on the basis of the flour streams used. When all streams of flour are combined in the original proportion, whole wheat flour is produced. Straight grade flour is prepared from a blend of all the white flour streams except for a small percent of the poorest stream. Fine bran particles and outer layers of the endosperm are found in the poorest stream. The streams of flour may be divided to yield long patent, fancy patent, and clear flours.

Patent flours come from the most refined portion of the endosperm. Long, medium, and short patent flours contain from 95 to 40 percent of the millstreams. The longer patent flours contain a higher percentage of protein than shorter patent flours from the same wheat. Clear grade flour is that remaining after the patent is removed. Patent flours are generally available on the market and are used for home and commercial baking. The larger patent flours are used for bread making, and short patent are used for cake flour.

Types of Flour

All-Purpose.   All-purpose flour may also be designated as family or general-purpose flour. It is prepared from a blend of wheats and may contain both hard and soft wheat. It contains less protein than bread flour but more protein than cake flour. It is not as coarse as bread flour or as fine as cake flour. It yields satisfactory breads, rolls, pastry, cookies, and some cakes. All-purpose flour suitable for all baked products except delicate, fine-textured cakes. The protein content of all-purpose flour may vary from one section of the country to another, but generally is about 10.5 percent.

Bread Flour.   Bread flour is made from the long extraction of hard wheat and contains a high percentage of protein. This flour is available to commercial bakers.

Cake Flour.   Cake flour has a relatively low protein content (7.5 percent). It is a short patent flour prepared from soft wheat. Cake flour holds its shape when pressed firmly, is white and fine in texture. The protein of cake flour forms a weak-quality gluten highly desirable for the preparation of delicate, fine-textured cakes.

Pastry Flour.   Pastry flour is produced from soft wheat or low-protein fractions of some varieties of hard wheat. It has a protein content less than that of all-purpose flour but approximately the same as cake flour. It is available to commercial bakers for pastry and cookie products.

Self-Rising Flour.   Self-rising flours are blends of hard and soft wheats (protein levels are 9.3 percent) and are often used in quick-bread preparation. They contain salt and leavening agents (such as monocalcium phosphate and sodium bicarbonate) in proportions desirable for home baking. No additional leavener is required.

Instantized Flour.   Instantized flours are granular in texture and are also identified as instant blending, instant, or agglomerated. In one method of producing instantized flour moisture is added on the surface of all-purpose flour, making it sticky so that the flour particles adhere and form agglomerates of uniform size. Those are then dried. Another instantized flour is made of cracked endosperm too coarse to be considered for regular flour. Particles of instantized flour are larger than of regular flour. They are heavy enough to sink when combined with liquid instead of floating as does regular flour. Instant flour does not pack and therefore requires no presifting. It flows freely, disperses quickly in water, and is dust free.

Whole Wheat Flour.   Whole wheat flour is also known as graham flour or entire wheat flour. These flours essentially contain the entire wheat kernel. They may be ground to varying degrees of fineness. The bran and germ these flours contain reduce their shelf life because the fat in the germ may become rancid.

Market Units

Although all-purpose flour may satisfy general food-preparation needs, specialty baked products may require cake, whole wheat, rye, or other flours. Flour should be purchased in quantities to meet short-term needs, since it is subject to insect infestation.

All-purpose flour is sold in two-, five-, ten-, and twenty-five-pound bags. Cake flour is available in two-pound boxes, whole wheat in two-pound boxes or five-pound bags. Table 7–3 lists the sizes and measures per common market units in which flour is purchased. This information can aid in determining the quantity of flour to buy.

GLUTEN

Gluten forms the structure or framework of baked products. Since flour affects the characteristics of the product, recipes are developed for specific flours. Much of the difference between flours is related to protein content. Bread flour forms the most gluten, all-purpose flour an intermediate amount, and cake flour the least. The quality of the gluten among the flours differs. Gluten from all-purpose and bread flours is elastic and can be stretched while that from cake flour is likely to

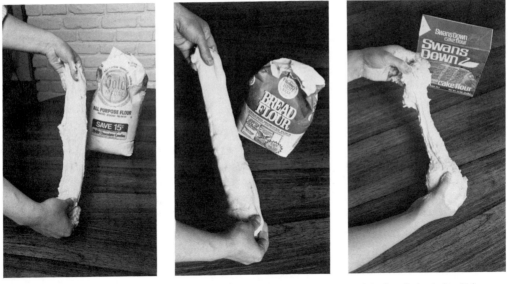

(a) All-purpose flour (Laimute Druskis)   (b) Bread flour (Laimute Druskis)   (c) Cake flour (Laimute Druskis)

tear and is soft. For bread a large amount of gluten is desirable; for cake a small amount of soft gluten is desirable.

Proteins

Proteins present in the flour contribute to its baking performance. Wheat flour proteins include the water-soluble albumins and globulins, and the water-insoluble gliadins (alcohol soluble) and glutenins (dilute acid soluble). The gliadins and glutenins play a major role in baking performance while the albumins and globulins do not. The glutenins are the least soluble and largest component of the gluten-forming complex. Glutenin consists of subunits with varying molecular

Table 7–3 Selected Flours: Measures per Market Unit Purchased

Flours	Market Unit	Measure per Market Unit (unsifted, spooned)
Wheat		
All-purpose	5 lbs	18 cups
Cake	32 ozs	8¼ cups
Gluten	32 ozs	6¾ cups
Self-rising	32 ozs	7¼ cups
Whole wheat	5 lbs	19 cups
Rye, pumpernickel	16 ozs	5½ cups
Corn	16 ozs	4 cups

Adapted from USDA, Science and Education Administration. *Buying Food*, Home Economics Research Report no. 42 (Washington, D.C.: Government Printing Office, 1978).

weights joined by disulfide (-S-S-) bonds. The subunits of glutenin appear to be heterogeneous and differ from those of gliaden (Ewart 1979). The quantity and quality of protein affects the baking quality of the flour. As the protein content of flour increases, the volume of bread baked from it increases.

Other Constituents

Gluten proteins, lipids, and other constituents may interact in the dough. Wheat flour contains some bound and some free lipids. Polar glycolipids appear to be essential for gluten to function in the production of good-quality bread (Pomerzna and Chung 1978). They may bind to gluten protein during mixing and to starch. The free lipids may form a lipoprotein complex with glutenin. When flour lipids are removed, loaf volume is low.

Gluten Formation

Water. The starch and protein components of flour bind water. Hard wheats have a greater water-binding capacity than soft wheats. Flour can firmly bind or adsorb water that approximates about one-fourth of its weight. Succeeding layers of water are less firmly bound, and the water not needed to hydrate flour contributes to the rheological property (flow/mobility) of flour-water mixtures.

Manipulation. When flour and water mixtures are manipulated (kneaded, beaten, stirred), gliadin and glutenin combine to form gluten. Glutenin molecules may bond together by the formation of disulfide (S-S) bonds between the protein chains. Manipulation of wheat flour-water mixtures (doughs) appears to associate long strands of glutenin with gliadin to form strong elastic films that enclose starch granules in the dough.

When water comes in contact with particles of flour, films of protein separate into fibrils and emerge from the fractured surface of endosperm cells. These emerged fibrils carry grains of starch with them and unite to form a network. Manipulation moves fibrils past each other and aligns them to bond at appropriate points to make gluten. Gluten forms a continuous three-dimensional network in which starch granules are embedded.

The development of gluten contributes elasticity and viscosity to dough, and starch grains contribute a plastic quality. When manipulated dough develops a satiny surface, gluten is well developed. Optimally kneaded dough is elastic, springy, and extensible. Hard wheat flours require more manipulation than soft wheat flours to yield elastic and extensible dough. Overdevelopment of gluten decreases tenderness and volume of products.

Gluten Inhibitors

Sugar and fat in relatively large amounts limit the quantity of gluten that can be developed. Sugar avidly competes with flour for water and thus inhibits gluten formation. Fat coats particles of flour and keeps them from easily contacting the water needed for gluten development.

Gluten Function

In a flour mixture gluten stretches with the pressure of expanding gases and thus permits their retention in the dough. The pressure of expanding steam maintains the gluten volume until heat coagulates the protein. Inflated gluten collapses when removed from heat before it coagulates. Coagulated gluten contributes to the structure of baked products.

SUMMARY

Starches function primarily as thickening agents and contribute viscosity and/or gel characteristics. Sugar and acids weaken starch gels. Gelatinization converts a temporary starch suspension to a colloidal sol through the action of moisture and heat. To avoid lumps starch should be completely dispersed by blending it with cold water, fat, or dry ingredients and stirring during cooking.

Factors influencing the viscosity of cooked starches include type and concentration of starch, presence of acid and sugar, and temperature reached during cooking. Starch sols become more viscous as they cool and often form gels.

Dextrinization is the reduction of starch molecules to dextrins by dry heat. Dry heat effects changes in starch that reduce its thickening power and bring about a browning in color.

Hard wheat flours are used for yeast-leavened products and soft wheat for cake, cookies, and pastry. Durum wheat is used for macaroni products. The short patent flours are the highest grade and the most refined flours. Enrichment restores the B vitamins and iron to refined flour and cereals.

The quantity and quality of gluten formed with flour is made into a dough determine its use in baking. Yeast breads require a flour with a high protein content (hard wheat) that forms a strong, elastic gluten to retain the leavening gases. The gluten of soft wheat is tender and is suitable for chemically leavened products. The gluten complex is formed from the flour proteins, gliadin and glutenin. Gluten forms a continuous network, which offers structure to baked products. Lipids influence gluten development.

SELF-STUDY GUIDE

1. Define starch, amylose, amylopectin, waxy starch.
2. Describe the function of starch in cookery and give two examples.
3. How is starch gelatinization influenced by agitation, temperature, sugar, and acid?
4. Explain what occurs when starch gelatinizes, dextrinizes.
5. Define synersis, retrograde, gel, sol, gelation.

6. Explain the procedure for preparing white sauces.
7. Discuss the application of starch-cookery principles to gravies and cornstarch puddings.
8. What processes are involved in production of flour?
9. Identify the types of flour available and suggest uses for each.
10. Discuss the formation of gluten and its contribution to baked flour products.

SUGGESTED READINGS

BAKSKI, A. S., and SINGH, R. P. Kinetics of water diffusion and starch gelatinization during rice parboiling. *Journal of Food Science* 45:1387, 1980.

BANKS, W., and GREENWOOD, C. T. *Starch and its components.* New York: John Wiley and Sons, 1975.

BIETZ, J. A.; HUBNER, F. R.; and WALL, J. S. Glutenin—the strength of wheat flour. *Baker's Digest* 47:26, 1973.

BILIADERIS, C. H., et al. Starch gelatinization phenomena studies by differential scanning calorimetry. *Journal of Food Science* 45:1669, November/December 1980.

DAVIS, K. R., et al. Evaluation of the nutrient composition of wheat. I. Lipid Constituents. *Cereal Chemistry* 57:178, 1980.

DERBY, R. I.; MILLER, B. S.; and TRIMBO, H. B. Visual observation of wheat-starch gelatinization in limited water systems. *Cereal Chemistry* 52:702, 1975.

EWART, J. A. Gluten structure. *Journal of the Science of Food and Agriculture* 30:482, 1979.

EVANS, L. T., and PEACOCK, W. J. *Wheat science—today and tomorrow.* New York: Cambridge University Press, 1981.

FERRINGTON, W. H.; WARWICK, M. J.; and SHEARER, G. Changes in carotenoids and sterol fractions during prolonged storage of wheat flour. *Journal of the Science and Food Agriculture* 32(9):948, 1981.

FLEMING, S. E. Influence of cooking methods on digestibility of legume and cereal starch. *Journal of Food Science,* 47:1, January/February 1982.

HARLAND, B. F., and HARLAND, J. Fermentative reduction of phytate in rye, white, and whole wheat breads. *Cereal Chemistry* 57:226, 1980.

HOSENEY, R. C. Dough forming properties. *Journal of the American Oil Chemists' Society* 56:78A, 1979.

HOSENEY, R. C.; LINEBACK, D. R.; and SEIB, P. A. Role of starch in baked foods. *Bakers Digest* 52:11, 1978.

HULSE, J. H., and SPURGEON, D. Triticale. *Scientific American* 231(2):72, 1974.

KAPPOR, A. C., and HEINER, R. E. Biochemical changes in developing wheat grains changes in nitrogen fractions, amino acids and nutritional quality. *Journal of the Science of Food and Agriculture* 33:35, 1982.

KNIGHTLY, W. H. The staling of bread. *Bakers Digest* 51:52, 1977.

KROCHTA, J. M., et al. Extraction with ethanol as an energy saving alternative to conventional drying of cornstarch. *Journal of Food Science* 46:1054, July/August 1981.

KUGIMIYA, M., and DONOVAN, J. W. Calorimetric determination of the amylose content of starches based on formation and melting of the amylose-lysolecithin complex. *Journal of Food Science* 46:765, May/June 1981.

LINEBACK, D. R., and WONGSRIKASEM, E. Gelatinization of starch in baked products. *Journal of Food Science* 45:71, 1980.

LORENZ, K. J.; WELSH, R.; NORMANN, N.; and MAGA, J. Comparative mixing and baking properties of wheat and triticale flour. *Cereal Chemistry* 49:187, 1972.

MAGNUSON, K. Vital wheat gluten update '77. *Bakers Digest* 51:108, October 1977.

MOD, R. R., et al. Chemical properties and interactions of rice hemicellulose with trace minerals in vitro. *Journal of Agriculture and Food Chemistry* 29:449, May/June 1981.

MORRISON, W. R. Lipids in flour, dough and bread. *Bakers Digest* 50:29, 1976.

NIELSEN, H. C.; BECKWITH, A. C.; and WALL, J. S. Effect of disulfide bond cleavage on wheat gliadin fractions obtained by gel filtration. *Cereal Chemistry* 45:37, 1968.

OTEY, F. H., et al. Starch-based blown films. *Industrial & Engineering Chemical Product Research and Development* 19:592, December 1980.

POMERANZ, Y. Molecular approach to breadmaking: an update and new perspectives. *Bakers Digest* 54(1):20; 54(2):12, 1980.

———, and CHUNG, O. K. Interaction of lipids with proteins and carbohydrates in breadmaking. *Journal of the American Oil Chemists' Society* 55:285, 1978.

RAFFI, J. J., et al. Radio-induced products in maize starch; glyceraldehyde, dihydroxyacetate, and 2-hydroxymalon aldehyde. *Journal of Agriculture and Food Chemistry* 29:548, May/June 1981.

RANUM, P. M. Nutrient levels in internationally milled wheat flours. *Cereal Chemistry* 57:361, 1980.

RAO, D. S., and DEOSTHALE, G. Mineral and trace element composition of wheat and flours of different extraction rates. *Journal of Plant Foods* 3:251, 1982.

SAVAGE, H. L., and OSMAN, E. M. Effects of certain sugars and sugar alcohols on the swelling of cornstarch granules. *Cereal Chemistry* 55:447, 1978.

SHEWRY, P., and MIFTEN, B. Gluten: A sticky phenomenon to understand. *Milling Feed and Fertilizer* 165:18, 1982.

TABEKHIA, M. M., and DONNELLY, B. J. Phytic acid in durum wheat and its milled products. *Cereal Chemistry.* 59:105, 1982.

WATSON, C. A.; SHUEY, W. C.; CRAWFORD, R. D.; and GUMBUMANN, M. R. Physical dough, baking, and nutritional qualities of straight-grade and extended-extraction flours. *Cereal Chemistry* 54:657, 1977.

WU, Y. V., and STRENGFELLOW, A. C. Protein isolate from alkaline extraction of air-classified high-protein soft wheat flour. *Journal of Food Science* 45(5):1383, 1980.

WURZBURG, O. B., and SYZMANSKI, C. D. Modified starches for the food industry. *Journal of Agriculture and Food Chemistry* 18:997, 1970.

8

LEAVENING AGENTS

OBJECTIVES

When you complete this chapter, you will be able to

1. Identify the leavens, list products in which they are used, and explain in general terms how they contribute leavening action.
2. Describe the characteristics leavening agents impart to flour mixtures.
3. Make appropriate baking powder and soda substitutions.
4. Identify products in which too much or too little leavening was used.

Leavening agents **aerate** and contribute porosity and lightness to products, thus enhancing their palatability. Leavening is dependent on the expansion of a gaseous substance when the leavening is subjected to heat. Air, steam, and carbon dioxide are gaseous leavening agents. In some products all three agents contribute in varying degrees to the leavening process; in others only one or two leavening agents are involved.

Air and water are incorporated into flour mixtures during their preparation, while carbon dioxide is formed within the products by chemical or biological action of some of the constituents. A light, porous texture requires a source of gas, a mixture that is elastic and capable of entrapping gas bubbles as they expand, and a structural framework that becomes rigid upon baking. The lightness and porosity achieved are dependent upon the type of leavener present, the gas-holding capacity of the flour mixture, and the baking conditions.

AIR

Some air is incorporated as ingredients are manipulated and combined. Air is thought to be an essential leaven in baked products. When the bubbles of air are exhausted from a batter, the effectiveness of other leavening agents is reduced. A pound cake utilizes both air and steam for leavening, but when the air is removed, the leavening action of steam is reduced severely, yielding a very heavy product.

Generally, specific techniques are used to incorporate all possible air during the preparation of products. Air is retained when whole eggs, egg whites, or yolks are beaten to produce a foam. Egg whites incorporate and retain air the most effectively; beaten whole egg and yolks retain considerably less air, producing foams of a lesser volume than egg whites alone. Egg whites beaten to optimum stiffness retain air, but beating to the stage of dryness causes loss of air. Overbeaten egg white foam is no longer elastic and releases air as it is manipulated. Egg foam must be folded into batters carefully to reduce loss of air.

Significant quantities of air can be introduced when plastic fats are creamed. Shortened cakes rely on air for a portion of their leavening. Most hydrogenated shortenings, which often are used in shortened cakes, contain about 12 percent air. In addition, useful amounts of air can be incorporated into a thoroughly creamed fat, sugar, and egg mixture. The sugar crystals promote the incorporation of air into mixtures. The egg also assists in trapping the air incorporated during creaming. A thorough creaming of fat and sugar produces many tiny air bubbles and a gas-in-a-solid foam, which is essential for fine-textured cakes. The air cells incorporated into the fat establish the textural character, which will be reflected in the baked shortened cake. The air cells act as nuclei into which both carbon dioxide and steam migrate during mixing and baking.

Mixing and beating are other techniques for incorporation of air into flour mixtures. Vigorous beating can incorporate some air into stiff batters or doughs. In some cases, however, mixing beyond the optimum can lead to loss of air.

Batters at room temperature incorporate and retain air more effectively than extremely cold or warm batters. Warm batters are extremely fluid and readily release trapped air. Viscous batters effectively trap and retain air, while thin batters are less able to do so.

Although some batters retain air more effectively than others, there is some loss of air from all flour mixtures. Products baked very soon after preparation receive maximum benefit from air leavening. Air contributes somewhat to the total increase in volume during baking because the increasing temperature expands the air in the cells and creates pressure, which stretches the cell walls. This effect is especially apparent in angel and sponge cakes.

STEAM

All batters and doughs include liquid in either small or large amounts, and some of this liquid is converted to steam for leavening action during baking. When water is converted to steam, it is capable of expanding to 1,600 to 1,800 times the original volume, making it an effective leavener.

The dramatic leavening capacity of steam is observed in the baking of cream puffs and popovers. Both of these products are leavened primarily by steam. They contain a high ratio of liquid to flour. Products utilizing steam as the primary leavening agent require a hot oven to convert water very quickly to steam. The steam presses against the cell walls in the baking batter or dough and stretches the cells until the protein denatures and loses its extensibility. The amount and distribution of steam pockets influence the size and number of pores in the crumb of baked products. Insufficient steam promotes a low volume and coarse texture in baked products.

Steam contributes some leavening action to all baked products, but other leavening agents also are needed to achieve the desired volume and texture when products with lower percentages of water are prepared. The water available for conversion to steam may be the added liquid or other ingredients with a high water content, such as eggs.

The amount of steam available for leavening is determined by the ratio of water to flour. When the ratio of water to flour is relatively small, as in puff pastry, sufficient steam is produced to aid in separating layers of pastry to achieve flakiness but not to form a hollow shell. The water content of egg generates enough steam to contribute significant leavening to sponge and angel cakes. However, some of the water in flour products is also bound into starch granules when the starch in the flour gelatinizes during baking. Also, not all of the steam produced in flour products is utilized for leavening; some of it is lost through evaporation.

CARBON DIOXIDE

Carbon dioxide may be introduced through chemical and biological agents. Carbon dioxide is formed by the action of acid on baking soda and the action of yeast on sugar. Chemical leaveners produce carbon dioxide more quickly than yeast. The chemical leavens—baking powder or soda and an acid—furnish carbon dioxide in many different baked products. The biological leavens—yeast or some bacteria—produce carbon dioxide to leaven bread products.

Baking Soda

The reaction of soda, also called sodium bicarbonate ($NaHCO_3$), and an acid results in the production of carbon dioxide and a salt. In the following reaction HX represents any acid.

$$NaHCO_3 + HX \longrightarrow CO_2 + NaX + H_2O$$

$$\text{soda} \qquad \text{acid} \qquad\quad \text{carbon} \quad \text{salt} \quad \text{water}$$
$$\text{dioxide}$$

Since this reaction is rapid and complete at room temperature, products leavened with acid (vinegar, sour milk) and baking soda must be baked immediately to avoid loss of carbon dioxide.

Buttermilk and sour milk contain lactic acid and are common acid ingredients to use with baking soda. Sweet milk can be made sour by removing one tablespoon of the milk in one cup and replacing it with one tablespoon of vinegar or lemon juice. One cup of either of these milks generally contains sufficient acid to react completely with one-half teaspoon of baking soda, thus producing adequate carbon dioxide for leavening about two cups of flour.

The degree of sourness in sour milk can vary. Milk that has just become sour is less acidic than very sour milk; however, the general rule of one-half teaspoon of soda to one cup of milk is still applied. When the milk is only slightly sour, all of the soda may not be neutralized, and a somewhat bitter flavor (due to excess soda) may be noted. The excess soda may cause a yellow color in the product, a coarse texture, and increased browning of the crust. The anthoxanthin pigments of flour turn yellow in an alkaline medium.

Fruit juices, brown sugar, honey, molasses and corn syrup contain variable amounts of organic acids such as citric or acetic. Generally, one-fourth teaspoon baking soda is used with one-fourth to one-half cup molasses or with one-half cup sour or buttermilk. Carbon dioxide is produced as soon as acid and soda are combined in a moist medium during the mixing process. The salts produced by the reaction of soda vary with the acid. For example, with acetic acid the salt is sodium acetate, with citric acid the salt is sodium citrate, and with lactic acid the salt is sodium lactate. These salts do not contribute unpleasant flavors.

Baking Powder

A baking powder containing soda, cream of tartar, and potato starch was produced in 1858 by Dr. William Price of Illinois. The formula today remains the same—soda, an acid, and starch.

Federal regulations require all baking powders to yield a minimum of 12 percent carbon dioxide. Most baking powders provide 14 percent or more to compensate for loss during storage. Cornstarch and calcium carbonate separate the acid ingredient and soda, so they do not react. The cornstarch and calcium carbonate are inert and act as a filler or standardizing agent so that a given measure of all types of baking powders produce the same amount of carbon dioxide. A small quantity (0.15 percent) of an optional ingredient, powdered dried-egg albumen, may be added to increase viscosity of the batter, thus helping to retain leavening gases.

Sodium bicarbonate (soda) is the alkaline ingredient used in all baking powders; the percent of soda incorporated in a baking powder formula varies with the acid salt(s) used.

Dry salts available for use in baking powder include **tartrate, phosphate,** sodium aluminum sulfate, sodium acid pyrophosphate, and sodium aluminum phosphate. Both phosphate and tartrate salts are classed as quick or single-acting because they liberate carbon dioxide quickly when they react with soda in the presence of cold liquid. The potassium salt of tartaric acid is cream of tartar and can be combined with soda to produce a homemade baking powder. Each teaspoon of baking powder in a recipe may be replaced with one-fourth teaspoon of soda and one-half teaspoon of cream tartar. The reaction with tartrate is as follows:

$$NaHCO_3 \ + \ KHC_4H_4O_6 \ \longrightarrow \ KNaC_4H_4O_6 \ + \ 2CO_2 \ + \ H_2O$$

| sodium bicarbonate | potassium acid tartrate | sodium potassium tartrate | carbon dioxide | water |

Dry acid salts available to commercial bakers range from those with very slow to rapid reaction rates. Some of these acid salts release 8–10 percent carbon dioxide before baking and the remainder during baking. Phosphate salts react at room temperature but more slowly than tartrate. Calcium acid phosphate (also called monocalcium phosphate) and sodium acid pyrophosphate are the commonly used phosphate salts. Sodium aluminum phosphate has a slow reaction rate and thus retains release of carbon dioxide for the baking period.

A leavening derived from glucose available for commercial use is glucono-delta-lactone (a lactone of gluconic acid). Quick breads leavened with glucono-delta-lactone and soda have the appearance and texture, but not the flavor, of yeast bread.

Leavening acids used alone or in combination in packaged mixes include sodium acid phyrophosphate, anahydrous monocalcium phosphate, and sodium aluminum phosphate. Because sodium aluminum phosphate accelerates development of rancidity in fats, it is not used in dry mixes containing fat. Instead, combinations of phosphate baking powders are used.

Although a variety of baking powers are available to commercial bakers, only the double-acting baking powder (some carbon dioxide liberated during mixing and the remainder during baking) is available to home bakers. Double-action baking powder contains sodium aluminum sulfate (SAS) and monocalcium phosphate monohydrate. Carbon dioxide is produced through a series of reactions. Monocalcium phosphate monohydrate and soda react to release carbon dioxide as soon as dry ingredients are moistened. The next reaction involves sodium aluminum sulfate, which liberates sulfuric acid when it is heated with moisture.

$$\underset{\substack{\text{sodium aluminum} \\ \text{sulfate}}}{Na_2Al_2(SO_4)_4} + \underset{\text{water}}{6H_2O} \xrightarrow{heat} \underset{\substack{\text{aluminum} \\ \text{hydroxide}}}{2Al(OH)_3} + \underset{\substack{\text{sodium} \\ \text{sulfate}}}{Na_2SO_4} + \underset{\substack{\text{sulfuric} \\ \text{acid}}}{3H_2SO_4}$$

The sulfuric acid then reacts with additional soda during baking.

$$\underset{\substack{\text{sulfuric} \\ \text{acid}}}{3H_2SO_4} + \underset{\substack{\text{sodium} \\ \text{bicarbonate}}}{6NaHCO_3} \longrightarrow \underset{\substack{\text{sodium} \\ \text{sulfate}}}{3Na_2SO_4} + \underset{\substack{\text{carbon} \\ \text{dioxide}}}{6\ CO_2} + \underset{\text{water}}{6H_2O}$$

Double-action baking powder is formulated to release carbon dioxide quickly during the mixing process at room temperature and to release additional carbon dioxide during baking. The residue remaining after the release of carbon dioxide tends to have a bitter flavor.

Uses of Baking Powder. Baking powder is the leavening ingredient in a variety of baked products: biscuits, cakes, coffee cakes, cookies, muffins, nut breads, pancakes, shortened cakes, and waffles. Ingredients, proportions of ingredients, mixing methods, and baking temperatures vary among the varities of baked products. All of these variations influence optimal levels of leavening ingredients. Too much baking powder yields products with a coarse texture and one which may overexpand and collapse during baking. Products with too little baking powder are low in volume and compact. The usual proportions of baking powder are one to two teaspoons per cup of flour for shortened cakes, one and one-fourth to two teaspoons per cup of flour for quick breads.

The leavening ingredients also influence the pH of the batter. Salts resulting from SAS baking powder are less acidic than from tartrate or phosphate powders. The flavonoid pigments of flour become yellowed in an alkaline pH and white in an acidic pH.

Baking Powder and Soda Substitutions. One teaspoon of baking powder contributes as much carbon dioxide as only one-fourth teaspoon baking soda. Soda, however, requires the addition of acid to release carbon dioxide. Therefore, the complete replacement of baking powder with soda must also include an acid, such as sour milk or fruit juice or pulp. Although the acidity of these products varies, a practical solution is to use one-fourth teaspoon of soda for one-half cup of acid (buttermilk, sour milk, or fruit juice or pulp). An excess of soda yields quick-bread products with an unpleasant flavor and yellow spots on the surface.

Yeast

Leavened-bread making is an ancient art cultivated first by the Egyptians and then the Greeks and Romans. They apparently allowed yeast organisms from the air to gather in a mixture of liquid, flour and/or sugar. These mixtures were used in bread doughs. The liquid mixture or a small portion of the dough, known as a starter, could be saved from one baking to the next. These starters contained wild yeast and often bacteria. Those organisms (which often promote sour fermentations) influence the flavor and other characteristics of the bread.

Wild yeast is readily available from the air, but some give bread an undesirable flavor. The yeast sold commercially is carefully selected for its breadmaking qualities and is identified as saccharomyces cerevisiae. Yeast may be purchased as active dry yeast or as a compressed cake. Compressed yeast has a higher moisture content than the active dry and must be refrigerated.

Yeast, a one-celled plant, is cultured in dilute molasses, recovered by filtration, and compressed into a cake. This cake is extruded and dehydrated to about 8 percent moisture and then ground to form active dry yeast. It is packaged in vacuum-sealed, foil-lined envelopes containing about one-fourth ounce (seven grams) or one level tablespoon of granular dried yeast. It keeps without refrigeration for a relatively long time.

Compressed yeast contains about 72 percent moisture, is sold in cornstarch-containing cakes weighing about one-half ounce (fourteen grams). A fresh cake is creamy gray in color, somewhat brittle, and breaks sharply. Compressed yeast is good as long as it crumbles easily even though it may appear slightly browned in color.

Fermentation.   Yeast can change most of the sugars (except lactose) found in batters and doughs to carbon dioxide and alcohol. (The latter is driven off during baking). The fermentation of sugar by yeast usually involves a complex anaerobic (without oxygen) process involving a series of reactions. Most of the enzymes involved in the fermentative process are contributed by yeasts, and some enzymes present in flour are also involved. The reactions in the fermentation process can be summarized as follows:

$$C_6H_{12}O_6 \longrightarrow 2\ C_2H_5OH\ +\ 2\ CO_2$$

$$\underset{\text{glucose}}{} \quad \underset{\substack{\text{ethanol} \\ \text{(ethyl alcohol)}}}{} \quad \underset{\text{carbon dioxide}}{}$$

A small amount of sugar is usually added to yeast-flour mixtures to speed the production of carbon dioxide. When sugar is not added, for instance, in French bread, yeast slowly produces carbon dioxide from the small amount of sugar present in the flour and from the maltose produced by the amylase enzyme in flour. The use of yeast as a leaven is discussed in chapter 10, which deals with breads.

A package of active dry yeast or a compressed cake will leaven about one to two loaves of bread. Compressed yeast is dissolved in lukewarm water for use in dough. Active dry yeast is rehydrated at temperatures between 100 and 105° F (40–45° C) to avoid inactivating the yeast. Active dry yeast may also be added directly to about one-third of the flour and other dry ingredients and blended before adding to all of the liquid, which has been warmed. The two forms of yeast, when appropriately handled, act at about the same rate in doughs.

Temperature. Yeast is sensitive to temperature. Temperatures of about 80 to 85° F (27 to 29° C) are considered ideal for proofing (rising) bread. A higher temperature may cause the dough to rise faster, but may also encourage growth of undesirable microorganisms. Lower temperatures require too long a proofing period. At refrigerator and freezer temperatures, yeast multiplication is slowed or stopped. Proofing is also retarded above 95° F (35° C), and the yeast is destroyed at about 130° F (54° C). A hot oven, as well as hot liquid, destroys yeast.

Bacteria

Some bacteria produce carbon dioxide as in sourdough and salt-rising breads. Sourdough bread is leavened with bacteria supplied by rye flour, and cornmeal provides the bacteria in salt-rising bread. The bacteria produce acetic and lactic acids, which contribute the sourness. The characteristics flavor of these breads is dependent upon conditions and the ingredients used to prepare the starter.

Cleanliness is essential; the starter must be covered with a cloth so that air is available and contaminants are minimized while the fermentative bacteria are cultured. The starter and the raw dough containing the starter should not be eaten or tasted. If bad color or odors develop, the starter, the dough, or the bread should be discarded. Commercial starters contain pure strains of bacteria and should be used rather than cultures developed from the ingredients or from the air.

SUMMARY

A leavener promotes porosity and lightness in a flour mixture. Air, steam, and carbon dioxide are the primary leavening agents. Carbon dioxide is produced within products by (1) yeast, (2) baking powder, and (3) soda in combination with acid. Yeast requires a fermentative process to yield carbon dioxide from glucose.

Tartrate and phosphate salts react at room temperature, and sodium aluminum sulfate requires heat. Generally one teaspoon of double-acting baking powder (SAS) is optimal per cup of flour. One-fourth teaspoon of soda plus one-half cup of sour milk is equivalent to one teaspoon of baking powder.

Too much leavening causes a coarse grain and an undesirable flavor and may cause excessive surface browning. If too much soda is used in relation to an acid ingredient, a yellow interior will develop. Insufficient leavening produces a compact product of poor volume.

SELF-STUDY GUIDE

1. Why are some leaveners classed as biological, chemical, and physical? Which leaveners are included in each class? In what ways do these leaveners differ? Give examples of products leavened by each.
2. Discuss fermentation. How is fermentation controlled?
3. Discuss the production of carbon dioxide by chemical leaveners. Identify the acid fraction.
4. How are baking powder and soda substitutions made? When may it be desirable to use these substitutions?
5. What are the results of too much leavening? of too little?
6. List three components of baking powder and explain their roles.

SUGGESTED READINGS

AHEA. *Handbook of food preparation.* 8th ed. Washington, D.C.: American Home Economics Association, 1980.

BENNION, M. *The science of food.* Chap. 29. New York: Harper and Row Publishers, 1985.

BRUINSMA, B. L., and FINNEY, K. F. Functional (breadmaking) properties of a new dry yeast. *Cereal Chemistry* 58:477, September/October 1981.

CHICHESTER, C. O. *Advances in food research.* Vol. 26. New York: Academic Press, 1981.

CONN, J. F. Baking powders. *Bakers Digest* 39(2):66, 1965.

CONSUMER GUIDE. *Food processor bread book.* New York: Simon and Schuster, 1980.

FREEDLAND-GRAVES, J., and PECKHAM, G. *Journal of Food Science* Chap. 31. New York: Macmillan Co., 1979.

HARLAND, B. F., and HARLAND, J. Fermentative reduction of phytate in rye, white, and whole wheat breads. *Cereal Chemistry* 57(3):226, 1980.

KAZANAS, N., and FIELDS, M. L. Nutritional improvement of sorghum by fermentation. *Journal of Food Science* 46(3):819, 1981.

KICHLINE, T. P., and CONN, J. F. Some fundamental aspects of leavening agents. *Bakers Digest* 44(4):36, 1970.

RAM, B. P., and NIGAM, S. N. Puffing and textural characteristics of chapati in relation to varietal differences in gluten composition. *Journal of Food Science* 47:231, 1982.

REIMAN, H. M. Chemical leavening systems. *Bakers Digest* 51(4):33, 1977.

9

LIPIDS: FATS AND OILS

OBJECTIVES

When you complete this chapter you will be able to

1. Discuss the composition and structure of fats and oils.

2. Discuss the nutritional quality of dietary fats.

3. Explain/discuss hydrogenation, antioxidant, winterizing, rearranged lard, rancidity.

4. Explain the differences between animal and vegetable fats; between oils and shortenings; between butter and margarine.

5. Discuss the use of fats in food preparation and select appropriate fats for each use.

6. Discuss the factors that influence fat absorption during frying.

Lipid is a general classification used to identify water-insoluble organic compounds present in animal and plant tissues. These compounds are extractable with fat solvents such as benzene, carbon tetrachloride, chloroform, and ether. On the basis of their form at room temperature, lipids fall into two general groups—fats (solid) and oils (liquid). Fats and oils are similar substances; it is only their physical form or state that differs. All fats liquefy at elevated temperatures and solidify when sufficiently cooled.

Variable amounts of fat are present in foods. The greasy nature of fats assists in identification of their presence. Some foods contain large amounts of invisible fats; for example, egg yolk, cheese, mayonnaise, chocolate, nuts, olives, and avocados. Other foods contain visible fat such as bacon, meat, and butter.

NUTRITIONAL QUALITY

Fats are a concentrated source of energy providing nine kilocalories per gram. They enhance the satiety value of meals, since fats leave the stomach slowly and thus delay the onset of hunger. Fats are the only source of linoleic acid, an essential fatty acid. They are carriers of the fat-soluble vitamins, A, D, E, and K. Fats transport many flavor components in food and thus contribute to food palatability.

Fats of animal origin may contain a high level of saturated fatty acids, whereas those of plant origin contain substantial amounts of unsaturated fatty acids. Butter, cheese, cream, eggs, and organ meats contain cholesterol. Nutritionists and health professionals express concern for the excessive consumption of fats by Americans. A high intake of fat, saturated fat, or cholesterol may increase the incidence of elevated blood lipids, coronary heart disease, and atherosclerosis for some individuals.

COMPOSITION/STRUCTURE

Fats are composed of carbon, hydrogen, and oxygen. Fatty acids are a component or building block of a variety of lipids. A fatty acid consists of a carbon chain with

$$-\overset{\overset{\displaystyle O}{\displaystyle \|}}{C}-OH$$

attached hydrogen and a terminal carboxyl group ($-C-OH$). The chains are of varying length ranging from 4 to 22 carbon. Most fatty acids in food contain an even number of carbon, and those with 16 or 18 carbon are prevalent.

Esters are formed when an organic acid (such as a fatty acid) and an alcohol (such as glycerol) combine. Esters of fatty acids and glycerol are known specifically as glycerides. Glycerol esterified with one fatty acid yields a monoglyceride, with two fatty acids a diglyceride, and with three fatty acids a triglyceride (Figure 9-1). Glycerides are classed as simple or mixed. Simple glycerides contain the same kind of fatty acid in all three positions on glycerol, while mixed glycerides contain two or more different fatty acids. Triglycerides (triacylglyerols is the new term) are the principle fats in food along with some phospholipids (phosphoglycerides), sterols (cholesterol), and a few free fatty acids.

Types of Fatty Acids

Most fats are composed of different fatty acids, some of which are saturated and some unsaturated (Table 9-1). Saturated fatty acids have no double bonds because they contain the maximum amount of hydrogen on each carbon atom, whereas unsaturated fatty acids contain one or more double bonds because two or more of their carbon atoms lack hydrogen. Those with two or more double bonds are known as polyunsaturated fatty acids. The long-chained fatty acids, those

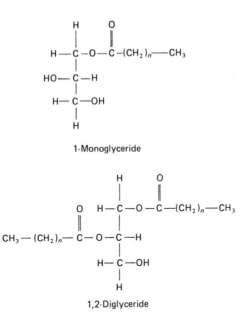

1-Monoglyceride

1,2-Diglyceride

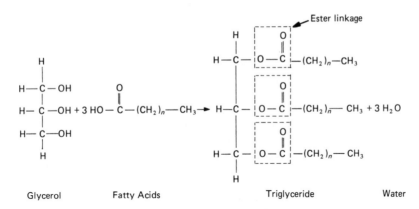

Glycerol   Fatty Acids   Triglyceride   Water

Figure 9-1   The Structure of Mono-, Di-, and Triglycerides.

with 18 or 16 carbons, such as stearic and palmitic, predominate in foods and are found along with smaller amounts of short-chained fatty acids, such as butyric and caproic.

The degree of saturation and length of the carbon chain influence the nature of the fat. The fat becomes harder as the proportion of saturated fatty acids increases and softer as the proportion of unsaturated fatty acids increases. Fats also harden as the proportion of long-chained fatty acids increase, and soften as the proportion of short-chained fatty acids increase.

Table 9-1 Some Common Fatty Acids in Food: Saturated and Unsaturated

Common Name	Number of:		Structure	Melting Point (°C)
	Carbon Atoms	Double Bonds		
Butyric	4	0	$CH_3(CH_2)_2COOH$	−7.9
Lauric	12	0	$CH_3(CH_2)_{10}COOH$	44.2
Myristic	14	0	$CH_3(CH_2)_{12}COOH$	53.9
Palmitic	16	0	$CH_3(CH_2)_{14}COOH$	63.1
Stearic	18	0	$CH_3(CH_2)_{16}COOH$	69.6
Oleic	18	1	$CH_3(CH_2)_7CH = CH(CH_2)_7COOH$	13.4
Linoleic	18	2	$CH_3(CH_2)_4CH = CHCH_2CH = CHCH_2)_7COOH$	−5.0
Linolenic	18	3	$CH_3CH_2CH = CHCH_2CH; = CHCH_2CH = CH(CH_2)_7COOH$	−11.0

PROCESSED FATS

Fats used in food preparation do not occur in a free form. They are extracted from animal or plant tissues and materials. For example, oils come from seeds, butter from cream, and lard from pork. The processes by which fats are separated vary with the product.

Oils

Oils are removed from oil-containing seeds by pressing, solvent extraction, or a combination of these processes. The extracted oils are refined, bleached, and deodorized. Salad oils are also **winterized** (chilled) to remove the fats that harden and give salad dressings a cloudy appearance at refrigerator temperatures. The common edible oils are corn, cottonseed, peanut, soybean, and olive oil. Olive oil contains few polyunsaturates and is valued for its flavor. Table 9–2 lists the fatty acid content of some plant and animal fats. Vegetable oils are used to produce shortenings, margarines, and salad dressings. (Salad dressings are discussed in chapter 14).

Hydrogenation

Oils and soft fats are hardened by the hydrogenation process. Liquid oils are exposed to hydrogen gas in the presence of a nickel catalyst and heat, which add hydrogen atoms to the double bonds present in the unsaturated fats. The hydrogenated fat is cooled, subjected to pressure in the presence of an inert gas (nitrogen), and then held at controlled temperatures for several days to permit small stable crystals to form.

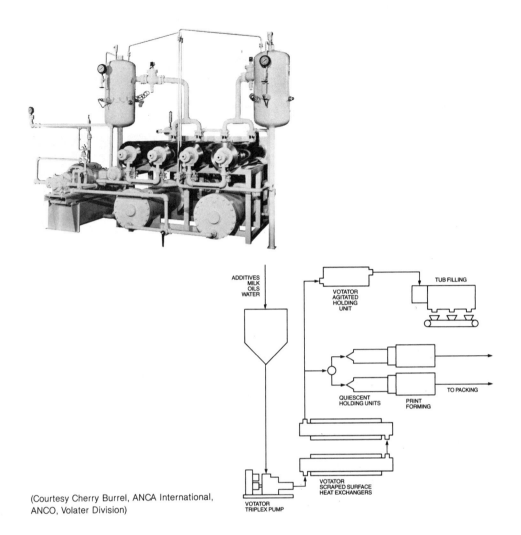

ADDITIVES
MILK
OILS
WATER

VOTATOR
AGITATED
HOLDING
UNIT

TUB FILLING

QUIESCENT
HOLDING UNITS

PRINT
FORMING

TO PACKING

VOTATOR
SCRAPED SURFACE
HEAT EXCHANGERS

VOTATOR
TRIPLEX PUMP

(Courtesy Cherry Burrel, ANCA International,
ANCO, Volater Division)

Shortenings

Vegetable shortenings are prepared from **hydrogenated** vegetable oils to yield a plastic fat. Some vegetable shortenings are whipped to incorporate air, thus increasing their plasticity, and some are **superglycerinated** (2 to 3 percent monoglycerides added) to improve emulsification properties. Some shortenings may contain both vegetable and animal fat. Labels on fats and oils must provide the common name of the fats used in descending order of percentage used.

Margarine

Margarine is prepared from vegetable oils (listed on label) churned with cultured-pasteurized skim milk, and with added salt, butter flavor (diacetyl), mono-

111

Table 9-2 Fatty Acid Content of Selected Fats

per 100 grams fat	Saturated Fatty Acids		Unsaturated Fatty Acids		
	Palmitic	Stearic	Oleric	Linoleic	Linolenic
Fats					
Butter	21.3	9.8	20.4	1.8	1.2
Cocoa butter	25.4	33.2	32.6	2.8	0.1
Lard	23.8	13.5	41.2	10.2	1.0
Margarine, hard	10.9	8.6	32.0	23.6	1.5
Margarine, soft	7.2	4.9	16.1	47.6	0.4
Shortening	14.1	10.6	44.5	24.5	1.6
Oils					
Coconut	8.2	2.8	5.8	1.8	—
Corn	10.9	1.8	24.2	58.0	0.7
Cottonseed	22.7	2.3	17.0	51.5	0.2
Olive	11.0	2.2	72.5	7.9	0.6
Peanut	9.5	2.2	44.8	32.0	—
Safflower	6.2	2.2	11.7	74.1	0.4
Soybean	10.3	3.8	22.8	51.0	6.8
Sunflower	5.9	4.5	19.5	65.7	—
Meats					
Beef	24.9	18.9	36.0	3.1	0.6
Lamb	21.5	19.5	37.6	5.5	2.3
Chicken	21.6	7.6	37.3	19.5	1.0

Adapted from USDA, Handbook no. 8-4, *Composition of Foods, Fats and Oils, Raw, Processed, Prepared,* 1979.

and diglycerides or lecithin for emulsification, sodium benzoate or benzoic acid for preservation, yellow color, and vitamins A and D.

Butter

Sweet or sour cream is agitated to break the oil-in-water emulsion thus releasing butterfat to form the water-in-oil emulsion of butter. Butter contains about 18 percent water dispersed in about 80 percent fat (Table 9–3). Salt to preserve and carotene for color may be added. Butter may be whipped to incorporate air and thus increase spreadability. Whipped butter contains about half the calories (per equal volume but not weight) of unwhipped butter because aerating doubles its volume. Butter contains a high proportion of butyric acid (saturated) and about 40 percent of the fatty acids in butter are unsaturated (oleic and linoleic).

Lard

Lard is fat rendered from the tissue of hogs. The composition of lard varies with feed consumed by hogs and what part of the animal it comes from. Prime steam lard comes from the fat trimmed from internal organs and various market cuts, leaf lard from the lining of abdominal cavity. Antioxidants are added during processing to retard rancidity. Lard is highly plastic with excellent shortening power.

Table 9-3 Fat Content of Selected Fats

Food Fat	Fat Content (percent)
Bacon fat	100
Butter	80
Cream	20
Cream (whipped)	35
Hydrogenated fat	100
Lard	100
Margarine	80
Peanut butter	46
Salad oil	100

Rearranged Lard

Interesterification is a chemical modification that rearranges fatty acids on the glycerol molecules, improving the creaming property of lard. Rearrangement occurs when fat is heated in the presence of nitrogen and a suitable catalyst. Then beta prime crystals do not convert to grainy beta crystals during storage.

Fat Crystals

Solid fats contain microscopic crystals including alpha, beta, prime, and intermediate. Alpha crystals are very small and transparent; beta are large and unstable. Intermediate crystals develop as beta prime change to beta crystals. Beta crystals impart an undesirable grainy character to food products. They form during prolonged storage or when fat is cooled slowly.

Acetylation

Acetin or acetylated fats form when fatty acid radicals are replaced with acetic acid. Acetin fats may be plastic or liquid at room temperature, depending on the fatty acid content. Crystalized acetin fats are waxy and translucent and are used as coatings for cheese, nuts, and dried raisins.

STORAGE

Animal fats tend to oxidize (become rancid) when exposed to air. They should be refrigerated to retard oxidation and may be frozen for prolonged storage. Hydrogenated fats and vegetable oils may be stored at room temperature since they contain some **antioxidants.** All fats easily pick up flavors and odors and should be kept tightly covered to minimize these changes. Refrigerated fats are easier to combine with ingredients when they are warmed to room temperature.

Rancidity

Oxidative Rancidity. The breakdown of fat is attributed to oxidation and enzyme action. Hydrogenated fats, composed primarily of saturated fatty acids, tend to resist chemical changes, but unsaturated fats are susceptible to oxidative changes. It is believed that the carbon atom next to a double bond picks up oxygen, leading to the formation of a hydroperoxide. As fats pick up oxygen, hydrogen is lost. The activated peroxide formed picks up another hydrogen from other unsaturated fatty acids to form a hydroperoxide. The hydroperoxides readily break into smaller volatile substances that have the characteristic odors of rancid fat. This is a self-catalyzing chain reaction. Once fats become slightly rancid, the reaction continues rapidly.

Oxidation of fat is accelerated by elevated temperatures, light, and the presence of metals such as copper, iron, and nickel. This type of **rancidity** is responsible for the spoilage of fats in foods. Iron present in meat proteins can initiate oxidation of the fatty acids in meats as iron can in wheat germ. Once begun, the reaction continues even in frozen foods. Even the small amounts of fat in cereal products stored improperly or for prolonged periods may become rancid. Proper storage conditions and use of antioxidants retard the development of rancidity. Rancidity is undesirable because it promotes objectionable changes in flavor, odor, color, fat consistency, and destruction of fat-soluble vitamins. The linoleic acid content of triglycerides is believed to be the chief precursor of the off-flavor in fats.

Hydrolytic Rancidity. Enzymes present in foods initiate hydrolytic rancidity. The enzyme lipase breaks down fat to free fatty acids and glycerol. Lipase is more active at room than refrigerator temperatures and thus accelerates the development of rancidity in unrefrigerated fats. An objectionable odor and a soapy flavor develop. The catalase enzymes are believed to inhibit enzyme-induced oxidation.

Antioxidants

Compounds that prevent oxidation are known as antioxidants. Some antioxidants occur naturally in fats and oils. Vitamin E designates a group of compounds known as tocopherols, which act as antioxidants. The high stability of vegetable oils as compared to animal fats is due to their tocopherol content. Other antioxidants, including lecithin, butylated hydroxyanisole (BHA), butylated hydroxytoluene (BHT), and propyl gallate, are used to protect fats against oxidation.

Antioxidants protect other compounds against oxidation by becoming oxidized themselves or by binding (sequestering) other substances such as metals which promote oxidation like EDTA in salad dressings. In addition to cooking fats and oils, other fat-containing foods, such as bacon, nuts, potato chips, baking mixes, and cereal products, must also be protected from fat spoilage. Fat-containing substances must be protected from air, light, and heat. Colored wrappers and colored glass offer protection against wavelengths that catalyze oxidation.

Reversion

An undesirable fishy or beany flavor, which precedes rancidity, is known as **reversion.** Oils that have a high proportion of linolenic acid are most likely to undergo reversion. This reaction is promoted by metals, heat, and ultraviolet light. Soybean oils readily undergo reversion, probably because they contain small amounts of iron and copper. The addition of EDTA (ethylenediaminetetraacetic acid) and phosphoric acid tends to control reversion. Some spoilage microorganisms (bacteria, mold) release enzymes capable of decomposing fats in dairy products, meat, and salad dressings, causing an unpleasant odor and flavor.

SELECTION

Fats and oils are purchased according to individual preference, intended use, special dietary needs, and cost. Label information identifies the actual fat content and permits selection of the product best suited to individual needs. Fats and oils are always listed in descending order of the quantity contained, from largest to smallest.

Butter may be preferred for table use because of its flavor. Highly polyunsaturated margarines may be chosen over butter for health or special dietary needs. Shortening and oil may be selected for specific cookery needs, or a general purpose shortening may be selected for both shortening and frying needs. Lard may be preferred for pastry and biscuits, hydrogenated plastic vegetable shortenings for shortened cakes. Oils are preferred for salad dressings.

FUNCTIONS

Fats serve a number of functions in food preparation. They contribute flavor, act as a leavening and tenderizing agent, serve as an emulsion ingredient, and serve as a frying medium.

Flavor

Fats such as butter, olive oil, and bacon fat contribute their own unique flavor to foods in which they are used. Fats are capable of dissolving certain flavor components contained in other foods. When flavorful foods such as celery, onion, and green pepper are cooked in fat, their flavors are incorporated into other foods cooked with them.

Tenderization

Fats act as a tenderizing agent in most flour products. Proteins in wheat flour develop gluten when mixed with water. Gluten contributes elasticity to the flour mixture. Because fat is insoluble in water, it separates gluten strands of the flour to produce a tender product. The ability of fat to tenderize flour mixtures is referred to as shortening value or power. Because butter and margarine contain 20 percent water and 80 percent fat, they have less shortening value than hydrogenated fats or lard, which contain 100 percent fat.

Leavening

Plastic fats have the ability to retain air when creamed or beaten. The air incorporated into the fat contributes some leavening action in flour mixtures.

Emulsion Ingredient

Emulsion refers to the dispersion of two liquids that do not normally mix. Oil and water are classic examples of liquids that do not mix. Fat is a major component of an oil-in-liquid emulsion, in which fat is dispersed in droplets in another liquid, such as water.

Emulsions are present in milk, cream, egg yolk, and a number of other foods. In these foods, the fat exists in tiny droplets and is dispersed throughout the liquid. Shaking, beating, and stirring are methods used to disperse one liquid in another. Cooked salad dressing, sauces, gravies, cream soups, and ice cream all contain fat dispersed in a liquid and are examples of emulsions. Emulsions are important systems in foods and food preparation. The use of fats in salad dressing is discussed in chapter 14.

Frying Medium

Fats serve as a medium for the transfer of heat to the food. Hydrogenated shortening and vegetable oils are excellent for frying because they have a high smoke point. Most forms of lard, butter, and margarine produce smoke when heated to temperatures used for frying. The temperature at which a fat begins to decompose is referred to as the smoke point. At this point, smoke rises from the surface, fats break down chemically to release free fatty acids, and **acrolein** (an irritating substance) is formed from glycerol. Foods cooked in decomposed fats pick up off flavors.

The use of and handling of fats influences the smoke point. Fats used repeatedly or for prolonged periods develop a lower smoke point. Emulsified fats have a low smoke point (Table 9–4). The smoke point is also lowered by increased

Table 9-4 Smoke Points of Selected Oils and Fats

Oil/Fat	Smoke Point	
	F degrees	C degrees
Corn oil	450[a]	232
Cottonseed oil	450[a]	232
Peanut oil	450[a]	232
Lard, rendered	360–400[b]	182–204
Shortening, not emulsified	450[b]	232
Shortening, combination, emulsified	319–376[c]	191–177

[a]K. Marril, F. Norris, A. Stirton, and D. Swern, *Bailey's Industrial Oils and Fat Products,* 3rd ed., edited by D. Swern. (New York: Interscience, John Wiley & Sons, 1964), p. 123. Copyright © 1964 by John Wiley & Sons, Inc.

[b]B. Lowe, S. Pradhan and J. Kastelic, The free fatty acid content and smoke points of some fats, *Journal of Home Economics* 50:778, 1958.

[c]M. Bennion and F. Hanning, Effects of different fats and oils and their modification on changes during frying. Reprinted from *Food Technology* 10:229, 1956. Copyright © by Institute of Food Technologists.

numbers of food particles dispersed through the fat. Fats heated in shallow, wide pans smoke at lower temperature than fats heated in small pans with vertical sides.

PAN AND DEEP-FAT FRYING

In frying, fats serve both as a lubricant to prevent sticking and to transfer heat. Pan-fried foods are cooked in a small amount of fat until the desired doneness is achieved. Pan-fried foods absorb some of the fat flavor and develop a crust.

Deep-fat-fried foods are submerged in hot fat and cooked until done. Deep-fat frying is done in a deep, heavy metal pan with straight sides and a small surface area. Deep-fat-fried foods are crisp and golden brown. Different foods require different frying temperatures (Table 9–5). A deep-fat-frying thermometer should be

Table 9-5 Deep-Fat-Frying Times and Temperatures

	°F	°C
Chicken	350	177
Doughnuts, fritters, oysters, scallops, soft-shell crabs, fish	350–375	177–191
Croquettes, eggplant, onions, cauliflower	375–385	191–196
French-fried potatoes	385–395	196–202

used to assure the fat is of proper temperature unless the pan is equipped with a thermostatic control. Vegetables should be free of surface droplets of water when deep-fat fried. With the exception of potatoes, most vegetables, meats, poultry, and fish are coated for deep-fat frying. The coating develops a crust and keeps the food interior moist.

FAT ABSORPTION

It is desirable to keep fat absorption to a minimum during frying to maintain palatability and promote ease of digestion. Absorption of fat is influenced by the temperature of the fat when the food is added, the amount of surface exposed to fat, composition of the food, and cooking time. The greater the surface area exposed to fat and the longer the cooking, the greater is the fat absorption. Foods with a high proportion of sugar absorb more fat than those containing lesser amounts.

Fat that is too hot overbrowns the surface of a food before the interior is cooked, resulting in a small volume in leavened products. Low temperatures cause the food to be greasy. Large quantities of food cooked at one time lower the temperature of the fat, and the foods become grease soaked and cook slowly and often unevenly. Fried foods should be drained on paper toweling and served immediately.

SUMMARY

Fats and oils are two general classes of lipids. Fats are essential for their linoleic acid content and are important as a concentrated source of energy. Foods of animal origin are high in saturated fatty acids, and those of plant origin are rich in unsaturated fatty acids. Triglycerides are the principal fat in foods. Fats are extracted from animal and plant tissues. Butter and lard are common animal fats. Vegetable oils are processed into shortening, margarine, and salad oils. In food preparation fats serve as flavor, leavening, and tenderizing agents, as an emulsion ingredient, and frying medium. Unsaturated fats and oils oxidize readily. Rancidity is attributed to oxidation and enzyme (lipase) action. Antioxidants retard the oxidation of fat.

SELF-STUDY GUIDE

1. What fats are used in cookery? Give uses for each.
2. Define hydrogenation, winterize. Why are these processes used?

3. What are the nutritive contributions of fats?
4. Identify the differences between animal and vegetable fats.
5. How do shortenings differ from oils? Suggest uses for each.
6. What influences the melting point of fats?
7. In what ways do butter and margarine differ?
8. Define shortening power and plasticity. When is each desirable in food preparation?
9. What four factors influence the choice of fats?
10. What five functions do fats serve in food preparation? Give examples.
11. What four factors influence absorption of fats during frying?
12. What fats are suitable for deep-fat frying? Why?
13. Why are some foods coated for deep-fat frying?

SUGGESTED READINGS

ALLEN, C. E., and FOREGEDGING, E. A. Some lipid characteristics and interactions in muscle food: a review. *Food Technology* 35:253, 1981.

AHEA. *Handbook of food preparation.* 8th ed. Washington, D.C.: American Home Economics Association, 1980.

ANDERSON, R. E. Lipase production: Lipolysis, and formation of volatile compounds by pseudomonas fluorescens in fat containing media. *Journal of Food Science* 45:1694, 1980.

BECKER, W. A., et al. Abdominal and carcass fat in five broiler strains. *Poultry Science* 60:693, 1981.

BUSHWAY, A. A., et al. Chia seeds as a source of oil, polysaccharide, and protein. *Journal of Food Science* 46:1349, 1981.

CHEN, I. S., et al. Comparison of methylene chloride and chloroform for the extraction of fats from food products. *Journal of American Oil Chemists' Society* 58:599, 1981.

ESKIN, N. M., and FRENKEL, C. A simple and rapid method for assessing rancidity of oils based on the formation of hydroperoxides. *Journal of American Oil Chemists' Society* 53:746, 1976.

GRAY, J. I. Measurement of lipid oxidation: A review. *Journal of American Oil Chemists' Society* 55:539, 1978.

GURR, M. I., and JAMES, A. T. *Lipid biochemistry: An introduction.* 3rd ed. New York: Methuen, 1980.

HSIEH, C. C., et al. Direct gas chromatographic estimation of saturated steryl esters and acylglycerols in wheat endosperm. *Cereal Chemistry and Technology* 58:106, 1981.

ITCH, T., et al. Triterpene alcohols and sterols of spanish olive oil. *Journal of the American Oil Chemists' Society* 58:545, 1981.

JANTAWAT, P., and DAWSON, L. E. Composition of lipids from mechanically deboned poultry meats and their composite tissue. *Poultry Science* 59:1043, 1980.

KILGORE, L., and BAILEY, M. Degradation of fats during frying. *Journal of the American Dietetic Association* 56:130, 1970.

KINSELLA, J. E., Dietary fat and prostaglandins: Possible relationship between food processing and public health. *Food Technology* 35:89, 1981.

LEE, F. *Basic food chemistry.* Chap. 5. Westport, Conn. Avi Publishing Company, 1975.

MAI, J., et al. Effects of microwave cooking on food fatty acids: no evidence of chemical alteration or isomerization. *Journal of Food Science* 45:1753, 1980.

MARSH, A. C. *Composition of foods, soups, sauces and gravies: Raw, processed, prepared.* Agriculture Handbook no. 8-6. Science and Education Administration. Washington, D.C.: Government Printing Office, 1980.

MILLER, R. L., et al. High intensity selection for percent oil in corn. *Crop Science* 21:433, May/June 1981.

MIN, D. B. Correlation of sensory evaluation instrumental gas chromatographic analysis of edible oils. *Journal of Food Science* 46:1453, 1981.

MOUNTS, T. L., et al. Selective hydrogenation of soybean oil: ix. Effect of pressure in copper catalysis. *Journal of the American Oil Chemists' Society* 53:402, 1978.

NES, W. R., and NES, W. D. *Lipids in evolution.* New York: Plenum Publishing, 1980.

OKOS, L., and HUBBARD, R. Use of low fat dairy spread. *Journal of Home Economics* 63:266, 1971.

PETROWSKI, G. E. Food-grade emulsifiers. *Food Technology* 29:52, 1975.

PHILLIPS, J. A., and VAIL, G. E. Effect of heat on fatty acids. *Journal of the American Dietetic Association* 50:116, 1967.

PONGRACZ, G. Antioxidant mixtures for use in food. *International Journal of Vitamin Nutrition and Research* 43:517, 1973.

ROTH, H., and ROCK, S. P. The chemistry and technology of frying fat. 1. Chemistry. *Baker's Digest* 46:38, 1972.

SLOVER, H. T., et al. Lipids in fast foods. *Journal of Food Science* 45:1583, 1980.

STROCCHI, A. Fatty acid composition and triglyceride structure of corn oil, hydrogenated corn oil, and corn oil margarine. *Journal of Food Science* 47:36, January/February 1982.

U.S. DEPARTMENT OF AGRICULTURE. *Composition of foods. Fats and oils: raw, processed, prepared.* Handbook no. 8-4. Human Nutrition Information Service. Washington, D.C.: Government Printing Office, 1979.

WEAST, R. C. *Handbook of chemistry and physics.* 61st ed. Cleveland: CRC Press, 1980.

10

BREADS: QUICK AND YEAST

OBJECTIVES

When you complete this chapter, you will be able to

1. Identify differences in the preparation of quick and yeast breads, and explain the functions of ingredients used in quick and yeast breads.
2. Describe methods of mixing used for muffins and biscuits, and give examples of other flour products that use these methods or their variations.
3. Identify differences in methods of mixing yeast and quick breads.
4. Discuss changes that occur during the baking of breads.
5. Discuss the nutritional contributions of breads.

Breads, quick and yeast, make a distinctive contribution to the food customs and the traditions of most countries. They add satisfaction to meals and make special occasions more festive. The term *quick breads* distinguishes the quickly prepared products from yeast-leavened breads.

Quick breads include many different oven-baked breads such as biscuits, muffins, nut loaves, and cornbreads. Some are baked on a griddle, for example pancakes and waffles; others, such as dumplings and brown breads, are cooked by steam; still others, including doughnuts and fritters, are fried in deep fat. Quick breads are made with quick-acting leavening ingredients (baking powder or soda and an acid) or steam instead of the slower-acting yeast. They are easily made, and many of them are served hot.

Yeast breads are kneaded and molded into attractive shapes, which rise to a fluffy lightness and are then baked to a golden brownness. Breads are known by many names throughout the world, often reflecting the grains from which they were made. The basic grain is wheat, but corn, rye, oats, and rice are also widely used.

Although quick and yeast breads share a number of common ingredients, the proportions and kinds of ingredients used vary with the product. This chapter identifies the nutritional qualities and functional properties of ingredients common to bread products and considers the preparation techniques involved.

NUTRITIONAL QUALITY

The nutritional quality of baked products is determined by the kinds and amounts of ingredients used. Enriched or whole-grain flour, milk, and eggs are prime contributors of nutrients in baked products, and the quantities in which they are used determine the levels of certain nutrients the product will provide. That is to say, large quantities of egg, milk, or enriched or whole-grain flour contribute significant nutrient value, whereas small quantities provide minimal nutrient value. A high level of fat in any baked product increases calories.

FUNCTIONS OF INGREDIENTS

The preparation of batters and doughs for quick and yeast breads involves the same basic ingredients of flour, liquid, salt, fat, and possibly sugar, and eggs. Each ingredient serves a key function in the wide array of breads. The significant characteristics and unique contributions of these basic ingredients are reviewed in the following sections.

Flour

Flour provides the basic structure of all bread products because it contributes the gluten and starch to form the structural network. The structure is due to gluten, which is coagulated by heat and gelatinized starch. The various types of flour and their differences were discussed in Chapter 7.

The protein content of the flour determines the nature and amount of the gluten and therefore also holds the key to whether a specific flour is appropriate for the product being prepared. An elastic, strong gluten (hard wheat) is preferred for yeast dough and a softer, less tenacious gluten (soft wheat) for quick breads. All-purpose flour, a blend of hard wheats or soft wheats, is commonly used to prepare quick breads.

Gluten is developed during manipulation in a flour-water mixture to form the basic cell-wall structure. As the gases in the cells expand during baking, the cells also expand. That happens early in the baking process while the gluten is still elastic. Later, when the gluten becomes hot, it coagulates, the stretching ceases, and the walls become rather rigid.

The starch fraction of the flour becomes gelatinized and embedded in the gluten network during baking. The surface particles of the flour are also dextrinized to contribute to the desired browning. When the starch gelatinizes, it binds water in the granules, with the result that much of the excess moisture is bound and no longer free to contribute to the fluidity of the mixture. This explains, in part, why batters and doughs are transformed from relatively moist unbaked mixtures to the fixed structure of the baked products. Some special flours, such as whole wheat or rye, contribute a characteristic color and nutlike flavor to baked products.

Liquid

The liquids used in breads serve as solvents for some ingredients, provide water needed to produce steam, and hydrate the proteins and starch in flour. Liquids dissolve the sugar and soluble salts so that they can be dispersed uniformly throughout the mixture. The solvent action of water is important also in dissolving baking powder and baking soda so that they can participate in the chemical reactions required to release carbon dioxide for leavening of quick breads. Liquids hydrate the flour proteins for gluten development and thus are essential for the formation of the structural network of batters and doughs. They also provide the water that is essential to the gelatinization of the starch in flour.

Milk is the liquid used most frequently in baked products. The fat content of milk contributes to a softer crumb, which is less subject to staling. Milk enhances the food value, contributes to flavor, and because of its lactose and protein assists in browning the crust. Since milk contains about 13 percent solids, a slightly greater volume of milk than of water is needed in a recipe to achieve the appropriate moisture content. At times water, fruit juices, or cream may be used as well. Fruit juices contribute not only flavor but also acid, which generates carbon dioxide from baking soda.

The proportion of liquid to flour influences consistency and makes the difference between batter and dough. Doughs contain a higher proportion of flour to liquid than batters. A product with too much liquid or too little flour is of a thin consistency, tends to fall, is moist, and may be soggy. Conversely, too much flour or too little liquid yields a stiff dough and compact baked products low in volume.

Leavening Agents

Leavening agents provide gases to contribute porosity and lightness to baked products. Gases expand the cell structure during baking, increasing volume and tenderness of the product. Effective leaveners maintain the expanded cell structure until coagulation of the protein structure is completed at the end of baking. The common leaveners of carbon dioxide, steam, and air are discussed in chapter 8.

Salt

The primary function of salt is to enhance the flavor of all baked products. In yeast doughs excess salt retards the fermentation process. However, the correct amount of salt has a tightening effect on protein, which results in a slightly greater volume of bread. This action is in opposition to the action of sugar, which speeds fermentation in yeast doughs. Breads containing salt have a finer texture than salt-free bread.

Fat

Breads generally contain small amounts of fat. Both liquid and solid fats are used in baked products. The nature of the fat influences the nature of the baked product; therefore careful selection of fat should be made so that the type best suited to the product is used. Solid fats contribute to flakiness as well as tenderness, while liquid fats contribute only tenderness. Tenderness is desirable in all bread products. Rolled biscuits contain fat distributed in small pieces that melt on baking, leaving spaces between layers of dough that contribute to flakiness.

Fats contribute richness to a product, and some fats (butter, margarine, and cream) may also contribute a desirable flavor and color. The texture of baked products is influenced by the type of fat and the way it is incorporated. Bread products containing fat tend to have a softer crumb and crust.

Sugar

Sugar is present in breads in variable quantities. Its primary function is to add sweetness. Sugar also promotes tenderness, but its influence is not as great as that of fat. In relatively large amounts it interferes with gluten development because it competes with gluten for water. It also interferes with gelatinization because it competes with starch for water. Sugar may be involved in caramelization and thus contributes to browning. Because granulated sugar, or sucrose, is not a reducing sugar, it does not react with amino acids to promote **Maillard** browning.

Eggs

The functional roles of eggs in breads include the following: they are a source of liquid, promote emulsification, and contribute to structure, color, possibly flavor, and nutritional value. The coagulation of egg protein during baking adds stength to the cell walls and thus contributes to the structure of cream puffs and popovers. Eggs are a major ingredient in popovers, which depend on the coagulation of egg proteins for structure after steam expands their volume. The lecithin of egg yolks serves as an effective emulsifying agent in fat-containing baked products. A good example of the effectiveness of eggs as emulsifiers is provided by cream puffs. Unless the emulsion is stable, the water and fat will separate, and the puffs will fail to expand.

The high moisture content of eggs permits them to act as a liquid in the preparation of flour mixtures, assisting in hydration of gluten and starch, solution of dry ingredients, and steam production.

CHANGES DURING BAKING

Changes that occur during baking of breads include the production and expansion of gases, coagulation of protein, gelatinization of starch, evaporation of water, and browning of the crust; in yeast breads there is also evaporation of alcohol. The gases air, steam, and carbon dioxide expand to promote a leavening effect that increases the volume of the baked product. Upon cooling, the coagulated proteins stiffen, and cooked starches gel to produce maximum product strength.

The baking temperature should be sufficiently low to permit optimum volume to be reached before the proteins on the outer surface coagulate and crust formation takes place. The starch in the flour is hydrated by the liquid and gelatinized when heated sufficiently. The evaporation of liquid from the surface during baking promotes higher temperatures and the development of a crust. As has been pointed out, Maillard browning does not occur because sucrose (granulated sugar) is not a reducing sugar. In theory, caramelization of sugar could contribute to surface browning.

QUICK BREADS

The differences among the quick breads are more numerous than the similarities. The major similarity is in the basic ingredients. All quick breads require flour, liquid, and salt. They also may include all or some of the following ingredients: shortening, leavening agent, sugar, and egg. Other ingredients may be included to enhance flavor, contribute character, and add variety. Differences exist in the proportion of ingredients (Table 10–1), the manner in which the ingredients are incorporated, and baking temperatures.

Quick-bread mixtures are classed as pour batters (pancakes, waffles), drop batters (muffins, drop biscuits), and doughs (dumplings, rolled biscuits). This clas-

Table 10-1 Proportions of Ingredients for Selected Flour Products

	Biscuits	Cream puffs	Doughnuts	Muffins	Pancakes	Popovers	Waffles	Yeast breads
Baking powder (tsp)	1½–2	0	1½	1½	1½–2	0	1¾–2	—[a]
Flour (C)	1	1	1	1	1	1	1	1
Salt (tsp)	½	½	½	½	½	½	½	¼
Sugar (Tbsp)	0	0	3½	1–2	1	0	0–1	1–2
Eggs	0	4	1	½	1	2–3	1–2	0
Fat or oil (Tbsp)	2–3	8	1	1–3	1	0–½	1–3	0–1
Liquid (C)	⅓–½[b]	1	¼	½	¾–1	1	⅔–¾	⅓

[a] ⅓ package yeast in yeast breads.
[b] ½ cup liquid for drop biscuits, ⅓ cup for rolled biscuits.

sification recognizes the diversity in the proportion of flour to liquid. Batters are flour mixtures with sufficient liquid to permit beating or stirring. The stiffness of batters varies from those that may be poured (pour batter) to those viscous enough to be dropped from a spoon. Pour batters use two-thirds to one cup of liquid per cup of flour and drop batters about one-half cup liquid. Doughs use only about one-eighth to one-half cup of liquid per cup of flour and range in consistency from stiff to soft.

Muffins

The muffin method of mixing is a basic method used not only for muffins but also for a variety of other products such as pancakes, popovers, and some cakes. It uses a thick drop batter prepared with two parts of flour to one part of liquid. The ingredients are first assembled into two groups, dry and wet. The measured dry ingredients (flour, sugar, salt, baking powder) are placed in a sifter and then sifted directly into the mixing bowl. Or if a flour is being used that does not require sifting, such as whole wheat, the ingredients are stirred well in the mixing bowl. The egg is blended in another bowl and then the milk and the melted shortening or oil are added and blended with the egg. The assembled liquid ingredients are poured, all at once, into a well in the center of the dry ingredients. The ingredients are carefully mixed just enough to moisten the dry ingredients yet retain a lumpy appearance.

The prepared batter is spooned carefully into a greased muffin pan. Each muffin cup should be filled half full with a minimum of manipulation, to avoid overmixing the remaining batter. A flexible spatula or scraper should be used to push the muffin batter carefully from spoon into the muffin cup. Muffins are baked at a high temperature (425°F, 218°C).

The proportion of flour to liquid favors the rapid formation of gluten in muffins. Because the small proportions of sugar and fat in muffins are unable to retard gluten formation sufficiently, mixing and manipulation must be carefully controlled. Overmixed muffins become distorted in shape and progressively less tender as mixing is increased owing to the overdeveloped gluten. An overmixed muffin batter is shiny and flows in a smooth, long stream from the spoon. Baked muffins from overmixed batter have a smooth crust, a peaked top, and long, narrow tunnels extending from the bottom toward the peak. The muffins are tough, the cells uneven in size, and the texture heavy.

Although overmixing is a common problem, muffins can also be undermixed. Undermixed muffins have a low volume and a flat top with rough areas on the surface. The poor volume is caused by insufficient moistening of the baking powder and an incomplete release of carbon dioxide. The muffin usually contains some dry lumps of flour and baking powder and is crumbly.

A properly mixed and baked muffin has a golden brown exterior, symmetrical in that it is not peaked. The muffin is tender with a pleasant, slightly sweet flavor. The interior texture is even, medium coarse, and light.

Variations from the basic muffin recipe include using a higher proportion of sugar and fat. The result is muffins with a fine, cakelike texture typical of commercial muffin-mix products. Plain muffins may be varied with the addition of dried or fresh fruit, nuts, sweeteners other than granulated sugar, and varietal flours or cornmeal.

(b)Poor quality muffins (Laimute Druskis)

(a)Good quality muffins

Loaf Breads

The muffin method of mixing is used to make quick loaf breads. They are often flavored with nuts, banana, cranberries, or other fruits and flavorings.

Popovers

Popover batter contains an equal amount of flour and liquid. Popovers have a crisp crust with a hollow center and are steam leavened. The high ratio of liquid to flour produces a batter with gluten particles dispersed so that long strands of gluten are not likely to form. All of the ingredients (flour, salt, milk, unbeaten egg) are assembled in one bowl and beaten thoroughly until the batter is smooth.

Because the proteins of egg and flour form the supporting structure, egg size and the number in the recipe are important. Popover volume is related to egg content. Extra-large eggs and more than one egg per cup of flour produce popovers with greater volume.

The oven temperature also influences volume. Popovers require a high temperature (425 to 450° F, 219 to 232° C) to produce a large volume of steam before the protein structure coagulates. If the high temperature is maintained throughout the baking period, however, it may cause excessive surface browning before the interior is dried. The solution is to reduce the temperature after about twenty minutes, which is the time it takes for popovers to reach maximum volume.

High-quality popovers are crisp, nearly hollow shells, golden brown, and slightly moist. They are served hot with butter and/or other spreads.

Yorkshire Pudding

Yorkshire pudding is a type of popover, differing only in the way it is baked—in the meat drippings after a roast is removed from the pan. Because a roasting pan is rather large, Yorkshire pudding has a puddinglike texture and is somewhat crisp.

Timbale Cases

Timbale cases are made of the same batter as popovers but are cooked on special irons in deep fat. They are used as a base for cream dishes or as a dessert. The batter is held for about one-half hour to free it of bubbles, which would create a rough surface and cause the case to break. The timbale iron is heated to the appropriate temperature and dipped into the batter. The batter will not adhere to a cool iron and falls off an overheated iron. A popover batter may also be used as a cover batter for fritters. Fritters are pieces of fruit, vegetable, fish, or poultry dipped into batter and fried.

Pancakes

The same basic ingredients used for muffins are used to prepare pancakes or griddle cakes. Pancake batter has somewhat more liquid per cup of flour than muffins do. The muffin method is used to combine the ingredients, and the same precautions are observed to avoid an overmixed batter. Pancakes are baked on a preheated griddle, either the nonstick type or one that requires greasing. The desired amount of batter is poured on the griddle and the pancake turned when bubbles break on the surface and the bottom is pleasingly browned.

Crepes

Crepes, or french pancakes, are prepared from a thin batter with a high proportion of egg and no baking powder. A small amount of batter is poured into a small skillet or special crepe pan. Crepes are served as a dessert with sweetened fruit, nuts, or syrup; or with a meat, cheese, or other unsweetened filling as a main dish.

Waffles

Waffle batter is similar to that of pancakes but contains more fat and egg. Although waffles are made by the muffin method, the eggs may be separated, the yolks blended with other ingredients, and the beaten white folded in last. The batter is poured into a preheated waffle iron.

Cream Puffs

Cream puffs are hollow shells leavened with steam. Like popovers they contain equal amounts of flour and liquid but more fat and egg and are prepared differently. The butter is first melted in boiling water and the flour added all at once and blended thoroughly. The mixture is stirred while being heated until a ball forms as the starch gelatinizes. When a ball forms, the mixture is removed from the heat and the eggs added one at a time with rigorous beating. The completed batter is a smooth paste that retains its shape when dropped on an ungreased baking sheet. A sufficient volume of steam forms when cream puffs are baked in a hot oven. High-quality cream puffs have a large cavity and good volume and are tender and lightly browned.

Biscuits

Biscuits are cut from a soft dough made with three parts of flour to one part liquid. The other ingredients are fat, salt, and leavening. In the biscuit-pastry method the solid fat is cut into the flour-salt mixture until it resembles small peas or coarse meal. The milk is added all at once to the fat-flour mixture and stirred with a fork to form a soft dough. The dough is lightly kneaded, to promote flakiness, uniform mixing of the dough, and the development of the desired level of gluten. Kneading is done by folding the dough over and pushing gently with the

palm of the hand. This procedure is repeated ten to twelve times for biscuits. Kneading must proceed gently and only for a short time to avoid overdevelopment of gluten, which leads to toughness.

The kneaded dough is rolled, usually to one-half inch thickness. The rolling flattens the fat particles to form layers of fat between layers of gluten and yields flakiness. These layers of fat melt during baking to form spaces for the leavening gases (steam, carbon dioxide) to expand before the protein coagulates and the starch gelatinizes.

The biscuit cutter is pressed evenly into the rolled dough to make uniformly shaped biscuits, or the dough may be cut into desired shapes with a knife or a pastry wheel. The biscuits may be arranged next to each other or spaced on an ungreased baking sheet and then baked in a preheated oven (424° F, 218° C) for about fifteen minutes. Biscuits should have a golden brown exterior, symmetrical shape, tender and flaky texture, and pleasant flavor.

Drop Biscuits. Drop biscuits are made in the same manner as rolled biscuits except a little more liquid is required to produce a soft dough that can be dropped from the spoon onto the baking sheet.

Shortcake. Shortcake is a biscuit dough that contains more fat than biscuits do and sometimes a small quantity of sugar. Shortcake may be served as a dessert with sweetened fruit and milk, light cream, or whipped cream.

Scones. Scones are prepared from a rich dough similar to shortcake dough and usually include eggs as part of the liquid. Scones are cut into triangle or diamond shapes and served as bread with meals or, particularly in Great Britain, for afternoon teas.

Cake Doughnuts. Beaten egg, sugar, soft shortening, and liquid are combined with sifted flour and leavening to form a soft dough. The rolled dough is cut with a doughnut cutter and them fried in deep fat (370–380° F, 188–193° C). Too high a temperature browns the surface before the interior is cooked, while too low a temperature yields a pale crust that absorbs an excess of fat.

Microwaved Breads

Microwaved breads do not brown, but they have a greater volume than the conventionally baked products. Color from ingredients such as corn, bran, and spices, or colorful toppings can compensate for the lack of browning. Toasted coconut, cinnamon and sugar, or chopped nuts, for instance, may be sprinkled over the bread surface before microwaving. Glazes may be applied to the microwaved bread surface.

YEAST BREADS

Beginning as an ancient art, bread making paralleled the progress of civilization and evolved into the complex, mechanized, continuous process established in modern bakeries. The action of yeast (see chapter 8), through the process of fermentation, produces carbon dioxide from glucose to leaven bread.

Yeast-leavened products require the same basic ingredients as quick breads except for the type of leavener used. The kinds and amounts of ingredients used, the techniques of mixing, and the manner of baking influence the quality and characteristics of specific yeast breads. Yeast, flour, and liquid are essential for yeast doughs. Salt, fat, and sugar improve the texture and flavor of yeast dough when they are used. These ingredients serve many of the same functions in yeast bread as in other flour products and were discussed earlier in this chapter. Breads, rolls, and cakes are examples of yeast-leavened products.

Function of Ingredients in Yeast Dough

Flour. Although all-purpose flour yields a satisfactory yeast product, the volume and texture of yeast breads are best when they are prepared from bread flour (hard wheat). The protein content of these flours provides sufficient water-holding capacity and gluten development for a yeast dough structure capable of retaining the carbon dioxide produced by yeast. Breads prepared with bread flour have somewhat higher volume and finer texture than those prepared with all-purpose flour.

Liquid. Although water may be used, milk is commonly used in bread making. Milk contributes nutrients and flavor, promotes a finer texture, improves the color of crust, and delays staling of the baked bread. The quantity of liquid is determined by how much water the flour can absorb. The protein content of the flour determines the water-absorption capacity; the higher the protein content, the more water the flour absorbs. Therefore, hard-wheat flour absorbs more water than soft-wheat flour. Flour best suited for yeast breads can absorb one cup of liquid for each two and one-half to three cups of flour.

Salt. Salt is used to control the rate of yeast growth as well as for flavor. Salt also retards action of the enzymes, which tend to soften the dough and make it sticky and difficult to handle. Breads prepared without salt are very coarse, and those with too much salt are heavy.

Fat. An optimal level of fat in yeast dough will improve the volume, grain, texture, crust, and keeping quality. Plastic fats are considered to be more effective than oils. Fats make yeast doughs more tender and elastic.

Yeast. Yeast a microscopic, one-celled plant is the chief leavening ingredient in yeast breads. Yeast ferments sugar to produce ethyl alcohol, carbon dioxide, and other by-products. The basic functions of yeast in bread making are to leaven the dough, contribute flavor from the flavor components, such as acids, esters, and alcohols, and promote dough development during fermentation. (Yeast activity is discussed in chapter 8 "Leavening Agents"). Compressed yeast is used in the baking industry. Bread and roll mixes usually contain active dry yeast (rehydrated at 100–115° F, 37–46° C).

Sugar. The level of sugar as well as of salt influences the speed of fermentation. Most yeast dough formulas include sugar to promote rapid yeast growth even though enzymes in flour and yeast can convert starch in flour to glucose. The conversion of flour starch to glucose is a slow process.

Egg. Eggs are not an essential ingredient for yeast doughs. They are included in some yeast doughs to contribute to the structure, color, and elasticity of the dough and to promote browning.

Methods of Mixing

Either the straight-dough or the sponge method yields quality yeast products. The no-knead and cool-rise methods are alternate procedures for making yeast products.

Straight-Dough Method. The straight-dough method requires less time than the sponge method and is usually used for home-baked yeast products. All of the ingredients are mixed together to form a soft dough, and the dough is kneaded before it is risen.

Sponge Method. The sponge method yields a bread with a slightly different flavor from straight-dough bread. The sponge method proceeds in two stages. First, the yeast and liquid are combined with about half of the flour to make a thick batter. The mixture rises in a warm place until very bubbly and light. Then the sugar, salt, fat, and remaining flour are added to the light batter to make a dough that can be kneaded. The remaining procedures are the same as for the straight-dough method and include rising, shaping, and baking.

Batter-Yeast Method. This method requires less time to produce yeast products with a flavor and texture similar to those prepared by the straight-dough method. The batter method requires more fat and somewhat less flour, and the mixture is not kneaded. The ingredients are mixed by the straight-dough method, and the gluten is developed by beating instead of kneading.

Cool-Rise Method.   Some of the steps in bread making are reduced in the cool-rise method. The bread is permitted to rise in the refrigerator and the straight-dough procedure is used with the following modifications:

1. Warmed pasteurized milk is used instead of scalded milk.
2. Vigorous beating during the additions of flour replaces kneading and develops gluten.
3. The shaped dough is allowed to rise in the refrigerator only once.
4. The dough is shaped by first rolling it to give greater uniformity to the shape of the loaf.

Active-Dry-Yeast Alteration.   Active dry yeast is blended with a portion of the flour before it is hydrated with liquid. The active dry yeast is added directly to one-third of the flour mixture and blended thoroughly before it is added to all of the warm liquid.

Another method combines the active dry yeast with about two cups of flour. Then the hot liquid is added to the yeast-flour mixture along with the fat, and is vigorously beaten by hand or on a mixer at medium speed to develop gluten. The remainder of the flour is added to form the dough. The rising, shaping, and baking procedures are the same as for the straight-dough method.

Preparation Principles

Bread making involves an orderly sequence of events, which begin with the combining of ingredients to develop a dough. The soft dough is usually kneaded to develop gluten to retain the leavening gas. The kneaded dough undergoes a fermentation period during which it rises until it is doubled in volume and light. Then the fermented dough is punched down, shaped, proofed, and baked.

Mixing.   The yeast may be hydrated in lukewarm water, or active dry yeast may be mixed with part of the flour before it is added to the liquid. Fresh whole milk is scalded (190° F, 88° C) to inactivate substances that may interfere with yeast activity. The fat, salt, and sugar are melted and dissolved in the scalded milk. The milk mixture is cooled to lukewarm temperature to avoid destruction of the yeast. The hydrated yeast is added to the cooled milk mixture and blended. The flour is gradually added to the liquid mixture until a soft dough is formed. As the dough is mixed, the liquid is distributed evenly, and gluten develops. Mixing is continued until all of the ingredients are thoroughly blended.

Kneading.   The soft dough is **kneaded** to develop sufficient gluten and to thoroughly blend the ingredients. A light film of flour may be used on the board to facilitate handling of the dough and to avoid making the dough too stiff. Kneading further distributes the ingredients, and the dough becomes smooth, dry, and elastic.

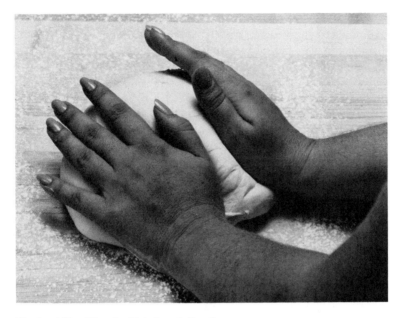

(Courtesy Hill and Knowlton/Fleischman's Yeast)

(Courtesy Hill and Knowlton/Fleischman's Yeast)

The dough is kneaded primarily with the heel of the hand. The dough is flattened somewhat with the heel of the hand and folded in half. Then it is pushed forward firmly with the heels of both hands to stretch it over the board. The dough is rotated a quarter of a turn and the folding and pushing continued until the dough becomes springy to the touch and is satiny smooth and the finger imprints rise as the finger is removed.

Rising. The surface of the kneaded dough may be lightly greased to avoid drying, and the dough is allowed to **rise** in a warm place (80–86° F, 27–30° C) protected from cold air currents until doubled in volume. As fermentation occurs, the volume of the dough increases. During the rising that accompanies fermentation, gluten becomes elastic and forms thin films around individual gas cells. The dough is sufficiently light when an imprint with two fingers remains in the dough. At this point the dough has reached its optimum gas-retention capability. The dough is punched down with the fist and kneaded gently several times to expel carbon dioxide. Pushing down the dough avoids overstretching of the gluten and rupture of cell walls. It also redistributes the yeast and tends to equalize the temperature.

Proofing. The fermented, punched-down dough is now ready for shaping into loaves and rolls. The shaped dough is placed into baking pans with greased bottoms and ungreased sides. The surface of the shaped dough is lightly greased to avoid drying. The dough is allowed to **proof** (rise a second time) until doubled in bulk. Technically, proofing refers to the rising of the fermented, shaped dough in pans before it is baked. A warm temperature (77–86° F, 25–30° C) should be maintained during proofing. When the product is proofed too long, the dough is too light, and the texture is coarse and crumbly. When the product is not proofed sufficiently, breaks occur along the sides because expansion continued after the crust started to become firm. The product has thick cell walls and a small volume and is heavy.

Baking. The proofed dough is baked in a preheated oven (400° F, 205° C). It undergoes **oven spring,** a rapid rise in loaf volume during the first few minutes of baking, before the yeast is inactivated by heat. The gluten begins to coagulate or set and the starch gelatinizes with the result that the risen volume and shape are retained by the baked product.

The baking temperature vaporizes the alcohol produced by yeast action. Evaporation of water from the surface dries the outer layer; the aldehyde group of the sugars and the amino groups of the protein react (Maillard reaction) and contribute to the brown color. Caramelization of sugar may also contribute to crust color. Dough containing milk, sugar, or eggs browns quickly. Color may serve as a guide but does not adequately identify completion of baking. A baked loaf of bread produces a hollow sound when lightly tapped. The baked bread is removed from the pan and cooled on a rack.

Microwaved Yeast Breads

Microwaved yeast breads do not brown or develop a crust as do conventionally baked breads. Because microwaved breads rise higher during baking than conventionally baked breads they should be placed in a larger loaf pan and timed carefully to avoid large air pockets, which collapse and cause an uneven shape. Properly microwaved breads are set and dry on top, and the surface springs back when touched. Toasted sesame seeds and other toppings can be used to add color to the bread surface.

Storage

Freshly baked, cooled breads may be stored in foil or plastic wrap for a few days at room temperature. These wraps prevent drying but do not inhibit mold growth or rope spoilage, which is caused by a fungus that attacks the interior of the bread. Refrigeration retards rope formation and mold growth. Commercially, calcium proprionate or sodium propionate is often added to retard mold growth and rope formation. Frozen storage maintains optimum quality of baked bread products.

Home-prepared frozen yeast doughs may have a retarded gas-producing capability because of the potential for some yeast destruction. Home-prepared yeast doughs may be refrigerated for a few days. The refrigerated dough is allowed to ferment before shaping if it has not risen to double its bulk. The shaped dough must be allowed to rise again before baking. Commercially prepared frozen breads are specially formulated and processed for freezing.

Staling

The flavor, texture, and aroma of bread begin to change soon after baking. The crumb gradually becomes firm and dry and the crust leathery. Staling of bread appears to be influenced by storage conditions and ingredients used. A high content of fat, milk, egg, and sugar may retard staling slightly in commercial breads. Freezing bread in an airtight wrapper very soon after baking delays bread staling.

The causes of staling have not been clearly identified. Staling appears to involve recrystallization (retrogradation) of starch. It has been suggested that the branches of amylopectin may fold up and associate with one another. Staled bread can be freshened temporarily by heating the bread in a wrapping until it softens. Bread freshened by warming should be used immediately before it cools and crystallizes again.

Homemade Mixes

Homemade bake mixes save time and energy as do the commercial mixes. Homemade mix for baked products can be prepared by sifting dry ingredients and cutting in the shortening. Liquid ingredients are added at the time of preparation. The mix will keep for several weeks at room temperature and several months in the refrigerator if shortening is used as the fat. Homemade mixes yield quality products and are especially suitable for biscuits, muffins, waffles, pancakes, and coffee cakes. In addition to saving time and energy, they save on cost.

Heating Baked Products

The microwave oven may be used to defrost frozen yeast breads and to cook the dough when a browned product is not essential. The defrost setting allows rapid defrosting and warming and maintains the tenderness of the product. For some microwave ovens it is necessary to remove foil or metal twists. When the cardboard container is not foil lined, the product may be warmed in the container. Other products may be placed on paper or pottery plates for reheating.

SUMMARY

Ingredients common to bread products include: flour, liquid, and salt; some breads in addition require eggs, leavening, shortening, and sugar. The proportion of ingredients and techniques of mixing and baking are variable among kinds of quick breads and among quick and yeast breads. Ingredients serve similar functions in all breads. Flour provides the structure; sugars sweeten, tenderize, and influence color of crust; liquids hydrate and act as solvents; eggs contribute structure and emulsify and may leaven; leavening agents contribute porosity and lightness; and salt enhances flavor. Whole grain or enriched flour, milk, and eggs contribute most of the nutrients in bread products.

SELF-STUDY GUIDE

1. Identify two basic methods used to prepare quick breads and list examples.
2. List ingredients common to quick and yeast breads and give their function.
3. Identify the characteristics of well-prepared muffins, biscuits, and yeast breads.
4. Define crepes, popovers, Yorkshire pudding, timbale cases, scones.
5. Contrast the preparation of muffins and cream puffs.
6. List three factors that influence the speed of fermentation.
7. Contrast the sponge and straight-dough methods for making yeast breads.
8. Discuss the kneading and rising process.
9. Identify three alterations used in mixing yeast dough. How do these breads compare with or differ from standard bread?
10. Discuss four principles of yeast-dough preparation.
11. Discuss bread staling. How can it be retarded?

SUGGESTED READING

BANNER, R.　Eleven-grain variety bread base. *Food Engineering* 53:97, March 1981.

BLOUIN, F. A. et al.　Role of flavonoids in production of color in biscuits prepared with wheat and cottonseed flours. *Journal of Food Science* 46:266, January/February 1981.

CARLSON, B. L., et al.　Influence of tomato seed addition on the quality of wheat flour breads. *Journal of Food Science* 46:1029, 1981.

CHICHESTER, C. O.　*Advances in food research.* Vol. 26. New York: Academic Press, 1980.

CONSUMER GUIDE.　*Food processor bread book.* New York: Simon and Schuster, 1980.

DAVIS, K. R., et al.　Evaluation of the nutrient composition of wheat. I. Lipid constituents. *Cereal Chemistry* 57:178, 1980.

EL-MINVAWI, M. A. and ZABIK, M. E.　Cottonseed flour's functionality in Egyptian baladi bread. *Cereal Chemistry* 58:413, September/October 1981.

EVANS, L. T. and PEACOCK, W. J.　*Wheat science today and tomorrow.* New York: Cambridge University Press, 1981.

HARLAND, B. F., and HARLAND, J.　Fermentative reduction of phytate in rye, white, and whole wheat breads. *Cereal Chemistry* 57:226, 1980.

HELDMAN, D. R., and SINGH, R. P.　*Food process engineering.* 2nd ed. Westport, Conn.: AVI Publishing Company, 1981.

JUNGE, R. C., and HOSENEY, R.　Mechanism by which shortening and certain surfactants improve loaf volume in bread. *Cereal Chemistry* 58:408, September/October 1981.

KHAN, N., et al.　Sorghums with improved tortilla making characteristics. *Journal of Food Science* 45:720, May/June, 1980.

KNOU, D., et al.　Enzymatic reduction of phytate in whole wheat breads. *Journal of Food Science* 46:1866, November/December 1981.

LEE, K., and CLYDESDALE, F. M.　Effect of baking on the forms of iron in iron-enriched flour. *Journal of Food Science* 45:1500, November/December, 1980.

MORRIS, C. E.　White bread matches nutrition of whole wheat. *Food Engineering* 52:69, July 1981.

NAGAO, S., et al.　Scanning electron microscopy studies of wheat protein fractions from doughs mixed with oxidants at high temperature. *Journal of the Science of Food and Agriculture* 32:235, March 1981.

RAM, B. P. and NIGAN, S. N.　Puffing and textural characteristics of chapati in relation to varietal differences in gluten composition *Journal of Food Science* 47:231, January/February 1982.

RANHOTRA, G. S., et al.　Expanded cereal fortification; bioavailability and functionality (flavor) of magnesium in bread. *Journal of Food Science* 45:915 July/August 1980.

REPETSKY, J. A., and KLEIN, B. P.　Partial replacement of wheat flour with yellow field pea flour in white pan bread. *Journal of Food Science* 47:326. January/February 1982.

SAAB, G. B., et al.　Fortification of bread with alphs-lysine HCl; Losses due to baking process. *Journal of Food Science* 46:662, March/April, 1981.

SATHE, S. K., et al.　Effect of addition of great northern bean flour and protein concentrates on rheological properties of dough and baking quality of bread. *Cereal Chemistry* 58:97, March/April, 1981.

TANGKONGCHITR, U., et al.　Phytic acid I. Determination of three forms of phosphorus in flour, dough, and bread. *Cereal Chemistry* 58:226, 1981.

TERADA, M., et al.　Rheological properties of dough made from flour exposed to gaseous ammonia. *Cereal Chemistry* 58:101, March/April 1981.

UNKLESBAY, N., et al.　Thermal conductivity of white bread during convective heat processing. *Journal of Food Science* 47:249 January/February 1982.

11

CAKES, COOKIES, AND PASTRY

OBJECTIVES

When you complete this chapter, you will be able to

1. Discuss and compare the basic methods used in making shortened cakes.
2. Discuss the functions of ingredients in shortened cakes.
3. Discuss the preparation of sponge/foam cakes and make comparisons with shortened cakes.
4. Discuss the functions of ingredients in sponge/foam cakes.
5. Discuss high-altitude baking.
6. Identify the basic types of cookies and compare preparation of cookies and cakes. Discuss functions of ingredients in cookies.
7. Discuss methods used to prepare pastry, and discuss functions of pastry ingredients.
8. Discuss the factors related to pastry tenderness and flakiness.

Although cake and pastry are prepared by a variety of methods, they usually contain the same basic ingredients. The ingredients must be balanced, in proportion, and of the correct type for the preparation of quality cakes and pastries. The term *cake* includes both shortened and sponge varieties. The term *pastry* includes conventional pies and often refers to a wide range of products made from doughs that usually have a high fat content.

NUTRITIONAL QUALITY

Most nutrients in cakes, pies, and cookies come from eggs, fruit, milk, and enriched flour. However, the quantities of these ingredients are restricted by the recipe and usually are relatively small, while the fat and sugar quantities are large. Small quantities of nutrient-rich ingredients provide minimal nutrient value, while large quantities of fat and sugar in any product provide an abundance of calories. In other words, cakes, pastry, and cookies mainly contribute many calories but very few essential nutrients. Preferably they are served only after adequate nutrient-rich foods are eaten, and then to make up the balance of calories yet needed. When these baked products replace nutrient-rich foods, they contribute to a caloric overload and lead to overweight, obesity, and malnutrition.

CAKES

Cakes are classified into two major groups: shortened and sponge or foam. Essential cake ingredients are flour, egg, sugar, salt, and liquid. Other ingredients are added to contribute distinctive qualities.

Function of Cake Ingredients

Ingredients serve the same general functions in cakes that they serve in other flour mixtures. Some of these ingredients have characteristics that make them especially suitable for cake baking. The essential ingredients must be present in proper proportions to produce cakes of high quality. The tenderizing ingredients in a cake formula (shortening and sugar) must counteract the toughening (structural) ingredients (flour, egg and milk solids).

Flour. Flour of smallest particle size and low protein content produce high-quality cakes. Cake flour has these characteristics and is generally preferred for cakes, although cakes of acceptable quality can be prepared with all-purpose flour. Cakes prepared with all-purpose flour are less tender and light than those prepared with cake flour and are not as fine grained. The small quantity of protein in cake flour is coagulated by heat and the starch gelatinized, and in this way both contribute to cake structure.

Sugar. Sugar exerts a tenderizing effect by interfering with gluten formation during mixing. Cakes with a high proportion of sugar are more tender than cakes with less sugar. Sugar also elevates the coagulation temperature of protein and the gelatinization temperature of starch, thus extending the time that the batter remains fluid and the leavening gases can expand during baking. The result is an increase in volume with increasing levels of sugar. There is a point, however, where the cell walls stretch to the breaking point before protein coagulation occurs. A fallen, compact structure then results. Sugar in crystalline form facilitates the incorporation of air into fats as they are **creamed.** Air adheres to the sharp edges of sugar crystals and is beaten into the fat.

Shortening. The nature of the fat determines the amount of air incorporated. Oils lack creaming quality and do not retain air. Butter, margarine, and lard are limited in their plasticity and therefore cream only moderately well. Along with other hydrogenated fats, these fats lack emulsifiers. Butter imparts very desirable flavor and color but yields a cake of lower volume than superglycerinated fats.

The creaming quality of plastic fats makes them especially suitable for cakes. Plastic fats entrap air during creaming, thereby contributing to the leavening effect. Superglycerinated shortenings (hydrogenated fat with emulsifiers) are preferred. Their excellent plasticity aids in the formation of the many small cells needed to produce a cake with fine texture. The mono- and diglycerides in superglycerinated shortenings act as emulsifiers and ensure a good distribution of fat in the batter. Superglycerinated shortenings also permit the use of cake formulas with higher proportions of sugar and liquid than cakes made from shortenings without emulsifiers.

During baking the batter becomes more fluid as the fat melts. As mentioned in the discussion of sugar, the expansion of gases is facilitated during this liquid state, directly affecting cake volume.

Eggs. Eggs exert a toughening influence unless shortening and fat are used in sufficient amounts and increased to compensate for a high egg content. Egg proteins coagulate when heated and stabilize the foam structure during the early stages of baking. Egg increases the concentration of protein and lowers the coagulation temperature of protein during baking, thus reducing the period of time during which leavening gases may expand.

Liquid. Liquid is essential for gluten formation and gelatinization of starch. Milk and eggs and at times water or juices contribute to the water content of a cake formula. Inadequate quantities of liquid produce a dry crumb and heavy texture. Excessive quantities of liquid weaken the cake structure and cause a low volume. Some causes of cake problems are summarized in Table 11–1.

Leavening. Air introduced when shortening is creamed, flour sifted, eggs beaten, and batter mixed provides air cells in cake batter that contribute to texture. Carbon dioxide liberated by the baking powder or baking soda plus acid and steam produced during baking collect in the spaces formed by air cells. Too much baking powder or soda produces a coarse, uneven texture.

The type of leavening may also influence the pH of the batter. The color of pigments in cocoa and chocolate change with the pH of the batter. In an acid

Table 11-1 Shortened Cakes: Problems and Causes

Failures	Causes
Coarse texture	1. Too much baking powder or sugar
	2. Insufficient mixing after flour was added
Poor volume	1. Not enough baking powder
	2. Insufficient mixing
	3. Too much fat, liquid, or sugar
	4. Insufficient creaming
	5. Overmixing after flour was added
	6. Low oven temperature
Heavy layer on bottom	1. Insufficient mixing
	2. Too much liquid or egg
Uneven peaked top	1. Too much flour
	2. Not enough milk
	3. Not enough fat or sugar
	4. Overmixing after flour was added
	5. Oven temperature too high
	6. Too deep a pan
	7. Placed too high in oven
Large holes and tunnels	1. Overbeating
	2. Too much baking powder
Sunken center	1. Insufficient baking
	2. Oven temperature too low
	3. Cake moved during baking
	4. Too much sugar, fat, or leavening
Tough crumb and dry	1. Too little fat, sugar or liquid
	2. Too much flour or egg
	3. Overmixing after flour was added
Crisp, sugary crust	1. Too much sugar, leavening, or fat
Overflowing pan	1. Too much baking powder or sugar
	2. Too small pan

pH below 7 they are yellowed; in an alkaline pH above 7 they become mahogany red. The soda in devil's food cake permits the characteristic red color to develop.

Methods of Mixing Shortened Cakes

Cake ingredients are mixed to incorporate a maximum volume of air and to **blend** them very thoroughly. The methods of mixing vary with the time needed to blend the ingredients, and they can affect the quality of cake produced. A variety of methods are used to combine ingredients for shortened cakes. The quick-mix and conventional methods are commonly used. Other methods include conventional-sponge, muffin, muffin-meringue, and pastry blend. The muffin method requires the least time and yields cakes that are acceptable when served warm but do not keep well. The conventional mixing method requires more time than the quick-mix method. The conventional-sponge is a variation of the conventional method. These methods vary primarily in the order in which ingredients are combined. Any of these methods can yield a successful shortened cake if the recipe was developed for the specific method.

Quick-Mix Method. The quick-mix method is known by a variety of names, such as one-bowl, single-stage, mix-easy, or dump method. The dry ingredients for the quick-mix method are **sifted** into a bowl; fat at room temperature and all or part of the milk and flavoring are added. The mixture is **beaten** for a specified time or specific number of strokes. Then any remaining milk and unbeaten eggs are added. The beating is again continued for a specified time or number of strokes.

Formulas for quick-mix cakes contain a high ratio of sugar, and liquid is near the maximal level. Emulsified shortening is recommended for quick-mix cakes.

Conventional Method. The conventional method begins with the creaming of shortening and sugar. Creaming yields an air-in-fat foam, and when eggs are added, a water-in-oil emulsion. Crystalline sugar promotes the incorporation of air into plastic fat. Plastic fat and fat at room temperature cream best. The sugar may be added all at once when a mixer is used. When the creaming is done by hand, the sugar is added in small amounts and thoroughly creamed after each addition. The longer the fat and sugar mixture is creamed, the more air is incorporated to yield a fine grain and optimum volume.

Eggs are added, usually one at a time, when the creamed fat-sugar mixture becomes fluffy and creaming is continued until the mixture becomes very light. The flavoring may be added to the creamed mixture for more effective distribution than when added at the end of mixing. The emulsion established when the eggs are blended into the fat-sugar foam also aids in the formation of a fine grain.

The sifted dry ingredients are added in four parts, alternately with the milk in three parts, beginning and ending with flour. This increases batter viscosity and helps to prevent curdling when milk is added. Mixing is kept to a minimum with each addition to avoid excessive gluten development.

Conventional-Sponge Method. The conventional-sponge method is a modification of the conventional method. The variation occurs in the addition of the egg and part of the sugar. The eggs are separated. Two tablespoons of sugar per egg white are reserved for preparation of the egg-white foam. The yolks are creamed into the fat-sugar mixture. The sifted dry ingredients in four parts and the liquid in three parts are added alternately to the sugar-yolk-fat mixture as for the conventional method. The meringue is prepared from the egg whites and remaining sugar and is folded in carefully after the last addition of flour. The egg white foam contributes to the volume of the cake.

Muffin Method. Cakes made by the muffin method contain a higher proportion of fat and sugar and can be stirred more than muffin batter. Eggs and milk are blended with the melted fat and then stirred into the sifted dry ingredients. The cake batter tends to be thin and the texture coarse because the ingredients are not well dispersed. This method is a time saver, and the cake is acceptable if it is eaten while very fresh.

Pastry Method. The fat and flour are blended together. The sugar, baking powder, and half the milk are mixed with the blended fat and flour. The egg and remainder of the milk are mixed in. The fat is well dispersed, and the cake has a fine texture and grain.

Methods of Mixing Sponge/Foam Cakes

Sponge and angel cakes are light and have a delicate flavor. They differ from shortened cakes in that they do not contain fat and are not leavened with carbon dioxide. They contain a high proportion of egg, sugar, and water to cake flour. Egg foams are essential in the preparation of these cakes. Egg whites form the most stable foam and are often separated from the yolk before beating. Acceptable cakes can be prepared from beaten whole egg. The preparation of egg foams is discussed in chapter 19.

Although eggs, flour, and sugar serve similar functions in shortened and sponge/foam cakes, there are special factors to consider.

Eggs. Medium-sized eggs are used to develop angel and sponge cake recipes. Eggs incorporate air during beating to produce the basic foam. The entrapped air is responsible for a large portion of the leavening action. During baking, egg proteins coagulate and set the foam, which is basic to sponge and angel cake structure. Eggs also provide moisture to hydrate flour protein and starch.

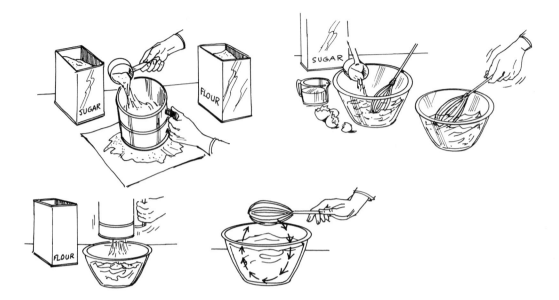

Flour. Flour proteins coagulate and hydrated starch gelatinizes during baking, contributing to cake structure. Cake flour has a fine granulation, or particle size, and a low protein content and is essential for high-quality sponge/foam cakes. To promote tenderness, the weight of the flour is less than half that of eggs.

Acid Ingredient. Cream of tarter is the most common acid ingredient in foam/sponge cakes. The addition of acid promotes the development of a fine texture—a stable foam, that improves the volume, texture, and tenderness of baked sponge/foam cakes. Angel cake without an acid ingredient is yellowed rather than snowy white, tough in texture, and low in volume.

Sugar. In addition to providing sweetness sugar stabilizes egg foam and is a tenderizing agent. It counterbalances the toughening effect of flour and eggs. Sugar elevates the coagulation temperature of egg proteins and in excessive amounts retards coagulation to the extent that the cake may collapse. A finely granulated sugar promotes a fine texture in all cakes. The higher the percentage of sugar, the more likely it is that a sugary crust will develop.

Angel Cake. Egg white foam is the basis of all angel cakes, although the method of mixing may vary. Egg whites, at room temperature, are beaten to the foamy stage. An acid ingredient, cream of tarter, salt, and flavoring are added and the foam beaten until the peaks barely bend when the beater is lifted. Then half the sugar is added gradually with continued beating, to yield a meringue. The sugar dissolves in the foam and stabilizes it. After the last addition of sugar, the foam is beaten only until it is fine grained. An overbeaten meringue is no longer elastic, and the cake becomes compact.

The remaining half of the sugar is sifted with the flour so that it can be readily and evenly distributed throughout the meringue in four additions. Each fourth of the mixture is sifted over the surface of the meringue and carefully **folded** into it. Folding is stopped as soon as the flour is evenly distributed. Overmanipulation results in a tough, compact, low-volume cake.

The prepared batter is carefully poured and pushed with a spatula into a tube pan, although loaf pans may be used. Any pockets of trapped air are eliminated by carefully cutting with a knife through the center of the batter. The tube pan supports the center of the cake and protects the delicate structure of angel and other foam cakes. The tube also facilitates the heating and resultant coagulation of protein before foam volume decreases.

Angel cakes are baked at 375° F (191° C). Higher temperatures cause cakes to overbrown. Some shrinkage does occur near the end of the baking period and as the cake cools. Because of their delicate and somewhat elastic structure, foam cakes are cooled in an inverted tube or loaf pan. In this position the cell structure remains stretched as it cools rather than becoming compacted by the weight of the cake. After the cake cools to room temperature, it is loosened and removed from the pan. The elastic crumb of a cooled angel cake is easily cut with a sawing motion of a serrated-edge knife.

A well-prepared angel cake is lightly browned, of good volume, moist, light, and has a moderately fine, uniform texture.

Sponge Cake.   Sponge cakes contain egg yolks and whites. Variations exist in their preparation. Most sponge cakes are made with separated eggs, but some are made with unseparated eggs and others from yolks alone with some added water.

Egg foams are basic in sponge cake preparation along with lemon juice, sugar, flour, and salt. In a basic or true sponge cake, egg yolk and white foams are prepared separately. The yolks are beaten first because yolk foam does not set on standing as egg white foam does. Lemon juice and/or water and a portion of the sugar are beaten with the yolk to a very thick, lemon-colored foam. Underbeaten yolks tend to separate and lead to the formation of a heavy layer near the bottom of the cake. The added liquids dilute the protein, thus tenderizing the cake while elevating the coagulation temperature.

The egg white foam is prepared as for angel cake with the addition of cream of tartar at the foamy stage and continued beating to a soft peak that bends slightly. Small portions of sugar are added gradually as beating is continued to yield a fine-textured meringue. The flour sifted with the remainder of the sugar is carefully folded into the beaten egg yolks. Care must be taken to avoid excessive folding at this point, and the yolk-flour mixture is carefully folded into the egg white mixture without loss of air. Folding is continued only until the mixtures are blended without visible white or yellow streaks. An alternate method folds the yolk foam into the egg white foam with the flour folded in last.

Sponge cake is baked in a tube or loaf pan at 375° F (191° C) and cooled in an inverted pan. A well-made sponge cake is light, tender, and nicely browned. The interior is golden yellow without streaks or layers.

Chiffon Cakes. Chiffon cakes are a blend of foam and shortened cakes. They have an appearance and texture similar to that of sponge cake. They contain egg foams along with oil and baking powder, neither of which is ordinarily used in foam cakes. The first step in chiffon cake preparation is to combine the dry ingredients—flour, baking powder, salt, and half the sugar—by sifting. The yolks and whites are separated. The liquid ingredients—oil, milk, and yolks—are assembled in a bowl. The dry ingredients are beaten into the liquid ingredients until the mixture is smooth. A meringue is prepared with egg whites, and the remaining sugar and is beaten until peaks just stand straight.

The yolk-flour mixture is poured slowly down the side of the bowl containing the egg white foam and gently folded into the foam. This procedure is continued until all of the yolk-flour mixture and meringue are uniformly blended. The batter is immediately poured into an ungreased tube pan and quickly placed into the oven.

The careful, thorough folding of the yolk-flour mixture and immediate baking are necessary to avoid drainage of liquid toward the bottom of the pan and the formation of distinct layers. The cake is cooled in an inverted pan as are angel and sponge cakes.

Microwaved Cakes

The tops of microwaved cakes are somewhat uneven, do not develop a dry crust, and do not brown. The cakes, however, are moist, fluffy, airy, and have greater volume. Since cakes are traditionally frosted, the difference in appearance is not a disadvantage. When a cake is to be served directly from the baking dish, the bottom of the pan is greased but not floured. When the cake is to be removed from the pan, the pan is lined with paper toweling cut to fit. Cake pans should be no more than half full of batter.

High-Elevation Baking

Some recipes for cake products may require changes to accommodate high elevations. However, it is recommended that recipes specifically developed for high altitudes (above 3000 feet) be used. Proportions of ingredients, baking temperatures, and times may be altered from those used at sea level. The lower atmospheric pressure offers less resistance to leavening gases. This problem is resolved by increasing the quantity of flour and egg and decreasing the quantity of sugar and baking powder. Water boils at a lower temperature at higher altitudes, permitting a rapid loss of moisture. This rapid loss of moisture is compensated for by the inclusion of more liquid in cake recipes. The internal temperature of cakes during baking is lower than at sea level due to the decreased boiling temperature of water. This causes the baking time to increase somewhat.

COOKIES

Cookies usually have the same ingredients as shortened cakes, but all-purpose flour is used rather than cake flour, and the egg may be the only liquid. They often contain more sugar than cakes, and some cookies, such as macaroons, contain no shortening.

The consistency and nature of cookies are determined by the kinds and amounts of ingredients used. Crisp cookies contain a high proportion of fat; chewy cookies, a high sugar and egg content; and soft cookies, a generous amount of liquid. Insufficient flour or too much fat produces a batter that spreads excessively when placed in the oven for baking.

Classes of cookies include bar, drop, filled, molded, pressed, refrigerator, and rolled. Bar cookies are also known as sheet cookies. The dough is richer and stiffer than cake batter. It is spread in a shallow baking pan and cut into bars after baking.

A slight modification of the conventional method of mixing is generally used to make cookies. The fat, sugar, and egg are creamed thoroughly to promote a good texture. The dry ingredients are sifted, added to the creamed mixture, and blended in. Overmixing results in a tough cookie.

Rolled cookies are cut from a dough sufficiently firm to roll easily. Rolling is done on a lightly floured pastry cloth or board. Chilling the dough for a short period facilitates rolling and cutting into desired shapes. It also helps to avoid the toughening that results when extra flour is worked in during rolling. **Molded** cookies are somewhat soft, yet firm enough to handle with ease. They are rolled with the fingers or the palm of the hand into desired shapes.

Filled cookies are rolled, cut, and then spread with a fruit filling. Another cut cookie is placed on top and the edges pressed together. A variation is to place filling on half the cookie and then fold the remainder of the cookie over the filling, pressing the edges together. The top of a filled cookie is slit or punctured with a fork to permit the escape of steam.

Pressed-cookie doughs have a high fat content, are fairly soft, and are forced through a cookie press into a variety of shapes. Drop cookies are made by dropping spoonfuls of stiff dough onto a cookie sheet, allowing spaces between each cookie for some spreading.

Refrigerator cookies are prepared from a fairly firm dough that has been shaped into a roll, covered with plastic wrap, and refrigerated for several hours prior to slicing for baking. The roll of dough may be wrapped for freezer storage and baked at a later time.

Microwaved Cookies

Bar cookies are suitable for microwaving since the microwave oven does not accommodate large batches. Large cookies microwave more evenly than small ones. Small cookies tend to have brown spots inside because cooking begins below the surface. Cookies are done when they are just set.

Storage

Although cookies come in many different textures, flavors, forms, and shapes, the original texture of the cookie is maintained when crisp cookies and soft cookies are stored in separate containers. All cookies are cooled before being stored in airtight containers or packed for freezer storage.

PASTRY

Good pastry is the hallmark of a good pie. The term *pastry* is used to identify a variety of baked products rich in fat ranging from Danish pastry to pies. In this chapter, pastry refers only to piecrust.

Function of Pastry Ingredients

Fat, flour, liquid, and salt are the ingredients required for pastry. Even though they are few in number, the ingredients, their ratios, and the methods used to combine them are all important factors in determining the characteristics of the baked pastry.

Shortening. Generally one-fourth to one-third cup of fat or shortening is used for each cup of flour for pastry of acceptable tenderness. All shortening promotes tenderness, but only solid shortenings contribute flakiness when cut into coarse particles. The coarse particles separate the dough into layers, which form flakes. Fats function as a shortening agent by coating some of the flour particles, interfering with their absorption of liquid and thus with the formation of gluten. The gluten strands are thereby shortened, making the pastry more tender; thus the term *shortening.*

Lard is plastic at low temperatures and has good shortening characteristics. It contributes more shortening power than other household fats and yields very tender and flaky pastry. Hydrogenated fats have a bland flavor and excellent shortening power, and are plastic at room temperature. They are easily cut into flour mixtures to promote flakiness and tenderness.

Margarine and butter contain a little more than 80 percent fat (rather than the 100 percent fat content of oils and shortenings) and about 14 percent water. Because of both the lower fat content and the higher water content butter and margarine contribute less shortening power. Consequently, when butter is substituted in equal measure for shortening in pastry, the pastry will be less tender.

Oils possess good shortening power because their fluidity enables them to coat each particle of flour. Their fluidity also interferes with the absorption of water by flour and thus inhibits gluten formation. Therefore, a crumbly or grainy pastry is formed.

Flour. Flour forms the structure of pastry and is the ingredient present in the largest amount. A tender pastry requires that only a small quantity of gluten be developed. All-purpose flour is generally used in the home, but commercial bakers use a soft-wheat pastry flour, which is lower in gluten-forming proteins.

All-purpose flour produces a cohesive dough because it contains more protein than pastry flour. Pastry flour makes a tender but crumbly pastry because it contains less gluten than all-purpose flour. All-purpose flour yields a very acceptable pastry when the amount of mixing is kept to a minimum.

Liquid. Although milk and other liquids may be used, water is usually the liquid in pastry. Liquids hydrate the flour so that sufficient gluten is developed during mixing to achieve a cohesive dough. When the amount of water in pastry is increased, more gluten develops from the flour proteins and the pastry is less tender than is considered desirable. Liquids also provide some steam to leaven pastry and actually help to form the flakes in a flaky pastry.

Salt. Salt enhances the flavor of pastry. The quantity of salt may be decreased or increased as desired without hindering tenderness or flakiness. It may be decreased when a salted fat is used.

Factors Related to Tenderness and Flakiness

Tenderness. The proportions of flour, fat, and liquid and the level of manipulation influence pastry tenderness. Pastry becomes progressively less tender as the quantity of flour or water is increased. Water hydrates gluten-forming proteins, but too much water increases toughness of pastry by hydrating more gluten than is needed. Additional flour incorporated during rolling also contributes to toughness since water is already present in the dough. Desirable tenderness is achieved with just enough liquid to barely form a dough. Some pastry problems and causes are listed in Table 11–2.

Soft-wheat flour contains less gluten-forming proteins than hard wheat and yields a more tender pastry. Tenderness of pastry decreases as the protein content of the flour increases. Manipulation is kept to a minimum after water is added to retard gluten formation and thus avoid tough pastry. Rerolling pastry overdevelops gluten and decreases tenderness.

Fats at room temperature blend easily with flour to aid in retarding gluten formation. The flour must be coated with fat to limit hydration before liquid is

Table 11-2   Pastry Problems and Causes

Failures	Causes
Tough Crust	Insufficient fat
	Too much water
	Overmixing
	Too much flour
	Too much handling
Crumbly Crust	Insufficient mixing
	Too much fat
	Too little water
	Self-rising flour

added to retain tenderness. A large portion of flour is coated with fat when solid shortening is cut in until the particles are the size of rice or cornmeal. Liquid fats blend easily with flour and produce short gluten strands and a tender pastry. A uniform distribution of fat promotes tenderness. The boiling-water method yields a more tender pastry than cut-in solid fat. Tenderness increases with increased amounts of fat but decreases with increased amounts of protein in flour.

Flakiness.   Too much or too little water in relation to the fat decreases **flakiness.** Flakiness is promoted by the expansion of steam produced from water in the dough. This expanded protein network is coagulated by the heat of the oven, and the flaky structure becomes firm. Flakiness develops as the small-to-coarse particles of fat are coated with moistened flour, flattened into layers by the rolling pin, melted in the oven, and absorbed by the adjacent dough to form hollow spaces between layers of baked dough.

A uniform distribution of fat can yield a flaky pastry. A firm but plastic fat at room temperature contributes to flakiness. Firm fat that remains in layers when rolled yields a flakier pastry than a soft or liquid fat. Some flakiness may develop when liquid fat is shaken with water to form a temporary emulsion and added immediately to the flour-salt mixture with gentle stirring. Fat that is thoroughly and evenly distributed tends to decrease flakiness while increasing tenderness. Hard-wheat flour has a high protein content, which promotes flakiness but decreases tenderness.

Methods of Mixing

Acceptable pastry can be prepared by several methods of mixing. Both flakiness and tenderness are prized characteristics of pastry and are promoted effectively when both fine and coarse particles of fat are present in the flour mixture.

Conventional Method.   The conventional or standard method of mixing promotes tenderness and flakiness and is commonly used to make pastry. Solid shortening at room temperature is *cut into* the flour-salt mixture with a pastry blender, two table knives, or two spatulas until the particles of fat resemble coarse cornmeal or small peas. Some favor coarsely cut fat in the flour mixture to promote flakiness, theorizing that rolling of large fat particles into thin layers promotes flakiness. A flaky pastry may also be prepared with finely cut fat particles.

The fat cut into the flour-salt mixture waterproofs the flour, that is, keeps it from becoming wet and thus retards gluten formation. Finely cut fat promotes the formation of short gluten strands and a uniformly tender pastry.

The liquid is sprinkled over the fat-flour mixture a tablespoon at a time and mixed lightly with a fork to moisten all the flour. Mixing and manipulation are kept at a minimum after water is added to avoid overdevelopment of gluten. The dough is gathered with the fingers and pressed into a ball. It may be rolled immediately or covered and allowed to rest for a short time at room or refrigerator temperature. This permits the water to penetrate uniformly throughout the dough and facilitates rolling.

Boiling-Water Method.   Boiling water is whipped into the fat, and the whipped mixture is stirred into the flour. This method distributes the fat evenly and yields a pastry more tender and mealy but less flaky than the conventional method.

Stir-and-Roll Method.   Oil or melted fat and milk or water are combined or shaken together and then stirred into the flour to form the dough. This method requires more manipulation than the conventional method to develop sufficient gluten to avoid an overly short and crumbly pastry. The pastry tends to be less flaky than conventional pastry.

Water-Paste Method.   The water-paste method controls the distribution of water and therefore of gluten. All of the measured liquid (two tablespoons per cup of flour) is combined with enough of the fat-flour mixture to make a lumpy paste. This paste is immediately stirred with a fork into the rest of the fat-flour mixture. This pastry is as tender and flaky as that prepared by the conventional method.

Rolling Pastry

Enough pastry for one crust is shaped into a ball and rolled immediately or placed into the refrigerator and allowed to stand a short time to hydrate for easy rolling. Pastry enough for one crust is rolled at a time to avoid toughening by rehandling the dough. Pastry may be rolled slightly less than one-eighth-inch thick between sheets of waxed paper, on a canvas-covered board, or on a lightly floured board. Rolling pastry between sheets of waxed paper eliminates the need for additional flour, which promotes toughness. The waxed paper is held securely in place if the counter is first lightly moistened with a damp cloth. Carefully rolling

(Laimute E. Druskis)

from center toward edge avoids wrinkles in the paper. Should wrinkles develop during rolling, the paper is rolled back to release them and rolling is continued.

Rolling always begins from the center of the pastry and stops at the outer edge. The dough is rolled into a circular shape about one-eighth-inch thick. The top crust should be about one inch larger and the lower crust about two inches larger in diameter than the top of the pie pan. When the dough is rolled on waxed paper, the top sheet is carefully removed, and the pastry lifted by the bottom sheet to place it over the pan, paper side up. The paper is removed and the pastry carefully shaped into the pan without stretching and without trapping air bubbles. Pastry rolled on a cloth or a board is carefully folded in half and lifted into the pan for shaping.

One-Crust Pie

A one-crust pie shell baked without filling must have a large number of holes pricked in it before it is baked to allow air to escape. An alternate method involves lining the baked pie shell with foil and dried beans to retain its shape during baking. Otherwise the shell develops large blisters caused by air trapped under the pastry and does not retain its shape. Custard-type fillings (pecan, pumpkin) are baked in raw, one-crust shells. Cooked or prepared fillings used in cream or chiffon-type pies are poured into baked crusts.

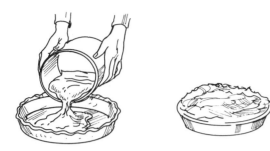

Two-Crust Pie

After the top crust is rolled, the filling is placed in the bottom pastry. The rim of the bottom pastry is moistened to facilitate subsequent sealing to the top crust. The top crust is centered over the filled crust and trimmed one-half inch larger than the pan. The top-crust extension is folded under the edge of the bottom crust and sealed by pressing. The edge is fluted to further seal the two crusts and to add eye appeal to the pie. Fluting is done by pressing the pastry between the index finger of one hand and the thumb and index finger of the other hand or between the thumb and bent finger of one hand. Several slashes are cut in the center area of the top crust to allow steam formed from the filling during baking to escape.

Baking Pastry

Pastry is baked at a relatively high temperature—425 to 450° F (218 to 232° C). The rapid production of steam separates the layers of dough formed as the rolled fat particles melt, promoting the development of flakiness. Baking temperatures are adjusted to the type of filling cooked in the pastry. The filling should be cooked adequately before the crust becomes too brown. Fresh fruit pies may be baked at a high temperature for ten to fifteen minutes, then at 350–375° F (177–190° C) for the remainder of the baking time. A hot oven aids in cooking the lower crust and avoiding a soaked crust. The use of a thickened filling or coating the upper surface of the lower crust with melted butter or margarine also protects against a soaked crust. Dull aluminum, dark pans, or glass pans usually bake the bottom crust of the pie more uniformly than shiny pans. Glass transmits radiant heat readily causing the outer crust to brown quickly. The oven temperature may be reduced by 25° F for glass pans. A high-quality pastry is evenly browned, crisp, tender and has a blistered surface and pleasing flavor.

Microwaved Pastry. Plain microwaved pastry shells cook quickly but do not brown. The top of the pastry will be dry and blistered; the bottom should look opaque and dry. The bottom should be checked for doneness. A clear glass pan permits viewing of the pastry bottom. Flavored pastry and toppings brushed on the surface add appeal.

Convenience Products: Cake and Pastry

Convenience cake and pastry products include mixes and frozen and ready-to-serve items. The acceptance of these products is determined by the satisfaction afforded to the person preparing the foods and to those who eat them. The factors of time, cost, energy, preparation skills, and satisfaction influence the decisions regarding the use of convenience items.

Defrosting Frozen Baked Products.   Frozen ready-to-eat cakes and pies may be defrosted in the refrigerator, on the counter, or in the microwave oven. Cakes are removed from foil-lined packages and placed on a plate or on the cardboard lid for defrosting in microwave oven. Frostings melt easily and should be watched closely. The microwave defrosted cake should be cooled before cutting. Cupcakes or pieces of cake should be arranged in a circle on a plate for microwave warming. Frozen baked pies may be placed on a glass plate to heat or defrost. The frozen pie may be cut into wedges and then placed on serving plates for defrosting or warming.

SUMMARY

Flour, eggs, sugar, liquid, and salt are essential cake and cookie ingredients; flour, fat, liquid, and salt are essential pastry ingredients. Other ingredients contribute distinctive qualities to cakes, cookies, and pastries. Ingredients serve the same general functions in these products as they do in other flour products. Coagulation of flour proteins and starch gelatinization contribute structure to these products. Fat and sugar are tenderizing ingredients. Eggs and flour are toughening ingredients. Plastic fats impart flakiness to pastries. Liquids hydrate flour proteins and starch and act as solvents. Air, carbon dioxide, and steam provide leavening action.

Methods of mixing vary in proportion of ingredients, in the order ingredients are combined, and in baking techniques. Sponge cakes do not contain shortening and carbon dioxide leavening as do conventional cakes. Cakes, cookies, and pastries contribute many calories but very few essential nutrients.

SELF-STUDY GUIDE

1. What are the functions of ingredients in shortened cakes?
2. Identify methods used to mix cakes and explain the differences among the methods.
3. Contrast the ingredients used and the methods of mixing and baking cookies with those of a standard shortened cake.

4. Identify the function of ingredients in pastry. What methods are used to prepare pastry? How do these methods influence tenderness and flakiness?

5. Discuss the factors that contribute toughness to pastry.

6. Identify the nutrient contributions of ingredients used in cakes, in pastry, in cookies. How significant is this contribution to your daily nutrient and caloric need?

7. Discuss the use of microwave ovens in the preparation of cake, pastry, and cookies. Compare the microwaved product with the conventionally prepared product.

SELECTED REFERENCES

ASH, A. J., and COLMEY, J. C. The role of pH in cake baking. *Bakers Digest* 47:36, 1973.

BEAN, M. M., and YAMAZAKI, W. T. Wheat starch gelatinization. 1. Sucrose: Microscopy and viscosity effects. *Cereal Chemistry* 55:936, 1978.

———, and DONELSON, D. H. Wheat-starch gelatinization in sugar solutions. 2. Fructose, glucose, and sucrose: cake performance. *Cereal Chemistry* 55:945, 1978.

BOYD, B. E. Making frozen dough, it's tricky. *Food Engineering* 52:148, 1980.

CHICHESTER, C. O. *Advances in food research.* Vol. 26. New York: Academic Press, 1980.

COLEMAN, P. E., and HARBERS, C. A. Z. High fructose corn syrup: replacement for sucrose in angel cake. *Journal of Food Science* 48:452, 1983.

Creating the combat cake. *Food Engineering* 53:111, 1981

CUDDY, M. E., and ZALL, R. R. Performance of lipid-dried acid whey in extruded and baked products. *Food Technology* 36:54, 1982.

DREHER, M. L.; BERGLUND, P. T.; and DREHER, C. J. Use of vegetable oils in pie crust. *Journal of Food Science* 48:1566, 1983.

DuBOSE, C. N., et al. Effects of colorants and flavorants on identification, preceived flavor intensity, and hedonic quality of fruit flavored beverages and cakes. *Journal of Food Science* 45:1393, 1980.

HESS, D. A., and SETSER, C. S. Alternative systems for sweetening layer cakes using aspartame with and without fructose. *Cereal Chemistry* 60:337, 1983.

HOWARD, N. H. Role of some essential ingredients in the formation of layer cake structure. *Bakers Digest* 46:28, 1972.

HSU, E. E., and DAVIS, E. A. Water loss rates and scanning electron microscopy of model cake systems made with different emulsification systems. *Journal of Food Science* 45:1243, 1980.

ISSHIKI, K. Gas chromatographic determination of proprionic acid in bread and cake. *Journal of the Association of Official Analytical Chemists* 64:280, 1981.

JOHNSON, R. M., and ZOBIK, M. E. Egg albumin proteins interactions in an angel food cake system. *Journal of Food Science* 46:123, 1981.

JOHNSON, T. M., and ZABIK, M. E. Response surface methodology for analysis of protein interactions in angel food cakes. *Journal of Food Science* 46:1225, 1981.

KIM, K., and SETSER, C. S. Presentation order bias in consumer preference studies on sponge cakes. *Journal of Food Science* 45:1073, 1980.

MARTIN, D. J., and TSEN, C. C. Baking high-ratio white layer cakes with microwave energy. *Journal of Food Science* 46:1507, 1981.

MILLER, B. S., and TRIMBO, H. B. Factors affecting the quality of pie dough and pie crust. *Bakers Digest* 44:46, 1970.

MONECRIEFF, J. Shortenings and emulsifiers for cakes and icings. *Bakers Digest* 44:60, 1970.

MORRIS, C. E. New emulsifier allows calorie-conscious cakes. *Food Engineering* 53:100, 1981.

PAINTER, K. A. Functions and requirements of fats and emulsifiers in prepared cake mixes. *American Oil Chemists Society* 58:92, 1981.

SALDANA, G.; MEYER, R.; and LIME, B. J. Potential processed carrot product. *Journal of Food Science* 45:1445, 1980.

U.S. DEPARTMENT OF AGRICULTURE. *Breads, cakes and pies in Family meals.* Home and Garden Bulletin no. 186. Washington, D.C.: Government Printing Office, 1979.

VOLPE, T., and MERES, C. Use of high fructose syrups in white layer cake. *Bakers Digest* 50:38 1976.

WALKER, J. Amateur scientist: The physics and chemistry of the lemon meringue pie. *Scientific American* 244:194, 1981.

12

VEGETABLES

OBJECTIVES

When you complete this chapter, you will be able to

1. Discuss the composition of vegetables and their nutritional contribution.

2. Name a number of vegetables that are less familiar than corn, beans, tomato, carrots, and cabbage.

3. List characteristics of high-quality fresh, frozen, and canned vegetables.

4. Describe the proper storage of fresh vegetables including greens and of frozen, canned, and dried vegetables.

5. Discuss the preparation of fresh vegetables for cooking.

6. Discuss retention of color, flavor, texture, and nutrients when vegetables are cooked.

7. List the pigments in vegetables and the factors that cause changes in their color.

8. Discuss changes that occur when vegetables are cooked.

9. Describe recommended preparation methods for fresh, frozen, canned, and dried vegetables.

Although vegetables are usually grown for the American table in the United States, many of our vegetables originated in lands adjacent to the eastern Mediterranean. Others were Asiatic in origin, imported to the West by people migrating to the New World.

The United States Supreme Court ruled in 1892 that the tomato, in the language of the people, is a vegetable since it is served in, with, or after the soup, fish, or meat. Our use of the term *vegetable* is compatible with the Supreme Court decision. It refers to the portion of the plant served with the main course while the term *fruit* designates portions of the plant served as dessert.

Menus exemplify the versatility of vegetables, which are featured as appetizers, salads, soups, side dishes, casseroles, and even dessert, in pumpkin or squash pie.

The marvels of modern technology make fresh vegetables available throughout the year along with a variety of canned, frozen, dried, and convenience items ready to heat and serve. Vegetables complement and enhance the food with which they are served. They contribute nutrients and through their color, flavor, texture, size, and shape, aesthetic qualities also. Vegetables may be served simply or elegantly.

This chapter considers the composition, nutritive quality, and classification of vegetables, their selection and storage, and principles of cooking them.

COMPOSITION

The composition of vegetables varies greatly because various parts of plants are used—bulbs, flowers, fruits, seeds, roots, and stems. Vegetables, just like all living systems, contain a variety of cells with different structures that make up the tissues. For example, parenchymal tissue comprises the edible parts of vegetables, and the dermal tissue forms the outer covering and acts as protection.

Because of their structural and chemical makeup vegetables are often described as either starchy or succulent. Although this variation exists among vegetables, they share a number of compositional features.

Carbohydrates

Vegetables are made up primarily of water and various kinds and amounts of simple and complex carbohydrates. One type of complex carbohydrate, cellulose, is a key structural unit of plant cells and therefore of vegetables. Cellulose provides structure and support to the entire plant, including the parts eaten as vegetables.

Hemicellulose is another form of the complex carbohydrate that contributes to the structure of vegetables. Somewhat different forms of cellulose and hemicelluloses are found in various plant parts. The kind of structural carbohydrate present influences tenderness. The cellulose in the skin of vegetables is tougher than that forming the interior cell structure, and cellulose may become progressively toughened as the plant matures. For example, matured green beans become toughened as lignin (made of phenylpropane) develops, to contribute a woody texture not softened by cooking.

Pectic substances are carbohydrate derivatives that bind cells together. The pectic substance in young vegetables is protopectin. As the vegetable matures, protopectin undergoes a gradual chemical change to pectin. Throughout the remainder of the maturation cycle, this conversion of pectic substances continues, and the formation of pectic acid is the result in very mature vegetables. The maturing vegetable becomes progressively less firm as protopectin in the immature vegetable undergoes conversion to pectin and finally to pectic acid.

Young vegetables contain carbohydrates in the form of sugar; as they mature the sugar is converted to starch. Some vegetables—corn, peas, and potato for example—are rich sources of starch. Vegetables with intermediate levels of carbohydrate include onions, carrots, and beets. Green beans, spinach, and asparagus are examples of the vegetables containing little starch or sugar and a lot of water.

The caloric contribution of vegetables varies with their starch and sugar content. Their caloric value is increased as these carbohydrates increase and water content decreases. However, compared with other foods, vegetables are low-calorie foods.

Water

Water swells or plumps the cells and is responsible for the crispness of vegetables. Fresh vegetables are at least 70 percent water by weight, and some are more than 90 percent, making water the most abundant constituent. The succulent vegetables, such as asparagus, green beans, lettuce, and tomato, contain the highest percentage; the starchy ones, such as sweet corn, mature peas, and sweet potato, are lower in water content.

Other Components

Vegetables contain small amounts of protein and fat. Legumes have the most protein and are relatively inexpensive sources of it. In addition to the abundant water and carbohydrate content, some protein and a little fat, vegetables contain a variety of color and flavor components and vitamins and minerals.

NUTRITIONAL QUALITY

Although varying amounts of all nutrient groups are present, vegetables are especially rich sources of vitamins and minerals. Their contribution of vitamins and minerals has established vegetables as part of one of the food groups recommended for a daily balanced nutrient intake. Table 12-1 shows the nutritive quality of some vegetables.

Vitamins

The green and yellow vegetables are given special recognition for their generous contribution of carotene, the precursor of vitamin A. The dark green vegetables (spinach, escarole, broccoli) have more vitamin A value than do those of a lighter hue (iceberg lettuce, cabbage). The deep yellow vegetables (carrots, sweet potato) contain more vitamin A value than pale or white vegetables (onions, white potato). The dark green, leafy vegetables are also prized for their generous contribution of ascorbic acid. Vegetables, as a group, also are valuable sources of thiamin, niacin, and riboflavin.

Minerals

The green color not only signifies vitamin A value but is a clue to mineral content. The leafy greens, along with broccoli, peas, and beans, are good sources of iron and calcium. Some of the other minerals contributed by vegetables include potassium, phosphorus, manganese, magnesium, copper, and cobalt.

Protein

Except for legumes (mature beans, peas), vegetables are relatively poor sources of protein. Vegetable proteins are identified as incomplete proteins because they are deficient in one or more of the essential amino acids. Vegetable proteins can be utilized effectively when they are supplemented with modest amounts of protein from animal sources, including meat, poultry, fish, cheese, or milk.

Fat

Vegetables generally are poor sources of fat and are regarded as low in kcalories. Some vegetables, however, such as tubers and mature seeds, are able to store starch, which serves to help increase their kcaloric value. Because soybeans and other legumes have a higher quality protein than other vegetables they can contribute important amounts of protein and complement other incomplete proteins when eaten at the same time.

Fiber

Vegetables are a valuable source of fiber, or cellulose, an indigestible component. Both the skin and pulp contribute cellulose (also called roughage or bulk), which promotes motility of the gastrointestinal tract, thus serving a laxative function.

Organic/Chemical

Research has not contributed any evidence to support the claim that vegetables grown organically—with natural fertilizers and without pesticides and chemical fertilizers—are superior to those grown with chemical fertilizers and pes-

Table 12-1 Nutritive Value of Selected Vegetables

Vegetable	Measure	Kcal	Calcium (mg)	Iron (mg)	Vitamin A (IU)	Thiamin (mg)	Riboflavin (mg)	Niacin (mg)	Ascorbic acid (mg)
Asparagus, cooked	1 cup	44	42	2.1	1480	.30	.27	2.1	49
Beans									
lima, cooked	1 cup	44	80	4.3	480	.31	.17	2.2	29
snap, cooked	1 cup	30	63	.8	680	.09	.11	.6	15
Beets, cooked diced	1 cup	55	24	.9	30	.05	.07	.5	10
Broccoli, cooked	1 cup	40	136	1.2	880	.14	.31	1.2	140
Brussels sprouts, cooked	1 cup	40	50	1.7	810	.12	.22	1.2	135
Cabbage, green, shredded	1 cup	20	44	.4	120	.05	.05	.3	42
red, shredded	1 cup	20	29	.6	30	.06	.04	.3	43
Carrots, raw	1 carrot	20	18	.4	5500	.03	.03	.3	4
cooked	1 cup	45	48	.9	15220	.08	.07	.7	9
Celery, raw diced	1 cup	15	39	.3	240	.03	.03	.3	9

Collards, cooked	1 cup	55	289	1.1	10260	.27	.37	2.4	87
Corn, canned	1 cup	170	10	1.0	690	.07	.12	2.3	13
Kale, cooked with stems	1 cup	30	147	1.3	8140	.11	.20	1.8	102
Lettuce, crisp head	⅛ head	8	11	0.3	188	.04	.03	.2	4
Peas, canned	1 cup	165	50	4.2	1120	.23	.13	2.2	22
Potatoes									
Sweet, baked	1 medium	155	44	1.0	8910	.10	.07	.7	24
white, baked	1 medium	90	9	.7	trace	.10	.04	1.7	20
Spinach, cooked	1 cup	40	167	4.0	14580	.13	.25	1.0	50
Squash, summer cooked, diced	1 cup	30	52	.8	820	.10	.16	1.6	21
Squash, winter baked, mashed	1 cup	130	57	1.6	8610	.10	.27	1.4	27
Tomato, raw	1 tomato	40	24	.9	1640	.11	.07	1.3	42
canned	1 cup	50	14	1.2	2170	.12	.07	1.7	41
Turnips, cooked	1 cup	35	54	.6	trace	.06	.08	.5	34
Turnip, greens cooked	1 cup	30	252	1.5	8270	.15	.33	.7	68

From *Nutritive Value of American Foods in Common Units.* Agriculture Handbook 456, Agricultural Research Service, USDA, 1975.

ticides. Chemical fertilizers and pesticides permit a greater yield per acre and in this way produce a greater nutrient contribution per acre than "organically" grown vegetables.

The nutritional contribution of vegetables depends upon such variables as variety, growth conditions, maturity, portion of the plant producing the vegetable, storage and marketing methods, and preparation techniques.

Organic Acids

Organic acids are metabolic products of plant cell metabolism and are present in vegetables. Most vegetables have low acidity, with a pH range of 5.06 to 5.6. Tomatoes have the highest acidity, with a pH range of 4.0 to 4.6 or above. Corn, peas, potatoes have a low acidity, with a pH range of 6.1 to 6.3. Oxalic acid is an organic acid found in spinach that may combine with calcium to produce calcium oxalate, which can hinder calcium absorption. On a normal mixed diet organic acids are not a hindrance to nutrient absorption.

SELECTION

Selection of vegetables is made from canned, dried, fresh, and frozen forms. Although fresh vegetables are available throughout the year, their price increases when the local growing season ends. All vegetables, fresh or processed, can vary in quality. Variations in appearance, size, texture, taste, and form usually make a difference in price. The decision leading to selection is influenced by price, availability, intended use, signs of quality, and personal preference. Table 12–2 lists servings of vegetables per unit purchased and Table 12–3 lists common can sizes.

Fresh Vegetables

Grading services are provided by the United States Department of Agriculture (USDA) Marketing Service. Most fresh vegetables at the wholesale level are sold on the basis of U.S. grades, which include U.S. fancy, U.S. no. 1, and U.S. no. 2. The chief grade for most fresh vegetables is U.S. no. 1, which identifies good-quality products. Premium quality is identified by the U.S. fancy grade.

Grading of vegetables is voluntary and is paid for by the processor or packer requesting the service. Grades are a reliable guide to quality. The nutritional value is similar among the grades; appearance is the main difference. Although grades are important in wholesale marketing, fresh vegetables on the retail market, except potatoes, generally do not display a USDA grade shield. Signs of quality in fresh vegetables include crispness, uniformity in size, characteristic color, degree of ripeness, and freedom from defects.

Table 12-2 Servings of Vegetables per Unit Purchased

Vegetable	Servings per lb as Purchased Fresh	Servings per 9- or 10-oz Package Frozen	Servings per 16 oz Can Canned
Asparagus	2 or 3	2 or 3	2 or 3
Beans, lima (in pod)	2 or 3	3 or 4	3 or 4
Beans, snap	5 or 6	3 or 4	3 or 4
Beets (without tops)	3 or 4		3 or 4
Broccoli	5 or 6	3	
Brussels sprouts	5 or 6	3	
Cabbage			
Raw, shredded	11 or 12		
Cooked	4 or 5		
Carrots (without tops)			
Raw, diced or shredded	5 or 6	3 or 4	3 or 4
Cooked	5		
Cauliflower	5	3	
Celery			
Raw, chopped or diced	8		
Cooked	6 or 7		
Corn, whole kernel		3 or 4	3 or 4
Kale (trimmed)	6	3 or 4	
Mushrooms	4		
Okra	5	2 or 3	3
Onions, cooked	3 or 4		3 or 4
Parsnips (without tops)	5		
Peas (in pod)	2	3	3 or 4
Potatoes	3 or 4	3 or 4	3 or 4
Spinach (prepackaged)	3 or 4	2	2 or 3
Squash	2 or 4	3	
Sweet potato	3 or 4	3	3 or 4
Tomatoes, raw, sliced or cut	4		3 or 4

From USDA, *Your Money's Worth in Foods,* Home and Garden Bulletin no. 183, (Washington, D.C.: Government Printing Office, 1979).

Table 12-3 Canned Vegetables: Common Can Sizes

Can Sizes	Net Weight
8 oz	8 oz
No. 1 or picnic	10½–12 oz
No. 303	16–17 oz
No. 2	20 oz (1 lb, 4 oz)
No. 2½	29 oz (1 lb, 13 oz)
No. 3 special	46 oz (2 lb, 14 oz)

Canned and Frozen Vegetables

Most canned and frozen vegetables are packed and priced according to their quality, even though a grade mark may not appear on the label. Sometimes stores use their own private brand names to indicate the quality of the vegetable. When a vegetable is packed under continuous USDA inspection, the individual packages or cans may bear the U.S. grade marks. The USDA has developed three grades to identify quality of canned and frozen vegetables. The grades are U.S. grade A or fancy, U.S. grade B or extra standard, and U.S. grade C or standard.

Grade A or fancy vegetables are of excellent quality and are used when appearance and texture are important. Grade B vegetables are quite good but are less uniform in color, size, and tenderness than grade A. Grade C vegetables are of fairly good quality and are as nutritious as the higher grades. They are less expensive and are good buys for use in casseroles, soups, and other combination dishes when uniformity in appearance is not important. Some generic vegetable products without brand names are now available. Most of these products are comparable to U.S. grade C.

Bulging canned-food containers indicate spoilage. The food in dented cans is not harmed unless the dent actually pierces the can. Packages of frozen vegetables should be firm at all times to avoid loss of quality. Wet or stained packages indicate that they have been defrosted and refrozen.

Labels on canned and frozen vegetables describe the contents; other information may include the grade, variety, style, seasonings, number of servings, and net weight in total ounces as well as in pounds and ounces. Directions for cooking and recipes may also be included, and some labels give nutrition information. Nutritional labeling is discussed in chapter 26.

STORAGE

The quality of fresh vegetables is retained when moisture loss is prevented and enzyme activity is kept to a minimum. The loss of moisture causes vegetables to wilt and become limp. Fresh green vegetables such as salad greens and celery retain crispness and firmness when kept in a covered container or plastic bag in the refrigerator. Storage containers suited to the quantity of greens permit only a minimum loss of water from the cells as the equilibrium becomes established between the moisture in the greens and the moisture held in the air surrounding the greens. When greens are washed before storage, they must be well drained to avoid decay.

The degree of maturity in harvested vegetables influences their color, texture, flavor, and nutritional value. The sugar content of young, tender corn and peas decreases progressively as the temperature is elevated. However, prompt cooling and refrigeration decreases the loss of sweetness.

Mature starch vegetables, such as potato, increase in sugar content and decrease in starch when stored in the refrigerator. Potatoes stored at 60° F (16° C) retain their starch content. Mature onions keep well in a dry, airy place; winter squash, tubers, and root vegetables should be kept in a cool place.

Enzymes contained in plant tissues continue to promote metabolic activity after harvest and are responsible for many changes that occur during storage. Cold or near-freezing temperatures retard enzyme activity and thus reduce deterioration of plant tissues. Vegetables also retain vitamins more effectively at refrigerator than at room temperature. Frozen vegetables are stored in the frozen food compartment at 0° F (minus 18° C). Canned vegetables are kept in a dry place to avoid rusting of cans. Dried vegetables are stored at room temperature in a dry place.

PRELIMINARY PREPARATION

Possible contamination by soil, dust, insects, insecticides, or hands necessitates a thorough washing of vegetables whether they are eaten raw or cooked. Greens trap soil and are fragile. They are placed in a large amount of cold water and lifted in and out repeatedly by hand. Lifting greens from the water removes soil and avoids redeposit of soil on cleansed greens. The soil and used water are discarded. This procedure is repeated until sediment is no longer evident in the rinse water. The clean vegetables are then inspected for blemishes and decay, which are removed.

Trimming and peeling procedures vary with the type of vegetable. Thin-skinned vegetables such as carrots or parsnips are scraped gently. Thick-skinned vegetables such as potato or eggplant may be pared. A discoloration may develop on the surface of some peeled vegetables held prior to cooking. Enzyme action causes this surface discoloration to develop.

Stems and woody stalks are generally removed or trimmed before cooking. They contain little nutritional value and require a longer cooking period than the remainder of the vegetable. Damaged or yellowed outer leaves are removed.

Preparation techniques, maturity, and size of the vegetables and the desired contrast in shape determine whether they are cut prior to cooking and use. Cutting decreases cooking time but increases the surface area and contributes to the loss of soluble constituents. Peeled or cut vegetables should not be soaked, to avoid loss of soluble components.

COOKING PRINCIPLES

The retention of color, flavor, textural qualities, and nutrient values are the concerns of vegetable cookery. The retention of these qualities is related directly to the techniques of cookery and to the palatability of the cooked vegetables. High-quality cooked vegetables are firm—just fork tender—retain characteristic color, and have a pleasing aroma and flavor. The techniques that protect the palatability also help to protect nutritive value. The choice of cooking methods is influenced by the color, flavor, texture, and nutrient components of the vegetable.

Texture

The cell walls in plant tissues are structural elements. The adhesion of cells to each other contributes to the textural qualities. High-quality raw vegetables are firm and crisp. The proteins of cell membranes are denatured when crisp vegetables are immersed in boiling water. Cells then lose water by diffusion, and the vegetable becomes limp. During cooking insoluble protopectin is converted to soluble pectin, cellulose is somewhat softened, starch absorbs water, and protein coagulates.

The softening of cellulose and the formation of pectin are responsible for the tenderness of cooked vegetables. This textural change contributes to the palatability of cooked vegetables. Overcooking promotes excessive softening of tissues.

An acidic pH retards softening of the structure, while an alkaline pH yields overly soft and mushy texture. Some of the organic acids contained in plant tissues are released during cooking and contribute to the cooking water a very weakly acidic pH, which can influence color pigments but is too weak to retard softening.

Flavor

A variety of organic compounds, such as acids, sugars, polyphenols, aldehydes, ketones, mercaptans, and volatile oils, contribute to the characteristic flavors of vegetables. Sugars contribute to the flavor of young, freshly harvested vegetables. Young vegetables contain a higher level of glutamic acid (an amino acid) than mature vegetables. Glutamic acid may be responsible for the pleasing flavor of young vegetables.

Vegetable flavors may be classed as mild or strong. Sulfur-containing compounds cause the characteristic strong flavors and odors of cabbage and onions. The flavor develops when the vegetables are cut or crushed, permitting the enzymes to act on the various sulfur compounds. Hydrogen sulfide is formed when the sulfur components of cabbage break down during cooking. Unpleasant sulfur components are intensified by heat, and undesirable flavors develop, especially in strong-flavored vegetables, from overcooking.

Some vegetables, such as garlic and onions, have volatile oils that contribute to their strong flavor. If they are cooked for a long time, the flavor becomes mild as the oil is liberated in the steam. Some flavoring components are decomposed during cooking and escape in the steam. The losses are minimized when the period of cooking is short.

Personal preference regarding the flavor and color of vegetables may determine the techniques used. Salt enhances the flavor of vegetables whether it is added before or after cooking.

A summary of the influence of cookery techniques on flavor components follows.

1. Flavor loss is reduced when mild-flavored vegetables are cooked in a minimum amount of water.
2. Vegetables in the cabbage and onion families may have milder flavor when cooked in water to cover than when cooked in a minimum amount.
3. The volatile flavor components are retained when vegetables are cooked with a cover.
4. A mild flavor develops when strong-flavored vegetables are cooked without a cover.
5. The flavor of cabbagelike vegetables becomes intensified progressively as cooking time is increased, while the flavor of onions decreases with longer cooking.

Color

Chemical compounds known as pigments provide the wide range of vegetable colors. These pigments may undergo changes during cooking. They may be influenced by heating time, pH, and metals (see Table 12–4). Plant pigments may be classified as **chlorophylls, carotenoids,** and **flavonoids.** A common structural characteristic relates the pigments within a specific classification. One pigment predominates even though more than one color component may be present in a vegetable.

Chlorophyll. Chlorophyll is the dominant color pigment of green vegetables. Chlorophylls are chemically similar to the heme portion of hemoglobin or myoglobin. Chlorophylls in raw vegetables contain an atom of magnesium in the center of each molecule. Another portion of the molecule, the phytyl of chlorophyll, is responsible for its solubility in fat and fat solvents.

When chlorophyll is heated in the presence of organic acids liberated from the plant cells, the magnesium atom is replaced with hydrogen, resulting in the formation of pheophytin. Chlorophyll, a bright green pigment, is sensitive to heat and acid, and becomes a drab olive green in the presence of acid or with prolonged cooking. The bright green of chlorophyll is thus changed to the drab green of pheophytin. When cooking time extends beyond the just-tender stage, the green color of vegetables progresses from green toward yellow. Most green vegetables show a marked color change with a relatively short period of overcooking in boiling water or in steam. The long cooking period required to sterilize canned vegetables promotes the conversion of chlorophyll to pheophytin.

Although chlorophyll retains the bright green color in alkali, the addition of soda to the cooking liquid is not recommended. Alkali or soda quickly softens the plant tissue to yield a mushy texture. Also the vitamins thiamin and ascorbic acid are destroyed in alkali.

Even though the use of a cover remains controversial, some choose to cook green vegetables without a cover to permit escape of volatile acids; others

Table 12-4 Factors Responsible for Color Changes in Plant Pigments

Pigment	Color	Alkali (effect)	Acid (effect)	Metals (effect)	Heat (prolonged)	Water Soluble	Fat Soluble
Carotenoids	Orange-yellow-red	Little effect	Little effect to paler	Little effect	May be less intense	Insoluble	Soluble
Chlorophylls	a. Blue-green b. Yellow-green	Bright green	a. Grayed green b. Olive green	Bright green with copper or zinc	Drab olive green	Insoluble to slightly soluble	Soluble
Flavonoids Anthocyanins	Red-blue	Blue-violet	Red	Blue-greenish-grayed with aluminum, iron, tin	Little effect	Highly soluble	Insoluble
Anthoxanthins (flavones and flavonols)	White/colorless cream	Yellowed	White/colorless cream	Bright yellow with aluminum, blue-black-brown-red with iron and copper	Pinkish, creamish	Highly soluble	Insoluble

prefer to use a cover and thus shorten cooking time. A shortened cooking time aids in the retention of the desired green color.

When vegetables are put into boiling water, the green color is intensified owing to the loss of some air from the tissues exposing the underlying chlorophyll. The intense green color of frozen vegetables developed during the brief blanching in boiling water or steam is retained when the vegetables are cooked with a cover until just fork tender.

Flavonoids. The flavonoid pigments, which may be subdivided into **anthocyanins** and **anthoxanthins,** are related chemically to phenolic compounds. The anthocyanins are soluble in water, relatively stable in heat, and sensitive to changes in pH. They become brighter red in acid and blue in alkali. Most foods containing these pigments are sufficiently acid to retain their color.

Until recently pigments in beets were considered to be anthocyanins. Beets contain purplish-red pigments called betacyanins and yellow pigments called betaxanthins. These pigments behave somewhat like anthocyanins. They are water soluble and less sensitive to changes in pH than the anthocyanins.

Vegetables and fruits containing anthocyanins are packed in enamel-lined cans or glass jars to avoid a blue purplish discoloration caused by contact with iron or tin.

Anthoxanthins are water-soluble pigments, colorless in acid and creamy yellow in alkali. As a group, the anthoxanthins differ in the structure of the center ring and on this basis may be subdivided into flavones, flavonols, and flavanones. Flavonols are chemically related to anthocyanins; contain hydrogen sulfide; and are present in cabbage, cauliflower, and onions, for example. Anthoxanthins may occur alone or in combination with other pigments, which may mask their presence.

Carotenoids. Chemically, the carotenoids are classed as carotenes and xanthophylls. Carotenes contain carbon and hydrogen, while xanthophylls contain oxygen in addition to carbon and hydrogen. Carotene is the most common carotenoid and is present in carrots, sweet potatoes, and winter squash. The carotenoids are also found in the chloroplasts of green plants but are masked by chlorophyll.

The carotenoids range in color from orange red to yellow. A system of conjugated double bonds is responsible for the color of these pigments. The carotenoid in tomato is **lycopene,** a red pigment. The lycopene pigment also contributes to the color of apricots, pink grapefruit, persimmons, and watermelon.

Carotenes are fat soluble and are not lost in the cooking liquid. Small amounts may dissolve in the butter or margarine used as seasoning. Prolonged cooking may cause some loss in color intensity. Carotenoids are susceptible to oxidation and may lose some of their intense yellow color when exposed to air. Acids and alkali usually have little effect on carotenoid pigments.

Some carotenoids are nutritionally valuable as precursors of vitamin A.

Beta carotene can be converted into two molecules of vitamin A; most other carotenes contribute only one molecule of vitamin A.

Nutrient Retention

Nutrient losses during cooking are results of solubility and heat. An increase in the cut surface of vegetables or in the amount of cooking liquid lead to an increased loss of soluble substances. Water-soluble compounds include the B vitamins, ascorbic acid, minerals, sugar, and flavor components. The loss of soluble substances in the cooking liquid is minimized when only small quantities of water are used and when any remaining liquid is served with the vegetable.

The extent of nutrient destruction increases as temperature and cooking time increase. Thiamin is unstable in heat, especially in an alkaline medium. Riboflavin, niacin, vitamin A, and carotenoids are stable at cooking temperatures and are well retained. Heat contributes to the loss of ascorbic acid. Enzymes present in the vegetable tissue may destroy ascorbic acid when vegetables are heated slowly to a boil.

The use of a covered container for cooking vegetables helps to control oxidation by limiting their exposure to air. Ascorbic acid is easily oxidized and its nutritive value lost. Baking, steaming, cooking in skins, and microwaving are vegetable-cooking techniques that retain food values more effectively than do some other methods.

COOKING METHODS

Cooking can bring about a change in flavor, texture, and color of vegetables; improve palatability and digestibility of some vegetables; and destroy surface microorganisms. Common vegetable-cooking methods include **boiling, baking, steaming,** stir-frying, and microwaving. Microwave cookery is discussed further in chapter 24. Some vegetables may also be **broiled** or deep-fat fried. The selection of a desirable cooking method is influenced by the type of vegetable, desire for variety, and nutrient retention.

Fresh Vegetables

Boiling.   Boiling is a popular basic method for cooking vegetables. Prepared vegetables are placed into just enough boiling water to prevent scorching and cooked in a covered pan. The water is again quickly brought back to a boil. When steam begins to emerge between the lid and the pan, the heat is lowered to maintain a slow boil. A rapid boil promotes the breaking apart of vegetables but does not increase speed of cooking. The objective is to have the vegetables just done when only a very small amount of water remains in the pan. Vegetables are cooked until just fork tender but slightly crisp. They should be of uniform size

and similar maturity so that all complete cooking at the same time. This method minimizes losses of soluble nutrients in the cooking liquid.

Some believe that green-colored or strong-flavored vegetables may not have the best color or flavor when cooked in minimum water with a lid. When these vegetables need more than five to seven minutes to become tender, they may lose some of their bright green color or develop an unpleasant strong flavor. When a longer cooking time is required, green vegetables or strong-flavored (cabbage or onionlike) vegetables may be boiled in water to cover the vegetable, without a lid. This permits the loss of volatile acids with the steam and dilution of nonvolatile acids. Undesirable changes in color of the green vegetables and flavors of the strong-flavored vegetables are minimized, but the loss of water-soluble nutrients tends to be increased.

Baking.   Baking time for vegetables is longer than boiling time. Heat of penetration is slower during baking than boiling; therefore a 350 to 425° F (177 C to 218° C) temperature is used. Vegetables such as potatoes, tomatoes, and winter squash may be baked in their skin to retain their moisture. The washed vegetable is usually placed in a baking dish in the oven.

Peeled and cut-up vegetables may be baked in a covered pan to retain moisture. When a white sauce is added before baking, they are known as **scalloped.** Vegetables may also be baked along with other foods, including meats. When a lower temperature is used to accommodate the meat, an increased cooking time offsets the lower oven temperature.

Broiling. Tender fresh vegetables, including whole, halved or sliced tomatoes, and canned or precooked vegetables may be broiled. The surface of the vegetables may be brushed with oil or melted fat to prevent excessive drying and covered with seasoned crumbs or grated cheese before broiling. Broiled vegetables make an attractive garnish, increase the variety of vegetable service, and add a festive touch. They should be served immediately.

Frying and Sauteing. Some vegetables may be cooked in shallow or deep fat. Before frying they can be cut up and coated with egg and flour or crumbs or dipped into a batter, as with onion rings. A pleasing flavor and texture develop during frying. Whether just a little fat or sufficient fat to completely immerse the vegetable is used, the heat should be controlled to prevent the fat from overheating and smoking. A thermometer is desirable to maintain deep fat at the selected temperature, usually 375° F (195° C), so the food will cook uniformly without excessive fat absorption.

Steaming. Nutrient retention is the advantage of steaming vegetables. Only the moisture from condensed steam reaches the vegetable. Prepared vegetables are placed in a perforated pan above vigorously boiling water and tightly covered. Heat is provided by the steam surrounding the vegetable. Because the cooking time is longer than for boiled vegetables, mild-flavored vegetables are preferred to strong-flavored or green vegetables for steaming. Steam under pressure, as in a pressure cooker, achieves a high temperature and cooks vegetables very quickly.

Stir-frying. The stir-fry technique was adopted from Oriental cookery. Finely shredded or sliced vegetables may be stir-fried. Tender succulent vegetables are best suited for stir-frying. A small amount of fat or oil is heated in a frying pan, prepared vegetables are added and stirred to ensure even cooking. Desired seasonings may be added. Tender succulent vegetables may be cooked without a lid; others are covered and cooked over low heat for a short time, stirred occasionally. The water present in the vegetable is usually sufficient for stir-frying, although a little water may be added to prevent burning if necessary.

Microwaving. Microwaved fresh and frozen vegetables retain their color, fresh flavor, and pleasing texture. Vegetables are microwaved in small quantities of water, just enough to form steam, and tightly covered. Juicy vegetables may be microwaved without added water. Cooking without added water or in small quantities of water decreases nutrient loss.

Vegetables cooked in the skin, such as potato, should be pricked with a fork before cooking to release excess steam. Microwaved vegetables continue to cook after they are removed from the oven. Some vegetables may have better color and flavor when microwaved than when cooked by conventional methods. Others may be preferred when cooked by conventional methods.

Vegetables of similar size, whole or pieces, cook uniformly. Canned vegetables may be heated by microwave just before serving. Frozen microwaved vegetables should be stirred midway through the cooking time to separate unthawed portions and distribute them toward the outer edges of the container.

Canned Vegetables

Canned vegetables are fully cooked and need only to be heated to serving temperature. The liquid in the can contains soluble nutrients and flavor components and should be used rather than discarded. The liquid is drained from the vegetable and simmered until about one-fourth of the original volume remains. This procedure allows excess water to dissipate as steam while the dissolved components are retained. The vegetable is then added and heated to serving.

Frozen Vegetables

Blanching in preparation for freezing and the freezing process itself tenderize the vegetable so that the cooking time is shorter for frozen than for fresh vegetables. Frozen vegetables are placed into about one-half cup of boiling water and covered. The water is again returned to a boil. When vegetables are frozen in a solid block, they should be separated with a fork for even cooking and the lid replaced. The heat is regulated to maintain a gentle boil. The directions on commercially frozen vegetables are good guides for cooking them.

Dried Vegetables

Because of their low moisture content dried vegetables can be stored at room temperature. Dried mature beans, peas, and lentils are **rehydrated** before cooking. A recommended method allows the dried vegetables to boil for two minutes in sufficient water to cover them. The vegetable then remains in the hot water for an hour before it is cooked. The short preboil softens the skins, so rehydration proceeds quickly.

Hard water prevents the softening of dried vegetables. Pectic substances in the dried vegetable form insoluble salts with the calcium and magnesium present in the water. The addition of one-eighth teaspoon of soda for each cup of dry beans prevents hardening. However, an excess of soda destroys thiamin and should therefore be avoided. Several methods are used commercially to dehydrate foods, and package directions are good guides for cooking dried vegetables.

Table 12-5   Herb Seasonings for Vegetables

Herb	Vegetable	
Basil	broccoli	onions
	carrots	peas
	eggplant	tomatoes
Dill	asparagus	greens
	cucumbers	new potatoes
	green beans	
Marjoram	brussels sprouts	peas
	carrots	potatoes
	onions	spinach
Mint	carrots	peas
	new potatoes	spinach
Oregano	broccoli	mushrooms
	cabbage	onions
	lentils	tomatoes
Rosemary	cauliflower	potatoes
	mushrooms	spinach
	peas	turnips
Sage	eggplant	peas
	lima beans	summer squash
	onions	tomatoes
Savory	artichoke	carrots
	beans	potato
	beets	tomato
Tarragon	beets	mushrooms
	cauliflower	spinach
	celery root	tomatoes
Thyme	asparagus	mushrooms
	beans	tomatoes
	carrots	zucchini squash

Seasoning

Seasoning contributes flavor appeal to vegetables. Several herbs may be used (Table 12–5), but sparingly—just enough to bring out and enhance the natural flavor of vegetables.

SUMMARY

Vegetables are obtained from various parts of plants and are valued for their vitamin and mineral content. They are classified according to their composition, flavor intensity, and the parts of plants they represent.

Wholesale grades established by the United States Department of Agriculture are used extensively in the vegetable trade. High-quality fresh vegetables are free from defects and are uniform in color, degree of maturity, and size.

Succulent fresh vegetables are highly perishable and are stored in the hydrator section of the refrigerator or in covered containers. Tubers and root vegetables are kept in a cool, well-ventilated place. The retention of color, flavor, textural qualities and nutrient values are the concerns of vegetable cookery. Methods of cooking include boiling, baking, broiling, frying, steaming, stir-frying, and microwaving.

Nutrient losses increase proportionally as the amount of water, the cut-surface area, and the cooking time increase. Nutrients are best retained by cooking vegetables in a covered pan in small amounts of water until fork tender. Cooking strong-flavored vegetables uncovered in a large quantity of water can result in a mild flavor. Cooking green vegetables without a cover may reduce pigment change.

SELF-STUDY GUIDE

1. What are five nutritional contributions of vegetables as a group?
2. Which nutrient contributions of vegetables are least affected, and which are greatly affected, by the techniques used to cook them?
3. Classify vegetables in two groups according to their most abundant constituents.
4. How are fresh, canned, frozen, and dried vegetables stored?
5. What information is listed on labels of packaged vegetables? Discuss the use of nutritional labeling.
6. What three factors influence palatability of vegetables? How are these characteristics of vegetables protected during cooking?
7. Identify the color pigments in vegetables and indicate the factors that influence the pigment color.
8. How is the nutritional quality of vegetables retained during their preparation and cooking?
9. Describe the methods used to prepare fresh vegetables.
10. How are canned and frozen vegetables prepared to retain maximum nutrients?
11. Describe the preparation of dried vegetables to maintain their quality and nutrients.
12. What four qualities other than nutrients do vegetables contribute to meals?

SELECTED REFERENCES

ABDUL-REHMAN, A. H. Nutritional value of some canned tomato juice and concentrates. Food concentrates. *Food Chemistry* 9:303, 1982.

ABOU-FADEL, O. S., and MILLER, L. T. Vitamin retention, color, and texture in thermally processed green beans and royal anne cherries packed in pouches and cans. *Journal of Food Science* 48:920, 1983.

AUGUSTIN, J.; MAROUSEK, G. I.; THOLAR, L. A.; and BERTILLI, B. Vitamin retention in cooked, chilled and reheated potatoes. *Journal of Food Science* 45:814, 1980.

_____. Retention of some water-soluble vitamins during home preparation of commercially frozen potato products. *Journal of Food Science* 46:1697, 1981.

_____. Vitamin retention during preparation and holding of mashed potatoes made from commercially dehydrated flakes and granules. *Journal of Food Science* 47:274, 1982.

BLUE GOOSE. *The buying guide for fresh fruits, vegetables, herbs, and nuts.* Hagerstown, Md.: Blue Goose, Inc.

BRODOWSKI, D., and GEISMAN, J. R. Protein content and amino acid composition of protein of seeds from tomatoes at various stages of ripeness. *Journal of Food Science* 45:228, 1980.

BUSHWAY, R. J., and PONNAMPALAM, R. α-chaconine and α-solanine content of potato products and their stability during several modes of cooking. *Journal of Agricultural and Food Chemistry* 29:814, 1981.

CARROAD, P. A., et al. Yields and solids loss in water and steam blanching, water and air cooling, freezing and cooking of broccoli spears. *Journal of Food Science* 45:1408, 1980.

CHEN, T. S., and GEORGE, E. L. Ascorbic acid retention in retort pouched green beans. *Journal of Food Science* 46:552, 1981.

EDIJALA, J. K. Effects of processing on the thiamin, riboflavin, and protein content of cowpeas. 1. Soaking, cooking and wet milling processes. *Journal of Food Technology* 15:435, 1980.

ESEN, A. A simple colorimetric method for zein determination in corn and its potential in screening for protein quality. *Cereal Chemistry* 57:129, 1980.

HANNIGAN, K. J. Developing new tomato paste products. *Food Engineering* 53:86, 1981.

HERRANZ, J.; VIDAL-VALVERDE, E.; and ROJAS-HIL-DALGO, E. Cellulose, hemicellulose and lignin content of raw and cooked processed vegetables. *Journal of Food Science* 48:274, 1983.

_____, Cellulose, hemicellulose and lignin content of raw and cooked spanish vegetables. *Journal of Food Science* 46:1927, 1981.

JACKSON, G. M., and MARSTON, E. Hard-to-cook phenomenon in beans: effects of accelerated storage on water absorption and cooking time. *Journal of Food Science* 46:799, 1981.

KAYISU, K., et al. Characterization of starch and fiber of banana fruit. *Journal of Food Science* 46:1885, 1981.

KILGORE, S. M., and SISTRUNK, W. A. Effects of soaking treatments and cooking upon selected B-vitamins and the quality of black-eyed peas. *Journal of Food Science* 46:909, 1981.

KLEIN, B. P., and PERRY, A. K. Ascorbic acid and vitamin A activity in selected vegetables from different geographical areas of the United States. *Journal of Food Science* 47:941, 1982.

KLEIN, L. B., and MONDAY, N. I. Comparison of microwave and conventional baking of potatoes in relation to nitrogenous constituents and mineral composition. *Journal of Food Science* 46:1874, 1981.

LAY, M. M. G., and FIELDS, M. L. Nutritive value of germinated corn and corn fermented after germination. *Journal of Food Science* 46:1069, 1981.

LEE, C. G.; BUREN, JR., L. M.; and VAN, J. P. Content of post-harvest handling and processing on vitamin content of peas. *Journal of Food Science* 47:961, 1982.

LEE, K., and CLYDESDALE, F. M. Effect of thermal processing on endogenous and added iron in canned spinach. *Journal of Food Science* 46:1064, 1981.

LEVINE, B. *Picked this morning: the California guide to fresh foods.* Colorado Springs: Chronicle Booksellers, 1980.

LOPEZ, A., and WILLIAMS, H. L. Essential elements in fresh and canned tomatoes. *Journal of Food Science* 46:432, 1981.

LOSH, J. M., et al. Sweet potato quality after baking. *Journal of Food Science* 46:283, 1981.

MASSEY, JR., L. M. Nutritive quality of long-distance shipped raw snap beans for processing. *Journal of Food Science* 48:1566, 1983.

MONDY, N. I., and PONNAMPALAM, R. Effect of baking and frying on nutritive value of potatoes; minerals. *Journal of Food Science* 48:1475, 1983.

PARK, Y. W., et al. Potential of near infrared (NIR) spectroscopy for estimating nutrient content of dehydrated vegetables. *Journal of Food Science* 47:1558, 1982.

PAULUS, K., and SAGUY, I. Effect of heat treatment of the quality of cooked carrots. *Journal of Food Science* 45:239, 1980.

PENG, A. C. Lipid composition of high solids cabbage. *Journal of Food Science* 47:1036, 1982.

RAO, M., et al. A kinetic study of loss of vitamin C: color, and firmness during thermal processing of canned peas. *Journal of Food Science* 46:536, 1981.

REYES, F. G., et al. Sugar composition and flavor quality of high sugar (shrunken) and normal sweet corn. *Journal of Food Science* 47:753, 1982.

SALDANA, G., et al. Potential processed carrot product. *Journal of Food Science* 45:1444, 1980.

SCHMITT, H. A. Effects of laboratory scale processing on chromium and zinc in vegetables. *Journal of Food Science* 47:1693, 1982.

SILVA, A. B., et al. Influence of soaking and cooking upon the softening and eating quality of black beans. *Journal of Food Science* 46:1716, 1981.

TALLEY, E. A.; TOMA, R. B.; and ORR, P. H. Composition of raw and cooked potato peel and flesh: amino acid content. *Journal of Food Science* 48:1360, 1983.

U.S. DEPARTMENT OF AGRICULTURE. *How to buy canned and frozen vegetables.* Home and Garden Bulletin no. 167. Washington, D.C.: Government Printing Office, 1977.

_____. *How to buy fresh vegetables.* Home and Garden Bulletin no. 143. Washington, D.C.: Government Printing Office, 1980.

_____. *A grade by any other name. Food News for Consumers.* Washington, D.C.: Government Printing Office, June 1980.

_____. *Vegetables in family meals.* Home and Garden Bulletin no. 105. Washington, D.C.: Government Printing Office, 1980.

_____. *Storing perishable foods in the home.* Washington, D.C.: Government Printing Office, 1980.

_____. Food yields summarized by different stages of preparation. Handbook no. 102. Washington, D.C.: Government Printing Office, rev. 1975.

13

FRUITS

OBJECTIVES

When you complete this chapter you will be able to

1. Identify the various classifications used for fruits and give examples.
2. Discuss the composition of fruits and their nutritional contribution.
3. List characteristics of high-quality fresh, frozen, canned, and dried fruits.
4. Discuss the factors considered when fruits are selected.
5. Suggest uses for the various forms of fruit available.
6. Describe the storage of fresh, frozen, canned, and dried fruits to protect their quality and nutrients.
7. Discuss preparation of fresh fruits for cooking.
8. Describe appropriate preparation methods for fresh, frozen, and dried fruits.
9. Discuss the changes that occur when fruits are cooked.
10. Discuss the effect of small and large quantities of sugar in the liquid in which fruits are cooked.
11. List pigments in fruits and the factors that cause changes in their color.

Fruits develop after a plant flowers and are the ripened ovaries and adjacent tissues of the plant. A pulp, or fleshy material, accumulates around and adheres to a core, as in apples and pears, or a hard pit, as in apricots and cherries. The fleshy material may be enclosed in a thick skin, as in citrus fruits, a thin skin, as in apples, or a hard rind, as in melons. Other fruits, such as blackberries and raspberries, develop around several ovaries. Pineapple develops from a cluster of several flowers.

(USDA Photo)

Several of our popular fruits—apples, cherries, grapes, and pears—were transplanted from the eastern Mediterranean-Caspian Sea area. Apricots, bananas, oranges, and peaches came from eastern India, Burma, and China.

Common usage and botanical classification of fruits may differ. Rhubarb, a stem, is a fruit in terms of common use but not in the botanical sense. Although botanically, cucumbers, tomatoes, and squash are fruits, in common use they are regarded as vegetables.

Good fruit is juicy, sweet, and fragrant, with aromatic flavors, delicious and good to eat just as picked. Fruit enhances the diet and the menu with its wide range of colors, flavors, and textures. This chapter covers the classification and composition of fruits, nutrient contribution, selection and storage, and the principles and methods of preparation.

COMPOSITION

Most fresh fruits commonly consumed contain about 85 percent water. Water retained in the cells contributes to firmness and crispness. When cells are ruptured, water escapes, altering texture.

Carbohydrates are the next most abundant component of fruits. In addition to the structural materials, cellulose and pectic substances, which are classed as carbohydrates, fruits contain sugars and some starch. The form or type of carbohydrate varies with the maturity of the fruit, although the total carbohydrate remains constant. Immature fruits generally contain more starch than the ripe fruits. As fruits ripen, starch is changed to sugar. The sweetness of ripe fruit is due to the high level of sugar in the forms of glucose, fructose, and sucrose.

Cellulose in the cell walls of fruits is essential to the water-retaining capability of the cells and tissues of fruits. Along with cellulose, pectic substances contribute to the structure of fruits. The protopectin in immature fruits contributes to their rigidity. The ripening process includes conversion of protopectin to pectin. There is considerable softening of the fruit as this chemical change proceeds.

Fresh fruits contain little protein, 1 percent or less, and what little there is, is classed as incomplete because it lacks the quantity and assortment of amino acids essential for growth and maintenance. Most fruits have a low fat content. They contain from a trace to about 1 percent fat, the exception being the avocado, which contains about 17 percent fat.

Pigments

The pigments are responsible for the appealing bright colors of fruits. As with vegetables, the chief classes of pigments are the carotenoids, flavonoids, and chlorophylls. The carotenoids and chlorophylls are fat soluble and are found in plastids.

Carotenoids.   The carotenoids contribute the predominant yellow to red orange. They are responsible for the yellow of apricots, oranges, peaches, and pineapple and the reddened color of tomatoes, watermelon, and red grapefruit. The carotenoid pigments are relatively stable to color change.

Flavonoids.   The flavonoids occur in cell sap, are water soluble, and are grouped as anthoxanthins and anthocyanins. The anthoxanthin and anthocyanin pigments often occur in the same plant tissues. Both the anthoxanthins and anthocyanins react with acids and bases. The anthoxanthins are creamy white in a neutral pH and shift to white in acid and to yellow in alkali. Anthocyanins are red in acid, and many of these pigments may shift to purple and blue as the pH becomes more alkaline. Because of their molecular structure, however, not all anthocyanins show a marked change in color with a pH change.

Most fruits contain more than one anthocyanin pigment, for example, strawberries, cranberries, blackberries, blueberries, boysenberries, ripe gooseberries, sweet and sour cherries, Tokay grapes, and the red pigment of apple skins.

Some anthocyanins possess free hydroxyl (−OH) groups and can react with aluminum, tin, and iron and become blue, green blue, or slate blue in color. Pigment reactions with these metals can promote undesirable color changes in some fruits. Cans coated with lacquer are used to prevent this discoloration.

Pigments can break down in the presence of a reducing sugar, oxygen, and a high pH. The bright red pigment in strawberries, an anthocyanin, becomes a brownish red during storage.

The anthoxanthins in fruits include the flavones, flavonols, and flavanones. Some of these phenolic compounds present in fruits may undergo a pigment change. For example, the pinkish color of some pears may be due to a change in a colorless pigment promoted by the presence of acid and heat. The presence of oxygen may cause some phenolic compounds to become brown. An enzyme, phenol oxidase, present in some fruit, catalyzes the color change that develops on the cut surface of fruits such as apples and peaches. This browning can be prevented by protecting the cut surface with a citrus fruit juice, a sugar syrup, or a sprinkling of sugar. Thus treated, the fruit surface does not come in contact with oxygen and does not discolor.

The color shift of pigments can be used advantageously in the preparation of fruit punches. The addition of pineapple juice along with lemon juice prevents the shift of bluish punch to red. The addition of lemon juice to blackberry juice shifts the color to red. The anthocyanin pigments in strawberry and cranberry juices have a somewhat different structure and are less likely to shift toward blue with added ingredients.

Flavor Components

Citric and malic acids are the most common **organic acids** in plant tissues, while tartaric and oxalic acids are found in certain plant tissues. Various organic acids and dissolved sugars are found in the aqueous cell sap and contribute to the characteristic flavors of fruit. Examples of organic acids and fruits in which they predominate are benzoic acid in cranberries, citric acid in oranges, malic acid in apples, oxalic acid in rhubarb, and tartaric acid in grapes. Most fruits have an intermediate pH range of 3.5 to 3.9. Banana and watermelon are the least acidic fruits with a pH of 6.4; lemons and limes are the most acidic among fruits with a pH range of 2.0 to 2.2.

Fruit flavors are a blend of organic acids, sugars, and various other organic compounds. Aldehydes, esters, and ketones serve to round out the flavor profile of the various fruits. These compounds provide distinctive aromatic overtones, which contribute to the unique flavor characteristics of individual fruits. These compounds are volatile, with the result that fruit flavors will become weaker with prolonged periods of cooking. The relatively mild flavors of fruit can best be retained when fruits are simmered in a covered pan.

NUTRITIONAL QUALITY

Fruits are valued for their abundant contribution of vitamins, minerals, and fiber. Table 13–1 lists nutritive values of selected fruits.

Table 13-1 Nutritive Value of Selected Fruits

Fruit	Kilocalories	Carbohy-drate (grams)	Water (%)	Vitamin A Value (IU)	Ascorbic Acid (mg)	Calcium (mg)	Iron (mg)
Apple 1 medium	70	18	85	50	3	8	.4
Apricots 3	55	14	85	2890	10	18	.5
Avocado 1	370	13	74	630	30	22	1.3
Banana 1	100	26	76	230	12	10	.8
Cantaloupe ½ medium	60	14	91	6540	63	27	.8
Grapefruit ½ medium	45	12	89	10	44	19	.5
Grapes 1 cup	95	25	81	140	6	17	.6
Oranges 1 medium	65	25	86	260	66	54	.5
Orange juice, fresh, 1 cup	110	26	88	500	124	27	.5
Orange juice, canned unsweetened, 1 cup	120	28	87	500	100	25	1.0
Orange juice, frozen concentrate with 3 parts water, 1 cup	120	29	87	550	120	25	.2
Orange juice, dehydrated, prepared with water, 1 cup	115	27	88	500	109	25	.5
Peach 1 medium	35	10	89	1320	7	9	.5
Pear 1 medium	100	25	83	30	7	13	.5
Pineapple, raw diced, 1 cup	75	19	85	100	24	24	.1
Strawberries 1 cup	55	13	90	90	88	31	1.5
Watermelon 4 × 8 wedge	115	27	93	2510	30	30	2.1

Adapted from *Nutritive Value of Foods*, Home and Garden Bulletin no. 72, Agricultural Research Service, USDA, rev. 1971.

Vitamins

Although there is some variation in vitamin content from one fruit to another, most raw fruits contribute some ascorbic acid. Citrus fruits, cantaloupe, and strawberries are rich sources. Yellow fruits, such as apricots, bananas, cantaloupes, and peaches, are excellent sources of carotene, a compound the body converts to vitamin A. Fruits contain moderate amounts of the B vitamins.

Canned fruits are usually eaten along with the syrup or juice, which has the water-soluble vitamins and other nutrients. Vitamin losses during canning are not serious, and vitamins are also well retained during freezing and frozen storage. Vitamins are less well retained in dried fruits than by other preservation methods. However, dried fruits are good sources of minerals and provide variety.

Fruits are sufficiently acidic to promote retention of ascorbic acid whether they are raw, canned, or frozen. All forms of orange juice—freshly squeezed, canned, dehydrated, or reconstituted frozen concentrate retain most of their ascorbic acid content even when stored for several days in the refrigerator.

Minerals

All fruits contribute some minerals. Oranges are especially good sources of calcium and dried fruits are good sources of iron. The nutritive value of selected fruits is shown in Table 13–1.

Carbohydrates

Fruits contain carbohydrates as sugars and polysaccharides. Sugars are the principal carbohydrate in fruits and include glucose, fructose, and sucrose. These fruit sugars contribute energy and sweetness. Other carbohydrates present in small amounts in fruits include cellulose, hemicellulose, and pectic substances. These polysaccharides are the structural material of fruits and are indigestible. They are valued as dietary fiber or bulk.

RIPENING PROCESS

The ripening process continues after the fruits are picked. Obvious changes in color, texture, sweetness, astringency, and flavor occur as fruits ripen. These changes are supported by changes in respiration that take place in the fruit. Changes during ripening usually involve a decrease in starch and an increase in sugar. Texture softens as changes occur in pectic substances. Organic acids decrease; flavor substances develop; and the fruit becomes less tart. Chlorophyll is degraded, and the carotenoid and anthocyanin pigments are synthesized.

As plant cells respire, oxygen is used, and carbon dioxide is given off. Hormones and enzymes within the plant appear to control the ripening process. A rise in respiration stimulates the production of ethylene gas, which appears to be involved in the initiation of the ripening process.

The ripening process can be controlled to a degree through the use of chemical compounds that mimic hormones produced by the plant. Low storage temperatures, but above freezing, slow down respiration and therefore the ripening process. Regulation of the concentration of oxygen and carbon dioxide and the use of inert nitrogen gas in the surrounding atmosphere also control plant respiration. Controlled-atmosphere storage is now used to prolong the storage life and quality of fresh fruits. Perforations in plastic bags permit an exchange of respiration gases while retaining moisture when fruits are displayed.

SELECTION

Most fruits come in a number of varieties, each with its special characteristics. Some varieties are good for eating raw, others have excellent cooking properties, yet others possess both eating and cooking characteristics. Flavor, texture, color, and storage ability tend to vary among the varieties of the same fruit. Consideration is given to variety, size, and grade when fruits are selected. Table 13–2 lists servings of fruits per unit purchased.

Fresh Fruit

High-quality fresh fruits are firm, crisp, free of decay or bruises, and of a good characteristic color. Fruits of a variety and size that best meet the specific

Table 13-2 Servings of Fruits per Unit Purchased

Fruit	Servings per Unit Purchased Fresh	Servings per 10- or 12-oz Package Frozen	Servings per 16-oz Can Canned	Servings per 8-oz Package Dried
Apples	3 or 4 per lb			8
Apricots	5 or 6 per lb		4	6
Bananas	3 or 4 per lb			
Blueberries	4 or 5 per pt	3 or 4	3 or 4	
Cherries	5 or 6 per lb		3 or 4	
Grapes	5 or 6 per lb			
Peaches	3 or 4 per lb	2 or 3	4	4 or 5
Pears	3 or 4 per lb		4	3 or 4
Plums	3 or 4 per lb		4	
Raspberries	4 or 5 per pt	2		
Strawberries	3 or 4 per pt	2 or 3		

From USDA, *Your Money's Worth in Foods,* Home and Garden Bulletin, no. 183, Washington, D.C.: Government Printing Office, 1979.

need should be selected. When fruits are used alone or for decorative purposes, uniformity in size, shape, and color is important. However, when they are cut or combined with other ingredients, uniformity becomes less important. Handle fruits carefully to prevent damaging them when evaluating quality and degree of ripeness. Purchase only the quantity that can be stored and used without spoilage.

Frozen Fruit

Good-quality fruits are used for the commercially frozen products. Select firmly frozen packages of fruit. Packages that are stained by the contents or are somewhat soft indicate thawing at some point during marketing and should be avoided. Labels on frozen fruits show product name, style, sweetener used, weight, and the name and address of the packer. Some labels may show grade marks such as grade A or fancy. Select frozen foods last during shopping and put them in bags to retard thawing.

Canned Fruit

Labels on canned fruits, like those on frozen fruits, must identify the product and the packer and indicate the sweetener used. The label may also include the USDA grade shield, serving directions, and recipes.

Canned fruits may be graded according to standards set by the U.S. Department of Agriculture. U.S. grade A or fancy designates the highest quality. When whole fruit, halves, or pieces are desired as a dessert, as a garnish, or as a decorative fruit accompaniment, this grade is ideal.

U.S. grade B or U.S. choice is the next grade and designates fruits of good quality and flavor suitable for all purposes. The color, uniformity of size and shape, and texture of the fruit are slightly less perfect than for grade A.

U.S. grade C or standard is the final grade and designates wholesome fruits with broken or uneven pieces and that have a less intense flavor than grades A or B. Grade C fruits are used when appearance and texture are less important, as in cobblers, pies, and sauces.

Dried Fruit

Although federal grades have been established for dried fruits, they usually are not used on labels. All methods of drying reduce the moisture content. High-quality dried fruits have a good color and are firm but pliable. The most popular dried fruits are raisins, prunes, and dates, followed by apricots, figs, apples, and pears.

More than one variety of a fruit may be dried. Seedless raisins are usually from Thompson grapes and those with seeds from Muscot grapes. Both light and dark raisins are from Thompson grapes, but the light raisins are treated with sulfur dioxide to retard darkening. Some dried fruits, such as prunes, are graded according to size, from small to extra large.

STORAGE

Controlled low temperature and humidity used commercially provide the best storage conditions for fresh fruits because they retard natural respiration and microbial spoilage. The controlled atmosphere technique regulates the levels of oxygen and carbon dioxide surrounding the fruit and thus delays ripening and extends the availability of several fruits. Ideal storage conditions are impossible to achieve at home, and quality is maintained best at refrigerator temperature although moisture loss does occur.

Underripe fruit may be ripened at room temperature and then stored in the refrigerator. Apples can be stored for an extended period at cold temperatures, but most other fruits should be used within a relatively short time. Berries cannot be stored for prolonged periods commercially or at home. Grapes and berries are stored with stems and caps intact. Fresh fruits should be stored in compartments, away from other food, because they absorb and emit odors. They may be placed in plastic bags to reduce moisture loss and stored on refrigerator shelves.

Dried fruits may be stored in covered containers at room temperature. When the climate is humid, it may be necessary to store dried fruits in the refrigerator to retard moisture absorption and mold growth. Frozen fruits are stored at $0°$ F ($-18°$ C) and thawed partially for serving. Fruits thawed in the refrigerator usually have a more pleasing texture than those thawed at room temperature.

PREPARATION METHODS

The principles of fruit preparation are concerned with the retention of wholesomeness, identity, texture, color, nutrients, and aesthetic qualities.

Raw Fruits

Most fruits are sprayed during the growth period to retard destruction by insects and plant-disease agents. Raw fruits are washed to remove most of the spray residue before they are marketed. Fresh, ripened raw fruits are ready to serve after they are again washed thoroughly at home to remove surface microorganisms and other residues.

Some raw fruits may be pared, cut, or sliced for service. Cut fruits of a low acid content, such as apples, bananas, pears, and peaches, discolor owing to tannin compounds in the fruit and to enzyme action. Some tannins, amino acids, and enzymes in the fruit cause the surface exposed to air to brown. This browning occurs only when fruits have been cut or injured. It can be slowed or reduced by coating the cut surface with acidic fruit juice, syrup, or sugar to protect it from contact with oxygen. Cut fruits with a high acid content, such as lemons, limes, and oranges, do not discolor.

Loss of ascorbic acid and other water-soluble substances is kept to a minimum when fruits are washed before cutting or removing stems and caps rather than afterwards. Cutting fruit just before serving further reduces losses of ascorbic acid. Uncut fruits or large pieces retain more ascorbic acid than finely cut fruit. Fruits retain their identity best with minimum handling and cutting.

Raw fruits, whole or cut, may be served as dessert, snack, fruit cup, combination plate, salad, an accompaniment, or ganish. Arrangement of fruits should be made with consideration for contrasts in color, shape, and size.

Cooked Fruits

Cooking extends variety and changes the texture, flavor, and color of fruit. Fruits are cooked to soften texture, enhance palatability, improve flavor of underripe fruits, and extend keeping quality. Cooking denatures the protein component of enzymes, thus making them inactive and prevents browning of the fruit.

Texture. Cooked fruits lose crispness and become tender. The pectic substances become more soluble and gradually break down to pectin or pectic acid. Constituents in the cell wall become softened. When heat is applied to fresh fruit, the cell membranes lose their selective permeability, and osmosis can no longer take place. Then both water and solute (sugar) can pass through the membrane by the process of diffusion.

The texture of cooked fruit is affected by the medium in which it is cooked. When fruit is heated in plain water, sugars diffuse out of the fruit cells, and water moves into the fruit so that the solute (sugar) concentration is equalized. However, when fruit is heated in a sugar syrup more concentrated than that in the cells, water is lost from the tissue causing the fruits to shrink, and a large amount of sugar enters the tissue and contributes firmness. Diffusion continues until the sugar concentration in the syrup and fruit are equalized. Preserved fruits are firm and hold their shape because of the heavy syrup in which they are cooked. However, fruits packed in their own juice maintain a desirable texture and contain less kcalories than syrup-packed fruits.

Color. The color change in cooked fruit may be due to the pH of the cooking liquid and reaction of metals with the pigments. Anthocyanins react with iron to form dark spots on the fruit. Lacquer-lined cans prevent discoloration of red pigments in canned fruits. Slow heating of refrigerated strawberries permits utilization of interior oxygen in cell respiration, which retains their bright red color.

Flavor. A variety of volatile organic compounds and sugars are responsible for the flavor of fruits. To minimize loss of volatile flavor components, fruits are cooked with a cover and for a short time only.

Many flavor components are water soluble. Water to barely cover the fruit reduces the loss of soluble flavoring compounds into the syrup. A minimum amount of water and a short period of cooking also retain nutrients and minimize heat destruction of ascorbic acid.

Cooking Methods. Fruits are commonly simmered, stewed, and poached. The juiciness of the fruit determines the amount of water required. Fruits are cooked sufficiently when they become translucent and tender.

The desired texture, firm or soft, determines whether sugar is added before or after cooking. The firm texture and retention of shape desired in **stewed** fruits require that the fruit be cooked in syrup. The preferred smooth texture of applesauce requires that the apples be cooked in water until tender and then sweetened. Fruits cooked in water and then sweetened are known as sauces. **Compote** or **poached** refers to a single layer of fruit cooked in a thin syrup until tender. **Glazed** refers to fruit cooked in a covered pan with half as much sugar as water, turned over once, and simmered until tender.

Fruits may also be baked, broiled, fried, and used as an ingredient in the preparation of other products. Slices or sections of fruit may be baked in a casserole, and some fruits may be baked whole. The firm skin of apples and pears, for example, holds the steam in, to cook the interior. Fruits that retain their shape, such as grapefruit and peach halves, pineapple rings, and lengthwise slices of banana, may be broiled, perhaps brushed with table fat and/or seasoned with sugar or a syrup first. Pieces of fruit may be sautéed in a small amount of table fat until just tender or dipped into a batter and deep-fat fried.

Dried Fruit. Rehydration prepares dried fruits for cooking. Hot water diffuses into the fruit more quickly than cold water. This process requires about an hour and depends upon size of pieces and the amount of cut surface. The fruit is then simmered in the water used for soaking. Tenderized dried fruits rehydrate as they simmer and usually do not need to be soaked prior to cooking. Sugar is added after the fruit is cooked to avoid toughening. The sugar diffuses into the fruit if it is stored overnight.

Microwaved Fruit. A microwave oven may be used to cook or defrost fruits. The short cooking time and the need for little or no added water account for the fresh flavor, texture, color, and shape of microwaved fruits. Fruits may be baked, stewed, or prepared as a sauce, compote, or soufflé in a microwave oven.

Before defrosting frozen fruits, remove any foil or metal from the package or place fruit in a casserole. The power level is usually set for defrost or lowest setting. Best results are achieved when directions provided with the oven are used for defrosting. Properly defrosted fruit should be cold, firm, and slightly juicy.

SUMMARY

Selections are made from fresh, frozen, canned, and dried fruits. Firm, sound, crisp, bright-colored fruits are of high quality. The label and U.S. grade marks are guides for selection of processed fruits. Fruits are cooked to increase variety, enhance palatability, soften texture, improve flavor of underripe fruits, and extend keeping quality. Fruits may be cooked in water or syrup, baked, broiled, fried, or used as an ingredient in other products.

Enzyme activity leads to browning of some fruits and can be retarded by coating cut fruits with an acidic fruit juice or sugar. A small quantity of sugar retards the flow of cooking liquid into the cell and retains the structure and shape of the fruit. A high concentration of sugar in the cooking liquid draws water out of the fruit, causing the fruit to shrivel and toughen. The principles of fruit preparation involve the rentention of wholesomeness, aesthetic qualities, color, nutrients, and identity.

SELF-STUDY GUIDE

1. Identify six classifications used for fruits and give examples.
2. Discuss the composition of fruits and give their nutrient contribution.
3. What three factors are considered when fruits are selected? Suggest uses for the various forms of fruits available.
4. How are fresh, frozen, canned, and dried fruits stored to protect their quality and nutrients?
5. Discuss six principles of fruit preparation.
6. How does cooking influence fruit flavor, texture, and color?
7. List five methods used to prepare cooked fruits. When and why may they be used?
8. Discuss the effect of small and large quantities of sugar in the liquid in which fruits are cooked.

SELECTED REFERENCES

AKHAVAN, I., and WROLSTAD, R. E. Variation of sugars and acids during ripening of pears and in the production and storage of pear concentrate. *Journal of Food Science* 45:499, 1980.

AKINYELE, I. O., and KESHINRO, O. O. Tropical fruits as sources of vitamin C. *Food Chemistry* 5:163, 1980.

ALBACH, R. F., et al. Seasonal variation of bitterness components, pulp, and vitamin C in Texas commercial citrus juices. *Journal of Agricultural and Food Chemistry* 29:805, 1981.

BERRY, R. E. Tropical fruits and vegetables as potential protein sources. *Food Technology* 35:45, 1981.

BOOTHBY, D. The pectic components of plum fruits. *Food and Biological Sciences* 19:1949, 1980.

CHAIROTE, G., et al. Characterization of additional volatile flavor components of apricot. *Journal of Food Science* 46:1898, 1981.

CHANDAN, R. C., and EREIFEJ, K. I. Determination of lysozyme in raw fruits and vegetables. *Journal of Food Science* 46:1278, 1981.

COOK, R. Quality of citrus juices as related to composition and processing practices. *Food Technology* 37:68, 1983.

HANNIGAN, K. Ingredients to fit today's trend: Dried natural fruit. *Food Engineering* 55:58, 1983.

KAYISU, K.; HOOD, L.; and VAN SOEST, P. J. Characterization of starch and fiber of banana fruit. *Journal of Food Science* 46:1885, 1981.

KELSAY, J. L., et al. Nutrient utilization by human subjects consuming fruits and vegetables as sources of fiber. *Journal of Agricultural and Food Chemistry* 29:461, 1981.

LII, C. Y., et al. Investigation of the physical and chemical properties of banana starches. *Journal of Food Science* 47:1493, 1982.

MAO, W. W., and KINSELLA, J. E. Amylase activity in banana fruit; properties and changes in activity with ripening. *Journal of Food Science* 46:1200, 1981.

MAZZA, G. Chemical composition of Saskaton berries. *Journal of Food Science* 47:1730, 1982.

MOHARRAM, Y. G., and MOUSTOFA, A. M. Utilization of mango seed kernel as a source of oil. *Food Chemistry* 8:269, 1982.

MONTGOMERY, M. W. Cysteine as an inhibitor of browning in pear juice. *Journal of Food Science* 48:951, 1983.

————; REYES, R. G.; CORNWELL, C.; and BEARERS, D. V. Sugar analysis and effect of heating on color stability of northwest concord grape juice. *Journal of Food Science* 47:1883, 1982.

NAGY, S., and ROUSSEFF, R. L. Lead content of commercially canned single strength orange juice stored at various temperatures. *Journal of Agricultural and Food Chemistry* 29:889, 1981.

NAGY, S., and WARDOWSKI, W. F. Diphenyl absorption by honey tangerines; the effects of washing and waxing and time and temperature of storage. *Journal of Agricultural and Food Chemistry* 29:760, 1981.

NELSON, P. E., and TRESSLER, D. K. *Fruit and vegetable juice processing Technology.* 3rd ed. Westport, Conn.: Avi Publishing Company, 1980.

OUGH, C. S.; DAUDT, C. E.; and CROWELL, E. A. Identification of new volatile amines in grapes and wine. *Journal of Agricultural and Food Chemistry* 29:938, 1981.

PARK, G. L., and NELSON, D. B. Analysis of sorbic acid in citrus fruit. *Journal of Food Science* 46:1629, 1981.

PROEBSTING, E. L., and MILLS, H. H. Effects of season and crop load on maturity characteristics of bing cherry. *American Society of Horticultural Science Journal* 106:144, 1981.

ROMAN, G. N. Moisture equilibrium in apples at several temperatures; experimental data and theoretical considerations. *Journal of Food Science* 47:1484, 1982.

SKREDE, G. Changes in sucrose, fructose, and glucose content of frozen strawberries with thawing. *Journal of Food Science* 48:1094, 1983.

STAROSCIK, J. A., et al. Nutrients in fresh peeled oranges and grapefruit from California and Arizona. *Journal of the American Dietetic Association* 77:567, 1980.

THOMAS, P., and OKE, M. Vitamin C content and distribution in mangoes during ripening. *Journal of Food Technology* 15:669, 1980.

WILSON, E. L. High pressure liquid chromatography of apple juice phenolic compounds. *Journal of Science and Agriculture* 32:257, 1981.

U.S. DEPARTMENT OF AGRICULTURE. *Fruits in family meals.* Home and Garden Bulletin no. 125. Washington, D.C.: Government Printing Office, 1975.

————. *Fruits and fruit juices: raw, processed, prepared.* Agriculture Handbook no. 8–9. Human Nutrition Information Service. Washington, D.C.: Government Printing Office, 1982.

————. *How to buy canned and frozen fruits.* Home and Garden Bulletin no. 191. Washington, D.C.: Government Printing Office, 1977.

————. *How to buy fresh fruits.* Home and Garden Bulletin no. 141. Washington, D.C.: Government Printing Office, 1977.

14

SALADS

OBJECTIVES

When you complete this chapter you will be able to

1. List the functions of salads and give examples.
2. Identify the major parts of a salad and give examples.
3. Discuss the preparation of salads to include selection, cleaning, crisping, cutting, and color retention of ingredients.
4. Define marinade and discuss its use.
5. Discuss the factors of color, shape, flavor, texture, and arrangement as they relate to salad composition.
6. Explain the differences among the three basic types of salad dressings and give examples of their use.
7. Discuss the nutritional quality of salads.

History reports that Roman emperors ordered the service of greens on plates of gold. The custom of mixing herbs and oil with greens originated in Italy and Greece and traveled to Spain and France, where it was readily adopted. The French and Spaniards introduced salads to America, where at first they were simply uncooked green leaves on stalks.

The popularity of salads has increased throughout the years, and now salads occupy a prominent place not only in meals at home but also in meals in restaurants, many of which feature salad bars. Each restaurant patron has the opportunity to demonstrate culinary artistry by combining ingredients of various shapes and colors to make a salad as pretty as a picture.

The salad continues to be served with the main course, as it originally was, or preceding the main course, and often it is the only vegetable. In this chapter we discuss uses of salads, their preparation and composition, salad dressings, and nutritional quality.

NUTRITIONAL QUALITY

The familiar command, Eat your salad, its good for you, focuses on the nutritional quality attributed to salads by almost everyone. Salads are deserving of this recognition, although the nutritional quality depends on the foods that compose the salads. Salads made with fresh fruits and vegetables are good sources of vitamins, minerals, and fiber. Salad greens—particularly the dark green ones—are rich sources of vitamin A, ascorbic acid, and iron. A salad made entirely of greens counts as one serving of leafy green vegetables, but the few greens that form the base on which other types of salads are arranged do not.

Salads containing meat, poultry, seafood, cheese, nuts, and hard-cooked egg contribute protein, vitamins, minerals, and fat. Those made of macaroni, potato, and mature beans provide carbohydrate, some vitamins, and minerals. Salad dressings and cream contribute kcalories and fatty acids.

The kind and amount of dressing eaten with a salad often determine the kcalories. Most salad dressings contain a high proportion of oil. The vegetable oils in the salad dressing contribute linoleic acid, which is an essential fatty acid, vitamin E, and kcalories. Mayonnaise provides the most kcalories per tablespoon (100), followed by French dressing (66), and cooked salad dressing the least (26).

Fresh vegetables and fruits are relatively low in kcalories and are preferred accompaniment salads. Salads used as a main dish may contain fewer kcalories than a number of other main course items. Salads used as dessert may contain fewer kcalories than a number of other dessert items.

SALAD FUNCTIONS

Salads are frequently grouped according to their use or function or according to the kind of food from which they are prepared. They are often designated as hearty or light, indicating their satiety and kcaloric value.

The original use of salad greens as an accompaniment to the main course has been extended so that salads now have a variety of roles on menus from appetizer to dessert. They may be served as a separate course between the main and dessert courses, although they continue to be popular meat or main-dish accompaniments. They also serve as party refreshments and as snacks and enhance the aesthetic qualities of food service.

Accompaniment Salad

Accompaniment salads are generally crisp and sometimes tart. They complement the meat or other main dish with which they are served. Combinations of crisp vegetables, greens, and fruits yield light salads with pleasing contrasts to meats and other main-dish foods. Accompaniment salads represent the most common salad function, appearing in nearly every dinner.

Gelatin salads are other popular accompaniment salads. These may be made with flavored or unflavored gelatins. Perfection salad can be made with unflavored gelatin, lemon juice, and shredded vegetables. Aspics derive their flavor from the combination of ingredients added to the unflavored gelatin. Tomato aspic is prepared with well-seasoned tomato juice.

Flavored gelatin is often combined with finely cut vegetables or fruits. Gelatin provides the structure for the salad, but the added foods contribute the nutritional value. These salads generally do not contain a sufficient quantity of added foods to be nutritionally important.

Main-Dish Salad

Main-dish salads are hearty and can be the basis of a lunch, supper, or party menu. Sometimes the main-dish salad is known as a salad plate or bowl. Included in this type of salads are crisp greens and vegetables along with such protein-rich foods as meat, poultry, fish, cheese, meat, and hard-cooked eggs. When these protein foods appear in julienne strips arranged over salad greens, the dish is called a chef's salad.

Some main-dish salads feature carbohydrate-rich foods, such as macaroni, potato, or red kidney beans, combined with crisp greens. Other hearty salads are prepared with fish, poultry, or meat and combined with raw or cooked vegetables.

A variety of fruits—fresh, canned, frozen, or dried—arranged attractively on crisp greens form main-dish fruit salad plates or bowls. These fruit salads often include additions of tiny sandwiches or slices of nut or banana breads, nuts, cheese, or sherbet, for the sake of satiety.

Appetizer Salads

Appetizer salads are designed to stimulate the appetite for the meal to follow. A combination of salad greens or of salad greens and other succulent vegetables, seasoned with a tart dressing, is a pleasing appetizer. Nearly all fresh fruits contribute a degree of tartness to fill the role of appetizer. Attractive arrangements of fresh fruits, with a variety of colors and shapes, on crisp greens or in hollowed-out half shells from fruits such as melons or oranges make appealing salads. Fruit appetizer salads usually provide a sufficiently satisfying flavor without a salad dressing, but a dressing may be used if desired.

Combinations of seafoods such as crab, lobster, shrimp, or anchovy, and greens, with flavorful sauces or dressings, also fill the appetizer role. Seafood in small quantities serves to stimulate the appetite but in large quantities can satisfy it, contributing a substantial portion of the daily protein need.

Garniture Salads

Vegetable and fruit garnishes offer an appealing contrast in color, shape, flavor, and texture and thus add to the enjoyment of the foods they enhance. A variety of interesting curls and shapes can be formed when thinly cut strips, slices, and rings of vegetables are crisped in ice water. Pickled fruits and vegetables also add exciting flavor accents. Small fruits remain whole, and large fruits may be cut into halves, sections, spears, cubes, or balls and arranged to accent the foods they garnish.

Dessert Salads

Dessert salads are less intensely sweet than most other desserts. They consist of various combinations of fresh, frozen, or canned fruits, gelatin, or frozen salads. Fruits are usually added to gelatin dessert salads, which may also include nuts and whipped cream. Frozen salads are prepared with whipped cream, cream cheese, or marshmallow base and often include fruits and nuts. Frozen salads tend to be somewhat richer than other dessert salads and are appropriately served with light lunches or dinners.

Refreshment/Snack Salads

Salads also serve as party refreshments or as snacks. The bright colors and arrangement of foods in a salad add attractiveness, festivity, and elegance to any occasion. All light or small salads are appropriate snacks and, except for plain gelatin, can enhance the daily nutrient intake.

The kind of party determines the salad selection. Accompaniment or garniture salads accent party sandwiches. Main-dish salads provide unusual and pleasing main courses for party luncheons and suppers. Dessert salads are elegant party refreshments or conclusions to a festive meal.

SALAD PREPARATION

Salads and triangles have one thing in common: they both consist of three parts. Salads consist of a base, a body, and dressing. Greens form the salad base. The body of the salad refers to the foods that give it structure, such as vegetables, fruits, meats, poultry, seafoods, macaroni, cheese, and hard-cooked egg. Salad dressings—french, mayonnaise, or cooked—provide the seasoning for salads when used.

Selection

Salad preparation begins with the selection of high-quality ingredients. Attractive salads require crisp, sound, firm vegetables and fruits with good color, texture, and flavor and uniform size and shape. Cooked or canned products should be sufficiently firm to retain their shape.

Cleaning

All raw vegetables and fruits are thoroughly cleaned for salad preparation. Leafy greens are lifted in and out of a large quantity of water or held under running water to remove soil and other residues. Iceberg lettuce cups are easily formed when the core is first removed either with a sharp knife or with a firm hit against the edge of the sink. The leaves separate readily when the portion from which the core was removed is held under cold running water. The washed greens are placed on a towel or rack to remove excess water and then stored in the refrigerator in a covered container or plastic bag to retain or restore their crispness. Other washed vegetables and fruits are drained and stored in the refrigerator hydrator.

Crisping

Refrigerator storage of washed greens, other vegetables, and fruits aids in maintaining maximum crispness. Some crispness can be restored to limp fresh vegetables by washing or rinsing them with cold water, and then refrigerating them in a plastic bag or covered container for an hour or more.

Cutting

Leafy greens used in the body of a salad are torn into bite-sized pieces to reduce possible damage to cell structure and provide a variety of shapes and sizes. A sharp knife is essential for cutting other salad vegetables and fruits to avoid bruising them. Head lettuce is often cut into wedges for lettuce salad. Firm vegetables, such as cabbage and carrots, may be shredded, chopped, grated, or cut.

Salad ingredients are cut into pieces that retain their identity and are easily eaten without cutting at the table. Raw fruits or vegetables should be cut just before serving to reduce exposure to oxygen and thus loss of ascorbic acid. Foods that can be easily cut with a fork may remain in large pieces, when desired.

Color Retention

Some fresh fruits—peaches, apples, and bananas—become brown after they are cut. This browning is promoted by enzymes present in fresh fruits and can be prevented by dipping the fruit in citrus fruit or pineapple juice as soon as it is cut. The enzymes react with polyphenols and some amino acids in the fruit to brown the cut surface exposed to air. When fruits are cooked or canned, the enzymes are inactivated by the heat treatment, and the color does not change.

Marinade

The **marinade** imparts additional flavor to starchy and firm succulent vegetables, meats, seafoods, and macaroni before they are used in salads. The marinade is a well-seasoned blend of oil and acid, such as vinegar, lemon juice or french dressing. The foods remain in the marinade for an hour or longer before draining so that the flavor will penetrate.

The salts in the marinade or salad dressing create an osmotic pressure. Water is then withdrawn from the vegetable cells in an effort to balance the salt concentration of the fluid within the cells and the liquid surrounding the cells. The loss of water from the cells causes them to weaken and begin to collapse. Succulent leafy vegetables, because of osmotic forces, begin wilting soon after they are coated with salad dressing. However, **marinating** firm foods such as potato, macaroni, and meat is an effective way to enhance and blend flavors.

SALAD COMPOSITION

Working much like any other artist, the culinary artist combines ingredients of various forms and colors to compose a salad for the intended function and considers the color, flavor, texture, and arrangement of salad components. The intended salad function determines the food items from which the salad should be prepared and its size. Appetizer, accompaniment, and dessert salads are of a moderate size; so-called salad plates or bowls and main-dish salads are large in size; garniture salads are small.

Color

Salads with well-chosen color combinations become the focal point of the meal. Fruit skins, with their vivid colors, should be retained for pleasing highlights in salads. Complementary and contrasting colors make attractive salads. A color range and contrast can be achieved by using a variety of greens to form the base of the salad. Colorful garnishes and bright accents enhance salads that are relatively neutral in color.

Most salads are prepared from raw fruits and vegetables, permitting the retention of the vivid colors of the fresh produce. But even those few salads that may be served hot, such as potato or chicken, can also be enhanced with colorful vegetable or fruit garnishes. Salad color combinations must be chosen as carefully as those of clothing or furnishings.

(Dudley-Anderson-Yutzy Public Relation Inc./United Fresh Fruit & Vegetable Association)

Shape

Salad materials cut in a variety of shapes and sizes contribute interest and aesthetic appeal. The ease with which the salad can be eaten and the dominant shapes of the foods with which the salad will be served should be considered. The shapes and sizes of salad materials should contrast with, rather than repeat, those of the foods they accompany. For example, when a casserole is featured as the main dish, the salad should contain relatively large or whole food items such as fruit halves on crisp greens. The salad should consist of few foods when the main course consists of a combination of several foods. A tossed salad would offer little variation or contrast to a stew, but it would offer a pleasing contrast when served with meat loaf or baked pork chops.

Flavor

Relatively bland or mild-flavored salads should be served with highly seasoned foods, and flavorful salads should accompany bland foods. Food flavors in a salad and the other foods that are served should complement each other and be coordinated. The distinct flavors of celery, green peppers, and radishes, for instance, accent the bland flavor of potato in a salad. Flavor accents and contrasts heighten the enjoyment of the salad and the meal it accompanies.

Texture

The **texture** of a salad should offer some contrast to the foods it accompanies, and textural contrast should be present in the foods in a salad. The soft texture of pasta contrasts effectively with a salad of crisp greens. The crispness of raw celery, onion, and radishes offer a pleasing contrast to the soft texture of potato in a salad. The crisp texture of fried food is accented when fruit and gelatin salads are offered with it.

Arrangement

The plate should be large enough to permit the salad to be eaten with ease and should be suited to the arrangement and size of the salad. All of the salad should be contained on the plate, with a margin of the plate serving to frame the salad, just as a picture is framed. Salad arrangements depicting specific objects and that detract from the natural beauty of foods should be avoided.

The arrangement of the components contribute to the beauty and pleasure offered by the salad. All salads, large and small, should have a center of interest, or a focal point, and should be attractively arranged. The arrangement should reflect a balance among the component parts of the salad. The greens or base of the salad serve to unify the salad and form a border for the other ingredients. The dressing, when used, is applied just before serving so that the crispness of the salad will be retained.

SALAD DRESSINGS

Common ingredients in salad dressing include oil, acid, egg yolk, cooked starch, and a variety of seasonings. Egg yolk promotes emulsification, the process by which one liquid is **dispersed** in another with which it usually does not mix. Other **emulsifiers** are often used in commercially prepared salad dressings. Oil and water are **immiscible,** that is, they separate rather than blend with each other. An emulsifier promotes the blending of immiscible liquids and thus the formation of an **emulsion.**

Emulsions are formed when one immiscible liquid, such as oil, is dispersed as droplets in another, such as water or acid. The emulsions formed by salad dressing ingredients may be permanent (do not separate), semipermanent (tend to separate on standing), or temporary (separate quickly). Emulsions may be classed as oil-in-water, that is, oil is dispersed (the discontinuous or dispersed phase) in the water (the continuous phase).

Emulsifiers retard the separation of oil droplets suspended in water. Emulsifiers form a protective coating for the droplets at the interface between the two liquids. This protective coating keeps droplets from coming in direct contact with each other and thus retards separation of the liquids.

Paprika, dry mustard, and various spices act as emulsifying agents in salad dressings. When used alone, these ingredients provide only limited stability, and the emulsion would be classed as a temporary emulsion. **Viscous** liquids, such as honey, syrup, or water or milk thickened with starch, slow the movement of droplets in the emulsion and cause the emulsion to be semipermanent. Salad dressing prepared with egg yolk is effectively stabilized at the oil-water interface and form permanent emulsions. The thick viscosity of a permanent emulsion also retards oil separation.

Salad dressings provide the seasoning for salad. The three types of salad dressing are identified as mayonnaise, french, and cooked.

Mayonnaise

Mayonnaise is an example of a permanent emulsion. A true commercial mayonnaise must contain egg or egg yolk, which acts as an emulsifier, and at least 65 percent oil. The high proportion of oil contributes to the thick viscous character of mayonnaise. The egg yolk assures the dispersion of oil in very tiny droplets and contributes to the permanent stability of the emulsion. It is the lecithoproteins of the yolk that are responsible for its outstanding emulsifying ability. The whole egg can form as effective an emulsion but yields a less viscous mayonnaise than the yolk alone.

The acid—vinegar or lemon juice—and the oil influence the flavor of mayonnaise. Oils must be free of rancidity and those that have been winterized are preferred. The winterizing process removes the oil fraction, which solidifies or cystallizes at refrigerator temperature.

Dry seasonings and egg yolk are used as emulsifiers in home-prepared mayonnaise. A portion of the vinegar is added and blended into the emulsifying agents. Then the oil is added very slowly, a teaspoon at a time, and thoroughly blended after each addition. When oil is no longer visible, the emulsification is complete. A rapid and thorough beating after the first additions of oil retards separation of the emulsion and promotes a viscous product. Should the emulsion separate dur-

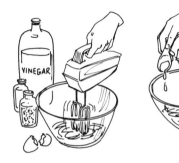

ing preparation, the emulsion can be reestablished by beating while adding the broken emulsion slowly to another beaten egg yolk.

Hand or mechanical beaters promote the formation of the emulsion essential in mayonnaise preparation. Emulsions can be established with a blender or food processor. The procedure may differ somewhat from that described for beater-prepared mayonnaise. Carefully follow the procedure for mayonnaise preparation in the use-and-care booklet for the specific appliance.

French Dressing

French dressing usually is a temporary emulsion that separates quickly and can be reestablished by shaking the dressing vigorously before each use. It is made with oil, acid, and seasonings. The insoluble seasonings, such as paprika and dry mustard, collect to the oil-water interface and contribute a small degree of stability to the emulsion. Vinegar or lemon juice, as the acid, is the continuous phase and the oil, the dispersed or discontinuous phase of the emulsion.

The oil, acid, and seasonings contribute to the flavor of french dressing. Corn, cottonseed, safflower, sunflower seed, soybean, and peanut oil retain their flavor during storage and are used in french dressing. Olive oil has a pleasing flavor but becomes rancid rather quickly when stored at room temperature. The acid ingredient may impart the distinct flavor desired in french dressing. Cider vinegar, white wine vinegar, or special vinegar flavored with herbs may be used. The seasonings may be salt, pepper, paprika, and sugar, or a variety of other herbs. Variations of the basic french dressing derive their characteristic red or orange color from paprika or tomato paste.

Commercially prepared french dressings contain seasonings, acid, and 35 percent vegetable oil. They also contain emulsifiers or stabilizers such as pectins, vegetable gums, or gelatin. Some commercial french-type dressings may have a creamy consistency and can be classed as a semipermanent emulsion.

Cooked Salad Dressing

Cooked salad dressing resembles mayonnaise whether home or commercially prepared. The appearance and flavor of home-prepared cooked salad dressing is somewhat different from commercial salad dressing because of the kinds and proportions of ingredients used.

Cooked salad dressings contain less fat and egg than mayonnaise. A cooked starch paste is the base of a home-prepared cooked salad dressing, and the dressing includes an acid—vinegar or fruit juice—egg, and seasonings. Butter or margarine may be added for flavor, but oil is not usually used.

Commercial cooked salad dressing contains a cooked starch paste, vegetable oil, an acid, seasonings, emulsifying agents such as pectin or vegetable gums, and sometimes eggs. It has a minimum of 30 percent oil compared to 65 percent for mayonnaise. Cooked salad dressing cannot be labeled mayonnaise because of its lower fat content.

Because of the difference in ingredients, mayonnaise is more expensive than salad dressing. French dressing and salad dressing have about the same kcaloric value.

Uses and Variations of Salad Dressings

Mayonnaise and salad dressing are suitable for most any salad, whether vegetable, meat, pasta, or fruit. French dressing is a favorite for crisp vegetable salads and may be used to marinate macaroni, meat, and potatoes.

Variety can be introduced to the basic salad dressings with the addition of one or more flavorful ingredients, such as pickles, olives, chili sauce, cheese, chives, mustard, horseradish, or tomato paste. Consistency and flavor of salad dressings can be varied with the addition of cream, whipped cream, honey, fruit juices, peanut butter, or cream cheese. These additions to the basic dressings are made with consideration for the foods with which they will be used.

SUMMARY

The nutritional, kcaloric, and satiety values of salads depend on the ingredients. Salads may be grouped as fruit, vegetable, protein, or gelatin. They serve the functions of appetizer, accompaniment, main dish, garnish, and dessert and are valued for their aesthetic and nutritional qualities.

The component parts of a salad include the base, the body, and often a dressing. Crisp greens form the base; vegetables, fruits, meat, poultry, seafoods, macaroni, and/or gelatin form the structure; mayonnaise, french, and cooked dressings or their variations are the seasoning for salads. The composition of a salad involves consideration for its function and its component parts, which are assembled with regard for its color, flavor, texture, and arrangement.

Salad dressings form temporary, semipermanent, or permanent emulsions between two immiscible liquids and may be stabilized with egg yolk and vegetable gums, which serve as emulsifying agents.

Marinating starch and protein foods in salad dressing enhances their flavor. Usually dressings are added just before salads are served in order to preserve crispness.

SELF-STUDY GUIDE

1. What are five functions of salads in meals? Give examples.
2. Discuss the nutritional quality of salads.
3. Discuss four techniques used in salad preparation.
4. What four factors are considered when salads are created?
5. How are vegetables crisped for salad preparation?
6. What are the differences in the basic types of salad dressings?
7. How is variety introduced to salad dressing? Give four examples.
8. Identify the emulsion in the basic salad dressings.
9. What factors influence these emulsions?

SELECTED REFERENCES

BENNION, M. *Introductory foods.* Chap. 7. New York: Macmillan Co., 1985.

CHEN, L. M., and PENG, A. C. Effect of acid dip on the shelf life of coleslaw. *Journal of Food Science* 45:1556, 1980.

Emulsifier based on soy protein. *Food Engineering* 51:32, 1979.

HANNIGAN, K. J. Crab salad with soy. *Food Engineering* 52:11, 1980.

_____. Dressing oil mimics butter—but at much lower cost. *Food Engineering* 53:91, 1981.

LEGENDRE, M. G., et al. Rapid instrumental technique for the analysis of volatiles in salad dressing. *Journal of the American Oil Chemists' Society* 57:361, 1980.

McDERMOTT, R. L., et al. Centrifugal method for characterization of salad dressing emulsions. *Food Technology* 35:81, 1981.

No-oil pourable creamy dressing. *Food Engineering* 53:100, 1981.

Pressure switch handles level control for highly viscous salad dressing. *Food Engineering* 52:189, 1980.

STILL, J. *Food selection and preparation.* Chap. 13. New York: Macmillan Co., 1981.

SULLIVAN, F. E. Sunflower oil processing from crude to salad oil. *Journal of the American Oil Chemists' Society* 57:845, 1980.

Tasty new toppings for salads are based on soy protein: Tasty toppers. *Food Engineering* 52:189, 1980.

15

GELATIN

OBJECTIVES

When you complete this chapter, you will be able to

1. Discuss the gelling process of gelatin.
2. Identify the factors in the formation of gelatin gels and explain their influence.
3. Discuss the sources and composition of gelatin.
4. Identify the uses of gelatin in home cookery and list its commercial uses.
5. Discuss the nutritional quality of gelatin.
6. Identify and define gelatin dessert products.
7. Explain the unmolding of gelatin gels.

Although pure **gelatin** is a colorless and tasteless substance, when combined with other ingredients, it yields a highly palatable and elegant product. Gelatin hydrates in cold water, disperses in hot liquid, and thickens or **gels** to a semisolid mass when cooled. The gel-forming capability of gelatin gives shape and form to food products. Gelatin provides the structure into which a variety of foods can be incorporated. The choice of those foods determines the position gelatin fulfills in a menu. The versatile nature of gelatin permits it to appear in meals as gelled soup, salad, or dessert.

The manner in which gelatin is handled during preparation affects the time of setting, the character of the gel formed, and the quality of the finished product. A properly prepared gelatin product retains the shape of the container at room temperature and is crystal clear, tender, and firm without being stiff.

SOURCES OF GELATIN

Commercially produced gelatin is derived from **collagen,** the connective tissue of mammals, the same connective tissue that has to be dealt with during the cooking of less tender cuts of meat. As connective tissues cook, large protein molecules of collagen are hydrolyzed to the smaller molecules of gelatin. Collagen is the chief protein component in bones, cartilage, skins, and tendons. A specific molecule, *tropocollagen,* is the basic molecule of collagen. Tropocollagen has a small rodlike structure consisting of three intertwined polypeptide chains. Aggregates of tropocollagen form collagen fibrils.

Collagen from bones, cattle hides, and pigskins is the basic raw material for gelatin and glue. The adhesive qualities of glue are derived from the presence of gelatin, but glue may contain impurities not permitted in gelatin that is added to food. Edible gelatin comes primarily from pigskins. The skins are washed, degreased, chopped, and soaked in dilute acid to prepare collagen for conversion to gelatin. This conversion to gelatin is further facilitated with the use of hot water and a neutral or lightly acidic pH. The extracted gelatin liquors are filtered, clarified, evaporated, sterilized, dried, ground, and screened. A good-quality plain gelatin is odorless and tasteless. Gelatin used in food must be manufactured under sanitary conditions and meet high standards of purity. Plain gelatin is sold in the granular form. Flavored gelatin mixes contain pulverized gelatin with sugar, acid, color, and flavor substances.

NUTRITIVE QUALITY

Although gelatin is derived from animal products, it is an incomplete protein as it does not contain all the essential amino acids. It is therefore a protein of lower biological value than muscle protein (meat). Gelatin contains a high proportion of nonessential amino acids—alanine, glycine, proline, and hydroxyproline and lacks the essential amino acids tryptophan, threonine, methionine, and isoleucine. Because of this lack gelatin cannot support growth and must be served with other protein foods if it is to make a contribution to the nutritionally adequate protein content of the diet. Obviously the claim that gelatin favors growth of fingernails cannot be substantiated. As noted, incomplete proteins do not support growth.

Gelatin, through its gelation capability, can bring nutritious foods into attractive combinations and serves as a base for palatable food combinations. In other words, the nutritional quality of gelatin-containing foods comes from the other foods that are added.

Only one tablespoon of gelatin is required to gel two cups of liquid. This amount is so small that its nutritive contribution becomes insignificant. One tablespoon of gelatin provides about six grams of protein and about twenty-five kilocalories spread throughout two cups of liquid.

GELLING PROCESS

The gelatin mixture is a **collodial dispersion.** Dispersed in water it forms a **sol,** and when the sol cools, a gel forms. This sequence is reversible for gelatin since the gel can be heated to re-form a sol and then chilled to produce a gel again. In the gelling process, gelatin undergoes hydration, dispersion, and gel formation.

Hydration

Gelatin swells as it **hydrates** in cold liquid. It is generally believed that cold-liquid hydration prepares gelatin for dispersion in hot liquid. The particles of granular gelatin must be hydrated to facilitate dispersion in hot liquid. Four parts of water to one part of gelatin allows adequate hydration. Hydrated gelatin may be heated over water to form a concentrated sol that can be carefully blended with other ingredients that are not overly cold. Granular gelatin may be blended with sugar and then dissolved in hot liquid without hydration.

Pulverized gelatin used in flavored mixes disperses sufficiently in a measured amount of boiling liquid when stirred. Stirring facilitates the solution and dispersion of gelatin. A rubbery layer on the bottom of the set gelatin product indicates insufficient hydration and dispersion of gelatin.

Plain granular and flavored gelatin mixes are used to prepare gelatin salads and desserts. The gelatin content of flavored mixes varies from 7 to 14 percent; the gelatin content in the prepared gel varies from 1.7 to 3 percent. A 1.5–2.0 percent gelatin content yields a gel of satisfactory consistency for salads and desserts. One tablespoon of granular gelatin (7 g) in two cups of water yields a gelatin concentration of about 1.5 percent.

Dispersion

Hydrated gelatin disperses at a temperature of 95° F (35° C) or above. The completely dispersed gelatin forms a colloidal solution. A portion of the total liquid should be added hot to the hydrated gelatin to disperse it, and then the remaining may be added cold. It is not desirable to add all of the remaining liquid as hot liquid because some volatile flavor substances are lost, thereby, and the mixture requires a long period to cool.

Gel Formation

Gel formation, or gelation, occurs as the gelatin mixture cools. Gelatin sets or solidifies over a temperature range of above 50 to 61° F (10°–16° C). Gel formation is a gradual process in which gelatin molecules link together at various places to form a three-dimensional structure. The gel will melt as it becomes warm. Although one tablespoon of granular gelatin in two cups of liquid yields a gel with a satisfactory consistency, the gel strength increases as the proportion of the gelatin is increased. Too much gelatin for the proportion of liquid yields a rubbery and overly stiff gel. Too little gelatin yields a weak gel or no gel.

FACTORS INFLUENCING GEL FORMED

Several factors influence the gel formed and include speed of cooling, gelatin concentration, sugar, acid, salts, and added foods.

Speed of Cooling

The rapidity of gel formation is related to gelatin concentration, sugar concentration, and speed of cooling. Gels with a higher concentration of gelatin set more quickly than those with less. Gelatins with a high sugar concentration set more slowly than those with less sugar. The speed of gel formation increases as the temperature at which the mixture is cooled becomes lower. However, very rapid cooling and setting of gelatin (accomplished by adding ice as a part of the liquid) results in a gel that softens more quickly than one set at refrigerator temperature.

Rapid cooling of gelatin promotes the formation of many weak links, while very slow cooling permits the links to form in a more orderly manner. Changes continue to occur in the gel during storage. Portions of the molecule between cross-linkages continue to undergo movement and new bondings may occur. It is desirable to hold gelatin mixtures for several hours or overnight at a low temperature to develop maximum stiffness.

Concentration of Gelatin

The proportion of gelatin to liquid determines the nature of the gel. The concentration of gelatin affects not only gel firmness as indicated but also the speed of gelling. Mixtures containing a high level of gelatin set more quickly than those with a low level. Excessive quantities of gelatin promote guminess in gelled products.

Sugar

The tenderness or firmness of gelatin is also influenced by sugar. Sugar serves to reduce the gelatin concentration, and as the quantity of sugar is increased, the firmness of the gel decreases.

Acid

Too high a concentration of acid may prevent gelation or cause a soft gel to form even though the gelatin concentration was increased. More gelatin is required for the same degree of firmness when the pH shifts from the isoelectric point of gelatin (pH 5). The addition of lemon juice as a portion of the one cup of liquid yields a desirable flavor and a satisfactory but more tender gel than without acid. Acid-containing gelatin mixtures require somewhat more time to set than neutral ones.

Salts

Salts in milk and in hard water appear to increase gel strength. Hard water yields a firmer gel than distilled water, and milk a firmer gel than water.

Added Foods

Chopped or shredded vegetables and diced fruits may interfere mechanically with a firm gel formation. The mechanical action of stirring interrupts gel formation. The added food should be well drained before it is added to the gelatin mixture to avoid dilution and thus an overly tender gel.

Fresh and frozen pineapple contain **bromelin,** an enzyme that breaks down gelatin, and therefore a gel cannot form. Fresh or frozen pineapple boiled for two minutes to destroy the enzyme may be added to gelatin. Canned pineapple is all right since the canning process inactivates bromelin.

Gelatin mixtures are generally cooled until they become viscous before other foods are added. Foods blended into a viscous gelatin remain uniformly dispersed rather than floating to the surface. Intercellular gases in fresh foods cause them to float. As it becomes firm, the gelatin entraps water, forming a structural network, and the result is a uniform distribution of added foods.

USES

Edible gelatin is carefully prepared and is highly purified. Gelatin as a food must meet specified standards of quality. A good quality gelatin is colorless and has very little flavor or odor. It must be of a specific gel strength and low microbial content. Dry gelatin is stable at room temperature; hydrated gelatin is perishable and must be refrigerated.

Commercially, edible gelatin is used in the production of marshmallows, gum, ice cream, and gelatin desserts. In home cookery, gelatin is used in gelled salads, desserts, and soups. In food preparation, gelatin commonly serves as a gelling agent and as an adhesive, binder, emulsifier, foaming agent, glaze, thickener, stabilizer, and inhibitor of crystal formation. Gelatin absorbs and binds water, thus interfering with crystal formation and promoting a smooth texture. It aids in emulsifying and stabilizing frozen dessert mixtures to achieve the smooth texture and body that are desirable in a quality frozen product. It is also used as a stabilizer for commercially prepared salad dressings. Gelatin concentrates on the surface of air bubbles in whipped desserts or whipped cream and thus stabilizes them.

As a jelling agent, gelatin yields a gel that may be beaten or combined with prepared fruit or vegetables, to be served as a salad or dessert. The dispersed gelatin, or sol, should be cooled to 50° F (10° C) to develop a consistency like that of thick egg white. Gelatin of this consistency is usually sufficiently thickened to retain an even distribution of added food or to retain air when beaten.

Salads

Gelatin gives structure as well as shape and form to salads in which it is used. For this reason, gelatin-containing salads can also be referred to as molded salads. Gelatins come in several flavors and colors and contribute variety as well as sparkle to salads. Gelatin salads may contain vegetables, fruits, meat, poultry, seafood, and cheese or cream products. Numerous combinations of these foods are used in gelatin salads.

The nature of a gelatin salad is determined by the added ingredients, which in turn influence its function. For example, gelatins containing poultry, meat, or fish function as the main course or dish, and those with sweetened fruits and whipped cream function as dessert. (See chapter 14 for a discussion of salads).

Gelatin Desserts

Foams, sponges, snows, and whips—all forms of gelatin desserts—are prepared with whipped gelatin.

Foam. A whipped gelatin yields a **foam** at least double the original volume of the gelatin solution. Dissolved gelatin cooled to the consistency of unbeaten egg whites incorporates air as it is beaten. After whipping, gelatin molecules in the fluid portion of the foam set the liquid. The setting of gelatin stabilizes the foam and retains its volume.

Sponges and Snows. Sponges and snows are whipped gelatins to which beaten egg whites are added.

Whip. A **whip** is a combination of a foam and a gel.

Chiffon Filling. Gelatin contributes to the large foam volume in chiffon pies. Chiffon fillings are usually prepared from a custard base thickened with gelatin. Beaten egg whites and/or whipped cream are added to a partially set gelatin.

Creams. Whipped cream is folded into the gelatin foam to yield a cream. Gelatin stabilizes the foam.

Bavarian Cream. **Bavarian creams** are prepared with a fruit juice set with gelatin into which whipped cream and beaten egg whites are folded.

Spanish Cream. **Spanish creams** are prepared by setting soft custard with gelatin. Beaten egg whites are folded into the partially gelled mixture.

Charlottes and Mousses. **Charlottes** and **mousses** are prepared by combining cream thickened with gelatin and whipped cream. Charlottes differ from mousses in that they are molded on sponge cake or lady fingers.

UNMOLDING GELATIN

Gelatin retains the shape of the container in which it gels. To facilitate unmolding the container may be oiled lightly before the gelatin mixture is added. The gel can be removed from the mold when the top circumference is larger than the interior. The mold is carefully and briefly dipped into warm water to the upper edge of the gelatin mixture. Then the edge is loosened with a sharp knife and gently shaken. Loosening the gel at one point from the container allows air to come between the gel and the container for easy removal of the gel. A plate rinsed with cold water is centered over the mold and then plate and mold are inverted together. The gelatin slips out onto the dish, and the mold is carefully removed.

SUMMARY

Gelatin is an incomplete protein derived from bones and skins of animals. It is available in granular form and pulverized in flavored mixes. Gelatin hydrates in cold water, disperses in hot water, and gels when cooled. It contributes structure and form and shape to food products. Gelatin lacks essential amino acids and is therefore unable to support growth. It must be served with other protein food to make a nutritionally adequate protein contribution to the diet.

One tablespoon of granular gelatin provides about six grams of protein and twenty-three kilocalories and gels two cups of liquid. Gelatin undergoes hydration in cold liquid and dispersion in hot liquid, and yields a gel when cooled. Gel formation is influenced by the ratio of gelatin to liquid, temperature, and level of acid and sugar. Foods added to gelatin are drained to maintain the gelatin-to-liquid ratio. Most foods can be added to gelatin but not fresh or frozen pineapple, which contain bromelin. That enzyme prevents gel formation. A thickened but not set gelatin can be beaten to a foam.

In food preparation gelatin serves as a gelling agent and as an adhesive, binder, emulsifier, foaming agent, glaze, inhibitor of crystal formation, thickener, and stabilizer. Gelatin appears in menus as a gelled soup, salad, or dessert. Desserts include plain or fruit gels, whips, snows, sponges, Spanish or Bavarian creams, charlottes, mousses, and chiffon pie fillings.

SELF-STUDY GUIDE

1. What is the source of gelatin?
2. What is the composition of gelatin?
3. Discuss the nutritional value of gelatin.
4. List and discuss six factors involved in the formation of gelatin gels.
5. List the function of gelatin in food preparation and discuss.
6. Discuss the uses of gelatin in food preparation.
7. Why are foods added to gelatin likely to float?
8. Give the direction for unmolding a gelatin gel.
9. Discuss the influence of gelatin proportions on the gel formed.
10. List and define four desserts prepared with gelatin.
11. How is the gelatin gel influenced by the speed of cooling?
12. Describe a high-quality gelatin gel.
13. What colloidal systems does gelatin form when in solution and when it coagulates?

SELECTED REFERENCES

BENNION, M.   *The science of food.* Chap. 21. New York: Harper and Row, Publishers, 1985.

CHARLEY, H.   *Food science.* Chap. 25. New York: John Wiley and Sons, 1982.

MCCLAIN, P. E.; CREED, G. J.; WILEY, R. R.; and GERRITS, R. J.   Cross-linking characteristics of collagen from porcine intramuscular connective tissue: Variations between muscles. *Biochimica Biophysica Acta* 221:349. 1970.

PECKHAM, G., and FREEDLAND-GRAVES, J.   *Foundation of food preparation.* Chap. 26. New York: Macmillan Co., 1979.

WARD, G., and COURTS, A., eds.   *The science and technology of gelatin.* New York: Academic Press, 1977.

16

MEATS

OBJECTIVES

When you complete this chapter, you will be able to

1. List the components of meat and describe the structure of meat.
2. Discuss the nutritional contribution of meat.
3. Distinguish between USDA quality and yield grades for meat and explain their value to the consumer.
4. Compare moist and dry media cookery and give examples of cuts prepared by each method.
5. Discuss heat-induced changes in meat and explain how they influence meat tenderness.
6. Discuss color changes in myoglobin.
7. List and discuss the factors that influence meat tenderness.
8. List and discuss the factors involved in meat identification and selection.
9. Store all meats properly.
10. List variety meats and discuss appropriate cooking methods.
11. Explain the cutting of meat into primal cuts and list some retail cuts from each.

Meat has been the mainstay and most prized item of the human diet since the beginning of time. The cave man fed himself and his family by hunting; medieval feasts included lavish servings of meat; and beef cattle were domesticated in parts of western Asia by the fifth millennium B.C. The aurochs, a huge, blackish, long-horned animal, was the wild ancestor of domesticated cattle (Ree, Dutson, and

Smith 1982). Today beef cattle are carefully bred and grown to yield a rich, tender, juicy meat.

The term meat refers to red meats (beef, veal, pork, lamb) as a group or to any one of them individually. Meat remains the focal point of many of our meals, and other foods are selected to complement it.

This chapter deals with the preparation of meats. Topics covered include meat structure and composition, types and cuts, selection and storage, and basic cooking principles.

NUTRITIONAL QUALITY

The high regard afforded to meat in the diet and menus is justified, at least partially, by its high nutrient content. Meats contribute high-quality proteins and a variety of other nutrients. Meat proteins provide both essential and nonessential amino acids, and are well utilized by the body for growth and maintenance. The protein content of meat ranges from about 10 to more than 20 percent and is inversely related to the amount of fat present. Meats with a high proportion of fat contribute less protein per pound than lean meats.

The fat content of meat is directly related to its caloric value. Fats contribute nine kcalories per gram, whereas proteins provide four calories per gram. The removal of visible fat prior to cooking or eating reduces the caloric content of the meat served or eaten, and cooking methods also affect the amount of fat. Frying contributes additional fat, whereas broiling decreases fat content.

Meats provide various amounts of all of the B vitamins. Lean pork is an especially rich source of thiamin. Other lean meats contain thiamin along with niacin, riboflavin, B-12, B-6, and tryptophan, an amino acid that can be converted in the body to niacin.

Meats are dependable sources of iron, copper, phosphorus, and other minerals. Liver contributes greater amounts of iron and copper than muscle tissue. However, meat is a poor source of calcium because bones are the chief source of calcium and cannot be eaten.

Meats retain most of their nutrients during cooking. Extremely high temperatures not usually used can alter protein structure and thus lower its availability, but the usual procedures and temperatures have little effect on protein quality.

Thiamin is more sensitive to heat than the other vitamins in meats. It is better retained by low cooking temperatures and in meats cooked to a low internal temperature.

Because of their solubility in water some of the B vitamins and minerals will be transferred during preparation to the cooking liquid or drippings. But when the liquid or drippings are used in soups or in the gravy or sauce served with the meat, these nutrients are not lost.

Some parts of the animal are not used as a source of table meats but are removed during slaughter and processed into by-products. The collagen in these products can be converted commercially into gelatin, which we discussed in chapter 15.

STRUCTURE AND COMPOSITION

Muscles vary in size, shape, location, direction, and the length of their fibers and in the amount and distribution of connective tissue. Muscle fibers increase in size but not in number as the animal grows.

Meat—the flesh of animals used for food—is derived from muscle tissue. Several different muscles are usually present within a single cut of meat. Most meats consist of voluntary, cross-striated muscles, which are responsible for body movement. The muscle is a complex structure of fibers held together with connective tissue. Muscle cells are long, slender fibers composed of contractile matter (protein) and surrounded by a very thin membrane called the sarcolemma.

Individual muscles are made of fibers, and the fibers or cells are made of myofibrils. The myofibrils are found in the cytoplasm of the cell called the sarcoplasm. They are tiny cylinder-like rods and contain an orderly arrangement of proteins that form thick and thin filaments. The myofibrils are the cross-striated, contractile elements of the muscle, which is made of myofilaments. Rows of thick and thin myofilaments overlap to form the dark and light bands visible on electromicrographs of muscle fiber.

The individual fibers are arranged into bundles within a network of connective tissue known as the endomysium. A bundle of muscle fibers is surrounded by a thin sheet of connective tissue, the perimysium. An outer layer of connective tissue, the epimysium, surrounds groups of muscle fiber bundles to form the muscle.

Muscle Proteins

The principal proteins of the muscle cell are **myosin, actin,** and tropomyosin. The thick filaments contain myosin, the thin filaments contain actin. Myosin is a large molecule of globular-type protein; it forms a gel when heated. Actin is a smaller molecule than myosin, is water soluble, and exists in two forms, globular actin and fibrillar actin.

Actin polymerizes, or becomes fibrillar, when the muscle contracts and combines with myosin to form actomyosin. During contraction the muscle shortens as the thick and thin filaments slide past each other. The formation of actomyosin (a reversible reaction) is thought to be the mechanism for muscle contraction and relaxation. Tropomyosin, a molecule somewhat smaller than actomyosin, is resistant to denaturation and is involved in the contractile action of muscle.

Muscles are classified also as red or white on the basis of their color intensity. Most muscles are mixtures of red and white muscle fibers. Red muscle fibers contain more myoglobin, an oxygen-carrying pigment, than white muscle fibers do.

Connective-Tissue Proteins

Connective tissue is a structural component of muscles and serves to attach muscle to bones (tendons) and bones to each other (ligaments). Connective tissue binds muscle cells (fibers) together in various bundles.

The fibrous proteins of collagen and elastin are the principal proteins of connective tissues. Connective tissue develops more extensively in muscles that are used to make movements, such as the legs and the neck. Collagen is a pearly white color and may be referred to as white connective tissue. Collagen fibers are flexible but not elastic. They are arranged to serve the functional purpose of the tissue in which they occur—in sheets as in muscle, in parallel fashion as in tendons, and randomly as in skin.

When moisture is present, collagen is softened and partially converted to gelatin, which is soluble in hot water. The conversion of collagen to gelatin increases with the length of cooking time. Sufficient water is present in meat to permit the formation of some gelatin even in dry-heat cookery. The short cooking time involved in most dry-heat cookery, however, limits the quantity of gelatin formed. Moist-heat cookery usually involves the addition of water and a low cooking temperature for a long time to facilitate the tenderization of less tender meat cuts by promoting collagen conversion to gelatin.

Although collagen fibers are the predominant type of connective tissue, small amounts of **elastin** are present in meats. Elastin tissues do not undergo conversion to gelatin, are only slightly softened by cooking, and can stretch. Elastin consists of branched fibers and is known as yellow connective tissue because of its color. It is generally found between large muscle bundles for example, in the neck and shoulder.

Usually more connective tissue is present in less tender cuts of meat than in tender cuts. Connective tissue is not the only factor affecting meat tenderness, however.

Bone

A compact bony tissue forms the shafts of long bones, and a central canal contains yellow marrow. Other bones contain a red marrow with many blood vessels. A connective-tissue sheath covers the outer side of bones. Bones facilitate movement and provide support for muscle tissues. Because they vary in size, shape, and appearance of the cross-section, they are useful in identifying specific cuts of meat. Bones are clues to meat tenderness and to the age of the animal.

The cross-sectional surfaces of bones from young animals are porous with a deep pink-to-red cast. Bones from mature animals are calcified more completely, are flinty, and are gray-to-white in color. The proportion of bone to lean tissue affects the cost and number of servings per pound of meat.

Pigments

The color of red meat is due to the concentration of the pigment **myoglobin** in the muscle. Beef contains more myoglobin and is therefore a deeper red than veal, lamb, or pork. Myoglobin is the chief pigment of the muscle and hemoglobin of the blood. Most of the hemoglobin pigment is removed in a well-bled animal. Both myoglobin and hemoglobin are made of the globin protein and the iron-containing pigment, heme. Because they both contain iron they can unite temporarily and reversibly with free oxygen.

The difference in the color of the pigment depends upon the presence of oxygen and the oxidation state of the iron atom contained in the compound. The oxygenated pigment, oxymyoglobin, is bright red in color; myoglobin has no oxygen and is purplish red.

The temporary loss of oxygen is responsible for the purplish red color of stacked meat slices and the inner portion of ground meat. The difference in oxygen permeability of the wrap used in packaging may cause the differences in color, ranging from bright red to a purplish red.

The oxidation of myoglobal iron (from ferrous to ferric) discolors fresh meat and promotes the formation of metmyoglobin, a brownish red pigment. The formation of metmyoglobin is accelerated by bacterial contamination, high temperature, ultraviolet light, freezing, some metals, and salt. Enzymes and bacteria can induce further oxidative changes in meat pigments to yield a series of brown and green compounds. These changes in color are associated with flavor and odor changes.

The pigment of **cured** meat is the result of the action of nitrite on myoglobin. The pink color of nitric oxide myoglobin is stabilized by heat with the formation of nitric oxide myochrome, which is the pigment of cured meat (Lee and Cassens 1976). Light and air can oxidize this pigment, changing the color from pink to brown, and further oxidation can produce products that are green. An iridescence sometimes present in cured meats is attributed to the refraction of light by structural components of the meat and not to changes in the pigment. Under some conditions oxidation of the porphyrin ring may lead to the formation of fluorescent yellow or green compounds.

The color of meat pigments changes during cooking from red to a tan or brown owing to the formation of denatured globin hemichrome (iron oxidized to ferric). The color of cooked meat is influenced by the amount of pigment in the raw meat. Well-done pork is lighter in color than well-done beef.

The discoloration of meat caused by oxidation or light can be controlled by proper packaging and storage. Airtight packaging aids in preventing the fading of color pigments in cured and frozen meats. Opaque packaging and storage away from light also protect the pigment of cured meats.

Fat

When an animal consumes more food than it needs for its maintenance and activity, the excess is converted into fat, which is stored throughout the animal. The fat is stored in cells called adipocytes. Adipose tissue contains accumulations of these cells. The adipocytes, or fat cells, are deposited in connective tissue in various body sites. A protective layer of fat is deposited in subcutaneous tissue around organs, then under the skin, next between muscles, and finally as marbling within the muscle. The subcutaneous fat beneath the skin becomes the outer covering on the carcass after slaughter.

Some fat is desirable; it contributes to the juiciness, enhances flavor, and increases the palatability of meat. Fats from different kinds of animals and different parts of the same animal differ in composition. Firm fats contain more saturated fatty acids than softer fats, which contain primarily unsaturated fatty acids.

Other Meat Components

As noted previously, meat consists primarily of muscle fibers, connective tissue, bone, pigments, and fat. Other meat components include minerals, nitrogenous and nonnitrogenous extractives, enzymes, and vitamins. Lactic acid is the chief nonnitrogenous substance, and the principle nitrogenous-nonprotein constituents are creatine and creatinine.

Water is the largest single component of muscle (75 percent), existing as bound and free water. Proteins in the muscle cells hold much of the water in a gel-type structure. There is some variability in the water content of meat, depending upon the kind of meat, type of muscle, and pH of the meat.

CHANGES AFTER SLAUGHTER

The series of complex changes that occur after slaughter convert animal muscle into meat. After the animal is bled, nutrients and oxygen are no longer provided to the muscle. Any glycogen present in the muscle is changed to lactic acid by enzymes. Lactic acid accumulates and causes a decrease in pH. Actin and myosin interact to form actomyosin, and the muscle contracts. The supply of ATP (adenosine triphosphate) is depleted as muscle metabolism gradually stops and the muscle stiffens—goes into **rigor mortis.** The muscle assumes a contracted or rigid state.

Microscopic examination of muscles in rigor shows dense nodes of contraction alternated with fibers pulled up in waves. When rigor passes, the fibers lose their wavy appearance. Rigor is resolved in a few days; then the muscles become soft, breaks appear in the fiber, and the fibers straighten.

If the animal is underfed or overly exercised before slaughter, the glycogen content of the tissue is too low, too little lactic acid is formed, and the pH of the meat may be higher than normal. The high pH yields a dark-colored meat, purplish red to brownish red, with a gummy or sticky texture. Animals are fed and rested before slaughter to avoid this undesirable darkening. The appearance and texture of dark-cutting meat is normal after cooking.

Aging

Aging refers to the holding of meat after rigor passes. As meat is held, the process of ripening occurs. The growth of microorganisms is controlled by keeping the temperature between 35.6° F (2° C) and 61° F (16° C) and the humidity at 70 percent. Aging occurs more rapidly at the higher than the lower temperature.

Aging contributes some additional tenderness to meat. The loss of cross striations and transverse breaks in muscle fiber, which may be due to changes in the myofibrils, possibly accounts for this tenderizing of meat during holding. The proteolytic enzymes present in muscles may account for some of the changes in structure that occur during aging. No changes have been observed in connective tissue as a result of aging. The increased tenderness of aged meat is also associated with an increase in the water-holding capacity of the proteins.

Aged meat is darker in color and more intense in flavor than unripened meat. Although aging improves the palatability of beef, it does not do so for pork.

Tenderness

Tenderness, a prized meat characteristic, appears to be related to sensory impressions created by muscle fibers and connective tissues. The ease of mastication and the apparent juiciness are associated with meat tenderness. Some of the factors believed to be related to meat tenderness include the location of the cut on the carcass, the amount and distribution of connective tissue, the size of muscle fibers, and the age of the animal. Muscles from the upper portion of the animal and along the backbone are less exercised than those from the neck and lower portion and yield tender meat. The quantity and firmness of connective tissue increase with age and with use. Meats containing the more exercised muscles tend to be less tender.

Although the carcass is cut in such a way as to separate the tender cuts from the less tender, different muscles within the same cut vary in tenderness. Cuts of meat usually classed as less tender may be prepared like tender cuts when they come from beef treated with enzymes. An enzyme preparation injected into the blood stream of an animal before slaughter is circulated throughout the animal.

Enzyme preparations are available for home use. The meat surface is repeatedly pierced with a fork and sprinkled with the enzyme mixture. The enzymes remain inactive until the meat is heated during cooking and then are inactivated when the meat temperature reaches about 185° F (85° C). The tenderizing compounds usually contain **papain,** a protein-digesting enzyme, obtained from the papaya plant, or bromelin from pineapple.

Meat can also be tenderized by grinding or cubing, processes that break up connective tissue. The method of cooking also greatly influences meat tenderness. Appropriate cooking methods can tenderize meat, while improper methods can even toughen tender meat.

INSPECTION/GRADING

The Federal Meat Inspection Act mandates inspection of animals for possible disease immediately before slaughter and after slaughter. Animals are inspected by qualified inspectors under the authority of the Food Safety and Quality Service of the United States Department of Agriculture. Meat carcasses that pass this examination bear the official stamp shown in Figure 16–1.

All ingredients used in processing and all procedures are continually monitored to ensure wholesomeness. Inspection is done under prescribed standards of sanitation. All meat products must also be labeled according to established regulations. Inspected products display the official inspection stamp shown in Figure 16–2. The federal inspection stamp indicates that the meat was safe for human consumption at the time of inspection. It is imprinted on each primal (wholesale) cut of the animal with an edible vegetable dye. This stamp does not indicate meat grade or quality.

Figure 16-1
Example of official inspection stamp on meat carcasses. (Courtesy U.S. Department of Agriculture.)

Figure 16-2
Example of official inspection stamp on primal cuts of meat. (Courtesy of U.S. Department of Agriculture.)

Grading

Inspected meat may be graded according to federal standards for quality and yield. Quality grades are based on palatability factors such as marbling, color and texture of the lean, and maturity of the animal. Yield grades are based on amounts of expected usable or salable meat and are used along with quality grades for beef or lamb. Yield grades are identified by numbers 1 through 5, with number 1 indicating the highest yield. Table 16-1 lists the meat quality and yield grades. The grades for pork are more concerned with yield than with quality, since much of the pork is processed before it reaches the retail market.

Meat grading is a voluntary service provided by the United States Department of Agriculture and performed by trained personnel according to established criteria. The meat may be classified by USDA grades or according to the meat processor's own grading system identified by brand names. This grading system enables consumers to select meats of desired quality. Figure 16-3 shows USDA grade marks for meat.

IDENTIFICATION

The size of the cut and the color of the lean, bone, and fat, as well as the distribution of fat, are clues to the animal source of the meat cut. The size of the cut is proportional to the size of the animal. The largest cuts of meat come from beef; veal cuts are next in size, followed by pork, with lamb cuts the smallest.

Beef comes from mature cattle, veal from young cattle, lamb from young sheep, and pork from relatively young pigs. Bones of young animals are reddish, porous, and relatively soft and often contain some cartilage, while those of mature animals are grayish in color and hard. The color of lean in beef is cherry red, veal a clear pink, pork a pale pink and lamb a dark red. The fat of beef is white to yellowish in color. Veal has very little fat, but the fat that is present is rather soft

Table 16-1 USDA Meat Quality and Yield Grades

Beef	Veal	Lamb and Yearling	Pork	Yield Grades	Percent Yield Carcass Weight
Prime	Prime	Prime	US no. 1	1	82.0
Choice	Choice	Choice	US no. 2	2	77.4
Good	Good	Good	US no. 3	3	72.8
Standard	Standard	Utility	US no. 4	4	68.2
Commercial	Utility	Cull	US utility	5	63.6
Utility	Cull				
Cutter					
Canner					

Figure 16-3   Examples of USDA shield-shaped grade marks for meat. (Courtesy U.S. Department of Agriculture.)

and pinkish in color. The fat of lamb is creamy white and hard in texture. Pork contains a generous amount of soft fat, white to pinkish white in color.

A knowledge of the retail cuts and their location on the carcass is very useful in meat selection and preparation. Carcasses are first cut through the backbone lengthwise into sides or halves to facilitate handling. Each side of beef is cut between the twelfth and thirteenth ribs into the fore and hind quarters. Each quarter is divided into primal (wholesale) cuts, and each primal cut is subdivided by the retail dealer into retail cuts for consumer selection.

Veal, pork, and lamb are smaller animals and can be handled easily by the dealer; therefore they are cut into somewhat different wholesale cuts than beef. The primal and retail cuts are shown in Figures 16–4 through 16–7.

The National Live Stock and Meat Board has developed a list of standard names for primal and retail cuts to be used in labeling fresh cuts of beef, veal, pork, and lamb currently offered in markets. The uniform identity label lists the type of meat, the primal cut, and the standard retail name and eliminates the confusion created with the use of various names for the same cut. Figure 16–8 shows a typical example of a uniform identity label.

Animals from which we get red meat have quite similar bone shapes and muscle structures. Cuts of meat can be identified easily by the bones and large muscles they contain. The shape of the bone identifies the location of a retail cut on the carcass and thus serves to classify cuts as tender or less tender. For example, the rib and T-bone identify tender cuts of meat in all four types of animals. The basic bone shapes useful in identifying retail cuts are shown in Figure 16- 9.

SELECTION

A knowledge of meat selection is particularly useful because the meats commonly used and purchased are among the most expensive items in the diet. It is necessary to consider the quality of meat purchased as well as the size and kind of cut. Quality meats can be consistently selected when USDA grades are indicated and there is a uniform identity label. A knowledge of primal cuts, their location on the carcass, and the basic bone structures aid in determining the degree of tenderness

RETAIL CUTS OF BEEF

WHERE THEY COME FROM AND HOW TO COOK THEM

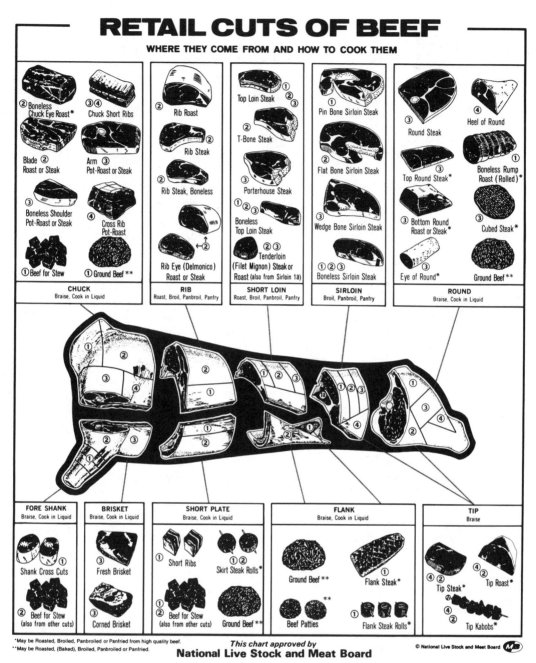

CHUCK
Braise, Cook in Liquid

② Boneless Chuck Eye Roast*
③④ Chuck Short Ribs
Blade ② Roast or Steak
Arm ③ Pot-Roast or Steak
③ Boneless Shoulder Pot-Roast or Steak
④ Cross Rib Pot-Roast
① Beef for Stew
① Ground Beef**

RIB
Roast, Broil, Panbroil, Panfry

② Rib Roast
② Rib Steak
② Rib Steak, Boneless
② Rib Eye (Delmonico) Roast or Steak

SHORT LOIN
Roast, Broil, Panbroil, Panfry

① Top Loin Steak
②③
② T-Bone Steak
③ Porterhouse Steak
①②③ Boneless Top Loin Steak
②③ Tenderloin (Filet Mignon) Steak or Roast (also from Sirloin 1a)

SIRLOIN
Broil, Panbroil, Panfry

① Pin Bone Sirloin Steak
② Flat Bone Sirloin Steak
③ Wedge Bone Sirloin Steak
①②③ Boneless Sirloin Steak

ROUND
Braise, Cook in Liquid

③ Round Steak
④ Heel of Round
③ Top Round Steak*
① Boneless Rump Roast (Rolled)*
③ Bottom Round Roast or Steak*
③ Cubed Steak*
③ Eye of Round*
① Ground Beef**

FORE SHANK
Braise, Cook in Liquid

① Shank Cross Cuts
② Beef for Stew (also from other cuts)

BRISKET
Braise, Cook in Liquid

③ Fresh Brisket
Corned Brisket

SHORT PLATE
Braise, Cook in Liquid

① Short Ribs
①② Skirt Steak Rolls*
①② Beef for Stew (also from other cuts)
② Ground Beef**

FLANK
Braise, Cook in Liquid

Ground Beef**
① Flank Steak*
** Beef Patties
① Flank Steak Rolls*

TIP
Braise

④② Tip Steak*
④② Tip Roast*
④② Tip Kabobs*

*May be Roasted, Broiled, Panbroiled or Panfried from high quality beef.
**May be Roasted, (Baked), Broiled, Panbroiled or Panfried.

This chart approved by
National Live Stock and Meat Board

© National Live Stock and Meat Board

Figure 16-4 Primal and retail beef cuts. (Courtesy of National Live Stock and Meat Board.)

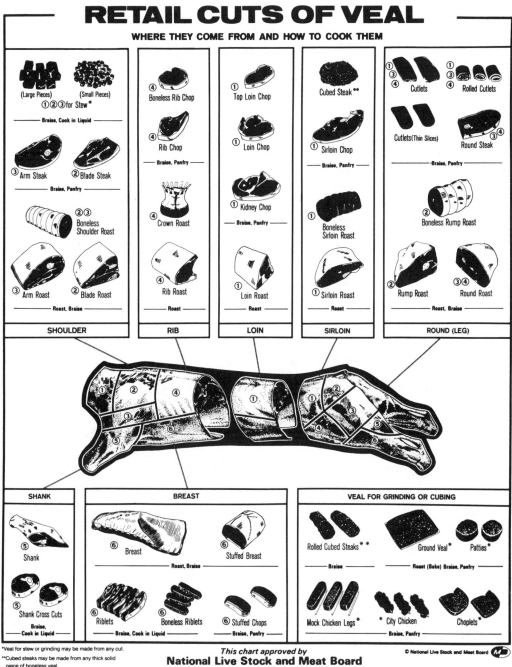

RETAIL CUTS OF VEAL

WHERE THEY COME FROM AND HOW TO COOK THEM

SHOULDER

(Large Pieces)　(Small Pieces)
①②③ for Stew*
— Braise, Cook in Liquid —

③ Arm Steak　② Blade Steak
— Braise, Panfry —

②③ Boneless Shoulder Roast

③ Arm Roast　② Blade Roast
— Roast, Braise —

RIB

④ Boneless Rib Chop

④ Rib Chop
— Braise, Panfry —

④ Crown Roast

④ Rib Roast
— Roast —

LOIN

① Top Loin Chop

① Loin Chop
— Braise, Panfry —

① Kidney Chop
— Braise, Panfry —

① Loin Roast
— Roast —

SIRLOIN

Cubed Steak**

① Sirloin Chop
— Braise, Panfry —

① Boneless Sirloin Roast

① Sirloin Roast
— Roast —

ROUND (LEG)

③④ Cutlets　③④ Rolled Cutlets

Cutlets (Thin Slices)　③④ Round Steak
— Braise, Panfry —

② Boneless Rump Roast

② Rump Roast　③④ Round Roast
— Roast, Braise —

SHANK

⑤ Shank

⑤ Shank Cross Cuts
Braise, Cook in Liquid —

BREAST

⑥ Breast　⑥ Stuffed Breast
— Roast, Braise —

⑥ Riblets　⑥ Boneless Riblets　⑥ Stuffed Chops
— Braise, Cook in Liquid —　— Braise, Panfry —

VEAL FOR GRINDING OR CUBING

Rolled Cubed Steaks**　Ground Veal　Patties*
— Braise —　— Roast (Bake) Braise, Panfry —

Mock Chicken Legs*　* City Chicken　Choplets*
— Braise, Panfry —

*Veal for stew or grinding may be made from any cut.
**Cubed steaks may be made from any thick solid piece of boneless veal.

This chart approved by
National Live Stock and Meat Board

© National Live Stock and Meat Board

Figure 16-5 Primal and retail veal cuts. (Courtesy of National Live Stock and Meat Board.)

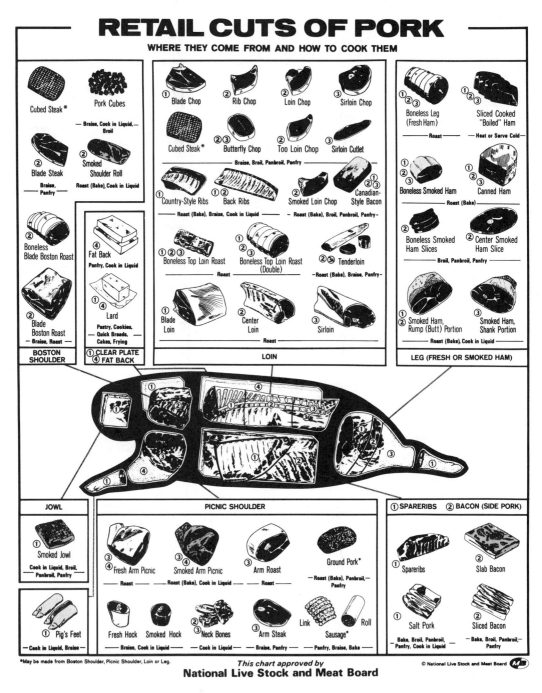

Figure 16-6 Primal and retail pork cuts. (Courtesy of National Live Stock and Meat Board.)

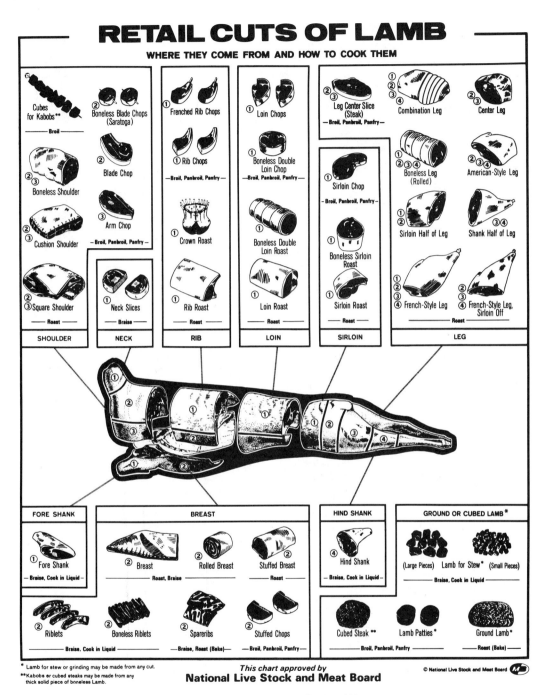

Figure 16-7   Primal and retail lamb cuts. (Courtesy of National Live Stock and Meat Board.)

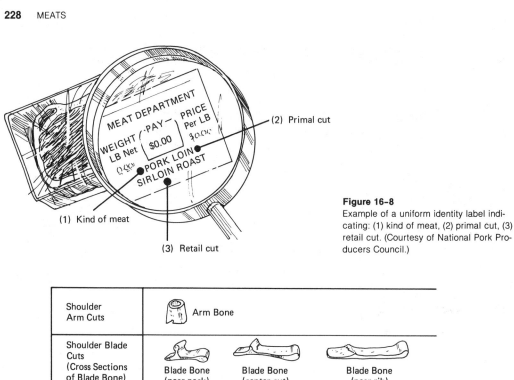

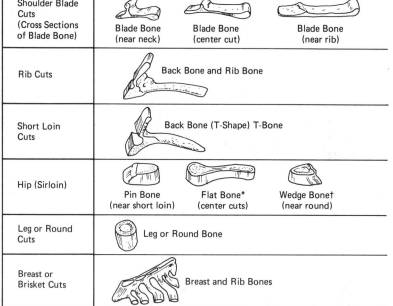

(2) Primal cut

(1) Kind of meat

(3) Retail cut

Figure 16-8
Example of a uniform identity label indicating: (1) kind of meat, (2) primal cut, (3) retail cut. (Courtesy of National Pork Producers Council.)

Shoulder Arm Cuts	Arm Bone
Shoulder Blade Cuts (Cross Sections of Blade Bone)	Blade Bone (near neck) Blade Bone (center cut) Blade Bone (near rib)
Rib Cuts	Back Bone and Rib Bone
Short Loin Cuts	Back Bone (T-Shape) T-Bone
Hip (Sirloin)	Pin Bone (near short loin) Flat Bone* (center cuts) Wedge Bone† (near round)
Leg or Round Cuts	Leg or Round Bone
Breast or Brisket Cuts	Breast and Rib Bones

*Formerly part of "double bone" but today the back bone is usually removed leaving only the "flat bone" (sometimes called "pin bone") in the sirloin steak.

†On one side of sirloin steak, this bone may be wedge shaped while on the other side the same bone may be round.

Figure 16-9 Basic bone shapes assist in meat cut identification. (Courtesy of National Live Stock and Meat Board.)

and juiciness of the retail cut. Because there is some variation in retail cuts, it is wise to compare the quality of similar cuts displayed, and select the cut with the least amount of trimmable fat, bone, and connective tissue.

The true cost of meat may not be revealed by the cost per pound. The best buy in meat depends upon the cost per serving. The determination of the cost per serving of edible meat takes into account the factor of waste and permits an accurate comparison of the cost of various meat cuts. The supply-and-demand factor is reflected in the cost per pound of meat. Cuts of meat in great demand are more expensive than less popular cuts. Money often can be saved by purchasing the less popular, less tender cuts or cuts of lower grades. Lower-grade cuts tend to contain less fat, are as nutritious, and may be more flavorful, but are less tender than comparable cuts from higher-grade carcasses.

Good meat selection is also made in terms of intended use, available equipment required for its preparation, and time. Cuts should be selected that are appropriate for the intended cooking technique. Cuts from portions of the animal considered as tender, such as the rib, from high-grade carcasses may be less tender from lower-grade carcasses. Conversely, less tender cuts, such as beef round or rump, from lower-grade carcasses, may be tender from a USDA prime carcass.

When meat is selected, the quantity needed must be considered. The amount to buy is determined by the number of servings needed and the number of servings the cut or pound will provide, the available storage space, and whether the meat is to take care of more than one meal. The proportion of bone and fat to lean affect the number of servings obtained from a pound of meat. Table 16–2 serves as a general guide for determining the amount of meat to allow for each serving. The purchase of meat is simplified when the shopping list includes specific cuts, grades, and quantities of meat to purchase.

HOME STORAGE

Cold temperatures prevent the growth of microorganisms and maintain the safety of meat during holding. Meat may be kept in home refrigerators at 35 to 40° F (−2 to 4° C) for a short period. See Table 16–3.

Fresh Meat

Fresh meat that will be used within the time interval shown in Table 16–3 should be stored in the coldest part of the refrigerator or in the special compartment designed for meat storage.

Retail markets prepackage many fresh meats for self-service. These meats are usually wrapped with oxygen-permeable films in order to retain the bright red color. Prepackaged meat may be placed in the refrigerator in the original wrapper if it will be used in one or two days. Fresh meat that was not prepackaged should

Table 16-2   Meat Buying Guide

Type of Meat	Servings per Pound
Fresh or Frozen	
Beef	
Rib roast boneless	2–2½
Round, rump	3–3½
Chuck	3
T-bone, porterhouse steaks	2–2½
Short ribs	2
Flank, round steaks	3–3½
Liver	3½–4
Cubed steak	3½–4
Ground beef	3½–4
Veal	
Chuck	3–3½
Leg	3¾
Loin chops	2½
Cutlet	3½–4
Liver	3½–4
Pork	
Shoulder roast	2–2¾
Cooked ham	3¾
Spareribs	1¾–2
Loin chops	2½
Lamb	
Leg, shoulder	3
Loin chops	2–2½
Canned	
Corn beef	5
Ham	3½

Adapted from USDA, *The Yearbook of Agriculture, Shopper's Guide*
(Washington, D.C.: Government Printing Office, 1974).

be removed from the market wrapping and loosely rewrapped in waxed paper, plastic wrap, or foil for refrigerator storage.

Grinding greatly increases the surface area of meat that may be contaminated by microorganisms. Ground meat should be cooked within twenty-four hours or packaged tightly in moisture-vapor-proof wrap and frozen. Ground meat may be shaped into patties or divided into desired portions before it is wrapped for frozen storage. Fresh variety meats are also highly perishable and should be cooked within twenty-four hours or frozen.

Frozen Meat

Meats purchased already frozen may be stored in the original wrap in home freezers. They should be stored at 0° F (−18° C) or lower immediately after purchase.

Table 16-3 Suggested Storage Time to Retain Meat Quality

Kind of Meat	Refrigerator 40° F (5° C) Days	Freezer 0° F (−17° C) Months
Fresh meat:		
Roasts		
Beef	3–5	6–12
Veal	3–5	4–8
Pork	3–5	4–8
Lamb	3–5	6–9
Steaks, chops		
Beef	3–5	6–12
Pork	3–5	3–4
Lamb	3–5	6–9
Ground meat	1–2	3–4
Stew meat	1–2	3–4
Sausage (pork)	1–2	1–2
Cooked meat:		
Meat, meat dishes	3–4	2–3
Meat broth, gravy	1–2	2–3
Processed meat:		
Bacon	7	1
Ham		
whole	7	1–2
half	3–5	1–2
slice	3	1–2
Frankfurters	7	½–1
Luncheon meats (opened vacuum-sealed package)	3–5	0
Sausage, smoked	7	0
Sausage (dry, semidry)	14–21	0

From USDA, *Safe Handling Tips for Meat and Poultry,* Food Safety and Inspection Service (Washington, D.C.: Government Printing Office, July 1981).

Cured Meat

Cured meat is stored in its original wrapper in the refrigerator. Canned hams should be stored in the unopened can in the refrigerator unless information on the can calls for different storage conditions. When cured meats are frozen, they should not be stored longer than sixty days.

Cooked Meat

Cooked meat should be tightly covered or wrapped and stored as soon as possible in the coldest part of the refrigerator. Large pieces of cooked meat should be frozen whole, rather than cut up, to avoid drying.

MEAT COOKERY

Heat-Induced Changes

The aroma, flavor, and appearance of cooked meats are especially appealing to most people. A number of changes occur when meats are cooked. The changes in flavor are due to melting and decomposition of the fat, coagulation and breakdown of proteins, loss of volatile components, and caramelization of any carbohydrate present. The flavor intensifies as the meat surface browns. The formation of flavor components takes place relatively rapidly in dry-media methods since the temperatures on the surface of the meat are usually high compared with moist-media methods. Some loss of aromatic, volatile substances occurs as meat is cooked. Volatile components are an important factor in identifying flavor since they make up part of the flavor profile.

The characteristic red color of raw meat is also changed as a result of cooking. Partial breakdown of protein, fat, pigments, and other components leads to the browning of the cooked meat surface.

Muscle-fiber proteins coagulate during heating, decreasing their water-holding capacity. The loss of water-holding capacity increases progressively as the temperature and cooking time increase.

Collagen, a type of connective tissue, hydrolyzes gradually to gelatin and thus softens. Because connective tissue tends to soften or tenderize, while my-ofibrils (protein) tend to harden or toughen during cooking, it is concluded that success in cooking tender meats with little collagen is dependent on the use of low-to-medium temperatures for as short a time as possible. Meats thus prepared remain juicy, are of maximum tenderness, show minimal weight loss or shrinkage, and are uniformly cooked throughout the cut. In contrast, less tender cuts of meat with abundant collagen will be more tender when cooked for a sufficiently long period of time to permit conversion of collagen to gelatin.

Considerations

Meat requires little preparation before cooking. The outer surfaces of the meat may be wiped with a clean paper towel and any bone splinters present removed. Cut meat should not be washed or soaked in water since water-soluble nutrients and extractives would leach out. Meat should be salted after it is cooked because adding salt before cooking promotes drip loss and retards browning. Salt added before cooking penetrates the meat only about one-fourth to one-half inch.

All raw meat may be somewhat contaminated with various microorganisms, and some raw meat may contain parasites. Cooking destroys microorganisms and parasites and makes the meat safe to eat. It is not necessary to trim the government stamp present, since it is applied with an edible dye. Cookery methods should conserve nutrients and flavor and contribute to the development of meat flavor.

Variations in the actual cooking time required are due to differences in oven temperature, the amount of bone, amount of fat, and degree of aging. Cooking should be terminated as soon as desired doneness is reached. Timetables are valuable guides for estimating how much time will be required. When cooking tender cuts of meat, a meat thermometer is the most accurate test for doneness. All less tender cuts of meat are cooked well done; therefore a meat thermometer is not necessary.

Beef and lamb are the only meats cooked to varying degrees of doneness. Veal and pork should be cooked well done. It is especially important that fresh pork be well done to destroy trichinella spiralis, a parasite that causes trichinosis. Most hams are heated during processing to protect against trichinosis and are identified as precooked on the label. Table 16-4 shows the recommended internal temperatures registered in the center of various meats for the stages of doneness ranging from rare to well done.

Dry-Media/Heat Methods

Roasting, broiling, and **pan broiling** are dry-media methods for cooking tender cuts of meat. These methods do not require added liquid, and the utensil is not covered. Frying is also classed as a dry-heat method because the meat is not surrounded by a moist environment. Fat is a better conductor of heat than dry air; thus the heat is applied more rapidly during frying than roasting.

Roasting. Large, tender cuts of beef, veal, lamb, pork, and ham are suitable for roasting. A temperature of 300° F (150° C) is used for large roasts and 325° F (160° C) for small roasts. These low oven temperatures permit even penetration of heat, avoid toughening, permit retention of juices, and reduce oven spatter. Beef may be roasted to suit individual preferences from rare, medium, to well done; lamb may be medium or well done; and veal and pork should be well done. See Table 16-5.

Table 16-4 Internal Temperature of Cooked Tender Meat Cuts

	Internal Temperatures		
Type	Rare	Medium	Well Done
Beef	140° F (60° C)	160° F (71° C)	170° F (77° C)
Lamb		175° F (79° C)	180° F (82° C)
Fresh Pork			170° F (77° C)
Veal			170° F (77° C)

Table 16-5   Meat Roasting Guide

Kind of Meat	Weight (pounds)	Oven Temperature °F	°C	Cook Minutes per lb	Internal Temperature °F	°C
Beef						
Standing rib	6–8	300–325	150–160	23–25	140	60 (rare)
				27–30	160	71 (medium)
				32–35	170	77 (well)
Rolled rib	5–7	300–325	150–160	30–32	140	60 (rare)
				35–38	160	71 (medium)
				45–48	170	77 (well)
Rolled rump	4–6	300–325	150–160	25–30	150–170	66–77
Sirloin tip	3–4	300–325	150–160	35–40	150–170	66–77
Beef loaf		325	160	30–45	160–170	71–77
Veal						
Leg	5–8	300–325	150–160	25–35	170	77
Loin	4–6	300–325	150–160	30–35	170	77
Rib (rack)	3–5	300–325	150–160	35–40	170	77
Shoulder	4–6	300–325	150–160	40–45	170	77
Pork, fresh						
Loin	5–8	325–350	160–175	30–45	170	77
Shoulder	5–8	325–350	160–175	30–45	170	77
Leg (fresh ham)	10–14	325–350	160–175	25–30	170	77
half (bone in)	5–7	325–350	160–175	40–45	170	77
Pork, smoked						
Ham (uncooked)	10–14	300–325	150–160	18–20	160	71
Ham half (uncooked)	5–7	300–325	150–160	22–25	160	71
Ham (cooked)	10–14	325	160	15	130	54
Ham half (cooked)	5–7	325	160	18–24	130	54
Lamb						
Leg	5–8	300–325	150–160	30–35	175–180	79–82
Shoulder	4–6	300–325	150–160	30–35	175–180	79–82

Adapted from National Live Stock and Meat Board, "Lessons on Meat."

The meat thermometer should be inserted in the center of the largest muscle so that it does not touch bone or fat. Then the roast is placed fat side up on a rack in a shallow pan and placed in the center of the oven. The rack may be omitted when the cut includes bone on which the meat may rest out of drippings,

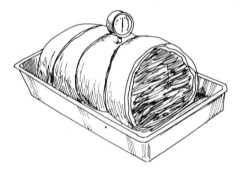

such as a standing rib roast. The meat is roasted until the desired internal temperature is reached. Residual heat usually causes the internal temperature to rise a few degrees after the roast has been removed from the oven. Roasts usually carve more easily when allowed to rest about ten minutes after removal from the oven.

Broiling.   Broiling is cooking with direct, radiant heat. Tender cuts about one-inch thick of beef and lamb, and ground beef, ham, and bacon are suitable for broiling. The fat surrounding meats to be broiled is cut to the lean at about one-inch intervals to prevent curling of the meat. Meats may be marinated in specially prepared dressings of oil, acid, and seasonings prior to broiling.

A thermometer may be inserted from the side into the thickest muscle to determine the internal temperature of broiled meat. The meat to be broiled is placed directly on the rack of the broiler pan. Aluminum foil should not be placed under the meat because the fat that collects may ignite. The broiler pan with the meat is placed on the oven rack so that the surface of the meat is about two to three inches from the source of heat for one-inch-thick meats or about three to five inches for thicker cuts. The distance the meat is placed from the source of heat regulates the speed of cooking during broiling. A meat broiling guide is presented in Table 16–6.

Broiled meats are about half done when the upper surface browns. They are turned with tongs and the second side browned and cooking completed. Meats may be sprinkled with seasoning before serving. Broiled meats are served immediately.

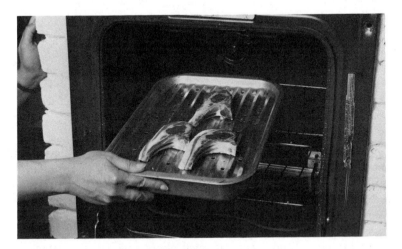

(Laimute E. Druskis)

Pan Broiling.   Pan broiling transfers heat from the surface unit to the skillet and by conduction to the meat. All tender cuts of meat suitable for broiling may also be pan broiled. As for broiling, the fat is scored at one-inch intervals to

Table 16-6 Meat Broiling Guide

Kind of Meat	Weight (pounds)	Minutes Cooking Time		
		Rare	Medium	Well done
Beef				
Club steak				
1 in	1–1½	15–17	18–20	22–25
1½ in	1½–2	25–27	30–33	35–40
Porterhouse steak				
1 in	1½–2	20–22	23–25	26–30
1½ in	2–3	30–32	35–38	40–44
Sirloin steak				
1 in	1½–3	20–22	23–25	27–30
1½ in	2–4	30–32	33–35	37–40
Ground beef patties				
1 in thick × 3 in	¼	13–15	18–20	22–25
Lamb				
Loin chops				
1 in	³⁄₁₆		10–15	16–19
1½ in	¼		15–18	19–22
Rib chops				
1 in	⅛		10–14	16–18
1½ in	¼		15–18	20–22
Shoulder chops				
1 in	¼–½		12–15	16–20
1½ in	½–¾		18–20	22–24
Ground lamb patties				
1 in thick × 3 in	¼		18–20	22–24
Pork, smoked				
Ham slice				
½ in	¾			10–12
1 in	1–2			16–20
Canadian-style bacon				
¼ in thick slices				6–8
Bacon				4–5

Adapted from National Live Stock and Meat Board, "Lessons on Meat."

prevent curling. The meat is placed in an ungreased heavy skillet without added fat or water and is not covered. The meat is heated slowly, and the fat drained as it accumulates. When the meat is browned, it is turned with tongs to avoid loss of juices from piercing. The browned meat may be salted, if desired. Pan-broiled meat is served immediately.

Pan Frying. Tender cuts of meat about one-half inch thick, including fresh pork and ham, may be pan fried. The fat around the meat should be scored at one-inch intervals to avoid curling. A small amount of fat is added to the skillet to prevent sticking of the meat. The meat is browned on both sides, and the fat is permitted to accumulate.

Meats are fried at a moderate temperature to avoid overbrowning before the interior is cooked to the desired doneness. High temperatures decompose the fat, cause it to smoke, contribute to an unpleasant flavor, toughen the meat, and yield a dry meat. Pan-fried meats are served immediately.

Moist-Media/Heat Methods

All less tender meats are cooked well done with the moist-media or moist-heat methods of braising or cooking in water. These methods require a covered utensil, which retains the steam and the liquid released from the meat or any water added. They involve a long, slow cooking period with moisture to promote the conversion of collagen to gelatin and thus facilitate the tenderization of the meat. These methods also promote the development of the meat flavors.

When a large piece of meat is cooked by braising, the process is often referred to as pot roasting. When very small pieces of meat are cooked in sufficient water to cover them, the process is called **stewing**. Cooking in water or simmering usually refers to cooking large pieces of meat in water to cover.

Braising. Convection currents from the moist atmosphere in the pan and conduction from the pan surface provide the heat for braising. Braising may be used for large or small cuts of less tender meats. Cuts from veal or pork, although tender, are often braised. Connective tissues in veal are softened by braising and pork is easily cooked to the recommended well-done stage. See Table 16–7.

(Laimute E. Druskis)

Table 16-7 Meat Braising Guide

Kind of Meat	Thickness or Weight (inches or pounds)	Cooking Time (hours)
Beef		
Fricassee	2-in cubes	1½–2½
Pot roast	3–5 lbs	3–4
Round steak	¾ in	1–1½
Short ribs	pieces 2 × 2 × 4 in	1½–2½
Swiss steak	1½ × 2½ in	2–3
Pork		
Chops	¾–1½ in	¾–1
Shoulder steaks	¾ in	¾–1
Spareribs	2–3 lb	1½
Tenderloin		
Whole	¾–1 lb	¾–1
Fillets	½ in	½
Lamb		
Breast	2–3 lb	1½–2
Neck slices	¾ in	1
Shanks	¾–1 lb	1–1½
Shoulder chops	¾–1 in	¾–1
Veal		
Breast	3–4 lb	1½–2½
Chops	½–¾ in	¾–1
Steak or cutlet	½–¾ in	¾–1
Shoulder cubes	1–2 in	¾–1

Adapted from National Live Stock and Meat Board, "Lessons on Meat."

Meat to be braised is first browned in a heavy pan on a surface unit for flavor and color. When the meat is floured or is lean, a small amount of fat is placed in the pan to avoid sticking. The meat is browned slowly and turned to brown all sides. A small amount of water or liquid is added to the browned meat, the utensil tightly covered, and then cooked at a low temperature on a surface unit or in the oven until tender.

The long period of cooking (about one and a half to three hours) permits collagen to be converted to gelatin without toughening the protein. Large cuts require more cooking time than small cuts. Large cuts of meat may be braised on a rack in the covered pan.

Cooking in Water. Heat is conducted from the surface of the pan and distributed by convection currents in the moist atmosphere to meat cooked in water. Large or small pieces of less tender meats and some variety meats may be cooked in water. Meats may be browned before water is added. A guide for cooking meat in liquid is presented in Table 16–8.

(Laimute E. Druskis)

Stewing is another term for cooking in water and is often applied when small pieces of meat are cooked. The meat is usually browned, and then covered with water and simmered in a covered utensil. Vegetables may be added when the meat is fork tender. **Fricassee** is yet another term used for small pieces of meat, usually fowl or veal, cooked by braising.

Table 16-8   Guide to Cooking Meat In Liquid

Cut	Weight (pounds)	Cooking Time (Hours)
Beef		
Fresh or corned beef	(4–6)	3½–4½
Cross-cut shanks	(1–2)	2½–3
Beef stew		2½–3½
Pork, fresh		
Spareribs		2–2½
Hocks		2½–3
Pork, smoked		
Ham (old style and		
country cured)		
Large	(12–16)	4½–5
Small	(10–12)	4½–5
Half	(5–6)	3–4
Ham (tenderized)		
Shank or butt half	(5–8)	1¾–3½
Picnic shoulder	(5–8)	3¼–4
Lamb		
Lamb for stew		1½–2
Veal		
Veal for stew		2–3

Adapted from National Live Stock and Meat Board, "Lessons on Meat."

Meats cooked in water may be served hot or cold, or deboned for use in salads and other combination dishes. The resulting meat-flavored broth may be used as soup stock or as the liquid in sauces or gravies for combination or thickened food products.

Cooking in Foil.   Foil-wrapped meat is cooked by moist heat since moisture is retained at the meat surface. Foil tends to increase weight loss and cooking time, and may give meat a steamed flavor.

Microwaving

The moving molecules in microwaved meats produce heat. The heat is conducted to the center of the meat when the area is greater than can be penetrated by microwaves. Because cooking time is shorter in the microwave oven, tenderization of less tender meats does not usually occur. Cooking losses may be greater than with conventional methods. The flavor of microwaved meat is generally very acceptable, but the browned appearance does not develop. Microwave reheating of meats gives a more meaty flavor than conventional reheating. Chapter 24 discusses details of microwave cookery.

Variety Meats

The organs of meat animals are known as variety meats and include liver, kidney, heart, tongue, brains, sweetbreads (thymus gland of veal, lamb, young beef), and tripe (stomach inner lining of beef). Liver is the most commonly used variety meat. Many variety meats have a distinctive flavor, and all are rich sources of nutrients, and some, for instance, sweetbreads, are considered a delicacy.

Some variety meats are tender and others are less tender. The liver and sweetbreads from young animals are tender, while the tongue and heart of all animals are less tender. The degree of tenderness determines the appropriate cookery methods for variety meats. Table 16–9 serves as a guide for cooking variety meats.

Frozen Meats

Frozen meats, muscle or variety, are cooked in the same manner as those not frozen. Most frozen meats, especially large cuts, are usually thawed before cooking. Thawing may be done in the refrigerator in the original wrapper, in a microwave with a defrost cycle, in warm water when the meat is in a watertight package, or during cooking.

Refrigerator thawing requires the removal of meat from the freezer to the refrigerator the day before it is to be cooked. A longer thawing period is required

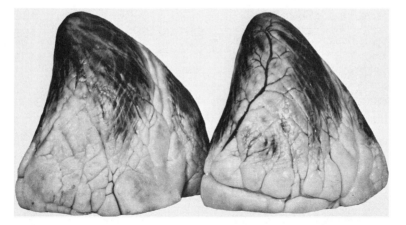

Hearts (Courtesy National Livestock and Meat Board)

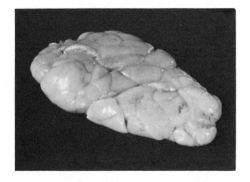

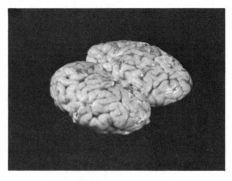

Sweetbreads (Courtesy National Livestock and Meat Board)

Brains (Courtesy National Livestock and Meat Board)

for extremely large cuts. Defrosting at room temperature is not recommended because of the accelerated growth of microorganisms.

Frozen meat requires a longer cooking time than thawed meat. Large pieces of frozen meat require about one to one and a half times as long to cook as thawed meat.

Soup Stock

Less tender meats and bones are used to make soup stock. Beef is the most commonly used meat for soup stock. Veal has little flavor, and mutton and lamb have too distinctive a flavor. Meat is usually cut into small pieces and bones cracked to increase the surface exposed to water and thus extract maximum meat flavor. Stock is prepared by simmering meat and bones for three hours or longer.

Table 16-9   Variety Meats Cooking Guide

Kind	Cook in Liquid	Braise	Broil
Liver			
Beef			
Piece (3–4 lbs)		2–2½ hours	
Sliced		20–25 minutes	
Veal (Calf)			
Sliced			8–10 minutes
Pork			
Whole	1½–2 hours		
Sliced		20–25 minutes	
Lamb			
Sliced			8–10 minutes
Kidney			
Beef	1–1½ hours		
Veal (Calf)	¾–1 hour		10–12 mintues
Pork	¾–1 hour		10–12 minutes
Lamb	¾–1 hour		10–12 minutes
Heart			
Beef			
Whole	3–4 hours	3–4 hours	
Sliced		1½–2 hours	
Veal (Calf)			
Whole	2½–3 hours	2½–3 hours	
Pork	2½–3 hours	2½–3 hours	
Lamb	2½–3 hours	2½–3 hours	
Tongue			
Beef	3–4 hours		
Veal (Calf)	2–3 hours		
Tripe			
Beef	1–1½ hours		
Precooked			10–15 minutes
Sweetbreads	15–20 minutes	20–25 minutes	
Precooked			10–15 minutes
Brains	15–20 minutes	20–25 minutes	
Precooked			10–15 minutes

Adapted from National Live Stock and Meat Board, "Lessons on Meat."

The scum is removed as it forms. Vegetables and seasonings are added during the last hour to avoid overcooking of vegetables. The broth may be strained and chilled to harden the fat for easy removal. Meat may be browned to develop flavor and color before it is simmered in water. The stock is then known as brown stock to distinguish it from white stock made without browning the meat.

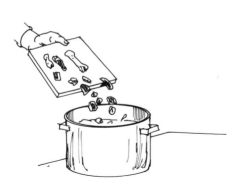

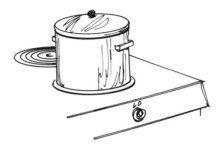

Gravy

Low-temperature meat cookery produces a minimum of drippings. However, the drippings that do accumulate from meats cooked by dry heat and the cooking liquors from braised or stewed meats may be used to make gravy. Oven roasts are generally served au jus (with the unthickened drippings). See chapter 7, "Starch and Flour," for gravy-making procedures.

SUMMARY

Meats supply high-quality protein with important quantities of iron, phosphorous, copper, and B vitamins. Less tender and lower grades of meat are equally as nutritious as the tender cuts and higher grades.

All meat is inspected under federal law. The grading of inspected meat is voluntary and may be identified by USDA grades. Meats are highly perishable and require careful maintenance of proper storage conditions.

Meats with relatively little connective tissue and good marbling are identified as tender and may be cooked by the dry-media/heat methods—roasting, broiling, pan broiling, and pan frying. The less tender cuts are cooked by moist-media/heat methods—braising and cooking in liquid. Moist-heat and long, low-temperature cooking tenderize less tender cuts by promoting the conversion of collagen to gelatin.

SELF-STUDY GUIDE

1. Identify five components of meat.
2. Describe the structure of meat.
3. Discuss three factors that influence meat color. What changes occur in the color of meat during cooking?
4. Discuss the influence of cooking on elastin and collagen.
5. Discuss four types of nutrients in meat.
6. Discuss three changes that occur in meat after slaughter.
7. Discuss four factors that influence meat tenderness.
8. What are the advantages of meat inspection and grading to the consumer? What meats are inspected and graded?
9. Identify the grades used for beef, veal, pork, and lamb.
10. Discuss storage of fresh, frozen, cured meats, cooked meats.
11. Identify the color of the lean and fat of beef, veal, pork, and lamb.
12. Which bone shapes in meat identify the tender and less tender cuts of meats? Discuss the cooking of tender and less tender cuts of meat.
13. Discuss four factors that are considered when meat is purchased.
14. Discuss three changes that take place in meat during cooking.
15. How are frozen meats cooked?

SELECTED REFERENCES

ADAMS, C. *Nutritive value of American foods in common units.* Agriculture Handbook no. 456. Agricultural Research Service. Washington, D.C.: Government Printing Office, 1980.

BERRY, B. W., et al. Cooking and chemical properties of raw and precooked flaked and ground beef patties cooked from the frozen state. *Journal of Food Science* 46:856, 1981.

BOUTON, P. E., et al. Effect of cooking temperature and time on the shear properties of meat. *Journal of Food Science* 46:1082, 1981.

BURTON, P. E., and HARRIS, P. V. Changes in the tenderness of meat cooked at 50–60° C. *Journal of Food Science* 46:475, 1981.

CHYR, C. Y., et al. Influence of raw ingredients, nitrate levels, and cooking temperatures on the microbiological quality of braunschweiger. *Journal of Food Science* 45:1732, 1980.

CONTREROS, S. Electrical stimulation and hot boning:

Cooking losses, sensory properties, and microbial counts of ground beef. *Journal of Food Science* 46:457, 1981.

CROSS, H. R., and TENNET, I. Effect of electrical stimulation and post-mortem boning time on sensory and cookery properties of ground beef. *Journal of Food Science* 46:292, 1981.

DREW, F., et al. Cooking at variable microwave power levels effects on energy use and quality of top round beef roasts. *Journal of the American Dietetic Association* 77:455, 1980.

GRAY, J. I.; REDDY, S. I.; PRICE, J. E.; MANDAGERE, A.; and WILKENS, W. F. Inhibition of N-nitrosamines in bacon. *Food Technology* 36:39, 1982.

GRIFFIN, C. L., et al. Effects of electrical stimulation, boning time and cooking method of beef roasts. *Journal of Food Science* 46:987, 1981.

HUFFMAN, D. L.; McCAFFERTY, D. M.; DORDRAY, J. C.; and STANLEY, M. H. Restructured beef steaks from hot-boned and cold-boned carcasses. *Journal of Food Science* 49:164, 1984.

HUHTANEN, C. N., et al. Flavor and antibotulinal evaluation of sorbic acid-containing bacon. *Journal of Food Science* 46:1796, 1981.

JOHNSON, M. B., and BALDWIN, R. E. Influence of microwave reheating of selected quality factors of roast beef. *Journal of Food Science* 45:1460, 1980.

KIMTO, W. I.; PENSABENE, J. W.; and FIDDLER, W. Isolation and identification of N-nitro-sothizolidine in fried bacon. *Journal of Agricultural and Food Chemistry* 30:757, 1982.

LEE, C. M., et al. Microscopical study of the structure of meat emulsions and its relationship to thermal stability. *Journal of Food Science* 46:1789, 1981.

LEE, K., and GREGER, J. L. Bioavailability and chemistry of iron from nitrite-cured meats. *Food Technology* 37:139, 1983.

LEE, R. Y., et al. Growth and enterotoxin A production by staphytococcus aureus in precooked bacon in the intermediate moisture range. *Journal of Food Science* 46:1687, 1981.

LEE, S. H., and CASSENS, R. G. Nitrite binding site on myoglobin. *Journal of Food Science* 41:969, 1976.

LIVINGSTON, D. J., and BROWN, W. Chemistry of myoglobin and its reactions. *Food Technology* 35:244, 1981.

MARCHELLO, J. J.; MILNE, D.; and SLANGER, W. D. Selected macro and micro minerals in ground beef and longissimus muscle. *Journal of Food Science* 49:105, 1984.

McCURDY, S. M., et al. Proximate analysis of cooked chuck and round roast from two beef breed-types on two feeding regimes. *Journal of Food Science* 46:1282, 1981.

MURRAY, A. C.; DOORNENBAL, H.; and MARTIN, A. H. Relationship of mineral content and tenderness of meat from cattle differing in breed, sex, and age. *Journal of Food Science* 47:49, 1982.

MURRELL, K. D. Preslaughter control of trichinosis. *Food Technology* 37:87, 1983.

NATIONAL PORK PRODUCERS COUNCIL. *Pork facts, consumer information* Des Moines, Iowa.

RAY, F. K., et al. Effect of soy level and storage time on the quality characteristics of ground beef patties. *Journal of Food Science* 46:1662, 1981.

REE, K.; DUTSON, T.; and SMITH, G. C. Effect of changes in intermuscular and subcutaneous fat levels on cholesterol content of raw and cooked beef steaks. *Journal of Food Science* 47:1638, 1982.

SEBRELL, JR., W. H., and HAGGERTY, J. L. eds. *Food and nutrition.* Chap. 2. Life Science Library. New York: Time, Inc. 1967.

SMITH, G. C.; SAVELL, J. W.; CROSS, R. R.; and CARPENTER, Z. L. The relationship of USDA quality grade to beef flavor. *Food Technology* 37:233, 1983.

WEST, R. L. Functional characteristics of hot-boned meat. *Food Technology* 37:57, 1983.

WILSON, N. R., et al. *Meat and meat products: Facts affecting quality control.* Philadelphia: International Ideas Inc., 1981.

U.S. DEPARTMENT OF AGRICULTURE. *Safe handling tips for meat and poultry.* Food Safety and Inspection Service. Washington, D.C.: Government Printing Office, 1981.

————. *Meat and poultry inspection—a program that protects.* Food Safety and Quality Service. Washington, D.C.: USDA, 1981.

————. *Composition of foods; sausages and luncheon meats: Raw, processed, prepared.* Agriculture Handbook no. 817. Science and Education Administration. Washington, D.C.: Government Printing Office, 1980.

————. *Meat and poultry products—a consumer guide to content and labeling requirements.* Home and Garden Bulletin no. 236. Washington, D.C.: Government Printing Office, 1981.

————. *Hamburger—questions and answers.* Food Safety and Quality Service. Washington, D.C.: USDA, March 1981.

————. *How to buy meat for your freezer.* Washington, D.C.: Government Printing Office, 1980.

————. *Lamb in family meals.* Washington, D.C.: Government Printing Office, 1980.

17

POULTRY AND FISH

OBJECTIVES

When you complete this chapter you will be able to

1. List the classes of poultry and suggest appropriate methods of cooking.
2. Discuss the nutritional contribution of poultry and fish.
3. List the factors to be considered when poultry and fish are selected.
4. Store poultry and fish properly.
5. Discuss the factors to be considered when poultry and fish are cooked.

6. List the classes of fish and give examples; identify their differences.
7. List the characteristics of fresh fish.
8. Compare the structure of fish to that of meat.
9. Explain how the spread of salmonella can be controlled.
10. Discuss the appropriate techniques for cooking fish.

Various types of poultry and fish are available throughout the world. Generally the term *poultry* refers to all types of fowl served as the main portion of a meal. Specifically, poultry includes chicken, ducks, geese, pigeons, and turkey. Of these chicken and turkey are consumed most frequently.

Thousands of species of fish are available, although only about two hundred are used commercially. Some human populations depend upon fish for their major source of animal protein.

Poultry and fish are flavorful, nutritious alternates for red meat. They have the advantage of a lower fat content, and their fat contains fewer saturated fatty acids than do fats from red meats.

This chapter is concerned with the factors related to the preparation of poultry and fish, including nutritional quality, selection, storage, and basic cookery principles.

POULTRY

Nutritional Quality/Composition

The nutritional quality of poultry is similar to that of meat. Poultry is an excellent source of high-quality protein capable of replacing meat in the diet. Poultry proteins contain the amino acids essential for building and maintaining body tissues. Unlike other meats, poultry has dark (thigh and leg) and white (breast) meat. The white or light meat contains shorter and more tender fibers than the dark meat. The myoglobin pigment is present only in the dark meat.

Poultry, like lean meat, is a good source of the B vitamins—thiamin, niacin, riboflavin, B-12, and B-6. Light meat is richer in niacin, but dark meat provides somewhat more riboflavin and thiamin. Poultry is also a good source of iron and phosphorus.

The fat content varies with age, sex, and species. Young birds contain little fat, and white meat is lower in fat than dark meat. Chicken contains less fat than turkey, duck, or goose. The fat is deposited in layers under the skin, in the abdominal cavity, and in muscle tissue. All poultry fat has a lower melting point and a somewhat softer consistency than the fat of other meats. The yellow color of poultry fat is due to the carotene and xanthophyll in the feed. Poultry tissues reflect the fatty acid content of the diet.

The amount of connective tissue varies with age and is more abundant in male and old birds. Dark meat has somewhat more connective tissue than white meat. The structure and composition of poultry are similar to that of large animals.

Classes

Poultry is classed on the basis of species, age, and sex. Common classes of chicken include broiler, fryer, roaster, capon, and fowl; classes of turkey include fryer-roaster, young hen or tom, and yearling hen or tom (Table 17–1). The weight and fat content vary with age. A relatively smooth skin, pliable breastbone, and pinfeathers are signs of young poultry.

Inspection

In preparing poultry for the market, it is first scalded to facilitate removal of feathers, then eviscerated and chilled. Most of the poultry marketed in the

Table 17-1 Poultry Classification and Cooking Method

Class	Age	Weight	Cooking Method
Young Chicken:			Roast/Bake, Barbecue, Broil, Fry, Rotisserie
Rock cornish	5–7 wks	1–1½lb	
Broiler/fryer	9–12 wks	1½–3½ lb	
Roaster	3–5 mos	3½–5 lb	
Capon (unsexed)	less than 8 mos	4–7 lb	
Stag (male)	less than 10 mos	3–6 lb	
Older Chicken:			Braise, Simmer, Stew
Hen (female)	over 10 mos	3–6 lb	
Stewing hen, fowl	over 10 mos	3–6 lb	
Cock (male)	over 10 mos	3–6 lb	
Young Turkey:			Bake/Roast, Rotisserie
Fryer, roaster	less than 16 wks	5–8 lb	
Young hen (female)	5–7 mos	8–24 lb	
Young hen (female)	5–7 mos	8–24 lb	
Young tom (male)	5–7 mos	8–24 lb	
Young Duck:			Bake/Roast, Rotisserie
Duckling	3–5 mos	3–5 lb	

United States is inspected for wholesomeness by the United States Department of Agriculture. This poultry-inspection service also approves facilities and processing procedures. Qualified inspectors examine the carcass along with its viscera. Birds that pass inspection are marketed with a stamp similar to that in Figure 17–1.

All canned and frozen poultry products must be prepared under federal inspection. Government regulations require that the label list the common name of the product, the net weight, and the name and address of the packer or distributor.

Grading

Dressed and ready-to-cook poultry are graded for class (age), condition, and quality. The official USDA grades are U.S. grades A, B, and C and apply to chicken,

Figure 17-1
Poultry inspection and grade marks. (Courtesy U.S. Department of Agriculture.)

turkey, duck, goose, and guinea. U.S. grade A is the highest grade for poultry and is the only grade of poultry commonly found on the market. The grading of inspected poultry, as with meats, is optional.

Grade A poultry is meaty, has a well-developed layer of fat in the skin, and is free from cuts or bruises. Grade B poultry has less flesh and fat but is of good table quality (Figure 17-2). Quality factors considered in grading poultry include freedom from defects and pinfeathers, conformation, fat distribution, and fleshing. The inspection and grade mark may be included together on the same tag or label.

Selection

Popular poultry meats include chicken, turkey, and duck. Inspection and grade marks aid in selection. The label lists the class of poultry and serves as a guide to tenderness and method of cooking. Poultry may be purchased fresh or frozen.

Chicken and turkey are sold whole, and packaged according to specific parts, such as breasts, legs, and wings. Heat-and-serve or ready-to-eat items such as poultry dinners, fried poultry, and canned chicken also are available but tend to be higher in cost than home-prepared products.

The amount of poultry to purchase depends upon the kind of poultry chosen, the cooking method, and number and size of servings. Usually one-half pound is allowed for each serving of whole broiler-fryer, stewing chicken, turkey,

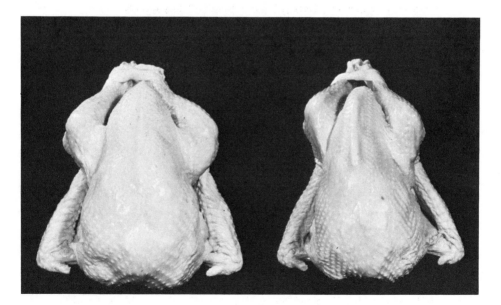

Figure 17-2   U.S. young turkey grades. (Courtesy U.S. Department of Agriculture.)

Table 17-2 Poultry Buying Guide

Type of Poultry	Allow per Serving
Chicken	
Fryer	½–¾ lb
Broiler	¼–½ chicken
Roaster	½–¾ lb
Capon	½–¾ lb
Turkey	½–¾ lb
Duckling	¼ duckling

duckling, or goose. One-fourth pound is allowed for each serving of a boneless turkey roast (Table 17–2).

Storage

Chilled and frozen poultry should be purchased only from refrigerated or freezer cases. Fresh poultry has a high moisture content, is very perishable, and requires prompt refrigeration or freezing. Fresh, chilled poultry can be stored for up to two days in its transparent wrap as purchased or loosely wrapped and stored in the refrigerator at 38° F (3° C). Table 17–3 suggests poultry storage times.

The transparent wrap on packaged, fresh poultry is not suitable for freezer storage. The whole bird or pieces should be repackaged in moisture-vapor-resistant

Table 17-3 Suggested Storage Time to Retain Poultry Quality

Kind of Poultry	Refrigerator 40° F (5° C) Days	Freezer 0° F (−17° C) Months
Fresh Poultry:		
Chicken		
whole	1–2	12
pieces	1–2	9
Turkey		
whole	1–2	12
pieces	1–2	6
Duck, whole	1–2	6
Goose, whole	1–2	6
Giblets	1–2	3
Cooked Poultry:		
Chicken, fried	3–4	4
Cooked poultry dishes	3–4	4–6
Pieces	3–4	1
Pieces with broth or gravy cover	1–2	6

From USDA, *Safe Handling Tips for Meat and Poultry*, Food Safety and Inspection Service (Washington, D.C.: Government Printing Office, July 1981).

wrap (freezer paper, clear plastic, or foil) for long storage in the freezer. Frozen poultry should be frozen solid at the time of purchase, and placed promptly in the home freezer, and kept at 0° F (−18° C).

Sometimes a color change is seen in the bones of frozen poultry. This harmless darkening of the bone is due to the liberation of hemoglobin from the bone marrow on freezing and thawing. The chief disadvantage is an aesthetic one and is not related to food safety.

Poultry can be a carrier of salmonella bacteria. To avoid cross-contamination and the disease of salmonellosis, utensils, surfaces, cutting boards, and hands in contact with poultry should be thoroughly washed with detergent and hot water. Also, the storage of partially cooked poultry is not recommended because the internal temperature of the meat is not high enough to destroy any bacteria that may be present.

Cooking

The tenderness of poultry determines the appropriate method of cooking and is mainly influenced by the age of the bird. Older birds tend to be tough and should be cooked by moist-media or moist-heat methods; young birds are tender and can be cooked by dry-media or dry-heat methods.

Roasting.   All young, tender, nearly matured poultry may be roasted. **Capons,** unsexed male birds, are usually roasted. If the bird is stuffed, the stuffing

(Courtesy Newman, Saylor & Gregory/The National Broiler Council)

is placed loosely into the body cavity and the neck opening, allowing for its expansion during roasting. The stuffed bird should not be refrigerated and held for later cooking because the warm dressing in the cavity is an ideal place for growth of microorganisms. If stuffing is made in advance, it should be thoroughly cooled and kept in the refrigerator until the bird is stuffed for roasting.

The bird is **trussed** by turning the wing tips back under the shoulder and tying the drumsticks to the tail. The legs and wings of a trussed bird are protected from overbrowning during roasting. A thermometer may be placed in the breast or the center of the inner thigh muscle of the turkey or in the dressing. The thermometer bulb should not touch bone.

The bird is placed breast side up on a rack in a shallow, open roasting pan. Poultry is roasted without added fat, usually at 325° F (163° C), until the thick part of the drumstick feels soft when pressed with thumb and forefinger, or the drumstick moves easily, or the internal temperature reaches 180–185° F (82–85° C). During roasting the poultry may be basted with melted table fat or drippings that accumulate in the pan. The required cooking time varies with the weight of the poultry (Table 17–4).

Some well-done roasted poultry meat may develop a pinkish color when components in the gaseous media of the hot oven react with compounds in the poultry. The other qualities of the meat are not changed, and the meat is safe to eat.

Table 17-4   Poultry Roasting Guide

Kind of Poultry	Roast-Ready Weight (lb)	Approximate Roast Time 325°F—162°C (hours)
Chicken, whole stuffed		
Broiler, fryer	1½–2½	1–2
Roaster	2½–4½	2–3½
Capon	5–8	2½–3½
Turkey, whole stuffed[a]	6–8	3–3½
	8–12	3½–4½
	12–16	4½–5½
	16–20	5½–6½
	20–24	6½–7
Halves, quarters, pieces	3–8	2½–3
Boneless roast	3–10	3–4
Duck	4–6	2–3
Geese	6–8	3–3½
	8–12	3½–4½

[a]Cooked, internal temperature in thigh 180–185° F, 82–85° C; in dressing 165° F, 74° C; in boneless roast 170–175°F, 76–79° C.

Adapted from USDA, *The Yearbook of Agriculture, Food For Us All,* (Washington, D.C.: Government Printing Office, 1969).

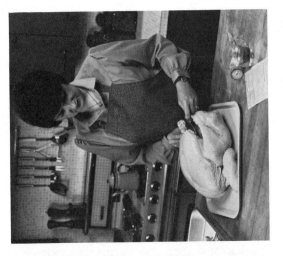

Preparing Poultry (Swift & Company)

Broiling. Poultry is broiled in much the same manner as meat. Halves, quarters, or pieces of very young poultry (broilers and fryers) may be broiled. Poultry is placed skin side down on the broiler rack to prevent sticking of flesh and to help retain juices. The broiler rack is placed about five inches below the heat source with the regulator set at broil. Poultry pieces are basted with melted fat during broiling to avoid drying.

Frying: Pan-, Oven-, Deep-fat. Young poultry may be pan-fried in shallow or deep fat or oven-fried. Pieces are usually rolled in flour or in egg and crumbs, to yield a crisp crust, and fried slowly to avoid overbrowning before they are fully cooked. Fried pieces are turned with tongs to avoid loss of juice from piercing. Pieces coated and rolled in fat may be placed in a shallow baking pan- and oven-fried at 350° F (175° C) for about one hour or until tender.

Deep-fat frying promotes the formation of a crisp outer crust and is a popular method for preparing young poultry. Serving-size pieces are coated with a prepared batter or crumb mixture. Vegetable fat is used for deep-fat frying because it has a high smoke point and does not contain emulsifiers. The fat is heated to 350° F (175° C) and monitored with a deep-fat thermometer. Too high a temperature browns the outside excessively before the interior is sufficiently cooked. Too low a temperature yields a greasy product and increases cooking time. Only a few pieces at a time are lowered into the hot fat, to avoid excessive cooling of the fat. The poultry is fried until golden brown and then drained on absorbent paper.

Braising. Mature poultry is tenderized by moist-media or moist-heat methods. Poultry is braised in the same manner as meats—first browning, then perhaps adding a small amount of liquid, and then covering the pan to complete the cooking. A gravy may be prepared from the pan drippings and served with the poultry.

Fricassee. Fricassee is an alternate term applied to braised meat. Specifically, it refers to small pieces of poultry cooked by braising, and it may also be applied to small pieces of braised veal or rabbit.

Cooking in Liquid: Stewing, Simmering. Mature poultry may be cooked in water, stewed, or simmered for use in casseroles, creamed dishes, salads, and sandwiches. The broth is used to make soup, sauces and creamed products, or as an ingredient in a variety of food combinations.

Stewing is an alternate term applied to poultry cooked in water. It usually refers to cut pieces of poultry cooked in a relatively small quantity of liquid. Stewing also applies to whole birds cooked in seasoned liquid to which vegetables may be added. *Simmer* is yet another term applied to poultry cooked in liquid. It means cooking in a liquid just below the boiling point (185–210° F; 85–99° C). The liquid bubbles slowly, and bubbles collapse below the surface.

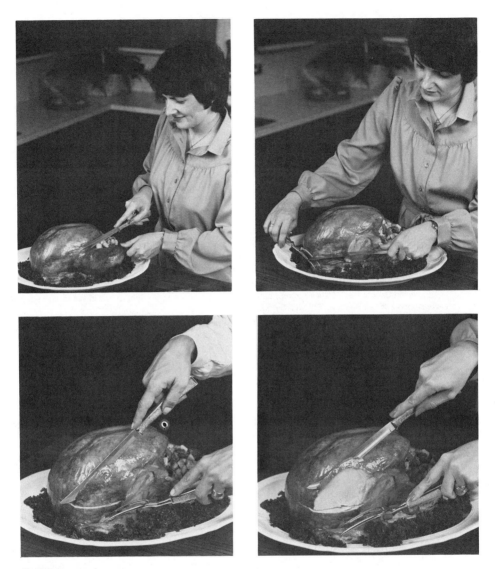

(Swift & Company)

Microwaving Poultry. Whole chicken or turkey up to about twelve pounds may be microwaved. Follow the directions for the temperature probe or those given by the manufacturer of the oven. Standing time allows the interior to finish cooking without toughening the breast meat. Chicken pieces cook quickly and do not brown. Plain microwaved chicken may be used for salads and casseroles. Poultry may be brushed with browning agents or coated with crumbs to

Table 17-5 Microwaving Turkeys

Time Interval	Approximate Cook Time (in minutes) in 625–700 W Microwave Oven Weight[1]						
	6 lb[1]	7 lb	8 lb	9 lb	10 lb	11 lb	12 lb
Stage I	Brush browning sauce[2] over turkey back, wings, and legs. Microwave breast down at 100% power (high). Rotate turkey ½ turn (180°) at end of each time interval. Also remove drippings and brush with well-blended browning sauce.						
1	12	14	16	18	20	22	24
2	12	14	16	18	20	22	24
Stage II	Brush browning sauce over turkey breast and legs. Microwave breast up at 50% power (medium). Rotate turkey ¼ turn (90°) at end of each time interval. Also remove drippings and brush with well-blended browning sauce.						
3	12	14	16	18	20	22	24
4	12	14	16	18	20	22	24
5[3]	12	14	16	18	20	22	24
6	12	14	16	18	20	22	24

[1]Weight = net weight minus 8-ounce gravy packet, if present.

[2]Browning Sauce: Melt ½ stick (¼ cup) butter in cup at 100% power (high). Blend in ¼ teaspoon paprika and ⅛ teaspoon Kitchen Bouquet. Stir well before use.

[3]Check for doneness after time interval 5. Meat thermometer (not touching bone) should reach 180–185° F deep in thickest part of thigh, 170° F deep in thickest part of breast, and 160–165° F in center of stuffing.

Cook time is the same for stuffed or unstuffed turkey. Total cook time = 12 minutes per pound (4 minutes per pound at 100% power plus 8 minutes per pound at 50% power).

From "Swift's New Method for Microwaving Turkeys," Swift & Company, 1929 Swift Drive, Oak Brook, Ill. 60521.

enhance its appearance. Refer to chapter 24 for microwave details and to Table 17–5 for microwave-roasting turkey.

FISH

Many species of fish and shellfish are sold in the United States, although the per capita consumption of fish is relatively low. Some species are known by more than one common name. Fish, as a group, are available in a variety of forms. Frozen fish and shellfish are available the year round. Edible fish are categorized as either finfish or shellfish. Finfish have a bony skeleton, while shellfish have hard or segmented, crustlike shells. Most edible fin- and shellfish come from salt water.

Nutritional Quality/Composition

The overall composition of seafood is similar to that of meat; therefore, the many varieties of fish can replace meat in the diet. Fish protein is of excellent quality and is an alternate for meat protein. The total fat content of raw fish generally is less than the fat content of equal amounts of raw meat or poultry. Fish

(Courtesy Wattenmaker Public Relations/North Atlantic Seafood Association)

(Gordon S. Smith, Photo Researcher, Inc.)

fat contains both saturated and unsaturated fatty acids, but the proportion of unsaturated fatty acids is higher than in meat. Fish are valuable protein alternates for diets restricted in total fat and in saturated fats.

The vitamin content of fish tends to vary with fat content. Fish with a high fat content are good sources of vitamins. Fish liver oils are concentrated sources of vitamins A and D. Fish in general are good sources of the B vitamins thiamin, niacin, and riboflavin. Iodine occurs more abundantly in saltwater fish than in any other food. Fish canned with bones—sardines and salmon—are good sources of calcium and phosphorus, if the bones are eaten. Oysters are very good sources of iron and copper, and fish in general provide some iron, but less than meat. The sodium content of fish is somewhat higher than of meat.

Raw fish are relatively low in calories owing to the low content of fat. However, calories increase as fish is floured, breaded, or dipped in batter or corn-meal in preparation for cooking. Pan or deep-fat frying increases the caloric content considerably.

Kinds of Fish

On the basis of anatomy, and also for convenience, fish are classified as finfish and shellfish. Usually the term *fish* means finfish—having a skeletal structure, fins, and gills. Fish may be further classed as saltwater or freshwater fish, or as fat or lean fish. Perch, flounder, and halibut are examples of lean fish (less than 5 percent fat). Salmon, tuna, and sardines are examples of fat fish (5 to 20 percent fat).

Shellfish are either crustaceans or mollusks, neither of which have a skeletal system. Instead they have a shell on the outside of soft tissue. Crab, lobster, and shrimp are crustaceans and have a segmented, horny covering. Clams, oysters, scallops, are examples of mollusks; they are enclosed in calcified shells, and their bodies are not segmented.

Structure

The flesh of fish consists of skeletal muscle similar to that of land animals. Fish muscle fiber cells display myofibrils (sarcoplasm) and are arranged into bundles and enclosed in connective tissue like the muscles in red meat discussed in chapter 16.

Fish muscles contain less connective tissue than meat muscle, and the tissue breaks down at a lower temperature. The muscle fibers of fish are shorter than red meat muscle fibers, and their ends are inserted into sheets of connective tissue to form small blocks or segments. The collagen of fish connective tissue hydrolyzes to gelatin during cooking, and then blocks of fiber separate as flakes. The flesh of most finfish is colorless, but some muscles near the skin are a reddish-brown. The pigmented muscles contain myoglobin.

Inspection/Grading

The Department of the Interior makes available the official inspection service for all types of processed fish products. Inspectors make continuous checks on quality of the raw product as well as on conditions under which the product is processed, prepared, and packed. The inspection service is voluntary and is available for a fee.

U.S. quality grades are based on appearance, absence of defects, uniformity, texture, odor, and flavor. Grades for prepared products also consider the quantity of fish compared to breading and bone. The grade designations are grade A for top quality; grade B for products that are of good quality and free from blem-

Figure 17-3
Example of U.S. inspection and grade shield for fish.

ishes but less uniform in size than grade A; and grade C for wholesome, nutritious products of fairly good quality. The inspected fish products may be labeled with the inspection shield and grade mark (Figure 17–3).

Selection

Fish is available in several market forms: canned, fresh, frozen, and prepared products. It can be purchased dressed; with entrails, head, tail, fins, and scales removed; or drawn, with only the entrails removed. Fish is also commonly marketed as boneless lengthwise slices cut parallel to the backbone, called fillets, or as cross-section slices of large fish, called steaks. Some shellfish is sold alive in the shell.

The odor and appearance of fish indicate its freshness. Bright eyes, bright pink gills, shiny skin, and a soft flesh that leaves no print when pressed identify fresh fish. The cut flesh is translucent and shimmering, with no unpleasant odor.

A great variety of canned fish is available. Popular canned finfish include salmon, tuna, and sardines. Among the canned shellfish are clams, crabs, lobster, oysters, scallops, and shrimp, all of which are generally considered to be delicacies. Some fish is cured, which preserves it and also gives it a distinctive flavor. Salted,

Fresh fish (top), stale fish (bottom) (Laimute E. Druskis)

smoked, and pickled fish are all referred to as cured fish. Smoked mackerel and salmon, finnan haddie, kippered herring, and salted cod are examples. Some fish, such as cod or herring, is cured by salting in brine or dry salt and then drying.

Mildly salted fish is sometimes treated with smoke to give it a special smoked flavor. Haddock that has been cured in brine and then smoked is known as finnan haddie. Pickled fish is cured in brine that contains vinegar and spices.

The form of fish determines the amount to purchase for each serving. Generally, 1/2 pound of dressed fish or 1/3 pound of steak or fillet is allotted for each serving. Some common market forms and the quantity to buy for an average serving are indicated in Table 17–6.

Storage

Fish spoils faster than meat. Prepackaged fish is refrigerated immediately in the original container. Fish purchased in market paper should be transferred to foil or plastic film and wrapped. Frozen fish should be placed immediately into the home freezer after purchase. Table 17–7 lists storage times for fish.

Most harmful bacteria grow best at 50–68° F (10–20° C), but some can

Table 17–6   Fish and Shellfish Buying Guide

Market Form	Market Unit	Allow per Serving
Fish		
Fresh or frozen		
whole or round	pound	¾ pound
drawn	pound	¾ pound
dressed	pound	½ pound
steaks	pound	⅓ pound or one steak
fillets	pound	⅓ pound
sticks	pound	3 ounces (cooked)
Canned		
mackerel	15 ounces	3 ounces
salmon	16 ounces	3 ounces
tuna	6 to 7 ounces	3 ounces
Shellfish		
Live		
clams, oyster	pound	6 oysters or clams
crabs	pound	3 crabs
lobster	pound	1 pound
Shucked		
oysters, clams	pint	⅓ pint
scallops	pound	⅓ pound
Fresh or frozen		
lobster tails	pound	½ pound
shrimp	pound	¼ pound

Table 17-7 Suggested Storage Time to Retain Fish and Shellfish Quality

Fish/Shellfish	Freezer 0°F (−17° C) Months
Raw fish	
Fillets—cod, flounder, haddock, halibut	6
—bass, ocean perch, sea trout	2–3
Salmon steak	2
Sea trout, dressed	3
Whiting, drawn	4
Cooked fish	
Fish with lemon butter	3
Fried fish	3
Raw shellfish	
Clams, shucked	3
Crabmeat—Dungeness	3
—King	10
Oysters, shucked	4
Shrimp	12
Cooked shellfish	
Shrimp creole	3
Fried scallops, shrimp	3

From USDA, *Home Care of Purchased Frozen Foods,* Home and Garden Bulletin no. 69. (Washington, D.C.: Government Printing Office, 1975).

continue to grow at temperatures as low as 32° F (0° C). Frozen storage of fish at 0° F (−18° C) delays bacterial growth. Fresh fish spoils very quickly and should be used as soon as possible. It can be stored covered in the refrigerator no longer than two days. For freezing a temperature of 0° F (−18° C) or lower is required to maintain fish quality.

Cookery

Fish contains little connective tissue and is more tender than red meats. The objectives of fish cookery are to coagulate the muscle fiber protein so that the fish can barely be separated into flakes and to heat the product to serving temperature. Because fish cooks quickly, it is easily overcooked. As fish is cooked, the translucent flesh becomes opaque. The flakiness of the flesh and loss of translucency are signs of doneness. Fish cooked beyond this point becomes progressively toughened as cooking continues. Tables 17–8 and 17–9 serve as guides for cooking fish and shellfish.

All techniques of frying—pan-, deep-fat, and oven-—and baking and broiling are popular methods for cooking fish. Moist-media or moist-heat methods are also suitable but are used for variety rather than for tenderizing.

Table 17-8 Cooking Guide for Fish

Method	Temperature	Time
Bake		
Pan dressed	350° F (175° C)	15–20 min/lb
Fillets	350° F (175° C)	10–15 min/lb
Steaks	350° F (175° C)	8–10 min/lb
Frozen–fried—2½, 3 oz portion	400° F (205° C)	8–10 min/lb
Broil (turn once)	(Place 3 to inches below broiler unit)	
Fillets	moderate	5–8 min
Steaks	moderate	5–8 min
Frozen-fried—2½, 3 oz portion	moderate	5–8 min
Deep-fat fry		
Fillets	350° F (175° C)	3–5 min
Steaks	350° F (175° C)	3–5 min
Frozen, breaded—2½, 3 oz portion	350° F (175° C)	3–5 min
Pan fry (turn once)		
Raw, breaded, or frozen, breaded	moderate	8–10 min
Poach		
Fillets	simmer	5–10 min
Steaks	simmer	5–10 min

Adapted from *Handbook of Food Preparation,* 8th ed., (Washington, D.C.: American Home Economics Association, 1980).

Table 17-9 Cooking Guide for Shellfish

Method	Temperature	Time
Bake		
Clams—live	400° F (230° C)	10–15 min
—shucked	350° F (175° C)	8–10 min
Crab—King	350° F (175° C)	8–10 min
Lobster—live	400° F (205° C)	20–25 min
—tails	350° F (175° C)	20–25 min
Oysters—live	450° F (230° C)	10–15 min
—shucked	350° F (175° C)	8–10 min
Scallops—shucked	350° F (175° C)	20–25 min
Shrimp—headless	350° F (175° C)	20–25 min
Broil	(Place 3 inches below broiler unit)	
Clams—live	moderate	4–5 min
—shucked	moderate	4–5 min
Lobster—tail	moderate	10–15 min
Oyster—shucked	moderate	4–5 min
Scallops—shucked	moderate	6–8 min
Shrimp—headless	moderate	8–10 min

Adapted from *Handbook of Food Preparation,* 8th ed. (Washington, D.C.: American Home Economics Association, 1980).

Poaching and steaming are popular moist-media methods. A single layer of fish is poached in enough milk or water to just cover the fish and is simmered until the fish can be flaked with a fork. Fish is steamed on a rack above boiling water in a tightly covered pan until the fish is easily flaked. Steamed and poached fish are served with a sauce, such as hollandaise or lemon butter.

Microwaving

The speed and moisture retention of microwaving are advantages in cooking fish. Fish should be microwaved until the outer area appears opaque but the center is still slightly translucent. The centers will finish cooking as the fish stands. Fillets and steaks may be microwaved in a sauce or steamed, or poached. Juices of salmon or halibut steaks coagulate on the surface whether microwaved or conventionally cooked. This can be eliminated by placing fish on a trivet or lining the dish, before microwaving, with a paper towel to absorb excess juices.

SUMMARY

Poultry is classed according to species, age, and sex. Most poultry marketed in the United States is inspected for wholesomeness and may display a grade mark. Poultry provides high-quality protein, B vitamins, iron, and phosphorus. The fat content varies among species, and dark meat contains more fat than white meat. Older birds contain more fat and are less tender than young birds. The tenderness of poultry is determined by age. Young poultry is cooked by dry media or heat and mature poultry by moist media or heat.

Fish is classed as finfish and shellfish. Inspection service and grading are available on a voluntary basis. The protein quality of fish is comparable to red meat. Fish contains less total fat and fewer saturated fatty acids than red meat. The fatty fish are good sources of vitamins A and D. All fish provide abundant iodine, the B vitamins, and some iron, calcium, and phosphorus. Fish is more perishable than red meats and must be immediately refrigerated or frozen. Fish contains little connective tissue and is quickly cooked by either dry- or moist-media methods.

SELF-STUDY GUIDE

1. Contrast the nutritional quality of poultry and fish with that of red meat.
2. List five available classes of poultry and suggest appropriate cooking methods.
3. What factors are considered when poultry is selected? When fish is selected?
4. How are poultry and fish inspected and graded?
5. How are the different forms of poultry and fish stored?

6. List two general classes of fish and give examples.
7. What factors determine the tenderness of poultry? The tenderness of fish?
8. Compare the structure of fish to meat.
9. Name five kinds of fish available and suggest cooking methods.
10. What three factors determine the amount of poultry and fish to purchase?

SELECTED REFERENCES

Poultry

ANG, C. Y. W. Vitamin B-6 and niacin contents of broiler meat of different strains, sexes, and production regions. *Journal of Food Science* 45:898, 1980.

BAKER, R. C., and BARFLER, J. M. A comparison of fresh and frozen poultry. *Journal of the American Dietetic Association* 78:348, 1981.

BENTON, H. J., and GARDNER, F. A. Effect of further processing systems on selected microbiological attributes of turkey meat production. *Journal of Food Science* 47:214, 1982.

BOWERS, J. Sensory characteristics of postmortem papain injected turkey cooked conventionally or by microwaves. *Journal of Food Science* 46:1627, 1981.

CUNNINGHAM, F. E., and TIEDE, L. M. Influence of batter viscosity on breading of chicken drumsticks. *Journal of Food Science* 46:1950, 1981.

GRAY, J. I., et al. Investigation into the formation of N-nitrosamines in heated chicken frankfurters. *Journal of Food Science* 46:1817, 1981.

HALL, K. N., and LIN, C. S. Effect of cooking rates in electric or microwave oven on cooking losses and retention of thiamin in broilers. *Journal of Food Science* 46:1292, 1981.

HAMM, D. Amino acid composition of breast and thigh meat from broilers produced in four locations of the United States. *Journal of Food Science* 46:1122, 1981.

——, et al. Mineral content and proximate analysis of broiler meat from two strains and three regions of production. *Journal of Food Science* 45:1478, 1980.

HAMM, D., and SEAREY, G. K. Mineral content of commercial samples of mechanically deboned poultry meat. *Poultry Science* 60:686, 1981.

KLOSE, A. A. Fluoride content of commercially prepared mechanically deboned poultry meat. *Poultry Science* 59:2570, 1980.

LEE, F. V. Effect of preparation and service on the thiamin content of oven-baked chicken. *Journal of Food Science* 46:1560, 1981.

LILLARD, H. S. Effect on broiler carcasses and water of treating chilled water with chlorine or chlorine dioxide. *Poultry Science* 59:1761, 1980.

LYON, B. G., and KLOSE, A. A. Sensory profiling of canned boned chicken. *Journal of Food Science* 45:1336, 1981.

SUDERMAN, D. R., and CUNNINGHAM, F. E. Factors affecting adhesion of coating to poultry skin: Effect of age, method of chilling, and scald temperature on poultry skin ultrastructure. *Journal of Food Science* 45:444, 1980.

SUDERMAN, D. R., et al. Factors affecting adhesion of coating to poultry skin: Effects of various protein and gum sources in the coating composition. *Journal of Food Science* 46:1010, 1981.

U.S. DEPARTMENT OF AGRICULTURE. *Poultry in family meals.* Home and Garden Bulletin no. 110. Washington, D.C.: Government Printing Office, 1979.

VAN DE BOVENKAMP, P., and KATAN, M. B. Cholesterol content of chicken skin. *Journal of Food Science* 46:291, 1981.

YOUNG, L. L. Evaluation of four purine compounds in poultry products. *Journal of Food Science* 45:1064, 1980.

——. Purine content of raw and roasted chicken broiler meat. *Journal of Food Science* 47:1374, 1982.

Fish

BIEDE, S. L., et al. Effects of mechanical processing on crab meat. *Lousiana Agriculture* 23:14, 1980.

BROOKE, P. J., and EVANS, W. H. Determination of total inorganic arsenic in fish, shellfish, and fish products. *Analyst* 106:514, 1981.

CANNED SALMON INSTITUTE. *Canned salmon fact book.* Seattle: Canned Salmon Institute, no date.

DENG, J. C. Effect of temperatures on fish alkaline protease, protein interaction and texture quality. *Journal of Food Science* 46:1950, 1981.

FINNE, G., et al. Minced fish flesh from nontraditional Gulf of Mexico finfish species: Yield and composition. *Journal of Food Science* 45:1127, 1980.

Fish farming heading upstream. *Institutions* 15:159, 1979.

HEIMELBLOOM, B. H.; RUTLEDGE, J. E.; and BIEDE, S. L. Color changes in blue crab (callinectes sapidus) during cooking. *Journal of Food Science* 48:652, 1983.

HUMAN, J., and KHAYAT, S. Quality evaluation of raw tuna by gas chromatography and sensory methods. *Journal of Food Science* 46:868, 1981.

JAUREGUI, C. A., and BAKER, R. C. Discoloration problems in mechanically deboned fish. *Journal of Food Science* 45: 1068, 1980.

LEE, C. M., and ABDOLLAHI, A. Effect of hardness of plastic fat on structure and material properties of fish protein gels. *Journal of Food Science* 46:1755, 1981.

LEU, S. S.; JHAVERI, S. N.; KARAKOLTSIDIS, P. A.; and CONSTANTINIDES, A. M. Atlantic mackerel (Scomber Scombrus, L): Seasonal variation in proximate composition and distribution of chemical nutrients. *Journal of Food Science* 46:1635, 1981.

LOPEZ, A., et al. Essential elements in raw, boiled, steamed, and pasteurized crabmeat. *Journal of Food Science* 46:1128, 1981.

LUTEN, J. B. An automated fluorimetric method for the determination of histamine in canned fish products. *Journal of Food Science* 46:958, 1981.

RUDFORD, T., and DALSIS, E. E. Analysis of formaldehyde in shrimp by high-pressure liquid chromatography. *Journal of Agricultural and Food Chemistry* 30:600, 1982.

SPINELLI, J., and KOURG, R. J. Some new observations of the pathways of formation of dimethylamine in fish muscle and liver. *Journal of Agricultural and Food Chemistry* 29:327, 1981.

TESHIMA, S. I.; PATTERSON, G. W.; and DUTKY, S. R. Sterols of the oyster, Crassostrea Virginica. *Lipids* 15:1004, 1980.

U.S. DEPARTMENT OF COMMERCE. *Import inspection services for fishery products.* Food Fish Facts no. 56, Washington, D.C.: USDC, no date.

WILLIAMS, S. K., et al. Moisture migration in frozen, raw breaded shrimp during nine months of storage. *Journal of Food Science* 46:137, 1981.

18

MEAT: EXTENDERS AND ALTERNATES

OBJECTIVES

When you have read this chapter, you will be able to

1. Extend the flavor of meat and thus increase the number of servings provided by a given quantity of meat.
2. Discuss the nutritional contribution of meat extenders and alternates and compare their nutrient contributions to those of meat.
3. Identify the various forms of processed soybean products and give examples of their use.
4. Describe the preparation of textured vegetable proteins.
5. Describe the preparation and use of dried legumes.
6. Select vegetable sources of protein to meet your protein requirement on a meatless diet.
7. Discuss various vegetarian diets and identify likely nutritional deficiencies.

Meat and other foods of animal origin continue to be regarded as dietary staples and as essential because of their protein content and quality. However, economic, cultural, religious, ethical, and spiritual factors, as well as availability, have directed some attention to meat extenders and alternates. **Meat extenders,** such as pastas and rice, carry the meat flavor throughout the food product so that a small amount of animal-protein food is required to yield a meat-flavored dish. **Legumes,** grains, and nuts are commonly used to replace meat in meals, and thus serve as **meat alternates.**

266

PROTEIN QUALITY: ANIMAL AND VEGETABLE

Proteins synthesized in animal and plant tissues consist of twenty-two or more amino acids. Some of these amino acids are classed as nonessential because they can be produced within human tissues. Others are known as essential since they are not produced by the body and must be provided by the diet. Human adults require eight essential amino acids—isoleucine, leucine, lysine, methionine, trypotophan, phenylalanine, threonine, and valine. Children require a ninth essential amino acid, histidine.

A high-quality (complete) protein must contain all of the essential amino acids in sufficient quantity and in the right proportion. High-quality proteins contain an amino acid pattern that is similar to the amino acid needs of humans. The amino acid pattern of egg protein is considered to be the most perfect and is used as a reference for assessing the quality of other proteins. Proteins of animal origin are considered as high-quality (except gelatin) protein and include those from meat, poultry, seafoods, eggs, milk, and cheese.

Vegetable proteins provide an inadequate amount of one or more of the essential amino acids and therefore are classified as incomplete proteins. The amino acid present in an unfavorable proportion or that is lacking is designated as the **limiting amino acid**. For example, the limiting amino acid in soybeans and other legumes is methionine; in grains and nuts, it is lysine (Table 18–1). The protein quality of soybeans and other legumes is higher than that of other vegetable proteins, which makes them useful as meat alternates. However, combinations of the various other vegetable proteins can contribute appropriate amounts of protein, enabling them to be substituted for animal proteins in the diet.

The quality of vegetable protein is enhanced when the limiting amino acid is supplied. This is easily accomplished when two or three vegetable sources of protein such as legumes, cereals, and nuts are consumed within the same meal. For example, corn can provide the methionine lacking in soybeans, while lysine and tryptophan are contributed by soybeans. Combinations of plant proteins are a practical way to meet human protein needs. The limiting amino acid can also be provided through enrichment of the vegetable protein or addition of synthetic amino acids. The quality of vegetable proteins is enhanced when small amounts of animal protein are included. The addition of milk, egg, or cheese increases the biological value of plant proteins.

Meat Extenders

Rice, other grains, and pastas are used as meat extenders. Their bland flavor provides an ideal base for extending the flavor and number of servings of foods of animal origin. Meat extenders are less expensive than foods of animal origin and can lead to a reduction in the overall cost of food. Enriched cereals and

Table 18-1   Protein, Limiting Amino Acids, Fiber, and kCalories in 100 Grams of Selected Plant Foods

	Protein (g)	Lysine	Methionine	Tryptophan	Fiber (g)	kcal
Legumes, cooked						
Beans, common	7.8		*	*	1.5	118
Beans, lima (immature)	7.6		*	*	1.8	111
Lentils	7.8		*	*	1.2	106
Peas, black-eyed	5.1		*		1.0	76
Peas, green split	8.0		*	*	0.4	115
Soybeans	11.0		*		1.6	130
Curd	7.8		*		0.1	72
Milk	3.4		*		0.0	33
Nuts						
Almonds	18.6	*		*	2.6	627
Brazil nuts	14.3	*		*	3.1	654
Cashews	17.2	*	*		1.4	561
Coconut	3.5	*			4.0	346
Hazelnut (filbert)	12.6	*	*		3.0	634
Peanuts, roasted	26.2	*	*	*	2.7	582
Pecans	9.2	*			2.3	687
Pistachio	1.9	*		*	1.9	635
Walnuts, English	14.7	*		*	2.1	651
Seeds						
Pumpkin	29.0	*			1.9	553
Sesame	18.6	*			6.3	563
Sunflower	24.0	*			3.8	560
Grains						
Barley, raw	9.6	*			0.9	348
Buckwheat, raw	11.7	*			9.9	335
Corn, sweet, cooked	3.2	*		*	0.7	83
Rice, cooked						
white	2.0	*			0.1	109
brown	2.5	*			0.3	119
Whole wheat flour	13.3	*			2.3	333
white flour	10.5	*			0.3	364

*Represents limiting amino acid in protein.

From USDA, *Composition of Food*, Handbook no. 8, Washington, D.C.: Government Printing Office, 1977.

pastas are good sources of the B vitamins and iron and make valuable contributions to the overall protein intake.

Meat Alternates

Legumes, grains, and nuts are the major vegetable sources of protein. Legumes are dried seeds of pod vegetables, grains are seeds of grasses, and nuts are

Table 18-2 Cup Measures of Dry and Cooked Legumes

Dry Legumes (1 cup)	Cooked Legumes (cups)
Black beans	2
Blackeyed beans (blackeyed peas, cowpeas)	2½
Cranberry beans	2
Great Northern beans	2½
Kidney beans	2¾
Lentils	2½
Lima beans, large	2½
Lima beans, small	2
Navy (pea) beans	2½
Peas, whole	2½
Pinto beans	2½
Soybeans	2½
Split peas	2½

Adapted from USDA, *Vegetables in Family Meals: A Guide to Consumers,* Home and Garden Bulletin no. 105 (Washington, D.C.: Government Printing Office, 1975).

fruits of trees. Cup measures of some dry cooked legumes are listed in Table 18–2.

Legumes.   Common varieties of legumes include the dried beans—lima, kidney, navy, white, pinto, and garbanzo—and lentils and dried peas. Lentils resemble peas but are smaller (see chapter 12). Soybeans contain the most complete of the vegetable proteins. In addition to protein, legumes contribute a moderate amount of starch, a little fat except for soybeans, a fair amount of the B vitamins, and moderate amounts of calories (Table 18–3).

Soybeans.   The cooked soybean is the most widely used legume. However, soybeans are not used raw because they contain a trypsin inhibitor that interferes with growth and metabolism. Soybeans are used as a soy flour, soy concentrate, and soy isolate.

Soy Flour.   The outer covering and oil are removed before soybeans are ground to yield flour. Soy flour contains about 50 percent protein and is used in making doughnuts, breads, rolls, cookies, and other baked products.

Soy Concentrate.   The oil and most of the soluble carbohydrates are removed from soybeans when soy concentrate is being manufactured. About 70 percent of the concentrate is protein. Soy concentrate in powdered form is used in sausage products, baby foods, cereals, and snacks. The granular form is used in

Table 18-3 Navy Beans: Percentage U.S. RDA

Nutrient	Percentage U.S. RDA 1 Cup Cooked Navy Beans
Protein	27
Thiamin	18
Riboflavin	7
Niacin	6
Calcium	11
Iron	28
Phosphorus	35
Zinc	12

Adapted from *The Bean Bag.* Michigan Bean Commission, winter 1984.

ground-meat products. Soy proteins have a tendency to gel when heated and are used in cream soups and pet foods.

Soy Isolate.   When the fat and carbohydrate are removed, the product becomes soy isolate, which is used in the manufacture of **textured vegetable protein.** About 90 percent of the isolate is protein.

Soy Milk.   Soy milk is prepared by grinding softened beans in water and then collecting the fluid drained from the mixture. The resulting soy milk contains most of the protein, oil, and solids of soybeans. When softened beans are ground while in hot water, the lipoxidase (an enzyme) is deactivated, and the off-flavor is eliminated. Soy milk contains only 25 percent as much calcium as cow's milk. When it is fortified with calcium salts (such as calcium carbonate) and with vitamin B-12 it becomes a good source of these nutrients.

Tofu.   Fermented soy milk can be made into a curd (cheese) called **tofu.** This tofu may be combined with vegetables or used in sandwiches. Dried tofu can be stored for considerable time.

Tempeh.   Tempeh requires a short fermentation period and is used in the same manner as tofu.

Soy Sauce.   Soy sauce is a popular fermented product made from defatted soy flakes mixed with wheat and salt.

TVP and TSP

Textured vegetable proteins (TVP) are food products made from high-protein flour, protein concentrate, and isolated proteins. Two methods used to give texture (make chewy or fibrous) to the high-protein mixture include (1) a spinning process similar to that used to make textiles and (2) an extrusion method used in cereal production.

The filaments formed in the spinning process are gathered into bundles. These flavorless textured fibers are used as a base for fabricated meat analogs. They are bound together with another protein material, such as egg albumen, and are blended with fat, flavoring, coloring, added nutrients, and stabilizers.

The extrusion method texturizes high-protein mixtures. The process of extrusion used to make breakfast cereals is also used with textured vegetable protein and textured soy protein (TSP). A mixture of protein, water, vitamins, flavor, and color is heated, subjected to pressure, and placed into an extruder. As this material passes through and out, it becomes puffed, and granules form. The granules are dried and vacuum packed to ensure shelf life. They are stored in a cool place and rehydrated for use.

Dried granules, sold as a grocery item, are rehydrated in the home with 1.5–2.5 times their weight in water. Excellent results are obtained when up to 25 percent rehydrated granules are added to ground-meat products, such as meat loaves, chili, spaghetti, and hamburger. They are used in fast-food items and frozen convenience products. TVP-meat mixtures are stored in the same way as meat. They require somewhat less time to cook and shrink less than meat since juices are absorbed by the TVP. When TVP is combined with meat, the methionine in meat supplements the nutritive value of soy protein. Textured soy protein is of a high nutritional quality and soy-meat products are generally acceptable.

Analogs.   Meat and seafood **analogs** are prepared from extruded soy protein blended with other vegetable proteins, fat, carbohydrate, vitamins, minerals, flavor, and color to form products resembling meat and seafoods. Meat analogs contain about 50 percent protein (meat contains from 15 to 20 percent protein). When methionine is added to meat analogs, the protein efficiency ration (PER) approaches that of meat. Meat analogs contain less saturated fat and cholesterol, and about one-third the total fat in meat. Seafood analogs have a seafoodlike texture and bland flavor. They are used with tuna, lobster, fish, and crabmeat. The analog may replace 30 to 50 percent of the seafood and retain the characteristic flavor.

Grains

Grains are a good source of incomplete proteins; they contribute moderate amounts of carbohydrate as starch, and they contain little fat. Grains combined with legumes and nuts can provide adequate amounts of essential proteins in the diet.

Grains are processed into cereals, flour, and a variety of pasta products. Pasta is a common term for macaroni products, which include spaghetti and noodles as well as macaroni. Pasta products made from durum wheat are produced in

Table 18-4 Yield Per Pound of Nuts Purchased in Shells and Shelled

Nuts	In Shells		Shelled	
	Kernels Cups	Chopped Cups	Kernels Cups	Chopped Cups
Almonds				
Hard shell	1½	1¾	3¼	3½
Paper shell	2	2½	3¼	3½
Brazil nuts	1¾	1¾		
Cashews			3¼	3¼
Filberts	1½	1¾		
Peanuts,				
roasted	2¼	2¼	3	3¼
Pecans	2	2	4¼	4¼
Pistachios	1¾			
Walnuts,				
black		¾		
English		1¾		3¾

Adapted from USDA, *Buying Food,* Home Economics Research Report no. 42. Science and Education Administration (Washington, D.C.: Government Printing Office, 1978).

varying lengths, sizes, and shapes. Rice is commonly prepared as a whole kernel and is the dietary staple in the Far East and other countries (see chapter 6).

Nuts

Nuts are high in fat, a good source of incomplete proteins, and a fair source of the B-vitamins. Although peanuts are a legume, they are usually grouped with nuts. Lysine is the limiting amino acid in most nuts. Some nuts lack tryptophan, and a few lack methionine. When nuts are consumed with grains and legumes, they make a substantial contribution toward a high-quality combination of proteins in the diet. Table 18–4 lists the yield per pound of purchased nuts.

COMPARATIVE SUMMARY: LEGUME NUTRITIONAL QUALITY

Comparatively, on the basis of a serving, legumes contain about twice as much protein as cereals, one-half as much protein as lean meat. Soybeans contain more protein than most other legumes. The quality of the protein is as important as the quantity. Legumes contain a higher protein quality than do cereals. Legumes are a better source of essential amino acids than cereals. They are especially good sources of lysine, an essential amino acid, lacking in cereals. However, the sulfur-containing amino acids of legumes, methionine and cystine are poorly utilized. Cereals can complement legume protein with cystine and methionine and when consumed with legumes contribute to a high-quality protein combination.

Soybeans have a better balance of essential amino acids and protein than other legumes. Soybeans and peanuts have a high fat content. Legumes contain a high level of phosphorus and somewhat more iron than cereals. Legumes also provide more riboflavin than cereals but less niacin than whole wheat. Lean meats contribute more riboflavin and niacin than whole-grain cereals. Legumes lack ascorbic acid and vitamin A. They have a high starch content and are a good source of energy.

MEATLESS MEALS: VEGETARIANISM

Although **vegetarianism** may be practiced in a variety of forms, there are two basic forms—lacto-ovo and **vegan.** The lacto-ovo vegetarian consumes milk products and eggs. The vegan, or pure vegetarian, does not eat any animal products but follows a diet of legumes, grains, nuts, vegetables, and fruits. Within these two classifications are the lacto-vegetarians, who consume milk products but not eggs; the ovo-vegetarians, who eat eggs but not milk products; and the fruitarians, who eliminate all food except fruit, nuts, honey, and olive oil. The vegan may have difficulty in getting enough energy (kilocalories) from only food of plant origin, since these foods are bulky. When the kcalorie intake is inadequate, the body is forced to use protein for energy rather than for body building and maintenance.

The vegan diet may be inadequate in essential amino acids and in total protein unless food selections are made with extreme care. Legumes and grains are the chief sources of proteins in the vegetarian diet. When foods of animal origin are not consumed for extended periods, a vitamin B-12 deficiency can develop. The high-fiber diet of the vegetarian may limit absorption of trace elements. The vegan may also have an inadequate intake of calcium and riboflavin owing to the exclusion of milk unless generous amounts of dark green, leafy vegetables are included.

When dairy products and/or eggs are consumed (lacto- or ovo-vegetarians), it becomes easy to secure adequate amounts of protein and other nutrients. The vegan diets (including fruitarian) can easily produce nutritional problems among growing children and pregnant and lactating women.

Meals can be planned to ensure an adequate vegetarian diet when appropriate combinations of foods are eaten. When diet selections are made only from plant foods, two of the four food groups are eliminated—milk-dairy products and meats. These groups include the foods of animal origin and are the primary sources of calcium, riboflavin, vitamin B-12, vitamin D, iron, and zinc. Plants provide nearly all of the vitamins A and C.

Legumes are the richest plant sources of protein and when supplemented with grains in the same meal, they can contribute appropriate combinations of amino acids. Meat analogs may be used to advantage in vegetarian diets. Dark green, leafy vegetables are the richest plant sources of calcium and iron, and they contribute significant amounts of riboflavin.

Because plant foods are bulky, in relation to protein content, vegetarians must eat a greater amount of food than those consuming meat to provide an adequate supply of protein. It takes two cups of legumes to match the quantity of protein in one serving of meat. Since plants to not provide vitamin B-12, the vegan must take a vitamin B-12 supplement or use soy milk fortified with the vitamin. A strict vegetarian diet is not recommended for children because of the difficulty in ensuring that their nutrient needs are met.

The four-food-group plan is easily followed by lacto-ovo vegetarians when the following are used:

1. Four servings of whole-grain products
2. Two servings of legumes, nuts, seeds, and meat analogs in place of meat, and eggs
3. Two servings of milk and milk products
4. Four servings of a variety of fruits and vegetables

The four-food-group plan for the vegan is as follows:

1. Four servings of whole-grain products
2. Two servings of protein-rich foods (include two cups of legumes daily to meet the iron needs of women; count four tablespoons of peanut butter as one serving)
3. Two servings of milk and milk products (or use soy milk fortified with vitamin B-12)
4. Four servings of fruits and vegetables (one cup of dark greens)

The four-food-group plan simplifies the selection of nutrient-rich foods for the vegetarian.

COOKING LEGUMES

Legume proteins become more available when cooked. The process of cooking alters the texture by weakening the intercellular structural components. Cooking gelatinizes the starch, improves the texture and flavor of legumes, and destroys some objectionable substances, including a trypsin inhibitor present in soybeans.

Because dried legumes have a low moisture content, they cook more rapidly when soaked. They may be soaked overnight or by heating them in boiling water for two minutes and then continuing the soaking for one hour. Legumes soaked in hot water should be cooked in the soaking water to conserve water-soluble vitamins and minerals. Most soaked legumes should boil gently for about 1½ hours. Fully cooked legumes, except soybeans, have a mealy texture.

Hard water extends cooking time of legumes. Hard water contains calcium and magnesium ions, which react with pectic components and retard tenderization. Dried beans do not cook tender in extremely hard water. The addition of a small amount of soda (⅛ teaspoon per cup of beans) to the cooking water shortens the cooking time but is not recommended because soda promotes the loss of thiamin, darkens the beans, and makes them mushy.

To cook legumes:
1. Cover dry legumes with water, boil 2 minutes and let soak for one hour, or cold-soak overnight. Legumes increase in size as they hydrate.
2. Drain beans, rinse and prepare according to selected recipe.

A pressure saucepan shortens cooking time of soaked legumes. The addition of one tablespoon of fat per cup of beans reduces foaming in the pressure saucepan or regular saucepan. Cooking time is prolonged when molasses or tomato juice is added to fried legumes. The calcium in molasses and the acid in tomato tend to retard tenderization. Therefore beans should be partially cooked before adding molases or tomato to keep cooking time relatively short. Generally, legumes increase in volume two to three times when cooked.

Cooked dried soybeans may be used in a variety of casseroles. Green soybeans are cooked in the same way as green peas. Soy milk is prepared from soaked soybeans, and it can be prepared at home.

SUMMARY

Meat alternates and extenders all extend the flavor of meat. Meat alternates serve to replace meats in meals and include legumes, grains, and nuts. Extenders include rice, other grains, and pasta. Vegetable proteins lack one or more essential amino acids in quantity or appropriate proportion. Carefully chosen combinations of vegetable proteins can contribute appropriate amounts of proteins and other nutrients. The four-food-group plan is adaptable to the needs of vegetarians.

SELF-STUDY GUIDE

1. Define meat extenders and alternates and give examples of each.
2. Compare the nutritional contribution of animal and plant sources of protein.
3. Define limiting amino acid, nonessential amino acid, and essential amino acid.
4. What are the differences between soy flour, soy concentrate, soy isolate, and soy milk?
5. Define textured vegetable protein, analog. How are they used?
6. Explain the dietary differences between vegans, ovo- and lacto-vegetarians, and fruitarians.
7. Which individuals are most likely to develop nutritional problems on vegetarian diets? Why?
8. List the four-food-group plan for vegans and lacto-ovo-vegetarians. Plan a day's menu for each.

SELECTED REFERENCES

AKPAPERMAN, M. A., and MARKAKIS, P. Protein supplementation of cowpeas with sesame and watermelon seeds. *Journal of Food Science* 46:960, 1981.

AMERICAN HOME ECONOMICS ASSOCIATION. *Handbook of food preparation.* 8th ed. Washington, D.C.: American Home Economics Association, 1980.

BRADFORD, M. M., and ORTHOEFER, F. T. Nutritional properties of soy protein concentrate. *Cereal World* 58:457, 1983.

DRYER, S. B.; PHILLIPS, S. G.; POWELL, T. S.; UERBERSAX, M.; and ZABIK, M. E. Dry roasted navy beans incorporated in a quick bread. *Cereal Chemistry* 59:319, 1982.

HALABY, G. A.; LEWIS, R. W.; and REY, C. R. Variation in nutrient content of commercially canned legumes. *Journal of Food Science* 47:263, 1982.

HANNIGAN, K. G. Nutrition spread from sunflower seeds. *Food Engineering* 53:85, 1981.

HAYTOWITZ, D. B., and MATTHEWS, R. H. Effect of cooking on nutrient retention of legumes. *Cereal Food World* 28:362, 1983.

KLEIN, M. A., and LEE, R. P. Thiamin content of freshly prepared and leftover Italian spaghetti served in a university food service. *Journal of Food Science* 47:2093, 1980.

MA, C. Y. Chemical characteristics and functionality assessment of protein concentrate from oats. *Cereal Chemistry* 60:36, 1938.

PAULIS, J. W. Recent developments in corn protein research. *Journal of Agriculture and Food Chemistry* 30:14, 1982.

POMERANZ, Y., and DIKEMAN, E. Mineral and protein content of hard red winter wheat flour. *Cereal Chemistry* 60:80, 1983.

SCHONAUS, I., and SGARBERIN, V. C. Inherited characteristics of composition and protein nutritive value of a new cultivar of maize in two stages of maturity. *Journal of Agriculture and Food Chemistry* 31:1, 1983.

U.S. DEPARTMENT OF AGRICULTURE. *Cereals and pastas in family meals.* Home and Garden Bulletin no. 150. Washington, D.C.: Government Printing Office, 1979.

————. *A guide to consumers: Nuts in family meals.* Home and Garden Bulletin no. 176. Washington, D.C.: Government Printing Office, 1977.

————. *How to buy dry beans, peas and lentils.* Home and Garden Bulletin no. 177. Washington, D.C.: Government Printing Office, 1970.

————. *Soybeans in family meals.* Home and Garden Bulletin no. 103. Washington, D.C.: Government Printing Office, 1978.

————. *Your money's worth in foods.* Home and Garden Bulletin no. 183. Washington, D.C.: Government Printing Office, 1979.

WILLIAMS, P. C.; PRESTON, K. R.; NORRIS, K. H.; and STARKEY, P. M. Determination of amino acids in wheat and barley by near-infrared reflectance spectroscopy. *Journal of Food Science* 49:17, 1984.

19

EGGS

OBJECTIVES

When you complete this chapter you will be able to

1. Discuss the nutritional quality of eggs and their use in the diet.
2. Select appropriate grades of eggs for specific cookery purposes.
3. Discuss storage and processing of eggs.
4. Identify the functions of eggs in cookery and cite examples.
5. List and discuss the factors that influence co-agulation of eggs, and compare the preparation of baked and stirred custards.
6. List and discuss factors that influence foam formation, and compare the preparation of meringue, puffy omelet, and soufflé.
7. Compare the methods of egg preparation and apply the principles of egg cookery.

Eggs serve a versatile and basic function in the diet and in food preparation. They are a prepackaged container of nutrients in their own disposable shell. They bind a meat loaf, coat a fish, emulsify a fat, add body to a sauce, thicken a custard, and contribute lightness to a cake and structure to a popover. Their nutrient quality, structure, composition, selection and storage, functional properties, and preparation principles are discussed in this chapter.

NUTRITIONAL QUALITY

Although the color of the egg shell varies from white to deep brown and of the egg yolk from yellow orange to pale yellow, this range in color does not influence egg quality or nutritive value. Because their proteins are comparable to those of meat in quality and quantity, eggs are suitable alternates for meat, poultry, or fish. The yolk is a more concentrated source of nutrients than the white. Both the yolk and the white contribute high-quality proteins. The white is also a good source of riboflavin. The egg yolk contains fat, minerals, and vitamins A and D and is an important source of iron. Yolks may be light in color, yet high in vitamin A value. Some carotenoids, such as zanthophyll, do not contribute vitamin A but may produce a deep-yellow yolk.

Both the yolk and white are good sources of riboflavin. Eggs also contribute some thiamin, niacin, phosphorus, and calcium. Eggs are relatively low in kcalories, yet high in essential nutrients. The nutritive values of the yolk, the white, and the egg as a whole are listed in Table 19–1 and the percentage of U.S. RDA per two large eggs in Table 19–2.

STRUCTURE

Calcium carbonate crystals are predominantly deposited with some magnesium carbonate and calcium phosphate in an organic matrix to form the shell surrounding the edible egg interior. The bloom, or cuticle, deposited on the shell surface

Table 19–1 Nutrient Values for a Large Egg

Nutrient	Whole	Yolk	White
Protein (g)	6.5	2.7	3.6
Fat (g)	5.8	5.2	trace
Carbohydrate (g)	0.5	0.1	0.3
Calcium (mg)	27	24	3
Iron (mg)	1.2	0.9	trace
Phosphorus (mg)	103	97	5
Thiamin (mg)	0.05	0.04	trace
Riboflavin (mg)	0.15	0.07	0.09
Niacin (mg)	trace	trace	trace
Vitamin A (I.U.)	590	580	0
Kilocalories	82	59	17

From USDA, *Nutritive Value of American Foods in Common Units*, Agriculture Handbook no., 456, Agricultural Research Service (Washington, D.C.: Government Printing Office, 1975).

Table 19-2   Percentage of U.S. RDA: Two U.S. Large Eggs

Serving Size = Two U.S. Large Eggs (108 g Edible Portion)

Calories.. 164	Fat (Percent of Calories—68%).................12 g
Protein .... 13 g	Polyunsaturated .... 1.4 g
Carbohydrates .... 1 g	Saturated..3.8 g
	Cholesterol (480 mg/100 g)....................520 mg
	Sodium (130 mg/100 g ....140 mg

Percentage of U.S. Recommended Daily Allowances (U.S. RDA)

Protein 30	Vitamin B$_6$... 6
Vitamin A 10	Folic Acid...15
Vitamin C ....**	Vitamin B$_{12}$ 15
Thiamin 6	Phosphorus...20
Riboflavin...20	Iodine..35
Niacin ....**	Zinc...10
Calcium.. 6	Biotin.. 8
Iron 10	Pantothenic Acid 15
Vitamin D...15	Copper 4
Vitamin E 6	Magnesium 4

**Contains less than 2% of U.S. RDA of these nutrients.
From O. J. Cotterill and J. L. Glauert. Data published in *Poultry Science* 58:134, 1979.

retards moisture loss and impedes bacterial contamination. The shell is rigid, brittle, and porous, permitting an exchange of gases and moisture between the surrounding air and the interior of the egg.

The interior of the egg is separated from the shell by two shell membranes composed primarily of keratin and mucin. As the freshly laid egg cools, the egg contents shrink, causing the formation of a small air space at the large end of the egg when the two membranes separate. Figure 19–1 shows egg composition and structure.

The white is composed of four layers: the inner firm layer next to the yolk, a second layer of thin white, another layer of thick white, and another layer of thin white next to the inner shell membrane. The ratio of thick to thin white varies with the hen, storage conditions, and the age of the egg. As the egg ages, the ratio of thin white increases and is influenced by unfavorable storage conditions.

Two dense, cordlike strands (chalazae) are continuous with the inner firm layer of white enveloping the yolk and keep it in position within the egg. The vitelline membrane (yolk sac) encloses the yolk and separates it from the white. The yolk contains concentric layers or bands of white yolk and yellow yolk. The germ spot (blastoderm) is light in color and is on the upper side of the yolk. The xanthophyll (carotene) content of the ration fed the hen determines the color of the yolk.

Egg Composition

Shell
- Outer covering of egg, composed of calcium carbonate.
- May be white or brown depending on breed of chicken.
- Color does not affect quality, cooking characteristics, or nutritional value.

Yolk
- Yellow portion of egg.
- Color varies with feed of the hen, but doesn't indicate nutritional content.
- Major source of vitamins, minerals and fat.
- Germinal disc.

Vitelline (Yolk) Membrane
- Clean seal which holds egg yolk.

Chalazae
- Twisted, cordlike strands of egg white.
- Anchor yolk in center of egg.
- Prominent chalazae indicates high quality.

Air Cell
- Pocket of air formed at the large end of the egg.
- Caused by contraction of contents during cooling after laying.
- Increases in size with age.

Shell Membranes
- Two membranes – inner and outer shell membranes – surround the albumen.
- Provide protective barrier against bacterial penetration.
- Air cell forms between these two membranes.

Thin Albumen
- Nearest to the shell.
- Spreads around thick white of high quality egg.

Thick Albumen (White)
- Excellent source of riboflavin and protein.
- Stands higher and spreads less than thin white in high quality eggs.
- Thins and becomes indistinguishable from thin white in low quality eggs.

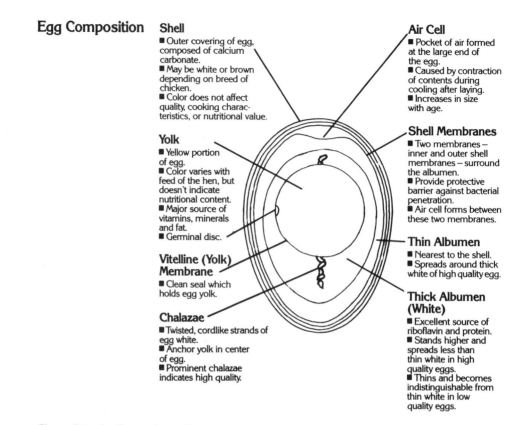

Figure 19-1 Egg Composition and Structure. (From American Egg Board. *The Incredible Edible Egg*, Park Ridge, Il., 1982.)

COMPOSITION

The whole egg has two distinct fractions—the white and the yolk. The white makes up more than half the egg, about 65 percent, and the yolk is 35 percent of the whole egg.

White

Water is the chief component of egg white (87.6 percent), with protein (10.9 percent) the next most abundant constituent. The remaining components include small amounts of minerals and sugars (glucose, galactose, mannose) and a trace of fat.

Egg white proteins are chiefly globular and often combined with carbohydrates to become glycoproteins. Ovalbumin, a glycoprotein, is the chief protein in egg white. It is **denatured** by beating and heat. Ovomucin, a mucoprotein, is responsible for the thickness of egg white. The thick white contains nearly four times as much ovomucin as the thin white.

Yolk

Egg yolk is composed of about 40 percent water, 32 percent fat, 16 percent protein, and a trace of carbohydrate. Nearly all of the egg yolk proteins are combined with lipids to form lipoproteins. The chief egg yolk protein is vitellin, also known as lipovitellin. The lipids of egg yolk include phospholipids, triglycerides, and cholesterol. Lecithin is the chief phospholipid and serves as an important emulsifying agent in food preparation.

SELECTION

Eggs should be selected from refrigerated, sound-shelled eggs. The USDA grade shield on the carton certifies the eggs were a specific grade at the time of grading. The United States Department of Agriculture administers a grading program to assure consumers that eggs and egg products are wholesome and properly packaged and labeled. This USDA grading program is a voluntary service paid for by the producer. Each carton of eggs must clearly display the grade, the size, and the packer or distributor. Only egg cartons bearing the special USDA shield have been inspected by federal inspectors (see Figure 19–2).

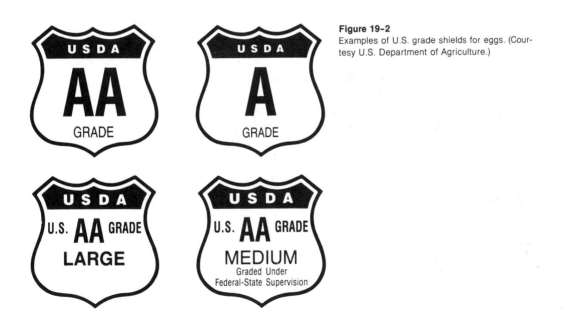

Figure 19–2
Examples of U.S. grade shields for eggs. (Courtesy U.S. Department of Agriculture.)

Egg Grades

The U.S. Department of Agriculture classifies eggs into four quality grades; U.S. AA, U.S. A, U.S. B, and U.S. C. Grade AA eggs are ideal for poaching and frying. They have a round, firm yolk and a high, thick white when broken. Grade A eggs are suitable for all uses. They have fairly well centered and rounded yolks, and the whites are relatively thick. Grade B eggs are suitable for general baking and cooking. The yolks are somewhat flattened, and the whites are less thick than those of Grade A eggs (see Figure 19-3).

In-Shell Grading

USDA quality standards specify clean, unbroken shells and identify the characteristics of quality yolks and whites. Candling is used to determine interior quality of eggs. As light passes through the egg, it shows the quality of the shell, the mobility and position of the yolk, the size of the air cell, and blood spots, if present. As eggs deteriorate, the chalazae weakens, and the yolk settles toward the shell rather than remaining suspended in the white.

When candling was done by hand, the candle was the source of light. Commercial grading operations have replaced hand candling with automated equipment and mass-scanning devices. The term *candling* continues to identify the method used to determine egg quality. The USDA grades for eggs are based on their candled appearance. The color of the shell is not considered in deter-

Figure 19-3
Eggs: Quality grades. (From American Egg Board, *The Incredible Edible Egg.* Park Ridge, Il., 1982.)

	GRADE AA	GRADE A	GRADE B
Break Out Appearance	Covers a small area.	Covers a moderate area.	Covers a wide area.
Albumen Appearance	White is thick and stands high; chalaza prominent.	White is reasonably thick, stands fairly high, chalaza prominent.	Small amount of thick white; chalaza small or absent. Appears weak and watery.
Yolk Appearance	Yolk is firm, round and high.	Yolk is firm and stands fairly high.	Yolk is somewhat flattened and enlarged.
Shell Appearance	Approximates usual shape; generally clean,* unbroken; ridges/rough spots that do not affect the shell strength permitted.		Abnormal shape; some slight stained areas permitted; unbroken; pronounced ridges/ thin spots permitted.
Usage	Ideal for any use, but are especially desirable for poaching, frying, and cooking in shell.		Good for scrambling, baking and use as an ingredient in other foods.

*An egg may be considered clean if it has only very small specks, stains or cage marks. Source: USDA

mining the grade of an egg since this factor has no influence on the flavor, quality, performance in cookery, or nutritive value.

Out-of-Shell Grading

Professional egg graders and researchers grade some eggs out of the shell, using more precise methods. Some tests used measure the height of the thick white in relation to the weight of the egg to determine the Haugh unit (an arbitrary unit), and the measurement of the height of the yolk in relation to the width of the yolk. The **albumen** index is determined by dividing the height of the thickest portion of the white (albumen) by the diameter of the white. The yolk index is determined by dividing the height of the yolk by the width of the yolk. The height of both the white and yolk is higher in high-quality eggs than in lower-quality eggs.

Egg Sizes

Large and small eggs can be the same grade. Egg grade and size are independent factors. Eggs are sorted into six weight classes based on minimum weight per dozen, ranging from jumbo (30 oz) to peewee (15 oz). Extra-large, large, and medium eggs are usually available in the three retail grades of U.S. AA, A, and B. Jumbo and peewee usually do not appear on the retail market. The carton identifies the size and grade of eggs and may list the minimum weight per dozen in ounces (see Figure 19-4).

Most recipes are formulated on the basis of large or medium eggs for uniformity in baking quality. Some recipes using large amounts of egg may specify a measured quantity of egg to avoid variations in egg sizes. The grade and size of eggs should be selected according to intended use. Although large eggs may be preferred for table use, it may be wise to consider the price in relation to grades and sizes for eggs used in cooking.

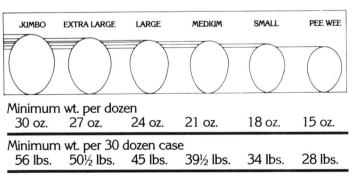

Figure 19-4
Egg sizes: Minimum weight per dozen. (From U.S. Department of Agriculture.)

JUMBO	EXTRA LARGE	LARGE	MEDIUM	SMALL	PEE WEE

Minimum wt. per dozen

30 oz.	27 oz.	24 oz.	21 oz.	18 oz.	15 oz.

Minimum wt. per 30 dozen case

56 lbs.	50½ lbs.	45 lbs.	39½ lbs.	34 lbs.	28 lbs.

STORAGE AND PROCESSING

The interior quality of an egg starts to deteriorate as soon as it is laid. The speed and degree of change are influenced by storage conditions. Proper conditions retard the deterioration of egg quality but do not stop the process.

Changes in Eggs

Moisture evaporates through the shell causing a gradual decrease in weight. Some carbon dioxide evolves from the egg as it ages increasing the alkalinity of the white above that of a fresh egg. The slightly acid yolk becomes alkaline. The thick white becomes thinned, increasing the percentage of thin white. The vitelline membrane of the yolk is weakened as water passes from the white to the yolk; the yolk flattens and breaks easily. The air cell enlarges as moisture is lost. These changes occur more rapidly at high storage temperatures.

Home Storage

Eggs should be refrigerated immediately after purchase. They should be kept covered in the carton or container to reduce absorption of flavors and odors from other foods. Although eggs deteriorate more quickly in a household refrigerator than under commercial cold-storage conditions, they keep satisfactorily for about two weeks. Leftover whites should be refrigerated or frozen immediately in a tightly closed container. Leftover yolks are best covered with a layer of cold water, tightly sealed, and refrigerated. Whole eggs broken out of the shell or yolks may be frozen with the addition of salt or sugar.

Commercial Storage

Egg quality is retained and deterioration minimized by controlled cold storage. Storage temperatures of 29 to 32° F (1.5 to 0° C) can maintain grade A quality of eggs for a period of six months. The cool temperature slows enzyme activity. In addition, commercial storage conditions maintain a relative humidity of 85 to 90 percent to reduce moisture loss from eggs.

Eggs may be dipped in light mineral oil prior to cold storage. The thin coating of oil partially closes the pores in the shell and reduces the loss of moisture and carbon dioxide. When the oiling is done properly, there is no significant rise in the pH of the egg during storage.

Processing

Because salmonella can be transmitted from poultry to eggs pasteurization of egg products produced in bulk is mandatory. The USDA requires that liquid whole eggs must be heated to at least 140–143° F (60–61.5° C) and held at this temperature for at least 3½ minutes. The objectives are to maintain the functional quality of the eggs and destroy pathogenic microorganisms.

Frozen, dried, or liquid egg products are used by commercial manufacturers of food products and quantity food buyers. Processed eggs retain their cooking functions and nutritive values and ensure uniformity in the prepared food product.

Freezing. Commercially frozen egg products are pasteurized before freezing to avoid salmonella infection. The pasteurization temperature required (140–143° F, 60–61.5° C) for liquid whole egg may affect somewhat the whipping quality of egg. Frozen egg products include whole egg, blends of yolk and white, egg yolk, and white. These products are used as ingredients in other foods.

Fluid whole eggs can be frozen alone, but they retain their functional properties somewhat better if a small amount of sugar or salt is added to control gelation of the yolk. Egg yolks frozen alone become viscous and gummy and lose their ability to blend with other ingredients. These changes also can be prevented by adding a small amount of sugar (one tablespoon per cup of yolk) or salt (one teaspoon per cup of yolk) to the yolk before freezing. The choice of salt or sugar depends upon the use to be made of the egg. Salt is suitable for eggs used in breads, noodles, or mayonnaise, and sugar for those used in cakes and other sweetened baked products.

Egg whites can be frozen alone satisfactorily. Functional properties of the white are not impaired by freezing, but pasteurization before freezing may affect whipping property to some extent. Egg white proteins are more sensitive to heating than those in whole egg mixtures; therefore, their whipping quality is slightly affected.

Cooked egg whites tend to become tough and rubbery when frozen. This may be due to the formation of large ice crystals and the separation of water from the coagulated white. Cooked egg yolks freeze satisfactorily without additions.

Drying. Eggs must be pasteurized before drying to avoid salmonella infection. Whole egg, yolks, and whites are dried. Moisture is removed from egg by evaporation. Egg whites are free of fat and can be dried without major changes in physical structure. Egg yolks contain fat, and the process of removing water appears to irreversibly change the structure of some lipid components in egg yolk. As a result, the lipid has a form-inhibiting effect when dried eggs are beaten.

For a stable product glucose must be removed from egg white before drying. This removal treatment controls the browning reaction (Maillard) that would occur during storage and permits the egg white to retain its functional properties, its flavor, and its color.

Dried egg products are subject to deteriorative changes during storage. They retain their quality best when kept in tightly sealed containers at a low storage temperature (40° F, 5° C). Dried eggs properly stored have about the same nutritive value as shell eggs.

Dried egg products are sifted before measuring. They may be sifted with the dry ingredients and the extra liquid used in the recipe, or they may be reconstituted before use. Dried eggs are reconstituted by sprinkling them over lukewarm water, stirring to moisten, and then beating until smooth.

Dried egg products are used commercially in angel food cake, salad dressing, noodles, candies, a variety of bakery products, and mixes. Dried-egg solids can replace fresh egg in recipes. Table 19–3 lists the amount of dried egg product and water required to replace shell eggs. Reconstituted dried egg whites require a much longer time to beat than fresh egg whites.

Egg Substitutes

Egg substitutes are of special interest to those on cholesterol-restricted or fat-restricted diets. Although the nutrient contribution of eggs makes them a valued food, the high cholesterol content of the yolk is of concern to some. Egg substitutes differ from eggs in that they are lower in fat, cholesterol, and calories. They are available in liquid or frozen forms, as complete-egg or partial-egg substitutes. The complete-egg substitute is made from soy or milk proteins. The partial-egg substitute retains the egg white but not the egg yolk.

Egg substitutes have about one-half the fat and calories of regular eggs and contain less sodium. The egg fat is replaced with vegetable oil (usually corn oil), giving egg substitute a higher ratio of polyunsaturated fat to saturated fat. Containers of egg substitute can be stored unopened in the refrigerator for about ten weeks and for two weeks after they are opened.

The flavor of egg substitute is different from that of real eggs but is quite acceptable. Egg substitutes blend easily with other ingredients. Acceptable omelets or scrambled eggs can be prepared from these products. They may replace eggs in recipes that call for whole egg except when eggs are used as a thickener, in

Table 19-3 Dried Egg Substitutions for Shell Eggs

Number (Large Size)	Sifted Dried Egg Product	Water
Whole eggs		
1	2½ tablespoons	2½ tablespoons
6	1 cup	1 cup
Egg yolks		
1	2 tablespoons	2 teaspoons
6	¾ cup	¼ cup
Egg whites		
1	2 teaspoons	2 tablespoons
6	¼ cup	¾ cup

Adapted from USDA, *Eggs in Family Meals*, Home and Garden Bulletin no. 103 (Washington, D.C.: Government Printing Office, 1975).

custard, for example. The milk protein used in egg substitutes does not have the thickening power of eggs.

COOKERY: FUNCTIONS

Eggs serve a variety of functions in food preparation and can replace meat as the main dish in a meal. They influence the color, texture, flavor, and nutrient value of food products in which eggs are used. The ability of egg proteins to **coagulate** enables them to act as thickening, binding, coating, and structural agents in the preparation of numerous food products.

Coagulation

Egg proteins, as is true of proteins in other foods, coagulate over a range of temperatures specific to each type of protein. As the egg white is denatured by heat, it loses its fluidity and transparency, becoming opaque and firm. The loss of flow properties results when water in the egg becomes trapped or bound as the proteins coagulate to form a gel. A number of factors influence the temperatures at which denaturation takes place, and these variables may also affect the characteristics of the final product.

Rate of Heating.   The rate of heating greatly influences the temperature range over which coagulation occurs. When eggs or other protein-containing foods are heated rapidly, coagulation will occur at higher temperatures than when a slow rate is used. Egg white may begin to coagulate at about 140° F (60° C) and become firm near 149° F (65° C). The yolk proteins begin to coagulate at near 149° F (65° C) and become firm at 158° F (70° C).

For the best results in egg-thickened products, a moderate rate of heating is desirable because there is sufficient time to determine that the desired end point has been reached before the protein is overheated. Heating proteins beyond the coagulation point causes them to shrink, toughen, and exude water and water-soluble compounds from the gel. Egg yolks have less tendency to toughen than egg whites, owing partially to the fat content, but overcoagulated egg yolks do become crumbly.

Concentration.   Eggs are often diluted by combining them with other ingredients, such as milk. The coagulation temperature of egg protein depends upon the concentration of egg protein. The coagulation temperature decreases as the concentration of egg in a mixture is increased; and conversely, the coagulation temperature increases as the egg concentration is decreased owing to the addition of other ingredients.

Salt.   Salt should be added before an egg mixture is heated so that curdling can be avoided during its addition. Salts (such as chlorides), lactates, phosphates, and sulfates that are contained in the ingredients added during preparation lower the coagulation temperature.

Sugar.   Sugar elevates the temperature at which coagulation occurs. As the sugar content of a mixture is increased, so is the coagulation temperature. Therefore a very sweet custard will need to be heated to a higher final temperature than one containing less sugar.

Acid.   Acids such as cream of tartar, lemon juice, or vinegar lower the coagulation temperature of egg protein or egg mixtures. Added acids may favor coagulation by enabling the protein to reach the isoelectric point (where the electrical charges on the protein are at a minimum). Overcooking or heating of the acid-egg mixture can cause protein to peptize (break), resulting in a thinned mixture.

Binding and Coating Function

The binding and coating functions of eggs are dependent upon the ability of eggs to coagulate. Eggs blended into croquette mixtures or meat loaf serve as a binder when the egg protein coagulates.

Foods may be coated with a batter containing egg, or the food may be dipped into beaten egg and then rolled in a crumb or flour mixture. Coatings that have egg in them coagulate when the food is cooked and adhere to the surface. Coatings are used to keep food such as fish from breaking apart, to help retain juices, and to enhance the appearance, texture, or flavor of the food to which they are applied.

Thickening Function

Egg proteins used in a sufficiently high concentration form a network that traps (enmeshes) fluid to form a gel. Egg-thickened products are known as custards, either baked or stirred. The basic ingredients of both baked and stirred custards are scalded milk, eggs, sugar, salt, and vanilla. The difference in the final product is due to the method of cooking. Baked custards are cooked in the oven while stirred custards are cooked over hot water.

Baked Custard.   The individual custard cups or a baking dish containing the blended custard mixture are placed into a pan of hot water on the center rack of a 350° F (177° C) oven. The water promotes an even distribution of heat and avoids overcooking of the outer surface before the center of the custard coagulates.

The custard is baked until a knife inserted in the center comes out clean. Care must be taken to remove the custard from the oven as soon as it is coagulated to avoid overbaking. An overbaked custard shows separation of liquid from the gel (**syneresis**) and a porous texture. A well-prepared custard is firm, tender, and uniformly coagulated with no signs of syneresis or porosity.

Stirred Custard.   The soft custard is stirred in the top of a double boiler while heating over hot water 158–167° F (70–75° C). Custards cooked slowly at a low temperature coagulate more completely than those heated rapidly. The flavor and consistency of stirred custards are better and curdling is less likely to occur when custards are heated slowly. Stirring is necessary to prevent lumping and promote a creamy consistency.

The custard is cooked until a thick layer coats the spoon. Because vanilla and other flavorings are volatile, they are added after the custard is cooked. The cooked custard is removed immediately from the heat and either it is poured into a cold dish or the pan is placed in cold water. Overheating yields a curdled custard. The consistency of a slightly curdled custard can be improved by beating with a rotary beater. A well-prepared stirred custard is the consistency of heavy cream. It may be served alone as dessert or as a sauce over fruit or cake.

Emulsifying Function

The lipoproteins in egg yolk are commonly used as **emulsifying** agents in food preparation. Emulsifiers facilitate the dispersion of fat in a liquid-based system. The eggs encourage the formation of an emulsion. Unless the droplets of oil are coated with a substance that keeps them from coalescing, water and oil will separate. Eggs, serving as an **emulsifier,** improve the textural quality of a number of foods. Egg yolk coats oil droplets so that an emulsion can form and be retained.

Egg yolks act as an emulsifier in the preparation of many foods including cakes, cookies, cream puffs, soufflé, ice cream, and mayonnaise.

Foaming Function

A **foam** consists of bubbles of gas trapped in a liquid. A thin elastic film of egg surrounds air bubbles. When eggs are beaten, they first become foamy, then form soft peaks, and with additional beating, stiff peaks. Part of the protein in the egg film surrounding air cells of beaten eggs is coagulated by the process of beating. As the egg foam is heated, the trapped air expands and stretches the egg film until the proteins coagulate or the cell walls rupture.

Egg foams are sufficiently stable to permit their incorporation with other ingredients. In this way egg foams contribute leavening action and structure to baked products in which they are used.

Egg white foams are used most often, but foam can also be prepared from whole egg or just yolks. Egg white foams are prepared quickly and are constituents of meringues, puffy omelets, soufflés, angel and sponge cakes, and some candies and frostings. Egg yolk foams require a relatively long beating time and are constituents of sponge-type cakes and puffy omelets. Egg foams make foods in which they are used light and porous.

A number of factors influence the volume, stability, and texture of egg white foam. The stages to which egg whites are beaten, utensils used, and added ingredients affect egg foam.

Beating. Egg proteins are responsible for the foaming property of egg. As beating denatures some of the protein, the egg foam becomes finer, whiter, and increasingly stiff and stable with a gradual loss of elasticity. The peaks formed progress from soft peaks with rounded tops to stiff peaks with sharp points. Eggs beaten to the stiff but not dry stage retain sufficient elasticity to permit their blending into food products to enhance the volume of baked products.

For most uses in food preparation egg whites are beaten to form moderately stiff peaks, the tips of which bend over when the beater is withdrawn from the beaten whites. The foam should retain a shiny, smooth surface, and the mass should flow very slowly when the bowl is partially inverted.

Continued beating after a stiff peak is formed yields a dry, brittle foam that does not incorporate with other ingredients. Once the desired stage is reached, the foam should be used immediately, otherwise it will stiffen and lose its elasticity.

Beater and Bowl.   Both the beater and bowl affect the foam. Good foams can be obtained with either a rotary beater (electric or hand) or a wire whip. The thinner blades and finer wires yield smaller air cells and a finer foam.

The bowl in which eggs are beaten should allow for expansion in foam volume. Bowls with rounded bottoms and sloping sides allow the beater to pick up the egg mass easily. Bowls other than those made of plastic should be used to beat egg whites because fat clings to plastic surfaces and thus interferes with foam formation.

Thick/Thin Whites.   The foaming ability of egg white depends upon the proportion of specific proteins in the thick and thin white. The thin egg white can be beaten to a greater volume than the same quantity of thick white, but the foam is less stable than that of the thick white. The volume of cooked meringues and angel food cakes is greater from thick whites than from thin whites.

Temperature.   Egg white foams are formed more quickly, reach a greater volume, and have finer texture when the whites are at room temperature rather than at refrigerator temperature. Apparently, cold egg whites are too viscous to whip effectively.

Sugar.   Egg whites without sugar are easily overbeaten and yield a foam with reduced stability and increased drainage. Adding sugar relatively early in the beating process reduces the possibility of overbeating the foam. Sugar retards coagulation and denaturation of egg proteins and extends the period of beating required to achieve the desired end point. Sugar should not be added before beating is begun and should be added gradually after foaming occurs. The ability of sugar to attract water may result in less drainage and thus promote stability of the foam. Sugar-containing foams are smooth and fine grained, and do not drain or collapse quickly. Sugared foams retain their elasticity for a period of time and can be spread or manipulated without rupturing cell structure.

Acid.   The addition of acid in the form of cream of tartar or lemon juice soon after foaming occurs lowers the normally alkaline pH of egg whites, bringing them nearer the isoelectric point of egg proteins and favoring coagulation and maximum stability. Acids also promote the formation of a stiff foam with a large volume and a fine texture.

Salt.   Salt delays foam formation and should be added after egg white is beaten to a foam. A small amount of salt is added to enhance flavor, but the foam may be less elastic than when beaten without salt.

Fat.   The fat in egg yolk or fat from other sources (cream, milk, shortening, or unclean bowls and beaters) retards form formation. For maximum foam volume the bowls and beaters must be completely free of egg yolk or other fat. Plastic bowls are not recommended for beating egg whites because it is difficult to remove traces of fat from them.

Liquid.   The addition of a small amount of water to egg white increases foam volume but decreases foam stability and increases leakage from soft meringues.

Interfering Function

The formation of large ice crystals can be retarded by the interfering action of beaten egg whites when they are added to mixtures to be frozen, such as sherbet. In the preparation of some types of candies and frostings, egg white foams interfere with the formation of large sugar crystals. In both instances the interfering action promoted by beaten egg white contributes to the desired smooth texture of frozen and sugar products.

FOAM PRODUCTS

The volume and texture of foam products, the meringues, puffy omelets, and **soufflés,** are dependent on such preparation factors as the texture and stability of the foam produced, the extent of beating, the technique used in incorporating the foam into other ingredients, and the conditions utilized in baking.

Meringues

Meringues are of two basic types: hard and soft. Hard meringues contain four tablespoons of sugar per egg white. Sugar is added to egg white beaten to the soft-peak stage, and then beating is continued until the foam forms a stiff peak. Swirls of egg white foam are placed on heavy paper on a flat baking sheet. They are baked at 250° F (120° C) for an hour and remain in the oven with the heat off and door closed for another hour to complete drying of the meringue shells. When shells are not dried sufficiently, they will be difficult to cut. Hard meringues should be dry, crisp, puffy, and a delicate brown.

Soft meringues are used as toppings for cream pies. They are usually prepared with half as much sugar (two tablespoons per white) as in hard meringues. When the foam forms a soft peak, the meringue is spread gently onto the hot filling to the point where it meets the crust, thus sealing the edge, and then it is baked.

Beading and leakage are two undesirable features associated with soft meringues. Droplets of amber syrup on the surface of baked meringues are due to overcoagulation of protein in the egg foam. Meringues baked in a hot oven (425° F, 218° C) for a short time (about 4½ minutes) are less likely to bead. The meringue is tender and less sticky. Meringues baked at a moderate oven temperature (350–375° F, 177–191° C) for fifteen to eighteen minutes may be somewhat sticky compared to those baked in a hot oven.

The accumulation of liquid where the meringue and crust meet is often termed *weeping*. This leakage from the meringue is due to undercoagulation of protein. There is less leakage when meringue is spread on a hot filling and baked in a hot oven for a short time.

A high-quality soft meringue is slightly moist, tender, fluffy, lightly browned, easy to cut, and free of syrup droplets on the surface and it shows no leakage near the crust edge.

Puffy Omelet

Puffy, or fluffy, omelet preparation begins with the separation of egg yolks and whites. Egg yolks with the desired seasonings and added liquid are beaten until very thick and light lemon in color and set aside. Egg yolks do not stiffen on standing as do egg white foams. Next the egg whites are beaten until they are just stiff but not dry. The egg yolk mixture is folded quickly but gently into the beaten egg whites. The folding is continued only until the white and yolks are completely blended. The omelet mixture is unstable and easily separates into dense and foamy layers when cooking is delayed.

The omelet mixture is poured immediately into a preheated, but not hot, heavy skillet containing a thin layer of margarine or butter. The mixture is spread gently and evenly in the skillet and cooked over medium heat without stirring until the bottom is lightly browned. The omelet then may be placed directly into a preheated oven at 325° F (163° C) to bake about twenty minutes to complete coagulation.

Omelets also may be completely cooked on the surface unit. When the omelet is set around the edges, the heat may be lowered and the pan covered to retain steam, which cooks the surface of the omelet. An alternate method places the omelet under the broiler for a short time to complete cooking.

High-quality puffy omelets are light, uniformly cooked, slightly moist, lightly browned, and tender. The interior has a homogeneous, yellow color, cells of uniform size, a pleasing flavor, and no trace of layers.

Soufflé

A starch-thickened, yolk-containing sauce rather than a yolk foam distinguishes a soufflé from a puffy omelet. Egg white foam is also an important ingredient in both products. The heat-coagulated protein of both the egg yolk and white

Souffle (Courtesy American Egg Board)

give structure to soufflés and puffy omelets. The expansion of air in the egg foam as these products bake causes them to rise and appear puffed.

Soufflé preparation begins with the blending of beaten egg yolks into a very thick white sauce. Grated cheese or other finely chopped foods may be added to the sauce-yolk mixture. Whites beaten to the soft-peak stage are carefully folded into the sauce-yolk mixture. The soufflé mixture is baked in an ungreased dish so that it can cling to the sides and reach maximum volume. The dish containing the soufflé is placed into a pan of hot water to protect the outer edges of the soufflé from overbaking. The soufflé is baked immediately in a 350° F (177° C) oven.

Baking of soufflés should be timed so they are served as soon as baking is completed. Even fully baked soufflés shrink slightly when removed from the oven. Overbaking can cause the soufflé to begin to shrink even while in the oven.

The food items added to the soufflé contribute flavor and determine its use as a main dish or dessert. Main-dish soufflés often contain grated cheese, chopped meat, fish, poultry, or vegetables. Dessert soufflés contain the basic ingredients of main-dish soufflés along with sugar, flavorings such as chocolate, chopped nuts, puréed fruits, and vanilla. All soufflés, regardless of flavor, should be light, tender, fluffy, well blended, of good volume, slightly moist, and delicately browned.

METHODS OF EGG PREPARATION

Eggs are often prepared and served as the main protein food in a meal. Controlled coagulation of egg proteins underlies successful preparation of egg in the shell or out of the shell. The use of low-to-moderate temperatures avoids toughening of egg proteins and applies an important principle in egg preparation. Toughening of egg proteins results from the use of too high a temperature or too long a period of heating. Egg whites begin to coagulate at a slightly lower temperature than egg yolks. Coagulation is a gradual process, but the rate of coagulation increases with increases in temperature. The application of the principle of low-to-moderate temperature for heating eggs rules out the use of boiling water.

In-the-Shell Eggs

Eggs in the shell may be cooked to the soft or hard stage. They are immersed in cold or simmering water (185° F, 85° C) and simmered three to five minutes for soft-cooked eggs and fifteen to twenty minutes for hard. The simmering period must be carefully timed to achieve the desired degree of coagulation (doneness). The simmer temperature allows time for heat to penetrate and coagulate the yolk before the white overcoagulates. Boiling toughens egg protein and should be avoided; therefore, *hard-cooked* or *soft-cooked* are more appropriate terms than *hard-boiled* or *soft-boiled.*

In an alternate method, eggs are placed in one pint of boiling water for each egg, the heat turned off, the pan covered, and the egg retained in the water for four to six minutes for soft-cooked and forty to forty-five minutes for hard-cooked eggs. If eggs are at refrigerator temperature, an additional two minutes should be allowed.

Overcooked eggs usually develop a green ring around the yolk. This ring is due to the formation of iron sulfide. The iron from the yolk and hydrogen sulfide from the white combine. This discoloration is harmless but unattractive. Formation of iron sulfide can be avoided by careful timing of the simmering period and rapid cooling of hot eggs in cold water.

A proper hard-cooked egg has a completely coagulated yolk, no ferrous sulfide ring, and a tender white. A proper soft-cooked egg has a firm but tender white and a slightly thickened but not firm yolk.

Poached

Successful **poaching** requires high-quality eggs. The large amount of thick white helps to minimize spread of the white and completely surrounds the yolk. A strong vitelline membrane makes it easier to handle the egg during poaching without breaking the yolk.

Eggs to be poached are broken individually into a small bowl or custard cup and gently slipped into simmering water. By directing the egg toward the side of the pan, the spreading of the white is minimized. Usually, as soon as the white is completely coagulated, the poached egg is removed from the water, resulting in the desired soft yolk. When a firm yolk is preferred, the egg is left in the water a few minutes longer to achieve the desired firmness. Poached eggs should be drained on paper towels.

Fried

A controlled low temperature and high-quality eggs are essential in the preparation of attractive fried eggs with a tender, compact white. Eggs are slipped one at a time into a preheated pan with a minimum of fat to prevent sticking. The egg may be turned or a lid placed on the pan to retain steam to cook the upper surface. The eggs are cooked slowly until the white coagulates, the yolk is slightly thickened, and a layer of coagulated white covers the yolk.

Scrambled

Eggs lower than grade A may be used for scrambling, since the yolk and white are blended with or without the addition of a small amount (one tablespoon) of milk per egg. The mixture is poured into a preheated buttered pan and heated slowly. The egg is pushed from the bottom and sides of the pan as it coagulates permitting the fluid egg to flow toward bottom of pan. This prevents the cooked egg from overcoagulating. Cooking is discontinued as soon as eggs are coagulated but still slightly moist. Additional heating causes liquid to squeeze out (syneresis) and the proteins to toughen. The eating quality of scrambled eggs is best when they are served promptly.

Plain (french) Omelet

Unlike the puffy omelet described earlier, the plain, or french, omelet is a flat disc lightly browned, usually rolled or folded. Often grated cheese or other flavorful items are added before folding. A sauce may be served over the completed omelet.

A mixture like that prepared for scrambled eggs is used for a plain omelet. The blended mixture is poured into a preheated pan containing a thin layer of fat. As the omelet coagulates, a small portion is lifted, rather than pushed, with a narrow spatula to permit the uncooked mixture to reach the bottom of the pan.

When necessary, the pan may be tipped to facilitate the flow of uncooked egg to the pan bottom for cooking. This procedure continues until almost no fluid egg remains. Slowly cook the omelet until it is lightly browned on the bottom.

Baked or Shirred

Eggs may be baked in individual baking dishes or together in a shallow baking dish. High-quality eggs are broken into well-greased baking pans. One-half teaspoon of table fat and one tablespoon of milk are placed over each egg. The eggs are seasoned as desired and baked in the oven at 325° F (163° C) until the desired degree of firmness is reached, usually about twenty minutes.

SUMMARY

Eggs are valued as a nutritious food and as an ingredient serving many functions. All eggs regardless of color are equally nutritious. They are a low-cost source of high-quality protein as well as an important source of iron, other minerals, and vitamins.

All eggs of the same quality perform equally well in cookery. Eggs are graded according to USDA quality standards, which are not related to egg size. Egg quality is determined in the shell by candling. Refrigerator storage is required at all times to retard egg deterioration.

The proteins of egg white coagulate before those of the yolk. Sugar raises the coagulation temperature, salt reduces it, and acids, on prolonged heating, peptize protein and cause thinning of thickened products.

The nature of egg foam determines the quality of the food product. The character of the foam is determined by egg quality, extent of beating, and added substances. Egg yolks can be beaten to a viscous foam. Egg white foams to be folded into other ingredients are beaten to the soft-peak stage, and to the stiff-peak stage for hard meringues. Beating beyond the stiff-peak stage results in a brittle foam, which functions poorly.

Eggs are an important staple food as well as a versatile ingredient. Grade AA is preferred for eggs cooked alone or for egg foams; grade A is satisfactory for all uses; grade B can be used for general baking and cooking purposes. The protein composition of egg mandates low-to-moderate cooking temperature and permits eggs to coagulate, leaven, thicken, and to act as binding, coating, and interfering agents. Egg yolk functions as an emulsifier.

SELF-STUDY GUIDE

1. Compare the composition and nutrient value of egg white and yolk.
2. Discuss the selection and storage of eggs.
3. List five changes that occur during the storage of eggs. How do these changes influence egg-containing products?

4. Discuss the characteristics of high-quality eggs. How does quality influence the product?

5. What temperature is appropriate for cooking eggs? Why?

6. How is coagulation of egg influenced by salt, sugar, and acid?

7. What characteristics of eggs permit them to function as a binder? As a coating agent?

8. Discuss the emulsifying function of eggs. In which products do eggs serve as an emulsifier?

9. What three factors influence the textural quality of egg-thickened products?

10. What five factors influence the formation of egg foams?

11. Identify three products dependent upon egg foam for their volume and texture.

12. Identify the types of meringues. In what ways do they differ? What are their uses?

13. List six functional purposes of eggs in cookery and give examples. Identify the egg constituent promoting each functional property.

SELECTED REFERENCES

ADAMS, C. *Nutritive value of American foods in common units.* Agriculture Handbook no. 456. Agricultural Research Service. Washington, D.C.: Government Printing Office, 1980.

AMERICAN EGG BOARD. *The incredible edible egg.* Park Ridge, Ill., 1982.

————. *Eggcyclopedia.* Park Ridge, Ill., 1981.

CHEN, T. C., and HSU, S. Y. Quality attributes of whole egg and albumin mixtures cooked by different methods. *Journal of Food Science* 46:984, 1981.

Cook in bag scrambled eggs for food service operations. *Food Engineering* 53:52, 1981.

DIXSON, D. K., and COTTERILL, O. J. Electrophoretic and chromatographic changes in egg yolk protein due to heat. *Journal of Food Science* 46:981, 1981.

ESSARY, E. O. Caloric content of eggs cooked by different methods. *Poultry Science* 59:1605, 1980.

GIL, V., and MACLEOD, C. Synthesis and assessment of three compounds suspected as egg aroma volatiles. *Journal of Agricultural and Food Chemistry* 29:484, 1981.

GOSSETT, P. W., and BAKER, R. C. Prevention of the green-grey discoloration in cooked liquid whole egg. *Journal of Food Science* 46:328, 1981.

HANDY, A. Eggs—nature's prepackaged masterpiece of nutrition. In *Food for us all: The 1969 yearbook of agriculture.* Washington, D.C.: Government Printing Office, 1969.

ISHIDA, M., et al. Occurrence of dibutyl and di(2-ethylhexyl) phthalate in chicken eggs. *Journal of Agricultural and Food Chemistry* 29:72, 1981.

JOHNSON, S. A. *Inside an egg.* Minneapolis: Lerner Publications Company, 1981.

KATO, Y., et al. Comparative study of aggregated and disaggregated ovomucin during egg white thinning. *Journal of Agricultural and Food Chemistry* 29:821, 1981.

————. Effect of Maillard reaction on some physical properties of ovalbumin. *Journal of Food Science* 46:1835, 1981.

————. Effects of some metals on the Maillard reaction of ovalbumin. *Journal of Food Science* 29:540, 1981.

KING, A. J., et al. Chemical and biological study of acylated egg white. *Journal of Food Science* 46:1107, 1981.

MARABLE, N. L., et al. Protein quality of supplements and meal replacements. *Journal of the American Dietetic Association* 77:270, 1980.

U.S. DEPARTMENT OF AGRICULTURE. *Eggs in family meals.* Home and Garden Bulletin no. 103. Washington, D.C.: Government Printing Office, 1975.

————. *How to buy eggs.* Home and Garden Bulletin no. 144. Washington, D.C.: Government Printing Office, 1977.

VAUPEL, J. W., and GRAHAM, J. D. Brief on behalf of eggs. *Science Digest* 87:58, 1980.

WAKAMATU, T., and SATO, Y. Studies on release of components from frozen-thawed low-density lipoprotein (LDL) of egg yolk. *Journal of Food Science* 45:1768, 1980.

20

MILK

OBJECTIVES

When you complete this chapter, you will be able to

1. Discuss the composition and nutritional quality of milk products and give examples of the use of milk products in cookery.

2. Discuss quality assurance of milk and explain how milk quality is maintained in the home.

3. Discuss the functions of milk in cookery and give examples.

4. Discuss the factors that influence denaturation and coagulation of milk proteins.

5. Identify the milk components influenced by heat and discuss the heat-induced changes that occur.

6. Identify and discuss the factors influencing the whipping quality of milk products that yield a foam.

Throughout the world milk from various animals makes an important dietary contribution. In the United States milk implies cow's milk unless otherwise identified. Milk products contribute wholesomeness, valuable nutrients, and variety to our diets. Milk and its derivatives, cream and butter, are versatile foods. They appear in meals throughout the day and between meals as snacks.

Milk is often served alone as a beverage. As an ingredient it appears in sauces, soups, puddings, custards, baked products, frozen desserts, and beverages. This chapter deals with the composition and nutritive value of milk and the processing and preparation techniques applied to milk and its products.

NUTRITIONAL QUALITY

Milk is often regarded as the most nutritious and nearly perfect food because of the quantity and quality of nutrients it contributes. It is especially valued for its content of calcium and high-quality proteins. Without milk it becomes very difficult to meet the calcium needs of children or adults. No other food in the usual American diet is as rich a source of calcium as milk. Table 20–1 lists the nutrient contributions of selected milk products.

Milk is generally considered a good source of minerals, except iron. The iron of milk is in a readily utilizable form, but the quantity is inadequate. Children restricted to diets of only milk for a prolonged period develop anemia unless iron supplemens are included. Milk is a rich source of phosphorous, and when calcium needs are met, a large portion of the phosphorous requirement is also met.

Varying quantities of all known vitamins are present in milk. The level of ascorbic acid is inadequate to meet nutritional needs. Milk is an excellent source of riboflavin, a good source of niacin, and a fair source of thiamin. Although milk contains only small amounts of formed niacin, it contributes important amounts of tryptophan, an amino acid precursor of niacin, making milk a good potential source of niacin.

Milk has a high vitamin A value consisting of the formed vitamin and the carotene precursor present. When cream—the fat—is removed in the production of skim milk, so are the fat-soluble vitamins. However, vitamins A and D are usually added to low-fat and skim milk, making them excellent replacements for whole milk. Although some vitamin D is present in fresh milk, the quantity is variable and unreliable. Vitamin D-fortified milk is a reliable source, providing 10 micrograms or 400 international units of vitamin D per quart. When vitamins A and D are added, the label will indicate this fortification.

Milk proteins are of excellent quality, providing all of the essential amino acids required for the synthesis of body proteins. The use of milk with plant protein sources, such as cereals and legumes, is nutritionally sound and economical. Milk provides methionine and lysine, the two amino acids notably low in cereals, thus promoting better utilization of the cereal protein.

LACTOSE INTOLERANCE

Lactose, or milk sugar, is found only in milk. Most humans produce the enzyme lactase, required to hydrolyze or digest lactose into its structural components of galactose and glucose. A few children and adults, however, are lactose intolerant because they lack the ability to produce adequate amounts of lactase and, therefore, are unable to digest lactose. Undigested lactose then remains in their intestinal tract and is subjected to the action of microorganisms, producing abdominal pain, diarrhea, and flatulence (gas).

Table 20–1 Nutrients in Selected Milk Products

Product	Measure	Kcal	Protein (gm)	Fat (gm)	Calcium (mg)	Vitamin A (IU)	Thiamin (mg)	Riboflavin (mg)	Niacin (mg)
Milk									
Whole (3.5% fat)	1 cup	159	9	9	288	350	.07	.41	.2
Lowfat (2% fat)	1 cup	145	10	5	352	200	.10	.52	.2
Skim	1 cup	90	9		296	10	.09	.44	.2
Evaporated	1 cup	345	18	20	635	810	.10	.86	.5
Sweetened condensed	1 cup	982	25	27	802	1100	.24	1.16	.6
Nonfat dry (instant)	1 cup	244	24	0.5	879	20	.24	1.21	.6
Cream									
Half & half	1 cup	324	8	28	261	1160	.07	.39	.1
Light/coffee	1 cup	506	7	49	245	2020	.07	.36	.1
Whipping, heavy	1 cup	838	5	90	179	2670	.05	.26	.1
Cheese									
American	1 cu in	65	4	5	122	210	trace	.07	trace
Cheddar	1 cu in	68	4	6	129	230	.01	.08	trace
Cottage, dry	1 cup	172	34	1.6	180	20	.06	.56	.2
Cottage, cream	1 cup	239	31	10	212	380	.07	.56	.2
Swiss	1 cu in	56	4	4	139	170	trace	.06	trace
Ice Cream									
Regular (10% fat)	1 cup	257	6	14	194	590	.05	.08	.1
Ice milk	1 cup	199	6	7	204	280	.07	.29	.1
Yogurt									
Whole milk	1 cup	152	7	8	272	340	.07	.39	.2
Skim milk (partially)	1 cup	123	8	4	294	170	.10	.44	.2

From ASDA, *Nutritive Value of American Foods in Common Units*, Agriculture Handbook no. 456, Agricultural Research Service, (Washington, D.C.: Government Printing Office, 1975).

Lactose-intolerant individuals can usually tolerate fermented dairy products such as buttermilk, cottage cheese, yogurt, acidophilus milk, and milk to which lactase has been added. Lactose intolerance is found most frequently among blacks, Orientals, South Americans, American Indians, and Mexicans. Lactose intolerance may begin early in life and may become more pronounced with age. Research studies show lactose-intolerant individuals have sufficient lactase to digest small amounts of milk (250 milliliters or 1 cup).

COMPOSITION

Although milk is primarily water, it is a complex system consisting of particles in solution (lactose, water-soluble vitamins, some minerals), and particles in colloidal dispersion in water (protein and some minerals). The opaqueness of milk is due to the colloidal particles.

Similar constituents are found in all milks, but their proportions are variable in the different forms of milk and milk products (table 20–1). Water is the chief component of milk, followed by the carbohydrate lactose, fat, protein, and minerals or ash. Fat is the most variable constituent of milk, and protein is the next most variable. A number of factors contribute to this variability and include the breed and diet of the cow. The fat and protein content show a seasonal variation, with both of these being somewhat lower in quantity in summer than winter.

Carbohydrate

Lactose, a disaccharide, is the chief carbohydrate of milk. Lactose is in true solution in the liquid fraction of milk but possesses a relatively low solubility, which permits it to crystallize in some milk products (ice cream, sweetened condensed milk), contributing a somewhat gritty texture. Lactose is less sweet than other sugars in foods.

Lipids

A layer of emulsifier surrounds the fat globules of milk so that they remain suspended in freshly drawn milk. On standing, the fat globules coalesce and rise to the surface of the milk. The minimum required fat content of whole milk ranges from 3.0 to 3.8 percent. Skim milk and reconstituted nonfat dry milk contain about 0.1 percent fat.

Triglycerides are the chief lipids in milk. Milk fat contains a high proportion of short-chain fatty acids. These short-chain fatty acids influence flavor and contribute to the soft consistency of butter. They contain chains of 4 to 8 carbon. Butyric, a saturated fatty acid, has the shortest chain of four carbons. Milk lipids contain significant amounts of linoleic acid (18 carbon, 2 double bonds), the essential fatty acid, and are carriers of the fat-soluble vitamins.

Protein

The two major groups of milk proteins are **casein** and **whey.** The alpha, beta, and gamma caseins represent about 80 percent of the milk protein. The whiteness of milk is attributed to casein. The casein proteins are associated with calcium as calcium caseinate and contain phosphoric acid in their structure, which also identifies them as phosphoproteins. Casein is coagulated by rennin, an enzyme, and by acids.

The whey proteins remain in the liquid portion during cheese making. They are coagulated by heat but not by acid or rennin. Whey portions are believed to contribute to the coating formed on pans in which milk is heated because they coagulate on heating.

Other Components

Fresh milk is bland in flavor, slightly sweet, and slightly salty. Among the many components contributing to its flavor are diacetyl (the flavor component of butter), organic acids, esters, and volatile substances. Other components of milk include vitamins and minerals.

The carotene (provitamin A) in the fat of milk gives cream and whole milk a slightly yellow tint. The water-soluble B vitamin riboflavin contributes a yellowish green color to the liquid fraction called whey.

The fat-soluble vitamins A, D, E, and K are associated with milk lipids, and the water-soluble C and B vitamins with the liquid fraction. The quantity of several of the vitamins in milk is dependent upon the diet of the cow. However, vitamin K is synthesized by bacteria in the digestive tract and is not modified significantly by diet.

Nearly all minerals are represented in milk, some in relatively large amounts (calcium and phosphorus) and others in trace amounts, such as copper and iron. The minerals in milk include aluminum, calcium, chlorine, copper, iodine, iron, magnesium, manganese, phosphorus, potassium, sodium, sulfur, and zinc as well as traces of others. Most of the sulfur is present as a component of protein.

Some minerals are associated with protein and fat and are partly in solution or suspension. Phosphorus occurs chiefly as calcium phosphate and is in suspension. Some phosphorus combines with casein to form phosphoproteins, and lesser amounts combine with lipids to form phospholipids.

PROCESSING

Immediate refrigeration of milk on the dairy farm and transport of milk in refrigerated and insulated tanks to the processing plant significantly reduce the growth of microorganisms. Despite precautions, however, raw milk still has the potential for causing illness in humans. For this reason the use of raw milk is not recommended.

Milk is an excellent medium for microorganismal growth. Various types of bacteria are present in raw milk; some cause disease, while some may promote souring of milk or other changes that are not detrimental to health. Some disease-causing organisms may be present in raw milk because cows can carry diseases.

Systematic federal and state inspection programs have greatly reduced the incidence of tuberculosis and brucellosis in cattle. The possible contamination introduced by milk handlers has been reduced by milk ordinances that require health examinations, certain production conditions, and sanitary practices in the milk industry.

Pasteurization

Milk safety is further assured by **pasteurization,** which destroys disease-producing microorganisms. Milk is pasteurized by the hold method or the alternative high-temperature short-time method (HTST). In the hold method, milk is heated to 145° F (63° C), held at this temperature for 30 minutes, and then quickly

Dean Abramson, Stock, Boston

cooled to 45° F (7° C) or lower. In the high-temperature short-time method, milk is heated to 161° F (72° C), held for fifteen seconds, and then quickly cooled to 50° F (10° C) or lower. Pasteurized milk is centrifuged to separate any sediment from the milk and is bottled automatically and sealed in sanitized containers. Enzyme testing determines the adequacy of pasteurization. Properly pasteurized milk has no phosphatase activity.

A new alternative to pasteurization uses ultrahigh-temperature treatment and aseptic packaging. Milk so treated will remain in good condition for several months without refrigeration.

Homogenization

The smooth, rich flavor of **homogenized** milk makes this type of milk readily accepted for use with cereals and coffee and as a beverage. Most pasteurized fluid whole milk is homogenized. During homogenization the fat globules are divided into many small droplets as the milk is forced through small openings under pressure (3,000 per square inch). The fat particles are so finely divided that they remain dispersed uniformly throughout the milk, even when it is allowed to stand undisturbed for several days.

During homogenization the casein and whey proteins participate in emulsifying the newly formed fat globules. Changes occur in the properties of these proteins and contribute to the overall characteristics of homogenized milk. Homogenized milk is more viscous, whiter, and blander in flavor than nonhomogenized milk. It foams readily, is less stable to heat, and curdles more easily when heated in cream soups and casseroles. Changes in milk proteins during homogenization also cause them to precipitate readily, forming a softer, more digestible curd than milk not homogenized.

MILK PRODUCTS

Fresh whole milk undergoes a number of processes to yield a variety of milk products. Some of the products are processed for storage without refrigeration; in others the curd texture and nutrient level may be altered. Some products contain a lower percentage of fat or water, or both, than regular whole milk; yet other products may be treated to develop a desired flavor or contain selected flavorings. Table 20–2 lists cups of milk or cream products in common market units.

Fresh Milk Products

Whole Milk. Most fresh milk sold is inspected, pasteurized, and fortified with vitamin A. Fresh whole milk is usually homogenized and contains not less than 3.25 milkfat.

Table 20-2   Cups of Milk/Cream in Common Market Units

Item	Market Unit	Cups per Unit Purchased
Milk		
Fresh		
Whole, skim, sour, buttermilk	1 qt (946ml)	4
Canned		1½
Condensed	15 oz (425 g)	
Evaporated	13 fl oz (384 ml)	1½
Dry	12.8 oz (363 g)	5
Nonfat, instant	(reconstituted)	14¾
	25.6 oz (726 g)	9¾
	(reconstituted)	29½
Cream		
Half and half	1 pt (473 ml)	2
Sour cream	½ pt (237 ml)	1
	1 pt (473 ml)	2
Light cream	1 pt (473 ml)	2
Whipping cream	½ pt (237 ml)	1

Adapted from USDA, *Buying Food,* Home Economics Research Report no. 42, Science and Education Administration (Washington, D.C.: Government Printing Office, 1978).

Low-fat and Skim Milk.   Low-fat and skim milk contains less fat (0.5 to 2.0%) than the minimum for standard whole milk. The milk fat is removed by centrifugation. Low-fat and skim milks are pasteurized and fortified with vitamins A and D.

Laimute E. Druskis

Flavored Milk.   Chocolate-flavored milk may be purchased or prepared at home with whole, low-fat, or nonfat milk and the addition of chocolate syrup or powder. Other popular flavorings include maple, strawberry, and vanilla. Flavored milks have the same nutrient values as those of the milks from which they are made except that their caloric content is increased with the addition of sugar or chocolate. Chocolate-flavored milk differs from chocolate milk in that cocoa is used instead of chocolate, and nonfat or skim milk instead of whole milk.

Canned Milk Products

Evaporated Milk.   Evaporated milk is whole milk from which about 60 percent of the water has been removed by heating under a vacuum. Most evaporated milks are fortified so that the reconstituted milk will provide 10 micrograms or 400 IU of vitamin D per quart. Evaporated low-fat and skim milks are also available. Evaporated milk is reconstituted with an equal volume of water and is used in the same manner as the original milk.

Condensed Milk.   Sweetened condensed milk is whole milk to which about 15 percent sugar has been added before it is evaporated and canned. The sweetness distinguishes it from evaporated milk. A browning reaction (Maillard reaction) occurs between the sugar and protein constituents of sweetened condensed milk when heated, yielding a thickened caramel-type product. Condensed milk is used in a variety of specially developed dessert recipes because of its sweetness. With the addition of an acid such as lemon juice, it thickens without heating to the consistency of pie filling or pudding.

Dried Milk Products

Dried milk products are prepared by evaporating milk under vacuum and then spraying the concentrated liquid into a heated vacuum chamber to dry. The dried particles are instantized by wetting with steam so they agglomerate (clump) to promote dispersion in water when reconstituted. Commercially available products include dried whole milk, nonfat dry milk, dry malted milk, dry buttermilk, and dry cream.

Dried Whole Milk.   Dried whole milk contains 26 percent fat and must be kept in a cool, dry place. It is used commercially in ice cream and candy.

Nonfat Dry Milk.   Nonfat dry milk is prepared from skim milk. Dried milk that has not been instantized readily clumps making it difficult to reconsitute. Vitamins A and D are generally added. Partially reconstituted nonfat dry milk solids can be whipped to yield a low-calorie foam.

Low-Sodium Milk.   Low-sodium milks are available dried or canned and are useful in sodium-restricted diets. Pasteurized and homogenized fresh whole milk is passed through an ion exchange resin to replace 90 percent or more of the sodium with potassium.

Cultured Milk Products

Lactic acid bacteria in milk change lactose into lactic acid giving a pleasant acid flavor. Pasteurized milk sours somewhat differently from regular milk, since most of the lactic acid bacteria are destroyed. Selected microorganisms are added to prepare **cultured** milk products to yield the desired flavor and consistency. Their nutritional quality is similar to the milk product used in their preparation.

Buttermilk. Cultured buttermilk is commercially available and is prepared from pasteurized skim or partially skimmed milk. The milk is inoculated with a lactic acid bacterial culture. Granules of butter may be added to increase palatability.

Sour Milk. Lactic acid bacteria are added to pasteurized milk to develop sufficient acid to partially coagulate the casein (protein) of milk.

Acidophilus Milk. Pasteurized milk is cultured with Lactobacillus acidophilus bacteria to produce acidophilus milk. These bacteria thus introduced into the intestinal tract may retard the development of putrefactive organisms.

Yogurt. Yogurt is a tangy fermented semisolid made from pasteurized skim, whole, or dried milk cultured with Lactobacillus bulgaris and Streptococcus thermophilus. Commercial yogurt usually contains added nonfat milk solids.

Imitation Milk

Imitation and filled milk are formulated to resemble milk. Filled milk is either a combination of skim milk and vegetable fat or a blend containing nonfat dry milk, vegetable fat, and water. Imitation milk is a blend of several nondairy ingredients such as sodium caseinate or soy solids, corn syrup solids, flavoring agents, emulsifiers, stabilizers, water, and vegetable fat. Filled and imitation milk are not governed by the same rigid standards as pasteurized grade A milk.

Dry whipped toppings, mixes, pressurized whipped toppings, and coffee whiteners are made from nondairy products. These products are generally a combination of vegetable fat, sodium caseinate, sweetener, emulsifiers, stabilizers, coloring, and flavor.

Cream Products

Creams. Cream is the fat separated from milk. Various creams are available, each with a different percentage of fat. Cream with a high percentage of fat is classed as heavy, that with somewhat less fat as light. Most cream is pasteurized, and some may be homogenized.

Whipping cream is regarded as a heavy cream and contains the highest level of milkfat (36–30%). Light cream contains a minimum of 30 percent fat, coffee or table cream at least 18 percent, and half-and-half (a mixture of milk and cream) about 10–12 percent. Pressurized whipped creams in cans are made from table or whipping cream with added sugar, stabilizer, and emulsifiers. Dry mixes and frozen whipped toppings are available.

Sour cream is cultured with lactic bacteria to develop a pleasant acid flavor. It contains at least 18 percent fat, and milk solids may be added to provide viscosity.

Butter. The lactic acid bacteria in pasteurized cream develop the aroma and flavor of butter. Butter contains at least 80 percent fat and about 15 percent water. It is prepared from sweet or sour cream by churning.

Ice Cream Products

Ice cream quality is related to fat content. Federal standards identify ice cream as containing at least 10 percent milkfat and 20 percent total milk solids, except for the diluting influence of added flavoring substances. Stabilizers and emulsifiers are limited to 0.2 percent. Milk fat contributes richness, body, and promotes a smooth texture. Milk solids contribute body, texture, and flavor.

Ice milk is made with skim milk. The fat content of ice milk ranges from 2 to 7 percent, while sherbets contain about 1 to 2 percent.

Some ice creamlike products, such as mellorine and parevine contain vegetables fats rather than milk fat. Another one of these products is made with tofu a fermented soy milk. The nutritional value of these products is determined by the ingredients used and should be listed on the label.

QUALITY ASSURANCE

Grades

Local, state, and federal cooperation assure movement of safe, wholesome milk. The milk sold across state lines must be inspected. The U.S. Public Health Service has set standards for grade A pasteurized milk and milk products. Milk produced, processed, and distributed under specified sanitary conditions is marked grade A.

The USDA has established grade standards for nonfat dry milk and butter. Certain other products are given "quality approved" ratings. The USDA grade shields signify the wholesomeness of milk products.

The highest quality of instant nonfat dry milk is labeled U.S. extra grade, indicating instantized milk that has the ability to dissolve quickly.

The U.S. grades for butter include U.S. grade AA, U.S. grade A, and U.S. grade B. Butter marked grade B is often made from sour cream and has a slightly acid but acceptable flavor.

Storage of Milk Products

A cold temperature and cleanliness are absolute essentials for maintenance of quality milk products. Milk is highly perishable and should be refrigerated immediately after purchase and kept in the coldest part of the refrigerator (45° F, 7° C) at all times, except for very brief periods during use. Also, riboflavin is quickly destroyed in milk exposed to light. Milk containers should be kept covered to avoid contamination and absorption of odor and flavor from other foods. Any remaining milk should not be mixed with that newly purchased. Suggested storage periods for milk and cream are listed in Table 20-3.

Foods with a high proportion of milk are equally good media for growth of microorganisms as milk. Staphylococci are widely distributed, and food may be easily contaminated by contact with unsanitary work surfaces, utensils, and hands. Milk-containing foods held in a warm place permit microorganisms to grow and to produce toxic compounds. Consumption of foods containing these compounds can cause gastrointestinal discomfort. The growth of microorganisms is retarded and controlled by immediate cooling and cold storage of foods.

Table 20-3 Storage of Milk/Cream

Product	In Refrigerator 35–40° F (2–5° C)	In Cool Room 60–70° F (16–21° C)
Milk, fluid		
Fresh whole, skim	1 week	
Milk, evaporated		6 months
unopened		
opened	3–5 days	
Milk, sweetened, condensed		
unopened		2–3 months
opened	3–5 days	
Milk, dry, nonfat		3 months
reconstituted	1 week	
Cream		
Table, whipping	1 week	
Pressurized, whipped	3 weeks	

Adapted from USDA, *Milk in Family Meals*, Home and Garden Bulletin no. 127, (Washington, D.C.: Government Printing Office, 1974).

Soured milk is wholesome as long as it remains sour. When an unpleasant odor or mold on the surface develop the milk is no longer safe for consumption. The presence of acid in milk slows bacterial growth, but mold can grow in an acid medium and often does grow on the surface of sour milk. Since most lactic acid bacteria are destroyed when milk is heated, pasteurized milk—which has been heated—is spoiled when putrefactive bacteria act on milk proteins. As soon as milk changes from acid to neutral, these bacteria act on protein, and an offensive odor develops and gas bubbles appear.

Unopened cans of milk are stored at room temperature in a dry, ventilated place to avoid rusting of cans. Once opened, the milk is refrigerated in the can. Containers of dried milk are kept at room temperature, and opened containers are tightly closed to avoid flavor change and lumping. Reconstituted dried milk is stored in the refrigerator in the same manner as fresh milk.

All fluid creams should be stored in the coldest part of the refrigerator. Warm temperatures promote souring. Soured cream is wholesome for use as long as it has a pleasing aroma and is free of mold. Cream kept at a cold temperature (45° F or 7° C) whips better than cream of a warm temperature. Fat particles readily clump in a cold cream and contribute to increased viscosity. A cold temperature, a viscous cream, and cold bowl and beaters enhance the whipping quality of heavy cream.

MILK IN COOKERY

Milk in food preparation serves as a major ingredient, a solvent, a dispersing and hydrating agent, and a rich nutrient source. Milk is the major ingredient in puddings, sauces, and soups. It hydrates the gliadin and glutenin of wheat flour to aid in gluten formation, disperses starch so that lumping can be avoided, and provides moisture for the gelatinization of starch. Milk enhances the nutritional quality of any food to which it is added.

Factors Affecting Milk Stability

A number of factors in cookery affect the stability of milk proteins. Cookery techniques may induce protein **denaturation** and **coagulation,** scum formation, and color and flavor changes in milk. The nature of milk can be altered by acid, heat, polyphenolic compounds, salts, and enzymes.

Acid. Casein may be precipitated as a curd by the addition of acidic foods or the action of lactic acid bacteria. As acid is formed from lactose by lactic acid bacteria, protein stability is disrupted and coagulation begins to occur. When the pH of milk falls below 5.2, casein is no longer colloidally dispersed; it forms a curd or gel. The acid of fruits lowers the pH of milk, causing the casein to become unstable and precipitate to form a curd.

Milk just beginning to sour contains too little acid to curdle casein unless it is heated. The acid sufficiently destabilizes the casein to make the protein sensitive to denaturation by heat. Continued heating causes the curd to shrink, squeezing whey from the curd. In the preparation of tomato soup, the acid in tomato may destabilize the casein sufficiently to promote curdling when heat is applied. The addition of hot tomato to the hot, thickened white sauce and the use of very fresh milk may help to minimize the tendency to curdle.

Heat.   Casein, the principal protein of milk, is relatively insensitive to heat and does not usually coagulate in fresh milk. When milk is heated, the globular whey proteins denature and coagulate, carrying with them some calcium and phosphorus as they settle on the bottom of the pan. The albumin protein in the coagulated material probably is the protein that scorches easily when milk is placed over direct heat.

Although pasteurization temperatures have little effect on milk protein, higher temperatures bring about a variety of changes. Changes increase in degree as the temperature and time of heating increase. Lactilbumin begins to coagulate at about 150° F (66° C) and the amount of coagulation becomes more intense as the temperature and time increase. Although usual cooking temperatures do not coagulate casein, it may coagulate when heated to a high temperature or for a prolonged period at the boiling temperature. As noted earlier, an increase in acidity accelerates the coagulation of milk protein when heated. In addition, heat affects the color and flavor of milk and promotes skin formation.

Color Change.   Milk scorches easily when placed over direct heat, owing partly to the film of coagulated albumin that collects on the sides and bottom of the pan. Stirring the milk while heating decreases the thickness of the film, but does not prevent scorching. When milk is heated over hot water, scorching is usually eliminated, and when milk is placed over direct heat, scorching can be retarded by keeping the heat low and the cooking period short.

The browning of scorched milk may be due to the Maillard reaction that occurs when lactose reacts with the milk protein. This browning also occurs in sweetened condensed milk with prolonged heating.

Flavor Change.   The heating of milk causes a flavor change. The length of time and temperature of heating determine the intensity of the cooked-milk flavor. This change in flavor may be due to the loss of dissolved gases, carbon dioxide and oxygen, and changes in protein due to heating. Volatile sulfides and sulfhydryl compounds liberated from the proteins of the fat globule membrane and the beta lactoglobulin may contribute to the cooked flavor.

Skin Formation.   A thin skin forms on the surface of milk heated in an open pan at a relatively low temperature, and it becomes pronounced and toughened as the temperature increases. The skin contains a variety of components and may include coagulated albumin, fat globules, and calcium salts. Its formation may be attributed to evaporation of water and the resultant concentration of casein, which occludes milk fat and calcium salts. The skin tends to retain steam; pressure develops beneath it and forces the milk to overflow.

As the skin is removed, another re-forms quickly. The formation of skin or scum is a troublesome feature of milk cookery. Techniques that aid in the prevention of skin formation include beating heated milk with a rotary beater to produce a layer of foam, covering the pan, introducing a layer of fat on the surface, and diluting the milk. Prepared puddings, gravies, and sauces are covered to minimize skin formation; whipped cream or marshmallows may be placed over the surface of hot beverages to avoid skin formation.

Salts. Heat coagulation of milk is also influenced by the kinds and amounts of salts present in foods. Foods high in salt, such as ham or dried beef, promote coagulation of casein and produce curdled products.

Polyphenols. Roots, seeds, and stems of vegetables tend to contain more phenolic compounds (tannins) than other parts of plants. These compounds are also present in brown sugar and cacao products. The curdling of vegetable-milk combinations such as creamed asparagus or scalloped potatoes is induced by **polyphenolic** compounds.

Enzymes. Casein can be altered by rennin, a **proteolytic** enzyme extracted from the stomach of a young calf. Rennin is heat sensitive and can form a custardlike gel when milk is heated to 104° F (40° C). High temperatures inactivate rennin, and the gel does not form. When milk is overheated, calcium ions are altered, so they are not available to react with protein to form the gel. Rennet is used with milk in the preparation of custards and puddings.

Some of the curdling that occurs when milk and certain fruits are combined is probably due to other enzymes contained in fruit. Although fruits contain organic acids, these probably are not present in sufficient quantities to promote curdling of milk.

Homogenization. Homogenized milk appears to coagulate more readily than nonhomogenized milk when used with some foods, such as potatoes. This may be due to the homogenization process or the protein surface on the newly formed fat globules. Starch-thickened products, puddings, and white sauces appear somewhat thicker when prepared with homogenized milk than with regular milk.

Milk-Product Foams

Creams with a high fat content, dried milk, and evaporated milk can be whipped to a foam. Whipped milk products are used as an ingredient or a topping for desserts. Air is incorporated during whipping to produce a foam. All milk products whip best when thoroughly chilled and when the bowl and beater are cold.

Cream.   Whipped cream foams are stabilized by fat globules clumping on the surface of air bubbles. The bubbles of air formed in whipped cream are surrounded by protein films, which contain clumps of fat. Although cream with at least 25 percent fat can be whipped, a stiffer, more stable foam is achieved with cream containing 30 to 36 percent fat. The viscosity of thin cream may be increased with added gelatin or lemon juice to permit whipping.

A cold temperature and a higher fat content increase viscosity of cream and enhance the whipping quality. Cream is sufficiently beaten when it nearly doubles in volume and when it mounds and holds its shape. Because sugar delays the formation of foam when a sweetened cream is desired, the sugar is folded into the whipped cream.

Beating of cream must be controlled to avoid overbeaten, curdled whipped cream. The clumping of fat droplets that leads to stiffening of cream is also the first step in breaking an emulsion.

Dried Milk.   Nonfat dried milk provides a more stable foam than dried whole milk. Dried milk sprinkled over equal amounts of cold water retains sufficient viscosity to permit whipping. Some of the protein in the foam is denatured, allowing it to set, but the structure is fragile. The stability of the foam is increased somewhat by adding a small amount of acid such as lemon juice or dispersing milk in gelatin before heating. Acid disperses milk protein and thus increases viscosity.

Evaporated Milk.   The large concentration of milk solids in evaporated milk and proteins that act as foaming agents contribute to its whipping quality. Evaporated milk whips most effectively when chilled to the point of ice-crystal formation, which increases viscosity and facilitates retention of gas bubbles. The addition of lemon juice also increases viscosity of milk and promotes stability. Whipped evaporated milk yields a foam with a good volume and fine air-cell structure but very limited stability. The addition of gelatin stabilizes the foam somewhat. Whipped evaporated milk foams become very thick but do not set and must be used promptly.

SUMMARY

The U.S. Public Health Service has set standards for grade A milk and some milk products. Milk consists of particles in solution, colloidal systems, and emulsions. Milk is considered a good source of vitamins and minerals except for ascorbic acid and iron. It is an excellent source of high-quality protein, calcium, phosphorus, riboflavin, and vitamin A.

In food preparation milk serves as a hydrating and dispersing agent and a source of nutrients. During cooking, milk proteins undergo denaturation and coagulation, and color and flavor changes may occcur. Changes in milk are induced by acid, heat, salts, polyphenolic compounds, enzymes, and homogenization. Scum formation and scorching are troublesome problems in milk cookery.

Dried and evaporated milk and high-fat creams may be whipped. Milk foams are used in food preparation, but cream foams are most stable.

SELF-STUDY GUIDE

1. What forms of milk are available for purchase? In what ways do they differ? Suggest uses for each type.
2. Identify four cultured milks and cultured milk products. How are they made? In what ways do they differ from regular milk?
3. Identify five cream and cream-type products and give their uses.
4. In what ways do imitation milk products differ from regular milk products? What are the advantages and disadvantages?
5. How is the quality of milk and milk products identified?
6. What two processing techniques are applied to milk and why?
7. Discuss the composition and nutrient quality of milk.
8. What three dairy products yield foam when whipped? What conditions permit foam formation? How are these foams used?
9. Which components of milk are involved in the formation of scum and the coating on the bottom of the pan in which milk is heated? Which cookery techniques will minimize their formation?
10. In what ways is milk influenced by heat, acid, salt, polyphenols, and rennin?

SELECTED REFERENCES

AMANTEA, G. F. Aseptic packaging of dairy products. *Food Technology* 37:138, 1983.

BASSETTE, E. A survey of milk flavor and quality. *Journal of Food Protection* 45:135, 1982.

COLMAN, N., et al. Detection of a milk factor that facilitates folate uptake by intestinal cells. *Science* 211:1427, 1981.

DEMAN, J. M. Light-induced destruction of vitamin A in milk. *Journal of Dairy Science* 64:2031, 1981.

DOUGLAS, F. W., et al. Color, flavor, and iron bioavailability in iron-fortified chocolate milk. *Journal of Dairy Science* 64:1785, 1981.

——————. Effects of ultra-high-temperature pasteurization on milk proteins. *Journal of Agricultural and Food Chemistry* 29:11, 1981.

DUNKLEY, W. L. Reducing fat in milk and dairy products. *Journal of Dairy Science* 65:442, 1982.

HARDY, J., and FANNI, J. Application of reflection photometry to the measurement milk coagulation. *Journal of Food Science* 46:1956, 1981.

HOTCHKISS, J. H., et al. Rapid method for estimation of N-Nitrosodimethylamine in malt beverages. *Journal of the Association of Official Chemists* 64:929, 1981.

JELEN, P. Reprocessing of whey and other dairy wastes for use as food ingredients. *Food Technology* 37:81, 1983.

JENNESS, R. Composition and characteristics of goat milk. Review 1968–1978. *Journal of Dairy Science* 63:1605, 1980.

JESSE, B. W., et al. Differences between cows and changes during lactation. *Journal of Dairy Science* 63:235, 1980.

KOSHAK, M. S., et al. Protein stability of frozen milk as influenced by storage temperature and ultrafiltration. *Journal of Food Science* 46:1211, 1981.

MAHONEY, R. R., and ADAMCHUK, C. Effect of milk constituents on the hydrolysis of lactose by lactase form kluyveromyces fragills. *Journal of Food Science* 45:962, 1980.

MARSILI, R. T., et al.   High performance liquid chromatographic determination of organic acids in dairy products. *Journal of Food Science* 46:52, 1981.

MILUS, S.   Is raw milk worth the risk? *Organic Gardening* 29:129, 1982.

MORRIS, C. E.   It's not butter nor margarine. *Food Engineering* 52:14, 1980.

OZIMEK, G., and POZNANSKI, S.   Influence of an addition textured milk proteins upon physicochemical properties of meat mixtures. *Journal of Food Science* 47:234, 1982.

RASHID, I., and POTTS, D.   Riboflavin determination in milk. *Journal of Food Science* 45:744, 1980.

RUEGSEGGER, G. J., and SCHULTZ, L. H.   Iodine in field milk samples. *Journal of Dairy Science* 63:115, 1980.

SCHMIDT, R. H.   Heat treatment and storage effects on texture characteristics of milk and yogurt systems fortified with oilseed proteins. *Journal of Food Science* 45:471, 1980.

SINGH, J., and KAUL, A.   Studies on degradation of different types of caseins and protein by lactobacilli. *Journal of Food Science* 46:1954, 1981.

U.S. DEPARTMENT OF AGRICULTURE.   *Federal and state standards for the composition of milk products and certain non-milkfat products.* Washington, D.C.: Government Printing Office, 1980.

————.   *Food and agriculture policy in the 1980's: Major crops and milk.* Washington, D.C.: Government Printing Office, 1981.

YUN, S. E., et al.   Increase in curd tension of milk coagulum prepared with immobilized proteases. *Journal of Food Science* 46:705, 1981.

21

CHEESE

OBJECTIVES

When you have completed this chapter, you will be able to

1. Predict and explain the effects of temperature and time as they relate to cheese cookery.
2. Suggest preparation techniques to promote the production of high-quality cheese products.
3. Suggest uses for specific cheeses in cookery and give examples.
4. Compare natural and process cheeses.
5. Discuss the composition and nutritional contribution of cheese.

Cheese making is an ancient art steeped in tradition and carried to this country by immigrants from many lands. **Cheese** consists of milk **curd,** a casein gel, from which most of the whey is removed. The great variety of cheeses is attributed to the kinds of milk used; the types of curd—acid or rennin; microorganisms used; and the degree of **ripening.** Most of the cheese consumed in the United States is commercially made and primarily cheddar, also known as American cheddar. Cheddar has many uses and is the most important cheese in cookery.

CHEESE MAKING

Although cheese is available in many flavors and textures, the same basic steps are followed in its preparation. Generally cheese is the curd of milk resulting from coagulation of nonfat or whole milk by lactic acid, rennin, or other suitable en-

(a) Cheddar is made from whole milk which may be pasteurized. The milk is then pumped into temperature-controlled cheese vats . . . and cheese-making has begun. Temperature is closely controlled because temperature plays a key role. (b) A "starter" is now added to the cheese. This "starter" is a harmless bacteria culture. (c) The curd is cut into small cubes by cheesemakers using wire knives. This permits the fluid material, which is referred to as whey, to separate from the curd. (d) Once the cheesemaker determines the curd is firm enough to be turned without breaking, it is "cheddared." During this stage, the trenched curd is cut into slabs. (e,f) The slabs are turned regularly then stacked and restacked. This procedure is called "Cheddaring," a technique from which Cheddar cheese derives its name. This releases additional whey and mats the curds into a solid form. (g) Some traditional

(g)

(h)

(i)

(j)

(k)

cheesemakers still use a copper kettle in Swiss production. (h) Swiss cheese is easily identified by the presence of holes or "eyes." The eyes result from a gas which is produced after the introduction of a special bacteria culture. (i) Provolone is sometimes smoked over metal wood burners or open hearths. Provolone also is available non-smoked. (j) Brick is a surface-ripened cheese. During the week-long curing process each cheese is manually washed and turned twice. This enhances the flavor development. The Brick name is credited to *how* the five pound pieces of curd were originally pressed to form a solid mass—with a brick! (k) Cheesemaking provides us with an especially delicious variety of mealtime and snacktime possibilities. Cheese is an excellent source of nutrition because it is a concentrated form of milk. (American Dairy Association of Wisconsin)

zymes or acid. The curd is cut, heated, drained of whey, salted, pressed, and ripened by bacteria or mold. The ripening process transforms the bland, tough, rubbery mass of cheese to a full-flavored, soft, mellow product.

Ripening occurs under controlled conditions for varying periods of time. Lactic acid fermentation is completed during ripening. Enzymes hydrolyze proteins and fat to produce changes in the texture and flavor of cheese. The flavor of cheese becomes more intense as aging time is extended and progresses from a mild flavor to mellow, sharp, and very sharp. The flavor of cheese is attributed to a blend of decomposition and hydrolytic products formed from the protein, lactose, and fat of milk during ripening.

NUTRITIONAL QUALITY

Cheese retains most of the nutrients of milk, but the nutrients are more concentrated. Cheese is an excellent source of high-quality protein and a rich source of calcium, phosphorus, and riboflavin; vitamin A value is also high when the cheese is made from whole milk. Most cheeses have a high fat content except those made from skim milk, such as cottage cheese (see Table 21–1).

The procedure used to coagulate the protein during the manufacture of cheese influences the calcium content of cheese. Acid-coagulated cheese loses more of its calcium in the whey than rennin-curd cheese. Other water-soluble constituents such as lactose, thiamin, and riboflavin tend to be lost in the whey. Whey cheeses and cheese spreads or cheese foods made with whey concentrates contain the valuable nutrients of whey. The high-quality proteins, lactoglobulin and lactalbumin, are also present in whey.

COMPOSITION

For convenience the composition of cheese can be roughly summarized as being one-third each protein, fat, and water. Cheese is an excellent source of high-quality protein. Casein is the principal protein since it coagulates during cheese making. The whey cheese contains considerable amounts of two proteins—lactalbumin and lactoglobulin. Cheese also contains a high percentage of fat, except for cottage cheese or cheese made from whey.

The water content of cheese varies from 30 to 75 percent. Soft cheese has a higher moisture content than hard cheese. Cheese with a high moisture content is more perishable than a low-moisture cheese.

A high proportion of calcium, phosphorus, and vitamin A is retained in cheese. Rennet-coagulated cheese retains more calcium than acid-coagulated cheese. The more acid the pH, the greater the amount of calcium released from casein molecules into the whey.

Table 21-1 Major Nutrients in Selected Cheeses

Cheese	Measure	Kcal	Protein (g)	Fat (g)	Calcium (mg)	Phosphorus (mg)	Iron (mg)	Vitamin A (IU)	Thiamin (mg)	Riboflavin (mg)	Niacin (mg)
Natural											
Blue/roquefort	1 cu in	64	8.7	5.3	54	59	.1	210	tr	.11	.2
Brick	1 cu in	64	3.8	5.2	126	78	.2	210	–	.08	tr
Camembert	1 cu in	51	3.0	4.2	18	31	.1	170	.01	.18	.1
Cheddar	1 cu in	68	4.3	5.5	129	82	.2	230	.01	.08	tr
Cottage, dry (sm. curd, spooned)	1 cup	125	24.7	.4	131	254	.6	10	.04	.41	.1
	1 oz	24	4.8	.1	26	50	.1	tr	.01	.08	tr
Cottage, creamed (sm. curd, spooned)	1 cup	223	28.6	8.8	197	319	.6	360	.06	.53	.2
	1 oz	30	3.9	1.2	27	43	.1	50	.01	.07	tr
Cream cheese	1 cu in	60	1.3	6.1	10	15	tr	250	tr	.04	tr
Limberger	1 cu in	62	3.8	5.0	106	71	.1	210	.01	.09	tr
Parmesan, grated	1 tbsp	23	2.1	1.5	68	46	tr	60	tr	.04	tr
Swiss	1 cu in	56	4.1	4.2	139	84	.1	170	tr	.06	tr
Process, pasteurized											
American	1 cu in	65	4.1	5.3	122	135	.2	210	tr	.07	tr
American cheese food	1 cu in	57	3.5	4.2	100	132	.1	170	tr	.10	tr
American cheese spread	1 cu in	50	2.8	3.7	99	153	.1	150	tr	.09	tr

From USDA, *Nutritive Value of American Foods in Common Units*, Agriculture Handbook no. 456, Agricultural Research Service (Washington, D.C.: Government Printing Office, 1975).

Cheese contains little carbohydrate or lactose. Freshly prepared cheese contains varying amounts of lactose. Lactose decreases during the ripening process and is lacking in aged cheese. Cheese is a concentrated source of essential nutrients and calories. A one-inch cube of cheese contains about 100 kcalories.

CHEESE CLASSIFICATION

Although all cheeses originate from milk, their specific characteristics permit useful classification. Cheeses are grouped into two general classes, as **natural** and **processed.** Combinations of natural cheeses are used to make processed cheese. Cheese may be further classified on the basis of ripeness and moisture content as soft, semisoft, and hard; and on the basis of flavor as mild and sharp. The uses and characteristics of some cheeses are listed in Table 21–2.

Table 21–2 Flavor, Texture, and Uses of Some Natural Cheeses

Cheese	Flavor	Texture	Uses
Soft Unripened			
Cottage	Mild, acid	Soft curd particles of varying size	Salads, with fruits, vegetables, dips
Cream, plain	Mild, acid	Soft and smooth	Salads, dips, sandwiches, snacks, desserts
Neufchatel	Mild, acid	Soft, smooth, similar to cream cheese but low in milkfat	Salads, dips, sandwiches, snacks, cheese cakes, desserts
Ricotta	Sweet, nutlike	Soft, moist or dry	Appetizers, salads, snacks, lasagne, ravioli, cooked dishes, grating, desserts
Hard Unripened			
Mozzarella, low-moisture (pizza)	Delicate, mild	Slightly firm, plastic	Snacks, pizza, lasagne, casseroles
Mysost	Sweetish, caramel	Firm, buttery consistency	Snacks, desserts, served with dark bread
Soft Ripened			
Brie	Mild to pungent	Soft, smooth when ripened	Appetizers, sandwiches, snacks, with crackers and fruit, dessert
Camembert	Mild to pungent	Soft, smooth, very soft when fully ripe	Appetizers, sandwiches, snacks, with crackers and fruit, dessert
Limburger	Highly pungent, very strong	Soft, smooth when ripened; usually has small, irregular openings	Appetizers, snacks, with crackers or dark breads, dessert

Cheese	Flavor	Texture	Uses
Semisoft Ripened			
Muenster	Mild to mellow	Semisoft, numerous small openings	Appetizers, sandwiches, dessert
Brick	Mild to moderately sharp	Semisoft to medium firm, elastic, many small mechanical openings	Appetizers, sandwiches, snacks, dessert
Hard Ripened			
Cheddar	Mild to very sharp	Firm, smooth	Appetizers, sandwiches, sauces, on vegetables, in hot dishes, toasted sandwiches, cheeseburgers, grated, dessert
Edam	Mellow, nutlike	Semisoft to firm smooth; small, irregularly shaped or round holes	Appetizers, snacks, salads, sandwiches, seafood sauces, dessert
Provolone	Mellow to sharp; smoky, salty	Firm, smooth	Appetizers, sandwiches, snacks, soufflés, macaroni and spaghetti, pizza, grating when cured and dry
Swiss	Sweet, nutlike	Firm, smooth with large round eyes	Sandwiches, snacks, sauces, fondue, cheesburgers
Very Hard Ripened			
Parmesan	Sharp, piquant	Very hard, granular	Grated for seasoning soups or vegetables, spaghetti, ravioli, pizza, lasagne, breads, popcorn
Romano	Sharp, piquant	Very hard, granular	Seasoning soups, casseroles, ravioli, sauces, breads, grating, when cured about a year
Blue Vein Mold, Ripened			
Blue (bleu)	Tangy, peppery	Semisoft, pasty, sometimes crumbly	Appetizers, salads, dips, salad dressing, sandwiches, spreads, with crackers, dessert
Roquefort	Sharp, slightly peppery	Semisoft, pasty, sometimes crumbly	Appetizers, snacks, salads, dips, sandwich spreads, with crackers, dessert

Adapted from National Dairy Council, *Newer Knowledge of Cheese*, 3rd ed. revised (Rosemont, Il.: National Dairy Council, 1983).

Natural Cheese

Although natural cheeses originated in Europe, many popular varieties are produced in the United States. Most natural cheeses are made from whole cow's milk; some are made from skim milk, whey, or a mixture of these.

Each natural cheese has its own characteristic flavor and texture. The flavor may be bland as in cottage cheese, tangy as in blue (bleu) cheese, or pungent as in Limburger. The texture varies from the creamy character of cream cheese to the firm and elastic nature of swiss cheese. The degree of ripening determines the flavor, body, and texture of cheeses. Some natural cheeses are used unripened.

Unripened.   Unripened cheese is ready for immediate use. The unripened cheeses do not undergo any curing or ripening, and they have a high moisture content. Neufchatel, ricotta, and cottage cheese are examples of soft unripened cheeses. Cream cheese is a popular unripened cheese made from whole milk with added cream. Neufchatel resembles cream cheese, but contains less fat. Of these, cottage cheese has the highest moisture content, about 80 percent. The fat content of cottage cheese is negligible unless it is creamed, and then it contains a minimum of 4 percent fat. Most other cheeses contain about 20 percent or more fat. The low-fat content of cottage cheese is an advantage when calories or fat are restricted.

Hard unripened cheeses made from whey include mysost and mozzarella. The low moisture content of hard unripened cheese permits a relatively long storage, while the high-moisture cheese must be consumed soon after it is made.

Soft Ripened Cheese.   Specific molds or bacteria, or both, produce the characteristic flavors and textures of soft ripened cheeses. The curing progresses from the outside toward the center so long as the temperature is favorable. Ripened cheeses vary in texture from soft to very hard. Brie, camembert, and limburger are examples of soft ripened cheeses. Limburger has a characteristic high aroma and a creamy white interior.

Semisoft Ripened Cheese.   Examples of semisoft ripened cheeses are bel paese, brick, and muenster. These cheeses are ripened from the interior as well as on the surface by characteristic bacteria or mold cultures or both. The ripening begins soon after the cheese is formed and continues as long as the temperature is favorable. Blue, gorgonzola, and roquefort are cured by blue mold and are mellow with a piquant flavor.

Firm Ripened Cheese.   Firm and very hard ripened cheeses are cured by bacteria. Because of their lower moisture content these cheeses require a longer curing time than do high-moisture cheeses. Cheddar, colby, edam, gouda, provolone, and swiss are examples of firm ripened cheeses.

Cheddar cheese was first made in Cheddar, England, and in the United States it is also referred to as American cheese. A bright red coating of wax distinguishes edam and gouda cheeses. Gases of bacterial origin during ripening produce the large holes that are characteristic of swiss cheese.

Parmesan, romano, and sap sago are very hard cheeses. Because of their low moisture and high salt content these cheeses are cured very slowly. They are easily grated and are often used to season foods and enhance flavors.

Process Cheese

Shredded fresh and aged natural cheeses are blended to yield a variety of processed cheeses. An emulsifier such as sodium citrate or disodium phosphate is added; the cheese is thoroughly blended and heated to pasteurize it. Pasteurization destroys bacteria and enzymes, and therefore no further ripening can occur. The flavor of process cheese is determined by the cheeses selected for blending and the other flavors added. One or more varieties of cheese may be blended and the variety of flavors further extended with the addition of flavoring materials, such as meat, smoke, pimiento, vegetables, or fruits. Process cheeses melt quickly and are easily combined with other foods.

Coldpack Cheese. The flavor of coldpack cheese is the same as the natural cheese used to prepare it. Coldpack, or club, cheese is made of a single cheese or a blend of two or more fresh and aged natural cheeses but differs from other processed cheese in that it is blended into a uniform product without heating. Coldpack cheese is soft and spreads more easily than natural cheese. Spices, coloring, salt, acid, and water may be added up to the quantity allowed for the variety of natural cheese used. The cheese is packed in jars or moisture-proof packages.

Coldpack cheese food is prepared in the same manner as coldpack cheese except that it may have added cream, milk, skim milk, whey, or nonfat dry milk. Also, it may be flavored with pimientos, fruit, meats, or vegetables.

Cheese Food. Cheese food has a softer texture and is more mild in flavor than other processed cheese because of its higher moisture content. Cheese foods spread more easily and melt more quickly than processed cheese. Pasteurized, processed cheese foods are prepared very much like processed cheese. Along with cheese they contain nonfat dry milk or whey solids and water. Therefore, cheese-food products contain less cheese and are lower in milk-fat content but higher in moisture than processed cheese. The flavor of pasteurized, processed cheese food may also be modified with added meats, smoke flavor, vegetables, pimiento, or fruit.

QUALITY ASSURANCE

Grades

Approved shields may be found on packages of cottage cheese and other processed cheeses, signifying USDA supervision and assurance of quality. Cheddar and Swiss-type cheeses may be designated as USDA grade AA and grade A.

Storage

Cheese is perishable and should be kept in the refrigerator. Cheese keeps well in the original container or wrapper. Once cut, a cheese tends to dry out rapidly and should be overwrapped with aluminum foil or plastic wrap or stored in a tightly covered container. The length of storage time depends on the kind of cheese and the wrapping. Cottage cheese should be used within two weeks. Hard cheese may be kept up to several months if protected from contamination and drying out. Table 21-3 lists storage times for cheese.

Freezing is not recommended for natural cheeses since some of them become crumbly and the soft cheeses separate upon thawing. However, brick, cheddar, edam, gouda, mozzarella, provolone and swiss may be frozen, especially in small pieces.

Table 21-3   Storage of Cheese Products

Product	In Cool Room (60-70°F/16-21°C)	In Refrigerator (35-40°F/2-5°C)
Cottage cheese		5-7 days
Fresh ricotta		5-7 days
Soft varieties		
Cream, neuf-chatel, others		2 weeks
Hard varieties		
Cheddar, swiss, others		2-3 months[a]
Grated		
Parmesan or romano		2-3 months[b]
Cheese Foods		2-3 weeks
Cheese Spreads		
Unopened	3-4 months	
Opened		1-2 weeks

[a]Unless mold develops.

[b]Some container directions suggest storing in cool, dry place.

From USDA, *Cheese in Family Meals*, Home and Garden Bulletin no. 112 (Washington, D.C.: Government Printing Office, 1980).

CHEESE IN COOKERY

Cheese appears in meals from appetizer through entrée to dessert. The many uses of cheese in cookery include in casseroles with pastas; with meat, poultry, and fish; with vegetables. The high protein content of cheese mandates the use of a low temperature and a short period of cooking. Cheese becomes tough and stringy when heated at too high a temperature or for too long a time. The flavor may change, and some fat may separate from the protein.

Cheese cookery involves melting it and/or blending it with other foods or liquids. The higher the moisture and fat content of cheese, the more easily it melts and blends. It melts quickly when it is first sliced, shredded, cubed, or grated. Hard cheese is grated on a fine grater, and soft cheese is shredded on a coarse grater. Cheese may be cooked in a double boiler or over direct low heat with constant stirring.

When cheese is heated, it softens and may melt. The fat content is partly responsible for the softening. Cheeses with a high fat content melt more quickly than those with a low fat content. As cheese is overheated, either by too high a temperature or by prolonged heating, the protein coagulates and shrinks, becoming toughened. The dry heat of the broiler or oven evaporates some of the moisture from the cheese and contributes to protein shrinkage and thus toughening.

Because high temperatures and prolonged heating toughen cheese protein, cheese may be protected from the intense heat by covering it with a sauce, a layer of the food with which it is used, or with bread crumbs. The cheese is also protected from overheating when the dish containing the cheese-food mixture is placed in a pan of hot water for baking. A cheese garnish should be added during the end of the baking period, just long enough to permit it to melt.

Cheese is frequently combined with a liquid in the preparation of a cheese sauce. Cheeses with a high fat and moisture content blend easily with liquid. The liquid should be heated sufficiently to melt the fat, but not so much as to toughen the protein. An overcooked cheese sauce becomes grainy or stringy and oily.

The emulsifier added to cheese promotes its blending with liquid. Ripened cheeses blend easily with liquids because their protein is dispersed in the curd. The cheese is usually added last to the sauce or product and stirred just until melted. Natural cheese imparts a somewhat grainy texture and pronounced flavor to sauces. The sauces made with processed cheese are not likely to curdle and are very smooth.

Other Uses

Cheese may be used as an appetizer in dips, spreads, or wedges; in sandwiches or salads as a main course or as an accompaniment to other main dishes; and as a dessert tray, often accompanied with an assortment of fresh fruits or candied and dried fruits.

The flavor and texture of cottage cheese and cream cheese are best when served directly from the refrigerator. Most other cheeses are best when served at room temperature.

SUMMARY

Cheese is the curd of milk and is classified as natural or process. Well-ripened and process cheeses blend easily and tend not to be stringy. The protein content of cheese requires the use of a low temperature and a short period of cooking. Cheese cookery involves melting cheese and blending it with other ingredients.

Cheese is a concentrated source of high-quality protein, calcium, phosphorus, and riboflavin; vitamin A value also is high in cheese made with whole milk. A one-inch cube of cheese provides about 100 kcalories.

Cheese products may display approved USDA shields. They are stored in the refrigerator. Cheese may be used as an appetizer, accompaniment, garnish, dessert, or in food combinations as the entrée.

SELF-STUDY GUIDE

1. Describe the process of cheese making.
2. List three major components of cheese. Which of these components determine the methods suitable for use in cheese cookery?
3. How is the quality of cheese identified in the marketplace? How is cheese quality maintained during storage?
4. Discuss the nutritional value of cheeses. How do cheeses vary in nutritional value?
5. How does processed cheese differ from natural cheese? Give examples of each. Suggest uses for each.
6. How does a product labeled as cheese food differ from one known as cheese?
7. How is cheese used in cookery? What preparation techniques are involved? Suggest cheeses for each cookery use.

SUGGESTED READINGS

AGBAVI, D.; ROULEAU, D.; and MAYER, R. Production and qualities of cheddar cheese manufactured from whole milk concentrate by reverse osmosis. *Journal of Food Science* 48:642, 1983.

AMERICAN DAIRY ASSOCIATION OF WISCONSIN. *A world of Wisconsin cheese.* Madison, Wis., no date.

AMERICAN HOME ECONOMICS ASSOCIATION. *Handbook of food preparation.* "Cheese," p. 48. Washington, D.C., 1980.

DEODHAR, A. D.; and DUGGAL, K. Nutritional evaluation of cheese spread powder. *Journal of Food Science* 46:925, 1981.

HANNIGAN, H. K. Fresh cheese made from powder. *Food Engineering* (Chilton's) 54:53, November 1982.

KAUTTER, D. A.; LYND, R. K.; LILLY, JR., T.; and SAL-

OMON, H. M. Evaluation of botulism hazard from imitation cheeses. *Journal of Food Science* 46:749, 1981.

KRAFT, INC. *Buylines on cheese.* Glenview, Ill., no date.

MAHONEY, R. R.; LAZARIDIS, H. N.; and ROSENAU, J. R. Protein size and meltability in enzyme-treated, direct-acidified cheese products. *Journal of Food Science* 47:670, 1982.

SHEERBON, J. W., and BARBANO, D. M. Seasonal changes in New York milk composition and their influence on theoretical yield of cheddar cheese. *Journal of Dairy Science* 63:62, 1980.

U.S. DEPARTMENT OF AGRICULTURE. *Cheese in family meals.* Home and Garden Bulletin no. 112 (Washington, D.C.: Government Printing Office, 1980).

22

BEVERAGES

OBJECTIVES

When you complete this chapter you will be able to

1. Identify and apply the principles involved in the preparation of high-quality coffee, tea, and cocoa/chocolate.
2. Identify the factors to consider in the selection of coffee, tea, cocoa/chocolate for beverage preparation.
3. Identify the factors that influence the quality of beverages.
4. Identify the stimulants in beverages and control the quantity released into the beverage.
5. Discuss the deteriorative changes that occur during storage of coffee, cocoa/chocolate, tea; and store these to avoid and minimize undesirable changes.
6. Discuss the merits of cocoa/chocolate, coffee, tea, and fruit beverages.

The coffee plant is thought to be a native of Abyssinia (Ethiopia) and parts of tropical Africa. A herdsman, centuries ago, noted the lively behavior of his goats after they ate berries from the "kaffa" shrub. He took some of the berries to a monastery, where they were dried and then boiled. The new black beverage delighted the monks, which they called kaffa after the shrub. The use of coffee spread by caravan to Arabia, India, Egypt, and Syria. Coffee houses were popular in England during the seventeenth century and then in colonial America.

      The preparation and service of tea is considered a ceremonial art in Japan and China. Tea came to England in 1866 as "tay." Coffee houses in London began serving tea and soon became tea shops. Tea was a popular custom in colonial America prior to the Boston Tea Party.

Chocolate was served as a beverage in golden bowls to guests by Montezuma, the Aztec emperor. The Aztecs also mixed roasted, ground cocoa beans with cornmeal, vanilla, spices, and herbs into a mush that was served cold. Cortez discovered chocolate in 1519 during the conquest of Mexico. He brought cocoa beans to Spain, and the Spanish added sugar to the beverage. The Dutch, Italians, Austrians, and French experimented with cocoa beans. A London newspaper in 1657 announced the service of an excellent West Indian drink, *jacolatte*. Chocolate houses became popular and the English colonists brought chocolate to America.

The worldwide popularity of these beverages continues yet today. This chapter includes coffee, tea, and chocolate/cocoa: their processing, characteristics, and preparation principles.

COFFEE

Coffee is imported into the United States from Brazil, Columbia, and Africa. Smaller amounts come from Arabia, Costa Rica, Jamaica, and the East Indies. Coffee is obtained from a reddish purple, cherrylike fruit from an evergreen tree. Each fruit contains two oval coffee beans. The fruit is picked by hand and may be either dried in the sun for a few weeks or soaked, depulped, washed, and dried by machine. The coffee beans develop the desired flavor during the curing or fermentation process. The sun-curing process is dependent upon spontaneous fermentation while the washed, machine-dried-coffee process uses enzymes from specially selected fruits.

Green Coffee

A parchment like layer and the silver skin are removed from the dried beans to yield green coffee. The dried green coffee beans are graded and classified by size into six groups and then packed for export. The green coffee keeps well for prolonged periods.

Roasting

The characteristic aroma and flavor of coffee beans develop during roasting, as the beans expand and the color becomes brown. Roasted coffee is classed by the color of the bean as light, medium, dark, or very dark roast. Most American coffee is a rather light to medium roast.

During roasting of coffee structural changes occur. Tiny bubbles of steam form as the green coffee beans are heated, making them porous and light. When the beverage is brewed, the contact area between the ground coffee and the water is increased by this porosity.

Chemical changes that occur during roasting are responsible for the color, aroma, and flavor of coffee. The caramelization of the sugar present in the bean

Columbia Information Service   Columbia Information Service

may be responsible for the color change in roasted coffee. The water-soluble compounds contribute to the characteristic flavor and aroma of the brew. Over- or underroasting results in an inferior coffee. The caffeine content is not altered by roasting and is not related to the color of the roasted bean.

Coffee is blended after roasting, since roasting time differs for each variety. Ground coffee is sold in vacuum-sealed cans to minimize flavor loss. Once opened, the cans must be kept tightly covered.

Caffeine

Caffeine is the stimulant in coffee. It contributes some bitterness to the brew and also acts as a diuretic. Bitterness also comes from the polyphenols, which become increasingly soluble as the temperature approaches boiling. Brewing coffee at just below the boiling temperature extracts sufficient polyphenols to achieve a mellow flavor without excessive bitterness.

Flavor/Aroma

Although they are not fully identified, some flavor components of coffee include sulfur compounds, organic acids, decomposition products of sucrose, and crude-protein fractions. Chlorogenic acid is the most prevalent organic acid and is somewhat bitter and slightly sour. It contributes some **astringency** to the brew. Other organic acids present include acetic, citric, malic, oxalic, and tartaric. A light-roast coffee contains the least acid.

When the coffee bean is heated, carbon dioxide collects in spaces formed by steam, and it is responsible for the floating of ground coffee when it first contacts water. Carbon dioxide influences the retention of flavor and aroma components and contributes some zest to the coffee flavor.

The sugar in coffee beans becomes caramelized during roasting and influences aroma and flavor. The caramelized sugar contributes both a sour and a bitter flavor component as well as color to the beverage.

Sulfur-containing compounds are thought to contribute significantly to the unique aroma of coffee. These volatile compounds also contribute to its flavor.

Kinds/Selection

Many brands of whole-bean, ground, and instant coffee are available, and each represents a special blend of different varieties of coffee. The degree of roasting greatly influences the flavor and aroma developed in coffee. A medium-roast coffee is generally preferred in the United States, although there is some preference for a dark or a light roast in some areas.

Instant Coffee.   Instant coffee is made by dehydrating a very strong brew or by freeze-drying. Freeze-dried coffee is first frozen and then placed in a vacuum chamber to change the ice directly to a vapor. The process of aromatization recovers the aromatic flavoring components that escape during freeze-drying. These are returned to the freeze-dried product to improve its flavor. The process of agglomeration makes instant coffee more soluble. The original fine powder is formed into particles resembling coarsely ground coffee.

Decaffeinated Coffee.   A ground or instant decaffeinated product is available for those preferring a less stimulating coffee. The liquid extract or the green coffee can be treated with solvents to remove most of the caffeine. Decaffeinated coffee is also prepared by a water technique that minimizes the danger of carcinogens. Decaffeinated coffee contains about 1 to 2 percent caffeine.

Ground Coffee.   Most of the coffee on the retail market is ground and packed in sealed or vacuum-packed cans. Vacuum packing removes the air before the container is sealed and protects the coffee from deterioration by moisture, air, and light. Coffee may also be purchased as whole beans and ground as needed at home.

Coffee Grind.   The preparation method determines the choice of coffee grind. Regular or coarse grind is selected for percolator or steeped coffee, drip or medium grind for dripolator, and fine grind for vacuum coffee makers. A coarser grind than regular may be used for electric percolators. A finer-grind coffee permits rapid extraction with less loss of desirable aroma and flavor components.

Deteriorative Change/Storage

Deteriorative Change.   The green beans retain the coffee flavors best, and roasted-coffee flavor is retained better in the whole beans than in ground coffee. When the beans are ground, flavor and aroma loss occur rapidly. The cell walls of the coffee bean are ruptured during grinding, releasing carbon dioxide and other volatile components.

Oils are naturally present in coffee, and the presence of oxygen promotes their deterioration. The oils in coffee stored longer than three weeks probably combine with oxygen, and they become rancid with prolonged storage.

Vacuum packing removes air before the container is sealed, preserving the flavor and aroma of roasted ground coffee. Carbon dioxide gas under pressure may be introduced in cans after the air is removed. Exposure to oxygen or moisture accelerate the loss of coffee flavor.

Storage.   As soon as the container is opened, there is a loss of carbon dioxide and volatile components. Coffee purchased in paper bags should be transferred to glass or metal containers and tightly covered. Losses of volatile aroma and flavor components can be minimized by carefully closing coffee cans and containers with tightly fitting lids. Instant coffee should also be kept tightly sealed. Storing coffee in the refrigerator or freezer further retards deteriorative changes and loss of flavor.

Coffee Preparation

Good coffee has rich flavor and color and is free of sediment. Coffee making involves the extraction of maximum amounts of flavoring substances with a minimum of polyphenols. The character of the beverage is influenced by the grind and freshness of the coffee, proportion of coffee to water, temperature and quality of the water used in brewing, the coffee maker, and preparation method.

Grind and Freshness.   The most satisfying coffee beverage is prepared with the grind appropriate for the coffee maker. A coffee ground too finely for the maker yields a cloudy beverage containing suspended insoluble coffee particles. Too coarse a grind will not permit complete extraction of flavor components and yields a weak brew.

The grind of the coffee influences the rate at which color and flavor components are extracted during brewing. More flavor will be extracted per given weight of coffee when a greater surface area of the coffee is exposed to water. A fine-grind coffee has a greater surface area than one of regular grind.

Fresh coffee has a maximum amount of aroma and flavor components and yields a beverage with a characteristic full coffee flavor. The loss of volatile aroma and flavor components and possible rancidity lead to staling and a beverage with an undesirable flat flavor. Fresh coffee of lower quality yields a better-flavored coffee than a coffee of higher quality that has staled.

Proportion. The proportion of water to coffee determines the flavor strength of the beverage (Table 22-1). A coffee of medium flavor requires 2 table-spoons of ground coffee per cup of coffee, or 3/4 cup of water; increasing the coffee to 3 tablespoons yields a stronger beverage; decreasing the coffee to 1 tablespoon yields a weaker beverage.

Temperature. Hot water extracts the flavor components of coffee. The optimum temperatures for brewing coffee are 185–203° F (85–95° C). These temperatures permit the extraction of caffeine and other soluble flavor-aroma components while restricting the solution of polyphenols, to yield a flavorful and stimulating brew. Higher temperatures extract more caffeine and allow the beverage to develop a bitterness. Coffee brewed for too long a time also develops an undesirable flavor. Too low temperatures and too short brewing time provide a flat, somewhat sour brew.

Coffee Pot/Water Quality. The coffee flavor may be influenced by the material of which the pot is made. Caffeine reacts with some metals to form insoluble compounds, imparting a perceptible metallic flavor to the beverage. Enamelware, glass, porcelain, pyroceram, stainless steel, and stoneware are not affected by caffeine and are preferred for coffee pots.

A coffee pot with an unpleasant odor is not sufficiently clean for the brewing of flavorful coffee. Coffee oils allowed to collect on the interior of the pot become rancid and contribute a stale coffee odor. Coffee pots should be washed thoroughly in hot soapy water after each use to avoid the buildup of oils and waxes and rinsed well to remove traces of soap or detergent, which would alter the coffee flavor.

The flavor of the water can be detected in the prepared brew. Water with a distinct hardness, alkalinity, or flavor detracts from the full, pleasurable coffee flavor. A trace of minerals in the water promotes a good coffee flavor and results

Table 22-1 Proportions for Brewing Coffee

Number of Servings (5½-ounce)	Coffee	Cups Water
2	4 tbsp	1½
4	8 tbsp	3
6	12 tbsp	4¼
8	16 tbsp	6
20	½ lb	16 (1 gal)
40	1 lb	32 (2 gal)

in a better beverage than one prepared with distilled water. The clarity and sparkle of the beverage may be decreased by the hardness of water. The extracted polyphenols of the coffee may react with the minerals of hard water to form precipitates, giving the beverage an opaqueness.

Methods. A good cup of coffee may be steeped, percolated, or filtered. Steeping heats the coffee and water together in a suitable utensil. The percolator, a special utensil, forces the water upward and over the coffee. Filtration permits water to flow down through the coffee. The dripolator coffee maker is a special utensil that uses the filtration method. In all methods the proportion of coffee to water remains the same.

STEEPED. Steeping refers to the extraction of flavor in water below the boiling point. The flavor of coffee is more desirable if the water is kept at a simmer and never allowed to boil. Boiling yields a strong, bitter brew. Measured regular-grind coffee is placed in a pot, and measured freshly simmered water is poured over the coffee. The pot is covered tightly while the beverage brews over low heat for seven to ten minutes.

A small amount of cold water or diluted egg white may be added to aid in settling the grounds. As soon as the grounds have settled, the brew is strained into a preheated pot. The coagulating egg traps the grounds, and causes them to settle quickly. The egg albumin combines with some polyphenols, yielding a somewhat blander coffee than without the egg.

PERCOLATOR. In the percolator, water filters through the coffee grounds repeatedly before the beverage is of desired strength. The percolator includes a pot, a coffee basket, and a hollow stem to support the basket. Regular-grind coffee is measured into the basket, which is placed on the stem, and then both are inserted into the pot. When heat is applied, the water under the dome attached to the stem is forced up the stem by steam and spreads over the coffee basket onto the grounds and down into the pot.

Only a small portion of the water at any one time reaches the basket. When percolation begins, the heat is adjusted so that water reaches the top of the basket about every two seconds. This gentle percolation is continued for six to eight minutes, until the desired strength is achieved.

Because the brew is maintained near the boiling point during percolation, some desirable volatile aroma and flavor components escape. Some percolators have a valve in the stem that serves to control the temperature of water reaching the grounds. The water flowing over the basket is generally just below the boiling point. The grounds should always be removed from the coffee maker at the end of extraction regardless of method used. Grounds absorb aroma from the beverage.

DRIPOLATOR.   The dripolator consists of three compartments. Measured drip-grind coffee is placed into the center section, freshly boiled water is measured into the top portion, and the brewed coffee collects in the bottom compartment. The hot water flows slowly over the grounds, extracting the flavor and aroma components before passing into the bottom container. A filter liner is usually placed in the bottom of the middle section to prevent very fine coffee particles from reaching the bottom compartment.

The dripolator uses water of optimum temperature 185–203° F (85–95° C), which contacts the grounds only once for a short time. The aroma and flavor components are retained well, yielding a most flavorful beverage.

The automatic electric drip machine brews coffee almost instantly. The coffee is placed under the heated water outlet, and the beverage receiver is placed on the warming plate. Freshly drawn cold water is put into the water container. Brewing occurs as soon as the coffee maker is turned on to yield a bitter-free beverage.

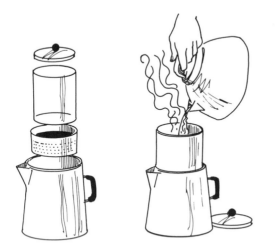

ACCENTED COFFEE.   Demitasse or café noir is strong black coffee, served after dinner in small cups. It can be prepared by any basic method using one and a half times or more the amount of coffee normally recommended (two tablespoons per cup).

Café au lait is prepared with regular or extra-strength coffee served with an equal amount of hot milk, preferably steamed to a foamy state. Equal amounts of coffee and prepared cocoa may be blended and topped with whipped cream. Coffee may also be accented with spices or flavorings, such as cinnamon, nutmeg, or lemon or orange peel.

Espresso coffee is brewed from a dark roast. A special apparatus passes a mixture of steam and hot water through finely powdered coffee. The beverage is dark in color, very strong, and relatively bitter. It is served in small cups, often with a small slice of lemon zest.

TEA

Tea is brewed from the leaf of an evergreen plant rather than from a bean, as with coffee. The use of tea began in China before the Christian era. Most of the world's supply of tea comes from China, India, Indonesia, and Japan.

Tea grows best in tropical climates with an abundant rainfall. The highest quality tea comes from the first and second leaves of the young unopened leaf bud. These leaves have the high polyphenol and oxidase content needed for colorful and flavorful tea. The quality of tea depends upon the kind of plant, growing conditions, time of picking, and curing conditions.

Types

The three major types of tea—green, black, and oolong—are processed from the same kinds of tea leaves by different methods.

Green.   Green tea is popular in Japan and is prepared from unfermented tea. The enzymes are inactivated to prevent fermentation by steaming the leaves at the beginning of processing. The leaves are rolled and then dried. The dried leaves are a green to dark gray in color. The beverage is a rather weak greenish color and has a suggestion of bitterness and astringency. The brewed green tea beverage is distinctly different and has its own uniquely appealing qualities.

The grades of green tea are gunpowder, young hyson, hyson, and imperial, according to leaf size and position on the plant. The smallest leaves are rolled into tight balls during drying and identified as gunpowder. The medium leaves are rolled lengthwise and identified as imperial.

Black Tea.   When the leaves wither and soften, the processing of tea begins. During machine rolling, enzymes and juices are released from the broken tissues, and then the leaves are allowed to ferment. Oxidative changes induced by enzymes occur during fermentation. The oxidative process begun during rolling is completed in a fermenting room where the leaves are spread thinly to facilitate contact with oxygen. Catechin and gallocatechin, which are new phenolic compounds, are produced from polyphenols by oxidation during fermentation.

Courtesy Thomas J. Lipton, Inc.

The dried fermented leaves are separated into grades according to size and so marketed. Broken orange pekoe is considered the best grade of black tea and consists chiefly of buds. Other grades in descending order are broken pekoe, orange pekoe, souchong, fannings (in tea bags), and dust (for quick brewing). Black tea is usually a blend of orange pekoe and pekoe. Black tea yields an amber-colored beverage with a rich aroma and flavor and little astringency.

Oolong Tea. Oolong tea is primarily produced in Taiwan. The leaves are wilted, slightly fermented, and dried. The resulting beverage has a color, flavor, and aroma intermediate to that yielded by green or black tea.

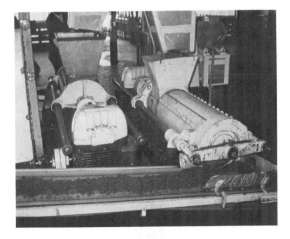

Courtesy Thomas J. Lipton, Inc.

Courtesy Thomas J. Lipton, Inc.

Courtesy Hershey Foods Corporation

Florida Sugar Cane League, Photo by Jeanne Mitchell

Instant Tea.   Instant tea is prepared from a concentrated brew from which the water is removed by spray or vacuum drying. Some tea is decaffeinated. Instant tea is soluble in hot or cold water and is used to make iced tea without heating water and steeping the beverage before pouring it over ice.

Speciality Teas.   Herbs and spices contribute distinctive flavors to speciality teas. The unique flavor of each tea develops from a blend of ingredients such as orange peel, hibiscus flower, rosehips, blackberry leaves, peppermint leaves, cinnamon, cloves, licorice root, and chicory root. The flavor may be sweet, flower-like, citrus with a spice accent, or cooling and penetrating as peppermint.

Tea Components

Theine was originally identified as the stimulant in tea, but it has since been shown to be identical with caffeine. The concentration of caffeine in the tea beverage is somewhat less than in brewed coffee. However, tea leaves contain more caffeine than roasted coffee. Green and oolong tea beverages contain less caffeine than black tea. Tea also contains theobromine and theophylline. Tea leaves contain a number of polyphenolic compounds, the flavonols and flavanols. The polyphenolic constitutents contribute to the flavor of tea and are chiefly responsible for its astringency.

Changes in the polyphenols during fermentation impart the characteristic aroma and flavor to black tea. New compounds, the theaflavins, are formed in black tea from flavanols. The orange theaflavins and brown thearubigins contribute sparkle and depth to the tea beverage. Volatile oils contribute to the aroma of tea and are known as essential oils. About thirty compounds have been identified in the aroma of green tea and more than three hundred in black tea aroma. The degree to which these components are dissolved in beverage preparation is related to temperature and steeping time.

Selection/Storage

Black tea is popular in America and may be flavored with lemon, orange, mint, and spices. Much of the tea brewed in the United States is prepared with tea bags and instant tea. Canned tea in a ready-to-drink form, either with or without lemon and sugar is also readily available.

Loose tea may be purchased in quarter-pound, half-pound, and pound packages. Tea bags and instant tea are available in containers of various sizes. Tea is less perishable than coffee, but there is some loss of volatile flavor and aroma components during storage. Tea can be stored in tightly covered containers for several months.

Tea Preparation

Tea preparation involves the use of freshly drawn water heated to a boil and then poured over tea leaves in a hot teapot. An alternate method involves a tea ball or tea bag immersed and steeped for three to five minutes in a covered teapot. After this time the tea leaves are strained out or the tea ball or tea bags removed to avoid bitterness and astringency in the beverage.

Water.   The dissolved oxygen present in freshly boiled water enhances the flavor of tea. During prolonged boiling of water oxygen is driven off, and a flat taste is imparted to the beverage. Soft water is preferred to hard water for tea. The polyphenols of tea interact with some salts in hard water to produce a precipitate that gives a cloudiness to the beverage, and they may form a film that floats on the surface and coats the cup.

Temperature.   The color, aroma, and flavor of tea are influenced by the temperature of the water when it comes in contact with the leaves. Flavorful tea contains a minimum of caffeine and a minimum of polyphenols. The water should be below the boiling temperature, or simmering (185–210° F, 85–99° C), as it contacts the leaves during steeping. Water temperatures above this range extract excessive amounts of polyphenols, which contribute a bitter flavor.

Proportion.   The strength of the beverage is determined by the quantity of tea used and steeping time. Generally, one teaspoon of tea or a tea bag per cup of water is recommended. Because tea leaves swell in hot water, a tea ball should be only half filled with loose tea. The strength of the tea is controlled by increasing or decreasing the quantity of tea per cup of water or by slightly increasing or decreasing the steeping time. Tea is usually steeped three to five minutes. Prolonged steeping yields a bitter tea. At the end of steeping, the beverage is poured through a fine strainer, or the tea bags are removed.

Teapot.   Polyphenolic compounds may interact with metal teapots to impart a metallic flavor to the beverage; therefore glass, enamelware, china, or earthenware teapots are recommended. The teapot should be warmed with boiling water before the tea is brewed to help maintain the temperature of the beverage at a sufficiently high level for optimal brewing and tea service.

Iced Tea.   Iced tea may be prepared with tea leaves or instant tea. A strong, hot tea (1½–2 teaspoons of tea per cup) is prepared and poured over ice cubes. The strong tea compensates for the diluting effect of the melting ice. An alternate method uses regular or extra-strength tea that has cooled and then is served over ice. Dissolved polyphenols may precipitate upon cooling and cloud the tea. The addition of lemon juice or a small amount of hot water restores clarity to the beverage. Iced tea is quickly prepared with instant tea and cold water. A regular or extra-strength tea is poured over ice. The flavor of the beverage may be less full and brisk than when prepared with tea leaves.

Flavor Accent.   Fruit juices, spices, mint, honey or other sweeteners and milk or cream may be added to enhance the flavor of hot or cold tea. The acid in fruit juice depresses ionization of certain tea components (thearubigins), producing a light-colored beverage. The astringency of the beverage is decreased with the addition of milk, owing to the formation of an insoluble casein-polyphenol complex.

Good Tea.   A well-brewed tea is sparklingly clear and free of surface film. Green tea is a pale greenish yellow color with a slightly bitter flavor, and little aroma. Oolong tea is an intermediate light brownish green color with a slightly bitter flavor and a mild aroma. Black tea is amber colored with a brisk, full flavor free of bitterness and a distinctive pleasing aroma.

CHOCOLATE

Cocoa and chocolate are derived from the cacao bean, which is the seed of a pod grown on a tropical tree, the Theobroma Cacao. The beans are removed from the pod and fermented for several days, at which time a rich brown color develops owing to polyphenolic oxidation. The graded dried beans are exported from Africa, Latin America, Java, and Samoa.

Processing

Cacao beans are dried and then roasted to develop flavor and aroma and to facilitate the removal of the shell. During roasting the composition of polyphenols is altered, lessening their astringency, and some volatile components and moisture dissipate.

A chocolate liquor or paste is formed from a variety of nibs or meat of the cacao bean. This liquor solidifies on cooling to form bitter chocolate. Sugar and flavoring are added to bitter chocolate to form sweet chocolate; milk, sugar, and flavor are added to make milk chocolate. When cocoa is made, the cocoa butter is pressed from the ground nibs. The pressed cakes of cocoa are crushed to a fine powder.

Cocoa and chocolate are classed as natural process and Dutch process. The nibs are treated with alkali during roasting of the Dutch process to improve their color and solubility. Dutch-process chocolate is less likely to separate from liquids and is darker in color than natural process. The pigments in cocoa and chocolate change in color with a change in pH. They are yellow at a pH of 5.0 and change to shades of brown and become mahogany red at a pH of 7.5. The added alkali changes the pH range from the 5.2–6.0 of natural-process cocoa and chocolate to 6.0-8.8 for Dutch process.

Compostion of Cocoa and Chocolate

Theobromine is the chief stimulant in cocoa and chocolate, along with some caffeine. The other major constituents of cocoa and chocolate include color and flavor compounds, lipids, and carbohydrate.

Although color and flavor components of cocoa and chocolate are not yet fully identified, it is known that partially volatile and phenolic compounds are involved. Some phenols are oxidized to reddish brown, water-insoluble pigments.

Courtesy Hershey Foods Corporation

The cocoa red and purple pigments are classed as **anthocyanins.** The chocolate flavor, at least in part, is attributed to phenolic compounds, which are converted to less astringent substances during fermentation. The flavor of unfermented cocoa is extremely bitter.

Natural-process cocoa and chocolate are only slightly acid, and the Dutch process is even less acid. For this reason, soda-leavened chocolate and cocoa flour mixtures should be prepared with sour or buttermilk rather than sweet milk, to avoid an unpleasant flavor.

Carbohydrates. Starch is the chief carbohydrate in cocoa and chocolate and functions as a thickening agent. Cocoa contains about 11 percent starch and chocolate about 8 percent. When the starch component is thoroughly cooked, cocoa and chocolate tend to remain dispersed rather than settling out. Cocoa has more thickening power than chocolate because of its high starch content. For this reason, cocoa is not substituted on a direct weight basis for chocolate. Usually, 3 to 3½ tablespoons of cocoa plus ½ tablespoon of table fat are considered equivalent to 1 ounce or square of chocolate.

Lipids. The lipid or fat constituent of cocoa and chocolate is cocoa butter. Cocoa has about half as much lipid as chocolate. Cocoa varies in fat content from 10 to 22 percent. Chocolate contains about 50 percent fat. The rather low melting temperature of chocolate, near 90° F (32° C) imparts a smooth texture and readily releases flavor components. Oleic and stearic fatty acids are most prevalent in cocoa butter, with some palmitic and a small amount of linoleic acid.

Storage

Cocoa and chocolate deteriorate quickly in the presence of moisture and heat. Cocoa becomes grayish in color and lumpy when stored at temperatures about 61–70° F (16–21° C) and in high humidity.

A mottled or gray surface known as the bloom may develop on chocolate when it is exposed to high heat and moisture. The melting of fat and recrystallizing in a different pattern on the surface is believed to contribute to the formation of bloom. Appropriate tempering procedures during processing and the use of stabilizers and modifiers retard the development of bloom.

Sugar bloom, a rough grayish layer, may appear on sweet chocolate. Moisture is believed to be responsible for the formation of sugar bloom; the dissolved sugar recrystallizes on the surface.

The chocolate flavor appears not to be altered by the development of bloom or lumping of cocoa products, but the texture may be grainy and the appearance grayed. Milk chocolate also may absorb flavors and odors when improperly stored. The quality of cocoa and chocolate is best retained when high temperatures and humidity are avoided. The best protection is tightly sealed containers kept in a cool, dry place.

Cocoa and Chocolate Preparation

Cocoa and chocolate do not require the extraction of flavor and color components involved in coffee and tea making. They are directly incorporated with milk. The methods used to prepare hot cocoa and chocolate beverages take into account their starch and fat content and their tendency to scorch.

Cocoa and fluid chocolate blend easily, but solid chocolate must be melted over low heat to avoid scorching. Beverage preparation begins with the blending of cocoa or chocolate with sugar and salt and then water. At this point the mixture is heated to boiling in order to gelatinize the starch, thus avoiding the raw-starch flavor and reducing the sedimentation of solids. The mixture thickens somewhat, and milk is blended slowly into the gelatinized cocoa or chocolate mixture. The beverage is now heated to serving temperature over low heat. Because of the high milk content a scum is likely to form on top. Scum formation can be controlled by covering the prepared beverage or beating it to form a layer of foam. Whipped topping or marshmallows also serve to reduce scum formation. A low temperature should be used after the addition of the milk to avoid scorching the milk or the chocolate.

Instant Cocoa/Chocolate. Instant cocoa mixes or chocolate syrups blend easily with hot or cold milk or water and only require heating over low heat to the desired temperature.

Good Cocoa/Chocolate. A good-quality cocoa or chocolate has a pleasing, characteristic chocolate flavor, with no hint of scorching or overheating, and it is free of sediment and scum.

FRUIT BEVERAGES

In addition to fresh and frozen fruit juices, canned, frozen, and powdered fruit drinks are available. Fruit drinks are prepared from regular or synthetic fruit juice or from a combination of the two. Fruit drinks contain natural or synthetic flavorings, sugar or non-nutritive sweetener, color, usually ascorbic acid, and preservatives. Federal standards of identity have been developed for orange drink, orange juice drink, pineapple-grapefruit juice drink, lemonade, and limeade. Fruit drinks are convenient and refreshing beverages, but they should not replace the use of fruit juices. Nutritionally, fruit juices are a better choice than fruit drinks, and fruit drinks a better choice than cola-type beverages. Table 22–2 lists the quantity of juice or concentrate in common market containers.

Table 22-2 Juice and Concentrate Containers and Yields

Containers	Cups
Chilled/canned juice	
6–8 fl oz	¾–1
12 fl oz	1½
1 pt	2
1 pt, 2 fl oz	2¼–2½
1 qt	4
1 qt, 14 fl oz	5¾
3 qt	12
Frozen concentrate	
6 oz	3
12 oz	6
Frozen ade concentrate	
6 oz	3¾
12 oz	7½

From USDA, *Fruits in Family Meals,* Home and Garden Bulletin no. 125 (Washington, D.C.: Government Printing Office, 1975).

NUTRITIONAL QUALITY/MERIT

The milk-prepared beverages provide a food value similar to that in the quantity of milk used. Cocoa and chocolate used in beverage preparation contain fat and starch, and sugar usually is added during preparation. All the nutrients in the milk used are present in the beverage plus the added energy or calories from cocoa or chocolate and sugar.

Of the fruit beverages, fruit juices provide a nutrient value similar to that of the fruit. Fruit drinks contain a relatively small quantity of fruit juice and therefore smaller quantities of nutrients than fruit juices. Although fruit drinks are less rich sources of nutrients than fruit juice, they are more nutritious than cola-type beverages, which provide only calories.

Tea and coffee are stimulating and satisfying beverages but are nutrient poor. The cream and sugar added primarily provide calories. When milk is used in coffee or tea, the quantity is so small that the nutritional benefit is not significant. The merits of tea and coffee are measured in pleasurable satisfaction rather than nutrients.

SUMMARY

Coffee is prepared from roasted, ground coffee beans by filtration, percolation, or steeping. Coffee makers include the dripolator, percolator, and vacuum. A water temperature just below boiling yields a desirable brew with a pleasing flavor, a minimum of polyphenols to avoid bitterness, and sufficient caffeine for stimulation. A satisfactory beverage can be prepared from ground or instant coffee. Except for green coffee, all coffee has a short shelf life and should be stored in a tightly covered container.

Tea is available as whole or broken leaves and is sold as packaged loose tea or teabags. The beverage is prepared from dried leaves, which are sometimes fermented to develop a less astringent flavor. Black tea is fermented, oolong is partly fermented, and green tea is not fermented. The beverage is prepared by the extraction of flavor and color components with freshly boiled water poured over tea leaves and steeped or with instant tea. Water temperature above simmer and prolonged steeping extract excessive amounts of polyphenols, and yield an unpleasant bitter tea. Tea stored in a tightly covered container has a relatively long shelf life.

Cocoa and chocolate are heated to gelatinize the starch before milk is added, thus reducing sedimentation and avoiding a raw-starch flavor. Scum formation and precipitation of milk protein are retarded by controlled temperature and heating period. The quality of cocoa and chocolate is best retained in tightly covered containers stored in a cool, dry place.

Milk is responsible for the nutritional quality of cocoa and chocolate, while tea and coffee are low in nutrients, but are valued as stimulants. Nutritionally, fruit juices are a better choice than fruit drinks, and fruit drinks a better choice than cola-type beverages.

SELF-STUDY GUIDE

1. What two values are derived from beverages?
2. Discuss three factors involved in selection of beverages.
3. Discuss three principles involved in preparation of quality beverages from coffee, tea, and cocoa.
4. What is the relationship of types of coffee to preparation methods?
5. What four factors influence the quality of beverages?
6. What stimulants are present in coffee, tea, and cocoa? How do they influence the beverage?
7. Compare the procedures for making coffee, tea, and cocoa.

SUGGESTED READINGS

ALM, L. Effect of fermentation on B-vitamin content of milk. *Journal of Dairy Science* 65:353, 1982.

Analysis of beverages. *Food Engineering* (Chilton's) 52:85, August 1980.

COHEN, B. L. Relative risks of saccharine sweeteners in drinks. *Science News* 199:983, 1979.

CRAIG, W. J., and NGUYEN, T. T. Carob products. *Journal of Food Science* 49:302, 1984.

DUBOSE, C. N., et al. Effects of colorants and flavorants on identification, perceived flavor intensity, and hedonic quality of fruit flavored beverages and cakes. *Journal of Food Science* 45:1393, 1980.

Fortified drinks. *Food Engineering* (Chilton's) 53:96, January, 1981.

HANNIGAN, K. J. Coffee in an instant: It's in the bag! *Food Engineering* (Chilton's) 54:57, June 1982.

HELBIG, N. B.; HO, L.; CRISTY, G. E.; and NAKAI, S. Debittering of skim milk hydrolysates by adsorption for incorporation into acidic beverages. *Journal of Food Science* 45:331, 1980.

HENNEKENS, C. H., et al. Effects of beer, wine, and liquor in coronary deaths. *Journal of the American Medical Association* 242:18, 1979.

HUOR, S. S.; AHMED, E. M.; CARTER, R. S.; and HUGGART, R. L. Color and flavor qualities of white grapefruit juice; watermelon juice mixtures. *Journal of Food Science* 45:1419, 1980.

HUOR, S. S.; AHMED, E. M.; RAO, P.; and CORNELL, J. A. Formulation and sensory evaluation of a fruit punch containing watermelon juice. *Journal of Food Science* 45:809, 1980.

HUSSEIN, M. M., and MACKAY, D. A. Application of large bore coated (LBG) columns to flavor analysis of beverages and confections. *Journal of Food Science* 46:1043, 1981.

IFT's expert panel on food safety and nutrition. Caffeine—a scientific status summary. *Food Technology* 37:87, 1983.

Machine produces stand up pouches for foods and beverages. *Food Engineering* (Chilton's) 52:129, July, 1980.

MACMAHON, B., et al. Coffee and cancer of the pancreas. *New England Journal of Medicine* 304:630, 1981.

PANDA, N. C., et al. Damage done to intestine, liver, and kidneys by tannic acid of tea and coffee. *Indian Journal of Nutrition and Dietetics* 18:97, 1981.

ROBERTS, H. R., and BARONE, J. J. Caffeine: History and use. *Food Technology* 37:32, 1983.

ROSSOUW, J. E., et al. The effect of skim milk, yoghurt, and full-cream milk on human serum lipids. *American Journal of Clinical Nutrition* 34:351, 1981.

ROSTON, D. A., and KISSINGER, P. T. Identification of phenolic constituents in commercial beverages by liquid chromatography with electrochemical detection. *Annals of Chemistry* 53:1659, 1981.

SMOLENSKY, D. C., and VANDERCOOK, C. E. Detection of grape juice in apple juice. *Journal of Food Science* 45:1773, 1980.

Soft drinks. *Food Engineering* (Chilton's) 53:111, August, 1981.

STALDER, R., and MARCHESINI, M. The effects of coffee consumption on the thiamin status of rats. *International Journal for Vitamin and Nutritional Research* 51:188, 1981.

VANDERCOOK, C. E.; STEVEN, D. L.; and SMOLENSKY, D. C. Rapid, automated, microbiological determination of orange juice authenticity. *Journal of Food Science* 45:1416, 1980.

23

CRYSTALLIZATION

OBJECTIVES

When you complete this chapter you will be able to

1. Discuss the factors that promote formation of small crystals in sugar products and in frozen dessert products.
2. Identify the function of ingredients in preparation of candy and discuss the differences in methods used to make crystalline and noncrystalline candies.
3. Identify the functions of ingredients in frozen dessert products and discuss differences in methods used to prepare frozen desserts.
4. Explain the difference between various frozen dessert products.

Water and sugar have in common the ability to form crystals. A smooth, creamy texture is desired, whether the product contains sugar or ice crystals. The specific ingredients of the sugar mixture as well as the mixture to be frozen affect crystal size and the consistency of the product. The techniques of sugar and ice-crystal formation, the factors influencing their formation, and some representative products dependent upon these crystals are presented in this chapter.

SUGAR

As an ingredient, sugar plays a variety of roles in food preparation, as discussed in earlier chapters. Sugar (1) enhances food flavors; (2) promotes tenderness, fine texture, greater volume, and browning in baked products; (3) stabilizes egg white foam;

(4) increases tenderness of starch-thickened gels, gelatin products, and egg dishes; (5) promotes production of carbon dioxide by yeast; and (6) acts as a dehydrating agent in pectin gel formation.

Sugar also modifies the temperature at which boiling and freezing occur and thus assumes a significant role in the preparation of candies and frozen desserts. Sugar crystals are the fundamental structural materials of candies. Sugar also influences the texture and the serving qualities of frozen desserts. Sugar lowers the freezing point of mixtures, permitting them to be stirred longer during freezing so that the ice crystals can be kept small.

Types of Sweeteners

Granulated white sugar is what is meant when a recipe calls for sugar, although other sweeteners may be used. Honey, molasses, and syrup also sweeten, and each contributes a distinctive flavor. Chemically, they are similar to sugar and serve similar functions in food preparation.

Granulated Sugar. The sugar derived from sugar cane and sugar beets is identical chemically and is called sucrose. The fibrous sugar cane stalks are crushed between rollers to extract the juice, and the juice is clarified with lime to remove nonsucrose materials. Then the water is evaporated under vacuum. Sugar crystals form when the solution becomes **supersaturated,** and they are separated out in a centrifuge. A revolving drum separates the molasses, the leftover product, from the sugar crystals. The yellow, sticky raw sugar is blended with water, passed through charcoal filters for purification, and recrystallized to form granules of a specific size.

Sugar beets are sliced into strips, soaked in hot water, clarified with lime and charcoal, and then concentrated in an evaporator and boiled in vacuum pans. A small amount of pulverized sugar is added to the thick liquid to encourage crystal formation. The crystals are then separated out in a centrifuge, yielding a refined table sugar, or sucrose.

The size of granulated sugar particles range from coarse to regular granulated to superfine. Finely granulated sugar dissolves more quickly than regular granulated sugar. The coarsely granulated is for special uses and decorative purposes. Regular granulated sugar is suitable for most uses.

Sugar pressed into cubes or cakes is convenient for sweetening hot beverages. Cube sugar dissolves more slowly than free-flowing granulated sugar.

Powdered Sugar. Powdered sugar, or confectioners' sugar, is a blend of pulverized granulated sugar and 3 percent cornstarch. The cornstarch helps to inhibit caking of the powdered sugar. The fineness of powdered sugar is designated by the number of Xs and ranges from coarse powdered to extrafine. Standard powdered sugar is identified as XXXX, or 4X; extrafine as 6X; and ultrafine as 10X, or confectioners'.

Florida Sugar Cane League, Photo by Jeanne Mitchell

Brown Sugar.   Some of the original molasses surrounds the crystals of brown sugar, contributing color and flavor. Brown sugars range in color from light to very dark. Dark brown sugar contains more molasses than the light brown sugar and is more intense in flavor. Brown sugar is sticky, and lumps form easily.

An **agglomerated,** or free-flowing, brown sugar contains relatively large granules. It is composed of small sugar crystals formed into granules. Free-flowing brown sugar weighs less per cup than regular brown sugar. On the basis of volume, each cup of regular brown sugar is replaced with 1⅓ cups of free-flowing brown sugar. A liquid brown sugar is also available. Only half as much, by weight, of the liquid brown is needed to replace the granular brown sugar specified in recipes.

Molasses.   The various stages in sugar refinement yield molasses of different qualities. A molasses with a high sucrose content is formed during the first stage of crystallization. The second and third crystallizations produce a molasses with less sucrose and more invert sugar.

The three types of molasses are unsulfured, sulfured, and blackstrap. Depending upon the stage of crystallization and refinement, sulfured molasses may be light or dark in color. Molasses from the second or third stages of crystallization is progressively darker than from the first crystallization. Sulfured molasses is a byproduct of sugar production and is exposed to sulfur dioxide fumes. When unsulfured molasses is prepared from ripe sugar cane, it is the principal product produced and is not exposed to the sulfur process. Blackstrap molasses remains after the sugar has been extracted. Much of it is used in preparation of animal foods. Blackstrap molasses has little nutritional value for humans.

Molasses may contain as high as 70 percent sugar, most of which is sucrose with some fructose. Different molasses fractions are blended to yield molasses products of desired viscosity, flavor, and color. Molasses contributes both flavor and color to the products in which it is used.

Sorghum.   Sorghum cane is similar to sugar cane and yields a syrup that resembles molasses in appearance. The total sugar content of sorghum is nearly the same as that of cane syrup.

Honey.   Bees produce honey from the nectars of flowering plants and deposit it in a comb. Alfalfa and clover nectars yield a light-colored honey with a pleasing flavor. Buckwheat nectar produces a dark honey with an intense flavor. Specialty honeys are made with nectars from blossoms such as citrus, tulip tree, and sage. Light-colored honey is generally milder in flavor than dark-colored honey. The color of honey does not determine its grade.

Honey contains a high level of fructose, some glucose, and about 2 percent sucrose. Fructose aids in attracting and holding moisture in food products made with honey. These products remain moist for a longer time than similar products made with other sweeteners.

Honey is sold as section-comb honey, but most often it is extracted and strained from the comb and sold as strained honey. Liquid honey may crystallize when stored for a period of time. This is more likely to happen when the honey is stored in the refrigerator and occurs less readily when honey is stored at room temperature. Crystallized honey is returned to a liquid state by placing the container in warm water.

Honey is also available as a dried, free-flowing, granular product. Its color and flavor are similar to the honey from which it was made. A blend of about 75 percent dried honey and starch is also on the market. Dried honey is used in confectionery making, in convenience baking mixes, and in commercial baking.

Corn Syrup.   Under pressure and heat, cornstarch can be hydrolyzed by acid to yield corn syrup. This syrup has a 40 to 50 percent sugar content as a mixture of glucose and maltose. Corn syrup can also be prepared by enzyme hydrolysis. Although enzyme-hydrolyzed syrup contains more sugar than acid-hydrolyzed syrup, it is less viscous and does not crystallize.

Corn syrup is primarily composed of glucose and contains some maltose and dextrin. It is used in baking to contribute sweetness and moisture and in frostings and confections to promote a smoother texture by helping to control crystallization of sucrose. Corn syrups are less sweet and less expensive than other syrups and are used in the preparation of table syrups and infant formulas.

High-Fructose Syrups.   The production of high-fructose syrups became possible with the availability of the enzyme glucose isomerase from the Streptomyces microorganisms. This enzyme converts the glucose in corn syrup to fructose. The resulting syrup is about 42 percent fructose and 50 percent glucose. Because fructose is sweeter than sucrose, the high-fructose syrup has an intense sweetness, which allows a smaller quantity to be used than of other sweeteners to achieve a desired sweetness. High-fructose corn syrup (HFCS) is used commercially in soft drinks, as a portion of the sweetener in pickles, relishes, and similar preserved foods, and in candy making to control crystal size.

Maple Syrup.   Maple syrup is made by evaporating the sap obtained from the sugar maple tree. During boiling, the maple flavor is developed from the organic acids present in the sap. High-quality maple syrup is light in color and clear. Dark maple syrup is made from the last run of sap and has an intense flavor. Additional boiling of the syrup yields maple sugar. Sucrose is the chief sugar in maple syrup, and some invert sugar is present.

CHARACTERISTICS OF SUGAR

Sugars are classed as carbohydrates. Glucose, fructose, and galactose are simple sugars and chemically are monosaccharides. All sugars contribute four kcalories per gram. Sugars vary in their degree of sweetness. Fructose is the sweetest, followed in sequence by sucrose, glucose, maltose, and lactose. In baked products, however, fructose is only about as sweet as sucrose. The solubility of these sugars varies and follows the same order as their intensity of sweetness, with fructose being the most soluble and lactose the least.

Disaccharides can be hydrolyzed into their component monosaccharides. Sucrose is the primary disaccharide involved in food preparation. It is composed of one molecule each of glucose and fructose. Maltose, a disaccharide composed of two glucose units, is usually not used in food preparation. It is present chiefly in malt extract and in small quantities in corn syrup and commercial glucose. Lactose, a third disaccharide, consists of glucose and galactose and is found only in milk. Because of its limited solubility and its relatively high cost, lactose is not commonly used. Lactic acid bacteria change lactose into lactic acid, and this process is used in the production of cheese and buttermilk.

Hygroscopic Nature

Sugars are **hygroscopic,** that is they are able to attract water. Sugar readily absorbs moisture from the atmosphere and becomes lumpy unless it is stored in a tightly covered container. Fructose is the most hygroscopic of the sugars. Since it is the sugar in honey, honey-containing baked products tend to remain moist for longer periods than sucrose products. Baked products with a high sugar content tend to pick up moisture, and candies tend to become sticky in a moisture-laden atmosphere.

Caramelization

Sugar is decomposed by heat. When dry sugar is exposed to heat it melts at 320° F (160° C) to form a colorless liquid. With continued heating it becomes yellow, and with additional heat the color change progresses to brown and then to nearly black. The heat-induced changes in sugar contribute a pleasing flavor and aroma and a brown color and are known as **caramelization.** Sweetness is decreased as caramelization progresses and is eventually lost as heating continues.

The caramelization process involves many complex chemical changes, which are not completely understood. Sucrose may first be decomposed to glucose and fructosan. A molecule of water is lost from fructose to form fructosan, and a molecule of water may be lost from glucose to form glucosan during heating. The dehydrated monosaccharide molecules may polymerize and combine to form large molecules. Sugar acids may also be produced by heat degradation of sugar.

Caramelized sugars are soluble in water. As soon as the desired degree of browning is reached, caramelization can be stopped with the addition of water, which promptly lowers the temperature below that required for caramelization to continue. Steam is produced when water is added to the intensely hot sugar, and caution must be observed. Caramelized sugar becomes very hard unless water is added to facilitate its blending with other ingredients.

Some caramelization may occur in concentrated sugar solutions as the final cooking temperature is reached. Caramelization takes place in the preparation of peanut brittle, caramels, and toffees. Organic acids as well as other unknown components contribute to the flavor and aroma of caramelized sugar.

Hydrolysis

The most common disaccharides present in food include sucrose, lactose, and some maltose. These disaccharides can be hydrolyzed to their constituent monosaccharides. **Hydrolysis** is promoted by heating sucrose in the presence of an acid, such as cream of tartar. The type and quantity of acid and the length of cooking time influence the extent of hydrolysis. Hydrolysis increases as acidity is increased, and a long, slow heating promotes more hydrolysis than rapid heating does.

Hydrolysis may be induced intentionally in sugar cookery to achieve desired textures and consistencies in sugar products. The mixture of sugars formed during acid hydrolysis yield somewhat softer candies with smoother textures than can be prepared when only granulated sugar and water are used. When hydrolysis is allowed to continue too long, candies become too soft.

Use of the enzyme invertase is another means of hydrolyzing sucrose. This enzyme hydrolyzes sucrose to invert sugar (mixture of equal amounts of glucose and fructose). Invertase is used in commercial candy preparation to achieve semi-isoft and fluid centers in chocolates but is not generally available on the retail market. Because heat inactivates the enzyme, it is added after the sugar mixture is cooked and cooled. After invertase is added to crystalline candies, the candies are allowed to ripen while the enzyme slowly hydrolyzes the sugar, softening the centers of chocolates.

Alkaline decomposition of sugar occurs in cookery. Alkalies present in the water added to sugar to form a solution may decompose sugar. Glucose and fructose are decomposed on standing or by being heated in alkaline solutions. Glucose and fructose are more easily decomposed by alkali than sucrose. The invert sugar produced from sucrose is also easily decomposed. The decomposition products of glucose and fructose are brownish in color and may have a strong flavor.

Solutions

Because sugars form true **solutions** in water they raise the boiling point of water. The boiling point of a sugar solution is directly related to the number of particles or molecules present; therefore, it is an indicator of the sugar concentration at any point in the boiling process. Candy and frosting preparation involve the solution of sugar in a liquid and application of heat to achieve the appropriate concentration of sugar.

As the sugar-water mixture is heated, all the sugar gradually goes into solution. As the sugar-water solution boils, the temperature rises above the temperature of boiling water, and the solution becomes saturated. A saturated solution has all of the sugar dissolved in it that can be dissolved at the temperature of the solution. Continued boiling evaporates more water; the solution becomes more concentrated; a higher sugar-to-water ratio develops; and the boiling point is gradually elevated. When the final temperature is reached, the sugar is cooked to the desired concentration for the candy product. Then the cooked, concentrated sugar mixture is carefully cooled to form a supersaturated solution. The final crystalline or amorphous solid is ultimately formed.

Sugar cookery begins with the formation of a solution. An excess of water is used to ensure that all of the sugar is dissolved. A solution is a homogeneous mixture of two substances, one (the solute) dissolved in the other (the solvent).

In a solution sugar exists as molecules and does not ionize as do some other solutes or salts. As the temperature is elevated, the solubility of sucrose and other sugars increases. The increased solubility of sugar upon heating permits larger quantities of sugar to dissolve in a specific quantity of water. About twice as much sugar dissolves in hot water as in cold water.

The solution of the solute is facilitated by stirring up to a point where no additional sugar can be dissolved unless the mixture is heated. When a solution cannot dissolve any more solute at a given temperature, the solution is known as a saturated solution. The temperature and the nature of the solute and the solvent determine the amount of solute that will dissolve. For example, lactose will not dissolve as readily in water as does sucrose, and sugar will not dissolve in alcohol as it does in water.

A saturated solution contains all of the dissolved solute that it can hold. When additional solute is present, an equilibrium will be established between the sugar (or other solute) in solution and the excess sugar, and sugar will crystallize at the same rate that sugar is going into solution. A constant amount of sugar will be in solution at a given temperature, and the solution will be stable.

A supersaturated solution contains more solute than theoretically is soluble at a specific temperature. It is unstable because the excess solute above the saturation level can recrystallize. Supersaturated solutions are created by (1) heating a saturated solution to the temperature required to achieve the necessary concentration of sugar for the desired firmness and (2) cooling the sugar mixture under controlled conditions so that the highly supersaturated solution is reached before crystallization begins. Supersaturation promotes rapid precipitation of many fine crystals rather than gradual crystal growth on existing nuclei once crystallization is initiated. When precipitation or crystallization begins, the excess sugar in solution will crystallize, and the sugar mixture will become a saturated solution, with crystals continuing to precipitate until room temperature is reached. Rapid crystallization is important to the texture of candy.

CRYSTAL FORMATION

Although sucrose crystallizes very easily, crystallization before a high degree of supersaturation is achieved is impossible. Slow crystal growth on a few nuclei as the candy cools results in large crystals and a grainy texture. A small quantity of corn syrup may be added to the sucrose mixture before cooking to promote many very small crystals. Corn syrup contains glucose, and the particles of glucose are very small; thus they interfere with the formation of large sucrose crystals.

The inversion of sucrose to glucose can be hastened with the addition of acids such as lemon juice or cream of tartar, thereby promoting formation of the desired small crystals. Both the amount of acid and the heating must be controlled carefully to avoid the very soft or fluid product that results from too much inversion of sucrose. A slow rate of heating promotes inversion, resulting in a final product with considerable breakdown of sucrose to invert sugar.

The high degree of supersaturation needed for rapid crystallization necessitates cooling of the candy mixture to about 110° F (43° C). As the mixture cools, it becomes increasingly supersaturated and more viscous. In crystalline candy products such as fondant and fudge, crystallization begins from a supersaturated solution.

Temperature influences the rate of crystallization and the size of crystals formed from a sugar solution. For example, sucrose in a fondant or fudge mixture will crystallize more rapidly if it is beaten when hot than if it is cooled to 104° F (40° C) before beating. Beating initiates crystallization by disturbing an unstable solution.

When the mixture is beaten before it cools, large crystals will form. The degree of supersaturation is less than at the lower temperature, and therefore fewer nuclei are available on which crystals may form. The few crystals present develop into large crystals. Beating promotes the formation of many small nuclei in a cooled sugar mixture.

In an appropriately cooled and beaten sugar mixture, a great number of small crystals form at once, changing the mixture rapidly from a liquid to a solid state. Beating must be continued until crystallization is completed. Agitation prevents formation of the large crystal aggregates that begin to form if crystallization is allowed to proceed undisturbed. The correct technique results in a smooth, creamy candy product.

CANDIES

Candies derive their structure from the concentrated sugar they contain. Although candies are often made from other sugars, sucrose is the primary sugar used. On the basis of their structure, candy products generally are classed as crystalline or noncrystalline (amorphous). The final temperature and doneness tests for various candies are listed in Table 23–1.

Crystalline Candies

Crystalline candies have a soft, smooth, creamy texture. They are prepared by dissolving the sugar, cooking the mixture to desired temperature, and then recrystallizing the sugar under conditions favorable to the formation of small crystals (see preceding section on crystal formation).

Table 23-1 Sugar Cookery Temperatures and Tests

Temperature[a]		Cold-water Test (dropped syrup forms)	Description	Product
Degree F	Degree C			
230–236	110–113	Thread	Syrup dropped from spoon forms 2-inch thread	Sugar syrup
234–240	112–116	Soft ball	Forms ball that flattens when removed from cold water	Fondant Fudge Panocha
244–258	118–120	Firm ball	Forms firm ball that does not flatten when removed from cold water	Caramels
250–266	121–266	Hard ball	Forms plastic ball that retains shape when removed from cold water	Divinity Marshmallows
270–290	132–143	Soft crack	Separates into hard threads in cold water	Butterscotch Taffies
300–310	149–154	Hard crack	Separates into hard, brittle threads in cold water	Brittle Toffee Lollipops
338	170	Brown, viscous liquid	Liquid becomes brown	Contributes color and flavor to products

[a]With each increase of 500 feet above sea level, subtract 1 degree Fahrenheit, or 1 degree Celsius for each 900 feet above sea level.

Adapted from *Handbook of Food Preparation,* 8th ed. (Washington, D.C.: American Home Economics Association, 1980).

It is the many small crystals that give structure to fondant, divinity, and fudge. Fondant is prepared with water, sugar, and usually a small amount of acid or syrup to promote small crystals. A hot syrup is beaten into egg white foam to prepare divinity—a creamy, delicate candy. Fudge contains milk, cocoa or chocolate, sugar, water, and corn syrup.

Crystals form easily in hot candy mixtures when they are moved or are seeded by contacting sugar crystals remaining on the sides of the pan or when they contact other surface disturbances. The cooked mixture should be shiny, smooth, and viscous when beating is begun. It becomes light in color as beating continues. Just before it becomes firm, the candy will lose its gloss and should be spread quickly. The basic steps in crystalline candy preparation are as follows:

1. Cook sugar syrup to the correct concentration.
2. Cool to a highly supersaturated state.
3. Beat until crystallization is nearly completed.

Crystallization Summarized. The formation of small crystals is promoted by the addition of corn syrup, acid ingredient, and fat. Corn syrup contains glucose, dextrin, and maltose, which inhibit crystallization. Sucrose and invert sugar mixtures crystallize less readily than do solutions containing a single sugar and thus produce a candy of fine texture. Acid promotes hydrolysis of sucrose to invert sugar (glucose and fructose). A sugar mixture heated slowly develops more invert sugar than one heated quickly. Excessive invert sugar retards crystallization and produces a candy that will not set. Fats coat sugar particles and prevent the formation of large sugar-crystal aggregates.

Particles on the surface of the candy or movement of the candy mixture before it cools induces crystallization before the mixture becomes supersaturated and also promotes the formation of large-crystal aggregates.

A high degree of supersaturation develops in candy cooled to 110° F (43° C). Beating promotes the crystallization of a large number of nuclei essential for making a smooth-textured product. Beating is continued until the gloss begins to disappear. Premature cessation of beating allows precipitating sugar to deposit on existing nuclei to form large-crystal aggregates.

Noncrystalline/Amorphous Candies

Noncrystalline, or amorphous, candies (caramels, toffees, brittles) are smooth, heterogeneous solids. Their texture ranges from hard to brittle to chewy. The temperature to which they are cooked and the ingredients used determine the nature of noncrystalline candies. Along with sugar, caramels contain corn syrup, cream or evaporated milk, and butter or margarine. These ingredients prevent crystal formation by acting as interfering agents.

The steps in the preparation of noncrystalline candy are as follows:

1. Dissolve the sugar completely and cook the mixture to the correct temperature for the candy to concentrate the sugar.
2. Avoid crystallization by adding relatively large amounts of ingredients that interfere with sugar crystallization, such as glucose, corn syrup, invert sugar, fat (cream, butter, margarine), and milk protein.
3. Carefully stir boiling syrup to avoid scorching, which leads to undesirable color and flavor.

Microwaved Candies

Because microwave energy is absorbed from all surfaces, microwaved candy requires less stirring than when prepared on a conventional range. Chocolate and caramelized mixtures cooked in the microwave oven require only occasional stirring rather than constant stirring, as on a conventional range. Chocolate squares can be melted in their paper wrappers with the seam side up. Chocolate bits can be melted in a paper bowl covered with plastic wrap. Since chocolate burns easily, a low or medium setting is used, and the progress of melting is checked at end of the minimum suggested time.

Uncooked Candies

Uncooked candies are prepared with confectioners' sugar. Ingredients, such as butter or margarine, concentrated milk products, cream, and corn syrup, are blended with the sugar. These candies may include any of several flavoring ingredients, for example, chocolate, coconut, nuts, vanilla, and other flavor extracts.

Chocolate Dipping

Dipping chocolate may be milk or bittersweet chocolate. Dipping chocolate contains more cocoa butter than regular chocolate. The increased cocoa butter gives a consistency that hardens appropriately and gives a glossy, smooth finish to dipped chocolates. Centers to be dipped are prepared in advance so that they may harden for easy handling.

Temperature and humidity must be controlled and the chocolate manipulated during melting and cooling, and while dipping. Manipulation blends cocoa butter with the other constituents of chocolate and ensures an even-coated product. When the fat of chocolate has not crystallized in stable form, the surface becomes dull and gray. Correct room and chocolate temperatures, optimum humidity, stirring, and cooling conditions avoid a grayed chocolate surface.

FROSTINGS

Boiled sugar mixtures are the foundation for cooked frostings, and confectioners' sugar is the foundation for uncooked frostings. Cooked frostings are related to crystalline candies and include fudge, seven-minute, and boiled. The same techniques used to induce small crystals in candy are applied in the preparation of smooth, creamy frostings.

Uncooked frostings differ from uncooked candies in that they are somewhat less viscous and can be spread easily. They are prepared in the same way as uncooked candies with confectioners' sugar, butter or margarine, and flavoring.

The frosting is applied to a cake brushed free of crumbs. The bottom layer is placed on a plate with its flat side up and is spread with frosting. The second layer is placed, flat side down, on the frosted first layer. The sides of both layers are spread with frosting; then the top of the cake is spread with frosting.

FROZEN DESSERTS

Frozen desserts are products in which water is crystallized as ice. Fruit ices, sherbets, ice cream, mousses, and parfaits illustrate the wide range of choices among frozen desserts.

Dessert ices are made of fruit juice and sugar and may include some fruit pulp. Sherbets also include fruit or fruit juice but differ in that they include a small amount of milk fat and milk solids. Ice cream is basically made from a combination of milk products, such as cream and milk, sugar, and flavoring. Gelatin and eggs are often included in ice cream. Mousses contain sweetened, flavored whipped cream and may include some gelatin. Parfaits are prepared with egg white, syrup, whipped cream, and flavorings. Mousses and parfaits are not agitated during freezing. Another type of parfait consists of alternate layers of ice cream, fruit, and syrup, topped with whipped cream.

Crystals form the structure of frozen desserts as they do in candies, but the crystals are of ice instead of sugar. Although the nature of the two crystals is different, some of the same techniques apply to the preparation of frozen desserts and candies.

The ingredients used, the rate and amount of beating, and the speed of crystal formation influence the texture and quality of frozen desserts and candies. The goal is to develop small ice crystals in frozen products and small sugar crystals in candy products for a smooth, creamy texture in both instances.

Frozen desserts consist of a mixture of ice crystals in a liquid syrup. Soft-frozen desserts contain somewhat fewer ice crystals in proportion to liquid syrup than firm, or hard-frozen, desserts.

Ingredients/Functions

All frozen desserts contain sweetener and liquid and may include varying quantities of milk products, eggs, gelatin, stabilizers, and emulsifiers.

Sweeteners.   Sugar contributes sweetness, enhances the flavor of other ingredients, and improves the body and texture of frozen products. Sugar forms a true solution and thus lowers the freezing point of the mix. Frozen desserts with a high sugar content freeze more slowly and at a lower temperature than those with less sugar. They also melt more quickly than low-sugar desserts. This delay of crystallization by sugar permits more agitation before freezing occurs and allows the formation of small ice crystals.

Although sugar, or sucrose, is a prime sweetener, other sweeteners, such as corn syrup or corn syrup solids, may replace a portion of the sugar. Corn syrup and solids promote a smooth texture and good body.

Lactose, the disaccharide in milk, is the least soluble dietary sugar. Lactose may precipitate out of solution because of its low solubility and impart a sandy texture to the frozen dessert.

Generally, sucrose is the principal and preferred sweetener for frozen desserts, but a blend of sucrose and corn syrup or honey may be used. Honey and corn syrup have a high monosaccharide content, which lowers the freezing point more than sucrose and yields a less solid frozen mixture.

Liquid. Water or some other liquid is essential for the formation of ice crystals. Fruit juices, fruit pulp, and milk products contribute liquid for ice-crystal formation. Each of these products contains sugars and salts, which cause their freezing points to be below that of pure water. Ice crystals, by entrapping some liquid, contribute the structure that changes a fluid dessert mixture to a solid.

Milk Products. Milk fat gives richness, promotes smooth textural qualities, contributes flavor, and acts as a carrier of other added flavors. Milk and cream are the sources of fat in frozen desserts. Commercially frozen high-quality ice cream contains 15 percent or more fat, and the standard product has 10 to 12 percent. Ice milk contains 2 to 7 percent butterfat.

Fat coats the ice crystals formed in the freezing mixture and prevents the aggregation of crystals on existing nuclei. Ice cream with a higher fat content is smoother than that with a low fat content because fat functions as an interfering agent and inhibits ice-crystal formation. Cream and homogenized milk are especially effective in promoting a smooth texture because their greater number of very small fat globules can cover a large surface area.

Undiluted evaporated milk and dry milk solids help to achieve a smooth texture. Too large a quantity of dry milk solids, however, may cause a somewhat grainy texture owing to the lactose. Milk solids increase the protein content and promote the development of a fine texture. Added milk solids increase the viscosity and foaming quality of frozen dessert mixtures.

Eggs. Egg whites are an effective means for introducing air into mixtures to be frozen. Egg yolk solids increase viscosity, improve body and texture, and enhance the flavor of frozen desserts.

Emulsifiers and Stabilizers. Ingredients such as milk solids, gelatin, and egg aid in emulsifying and stabilizing the mixture, thus promoting a smooth texture and body characteristic of high-quality frozen products. Monoglycerides and diglycerides are added as emulsifiers in commercial products. Lecithin is the emulsifier in egg yolk. Emulsifiers improve whipping quality, body, and texture of frozen products.

Most commercial frozen products contain stabilizers to promote smoothness, resist melting, and prevent ice-crystal formation during storage. Gelatin, pectin, vegetable gums, carrageenan, alginates, and carboxymethylcellulose are examples of stabilizers.

Gelatin absorbs and binds water, thus interfering with crystal formation and promoting a smooth texture. It inhibits crystal growth during storage and makes products easier to serve because it delays melting. Vegetable gums also bind water, and they contribute body to commercially frozen products.

Fruit Juices. Fruit juices are a source of liquid and impart flavor to frozen products. It may be necessary to increase the proportion of sugar to compensate for the acidic nature of fruit and achieve the desired flavor. For this reason fruit ices and sherbets may have a higher sugar content than other frozen items.

Freezing Processes

The process of freezing causes water to crystallize to ice, and agitation during freezing incorporates air into the mixture.

With Agitation. Ice cream freezers equipped with agitators are available for home use. The ice cream mixture is placed in a metal container until it is no more than two-thirds full and inserted into the outer container.

A mixture of six parts of crushed ice and one part of coarse salt by weight (by measure, one cup salt to twelve cups ice) is packed into the space between the two containers. The ice dissolves some of the salt, and as the ice melts, some heat is absorbed from the mixture. The temperature of the ice-salt mixture decreases until the freezing point of a saturated salt solution is reached.

The agitator inside the metal container incorporates air and rotates the mixture to bring it in contact with the cold sides of the metal container. Agitation promotes the formation of many nuclei, on which ice crystals form, resulting in a smooth texture. The ice cream mixture is agitated slowly at first to permit uniform cooling to the freezing point. When the mixture begins to freeze, beating should become rapid to maintain small ice crystals. Rapid agitation before freezing begins may cause the butterfat to separate and produce a curdled effect in the product. The freezing mixture is agitated until it stiffens and can no longer be turned. The agitator is removed, the container closed, and more ice and salt packed around the container to permit rapid freezing. The ice cream can be transferred to a freezer for storage.

Without Agitation. Because mechanical refrigerators do not provide a way to incorporate air during the process of freezing, coarse-crystal formation must be retarded with air provided by the ingredients and preparation methods used. Mixtures successfully frozen without agitation are those that are rich in fat and contain a cooked starch base, gelatin, custard, evaporated milk, or eggs. Air can be incorporated into the cream or milk product, egg white, or gelatin during preparation. Also the mixture can be partially frozen and removed from the freezer tray and beaten once or twice during the freezing process.

When the mixture is frozen without beating, it should be frozen as quickly as possible to promote the formation of small ice crystals. Stirring the mixture occasionally in the freezer tray allows the unfrozen part of the mixture to make contact with the cold tray.

Whether the frozen dessert is prepared with or without agitation, cream, gelatin, chocolate, egg, pectin, and nonfat milk solids interfere with large-crystal formation. Small crystals are essential for a smooth texture in frozen dessert products.

Commercial Ice Cream

Commercial ice cream mix is pasteurized, homogenized, and blended to obtain optimum body, texture, and flavor. It is then cooled, aged, flavored, frozen, packaged, and hardened in storage. Small ice crystals are produced with fast freezing and powerful agitation. Additional ice crystals form while the ice cream hardens at low temperatures.

Ice crystals and fat globules give structure to ice cream. Commercial ice cream is formulated to withstand variable freezing temperatures and short periods of exposure to heat due to usual marketing procedures. The minimum butterfat content is set by the United States Drug Administration standard of identity at 10 percent, with 20 percent total milk solids for regular or standard ice cream. Most commercial ice cream contains 10 to 12 percent fat.

Overrun. Overrun refers to an increase in volume above that of the mix, which occurs when dessert mix is frozen. It is chiefly due to the air incorporated during preparation and the expansion during freezing. The overrun in commercial ice cream is 70–80 percent and in homemade ice cream 35–50 percent. Ice cream with little overrun has a coarse, heavy texture, and that with too much overrun, a frothy texture.

Nutritional Quality

The nutritional quality of frozen desserts is determined by the ingredients used in their preparation. Milk provides most of the nutrients in frozen desserts. Cream contributes the fat-soluble vitamins and a higher fat content than milk. Cream lacks the water-soluble vitamins, calcium, and protein. The use of milk instead of cream in frozen desserts lowers the fat content and calories and increases the level of the B vitamins, calcium, and protein.

Although eggs and fruits are nutrient-rich foods, they are used in relatively small quantities in frozen desserts. Therefore, they add minimal quantities of nutrients to the frozen product. The nutrient values of some frozen desserts are listed in Table 23–2.

On the other hand, candies are concentrated sugar mixtures with small quantities of other ingredients. Their high sugar content provides generous amounts of kcalories but no other nutrients. The abuse of sugar is a factor in tooth decay and malnutrition.

Table 23-2   Major Nutrients in Selected Frozen Desserts (in one cup—about 8 oz)

Product	Kcalories	Protein (g)	Fat (g)	Carbohy-drate (g)	Calcium (mg)	Vitamin A (IU)	Riboflavin (mg)
Ice cream							
about 10% fat (regular)	257	6	14	28	194	590	0.28
about 16% fat (rich)	329	4	24	27	115	980	0.16
Ice milk							
hardened	199	6	7	29	204	280	0.29
soft-serve	266	8	9	39	273	370	0.39
Sherbet	259	2	2	59	31	120	0.06
Fruit ice	193	0.8	tr	63	tr	tr	tr
Yogurt							
partly skimmed milk	128	8.8	4.2	12.7	294	170	0.44
whole milk	152	7.4	8.8	12.0	272	340	0.39

Adapted from USDA, *Nutritive Value of American Foods in Common Units,* Agriculture Handbook no. 456, Agricultural Research Service (Washington, D.C.: Government Printing Office, 1975).

SUMMARY

Candies and frostings contain sugar crystals; ice crystals contribute structure to frozen desserts. A creamy, smooth texture is desired whether the product contains ice or sugar crystals. Ingredients included in the sugar mixture and those in the mixture to be frozen affect crystal size and the consistency of the product.

Candies derive their structure from the sugar crystals. They are classed as crystalline and noncrystalline, or amorphous. The control of crystallization is of prime concern in preparation of crystalline candies. Sugar solutions are cooked until the desired concentration of sugar is reached as indicated by temperature. This saturated solution is cooled to develop a high degree of supersaturation. Then the candy is beaten to promote the development of small crystals. The use of corn syrup or cream of tartar promotes the development of small crystals to achieve a smooth texture.

Cooking the sugar mixture to the correct temperature and the prevention of scorching are of prime concern in the preparation of noncrystalline candy. During the boiling period, acid hydrolysis converts sucrose to invert sugar and caramelization promotes a change in color and flavor.

Ice-crystal formation in frozen desserts is influenced by the component ingredients, the rate and amount of beating, and the speed of crystal formation. Sugar lowers the freezing temperature of the mixture, and both fat and sugar hinder the formation of ice crystals. Milk solids and gelatin stabilize mixtures to be frozen and aid in the retention of a smooth texture. Mono- and diglycerides and vegetable gums emulsify commercially frozen products. Nonfat milk solids and the presence of crystals aid in retention of air. Incorporation of air and agitation promote small ice crystal formation. Products agitated during freezing have a smoother texture and are lighter than those prepared without agitation.

The levels of fat and sugar determine the caloric value of candy and frozen products. The nutrient contribution of frozen products is determined by the component ingredients.

SELF-STUDY GUIDE

1. Compare the roles of sugar, fat, milk solids, and egg white in candy and frozen desserts.
2. What influence does the inversion of sucrose have on the boiling temperature of sugar syrup and on the texture of candy?
3. Define sugar solution, saturated sugar solution, and supersaturated sugar solution. When is a supersaturated sugar solution desirable?
4. Discuss five factors that influence sugar-crystal size; ice-crystal size.
5. Identify two basic types of candy and give examples. In what ways do they differ?
6. Compare the preparation of candy and frosting.
7. What ingredients serve as emulsifiers and stabilizers in frozen desserts?
8. Describe methods for preparing and freezing frozen desserts.
9. Compare the nutrient contribution of frozen desserts with candy products.

SUGGESTED READINGS

ABRIL, J. R., et al. Characteristics of frozen desserts with xylitol and fructose. *Journal of Food Science* 47:472, 1982.

BRANDAO, A. C. C.; RICHMOND, M. L.; ARAY, J.; MORTON, I.; and MSTINE, C. Separation of mono- and di-saccharides and sorbitol by high performance liquid chromatography. *Journal of Food Science* 45:1492, 1980.

Confectionary ingredients. Confectionary facts. National Confectioners Association, National Candy Wholesalers, and Retail Confectioners International.

DANIELS, E. W. Why children eat paint and other sweet tidbits. *Nutrition Today* 17:18, 1982.

FREEMAN, T. M. Polydextrose for reduced calorie foods. *Cereal Foods World* 27:515, 1982.

GIANGIANCOMO, R., et al. Predicting concentrations of individual sugars in dry mixtures by near infrared reflectance spectroscopy. *Journal of Food Science* 46:531, 1981.

GOFF, D. H., and JORDAN, W. K. Aspartame and polydextrose in a calorie-reduced frozen dairy dessert. *Journal of Food Science* 49:306, 1984.

HANNIGAN, K. J. Corn/soy-based frozen desserts: Taste and nutrition made to order. *Food Engineering* (Chilton's) 54:92, March, 1982.

———. The sweetener report 1982–1987. *Food Engineering* (Chilton's) 54:75, July, 1982.

HAYASHI, T., and NAMIKI, M. On the mechanism of free radical formation during browning reaction of sugars with amino compounds. *Agricultural and Biological Chemistry* 45:933, 1981.

HUGILL, J. A.; BIBBY, B. G.; CURZON, M. E. J.; and WALKER, A. R. P. Sugars and dental caries. *The Lancet* 1:598, 1983.

Institute of Food Technologists. Expert Panel on Food Safety and Nutrition. Sugars and nutritive sweeteners in processed foods. A scientific status summary. *Food Technology* May 1979, p. 101.

JOHNSON, J., and CLYDESDALE, F. M. Perceived sweetness and redness in colored sucrose solutions. *Journal of Food Science* 47:933, 1982.

LAWHON, J. T., et al. Utilization of membrane produced oilseed isolates in soft serve frozen desserts. *Journal of the American Oil Chemists' Society* 57:302, 1980.

LIUZZO, J. A., and WONG, C. M. Detection of floc-producing sugars by a protein dye-binding method. *Journal of Agriculture and Food Chemistry* 30:340, 1982.

NEWBURN, E. Sugar and dental caries: A review of human studies. *Science* 217:418, 1982.

PIHL, M. A.; STULL, J. W.; TAYLOR, R. R.; ANGUS, R. C.; AND DANIEL, T. C. Characteristics of frozen desserts sweetened with fructose and lactose. *Journal of Food Science* 47:989, 1982.

REES, F. M. Dehydrated maple syrup. *Journal of Food Science* 47:1023, 1982.

SANDERSON, G. R. Polysaccharides in foods. *Food Technology* 35:50, 1981.

SOMMONS, R. G.; GREEN, J. R.; PAYNE, C. A.; WAN, P. L.; and LUSAS, E. W. Cottonseed and soy protein ingredients in soft-serve frozen desserts. *Journal of Food Science* 45:1505, 1980.

Will dextrose replace sucrose? *Food Engineering* (Chilton's) 53:124, May 1981.

YOUNG, C. K.; STULL, J. W.; TAYLOR, R. R.; ANGUS, R. C.; AND DANIEL, T. C. Acceptability of frozen desserts made with neutralized, hydrolyzed, fluid cottage cheese whey. *Journal of Food Science* 45:805, 1980.

24

COOKING WITH MICROWAVES

OBJECTIVES

When you complete this chapter, you will be able to

1. Explain how microwaves cook.
2. Select appropriate utensils for cooking in the microwave oven.
3. Explain the uses of microwaves in food preparation.
4. Identify and explain the factors that influence cooking time in microwave ovens.
5. Give examples of techniques used to control the speed of microwave cooking.
6. Describe the influence of microwaves on water, sugar, starch, fat, proteins, vitamins, and enzymes.
7. Give examples of microwave-cookery applications.

The microwave oven utilizes electromagnetic radiation to excite water molecules in the food. The conventional oven obtains heat from an external source such as electricity or gas. The heat is transferred to the container holding the food by conduction. Further transfer of heat proceeds by convection in the liquid within the pan. Food also can be heated by radiation, as in a conventional broiler.

Microwaves are nonionizing electromagnetic waves. This is a common form of energy surrounding us at all times. It includes visible light from the sun or from an ordinary light bulb, infrared waves from a fireplace, and radio waves, as well as microwaves. The microwaves are of short-wave length and a high frequency, which places them between radio waves and infrared waves. Microwaves are shorter than radio waves; hence, the name. They should not be confused with ionizing waves, such as x rays or ultraviolet rays. They do not have the same strength or effect as ionizing waves.

Foods are complex substances and include molecules carrying both positive and negative charges, such as water. The water molecule carries a positive charge on one end and a negative charge on the other end. This charge arrangement is known as dipolar and will interact with the electric field of the electromagnetic radiation, when that radiation has a frequency that excites the vibrations made by the water dipole. Water participates as the absorber of radiation at microwave frequencies.

HOW MICROWAVES COOK

Ninety-nine percent of the microwave energy is lost within ten inches of the source. Microwaves must be enclosed in a small space to cook foods. Because they do not penetrate metal they can be contained in a small metal box, such as the microwave oven. Microwaves alternate between positive and negative directions and act like a magnet on the positive and negative particles in food, for instance, water, sugar, and fat molecules. The direction of the microwave field changes about 2½ billion times a second, so the food molecules vibrate at the same speed. Heat is produced in the food by the friction between molecules, thus causing it to cook.

Microwaves penetrate foods to a depth of ¾ to 1½ inches on all sides—top, bottom, and sides. They generate heat in the areas they penetrate but do not produce chemical change in food. The heat then spreads by conduction to the center of the food, as it does in conventional cooking. Some of the heat also reaches the surface and is lost in the surrounding air.

THE MICROWAVE OVEN

The Federal Communications Commission has assigned the frequencies of 915 and 2450 megahertz for use in microwave ovens, which will not interfere with communication systems. Satisfactory results can be obtained with either frequency. The shorter the wave length, the shorter the depth of penetration into the food being cooked. The magnetron tube converts electrical energy of an amplifier into microwave radiation.

A magnetron tube located in the oven produces microwaves, which pass through a channel into the oven cavity where they are reflected by a multiblade fan. Without a fan to distribute the energy, some parts of the food would be overcooked and others would be undercooked. The stainless-steel walls of the oven and the rotating fan reflect microwaves. As the microwaves are reflected within the oven, they are absorbed by the food, causing the molecules of water within the food to vibrate very rapidly and thus heat the food.

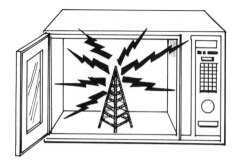

Safety

Microwaves are a nonionizing form of radiation and will not make foods and other material radioactive. Microwaves differ only in frequency; otherwise they are the same kind of energy as solar and that transmitted by power lines.

The wattage of the microwave oven should not be confused with microwave energy. With a higher wattage there are only more microwaves, but each microwave still has only one-millionth of the energy in ionizing waves such as x rays and gamma rays.

The metal container of the oven that encloses microwaves so they can cook also retains them safely inside. Federal standards require that microwave ovens be designed so that they cannot be operated when the door is open.

Two independent interlock systems prevent transmission of energy when the door is not securely fastened. A monitoring system assures that the oven will not work if the interlock system fails. Every oven must be tested to make sure it meets very strict government safety standards. Ovens are tested for possible leakage of microwave energy within two inches of the oven door. Any oven safe at two inches is definitely safe at operating distance.

The microwave oven manual recommends operating procedures and safety precautions. The microwave oven should never be operated when the door does not close firmly. A simple and harmless test can be made by tracing the door seal with the thumb while the microwave oven is used for cooking. When the skin of the thumb feels warm, the leakage should be measured.

Power Levels

Early microwave ovens had one power setting—on or off—which limited the variety of foods suitable for microwaving. The introduction of variable power made microwave cookery versatile and flexible. Microwave ovens with variable power automatically cycle energy on or off. Short pulses of energy alternate with periods of no energy. The internal temperature of the food equalizes during periods of no energy.

A panel representing consumers and manufacturers met to determine the percentages of power used most frequently and the terms that would be most meaningful to consumers in referring to microwave operation. In accordance with the guidelines set by this panel, the variable levels on the ovens are preset to provide a percentage of the oven's full power (see Table 24–1).

When a choice of **power levels** is given, the lower setting will cook and heat more evenly, although it will take a little longer. High power is full (100 percent) power and is used for fast cooking of foods that tolerate heat and speed. Medium-high power is about two-thirds (70 percent) the full power of the oven and is used for ease in heating and cooking amounts or types of food that require extra attention at high power. Medium power is about one-half (50 percent) of full power and is recommended for delicate foods that are not tolerant of fast cooking or foods that require slow simmering to tenderize them. Medium-low is 30 percent, and low, 10 percent of full power. The low power settings result in a reduction of microwaves, causing slower heating and cooking of food.

Some microwave ovens have a special defrost setting, which cycles on and off automatically so that frozen foods can be defrosted without being cooked. The intermittent heating and resting provide the opportunity for the heat generated in the on cycle to be conducted to the inner portions of the food.

Advantages of Microwaves

The advantage of a microwave oven is the speed of cooking. Microwaving can save energy, but savings depend on what and how much is cooked. The amount of food cooked affects energy consumption. Greater savings occur when medium or small quantities of dense foods are heated. Large quantities of food (such as a dozen potatoes) bake more efficiently in a conventional oven.

Table 24–1 Microwave Oven: Power Levels, Settings, Power Output

	Settings		Watts of Power Output	
Power Levels	Term	Number	700-W Oven	500-W Oven
100%	High	10	700	500
90%		9	630	450
80%		8	560	400
70%	Medium-high	7	490	350
60%		6	420	300
50%	Medium	5	350	250
40%		4	280	200
30%	Medium-low	3	210	150
20%		2	140	100
10%	Low	1	70	50

Microwaving consumes less energy than conventional cooking. Foods cook faster, the food is heated directly, rather than the pan or air or water surrounding it. The amount and type of food cooked determine the actual savings. Variable-power microwave ovens also save energy. Although 50 percent of power takes twice as long to cook a food, it takes exactly the same amount of energy as full power.

In addition to the advantage of saving time and energy, some foods may be microwaved because of the excellent flavor and texture achieved. Vegetables retain their fresh, crisp texture and bright color. Leftovers remain moist and retain the fresh-cooked flavor. Bacon becomes crisp and brown and remains flat.

Limitation of Microwaves

The major limitation of microwave cooking is the lack of browning. Foods do not brown as they do in a conventional oven. Even though they are fully cooked, pale baked products lack visual appeal. Some microwave ovens include a browning unit to somewhat overcome this problem. A special ceramic browning dish or grill is available for cooking foods that need to be browned. The tin-oxide undercoating can absorb microwaves and become heated to a high temperature. The food surface in contact with the preheated dish is browned by the intense heat. Meats can be browned on this special dish, or the conventional broiler can be used. Meats to be browned separately are microwaved to the desired doneness and then broiled. This procedure reduces the excess surface moisture of microwaved meat as well as inducing browning.

Spices, sauces, gravies, and browning aids can be creatively used to enhance the surface of microwaved meats. Browning agents are applied before the food is cooked.

Some foods do not microwave well. Eggs in shells may burst. Popcorn may be so dry that the magnetron tube may be damaged by the unabsorbed waves. Canning requires a prolonged, controlled high temperature, but the lack of temperature control in microwaving may result in the explosion of jars due to very high pressure buildup. Deep-fat frying in a microwave is also dangerous because of the probable overheating of the fat.

Cleaning

Cleaning the microwave oven is easy since foods do not burn onto the surface as they do in a conventional oven. But regular cleaning is essential in order to prevent a buildup of grease, which may cause door seals to weaken and warp. Should that occur, a leakage of radiation could result. The interior of the oven, the door, and the door seals should be cleaned very frequently with water and a mild detergent. Abrasives should not be used. Any lingering odors can be removed by boiling a small amount of a mixture of lemon juice and water in the oven.

MICROWAVE UTENSILS

Microwaves may be either absorbed, transferred, or reflected. Cooking utensils should transfer the microwaves, so that there is no interference with the cooking process.

Foods absorb microwaves because all foods contain moisture, and in the process they will become hot. Except for wood or straw, which contain a minimal quantity of moisture, most cooking utensils used in the microwave oven do not absorb microwaves. Wooden-handled spatulas and spoons become warm when left in the oven. With continued exposure to microwaves, wood and straw items become dry and may crack.

The ideal utensil is transparent to microwaves; it allows the energy to pass through the container and heat the food. However, once the food becomes hot, some heat is transferred to the utensil. In addition to utensils designed for microwaving, many conventional utensils are suitable.

The suitability of conventional utensils for microwaving can be determined easily by placing ½ cup cold water in a glass measure beside a utensil and microwaving for one minute on high. If the utensil remains cool but the water is warm, the utensil can be used for cooking. If the utensil is lukewarm and the water is warm, the utensil is suitable for heating or **reheating** food. If the utensil becomes hot while the water stays cool, do not use the utensil for any purpose in the microwave oven. This test is not satisfactory for plastic containers, however, because most plastics are transparent to microwaves. Microwaves do not cause distortion of plastic containers, but the contact with hot food may.

Paper

Paper absorbs moisture and fat and transfers microwaves without absorbing them. Paper plates, cups, and toweling are convenient for heating foods and for cooking food up to four minutes on high. White paper products are safest because some colored dyes may bleed or be toxic. Hot-drink cups may be used to heat beverages. Plastic-coated paper plates may be used for heating and serving moist foods. Paper plates without a coating absorb moisture and are suitable for heating crackers or other dry and crisp foods. Paper baking cups absorb excess moisture when cupcakes or muffins are microwaved. However, they should not be used when recipes contain very high levels of sugar or fat because they may ignite.

Waxed paper can serve as a cover to prevent spatters or to retain heat for faster cooking while allowing some escape of steam. Because paraffin or wax is transparent to microwaves it will not melt unless it comes in contact with very hot food. Items packed in paper can often remain in the package for heating or defrosting. "Ovenable" paper containers are designed for use in microwave and conventional ovens and withstand an oven temperature of 400° F (205° C).

Glass, Glass-Ceramic, China, and Pottery

Glass, glass-ceramic, china, and pottery products are generally well suited for microwaving and are among the most useful microwave utensils. Many are on hand for conventional cooking. The utensil may be a serving dish, a plate, a storage jar, a baking dish, or a measuring cup. It is wise, however, to microwave test the containers to make sure they can withstand the high temperatures when foods are cooked in them. Containers with gold or silver trim or a metal signature on the bottom should not be used. The metal or the trim may blacken or overheat the area next to it and crack the dish.

Ovenproof casseroles and baking dishes are recommended when cooking foods will be in contact with the container for a relatively long period. When the food is to be baked or broiled as well as microwaved, an ovenproof container is, of course, essential. Some ovenproof glass and ceramic containers may be used on a conventional burner and are convenient to use when the food is browned first and then microwaved.

Porcelain and stoneware are usually suitable for conventional ovens and can be good microwave utensils. Most kinds of pottery are suitable for microwave cooking and also as serving dishes. However, some pottery has a glaze that contains substances that attract microwaves, thus causing the food to cook slowly. Some paints and glazes contain metallic substances that make the containers unsuited for microwave use.

Plastics

Most plastics, except melamine, are transparent to microwaves, but they vary in the food temperatures they can withstand. Some plastic containers suitable for heating will melt or distort when prolonged cooking causes the food to reach a high temperature. Dishwasher-safe plastics are suitable for defrosting and heating in the microwave oven.

Purchased containers labeled "microwave-safe" should be used only as directed by the manufacturer. Most storage and tableware plastics can be used to heat foods to a serving temperature of 140° F (60° C). They should not be used for heating or cooking foods high in sugar or fat content.

Thermo-set-filled polyesters and polysulfone plastics can be used in a conventional or microwave oven and will withstand temperatures from 325 to 425° F (163 to 218° C). The manufacturer recommendations should be followed for the types of food to cook in these utensils.

Styrofoam containers are suitable for heating foods to serving temperature but show distortion at 170° F (77° C).

Boil-in-a-bag pouches may be used for defrosting or warming food. When foods are heated sufficiently to permit steam to form, a slot should be cut in the pouch before cooking to permit escape of steam.

Metals

Although the oven walls are continuous sheets of metal, to reflect and retain microwaves, metal utensils are not used. Metal cooking utensils would reflect microwaves and prevent them from reaching the food. In addition to slowing the cooking process, metal can cause "arcing," which is a static discharge of energy that can damage the magnetron tube.

When there is little or no food in the oven, small pieces of metal can also act as antennas and cause a sparkling, lighteninglike effect. These sparks can set paper or plastic on fire.

Although metal generally is not used in the oven, most new ovens are designed to prevent energy feedback to the magnetron tube and permit some use of metal. One should read the manufacturer's instruction booklet and warranty and not use metal when it is prohibited. Reflective properties of metal can be used to advantage in most microwave ovens.

Without **shielding,** areas that are already thawed will start to cook while the rest of the food remains frozen. During cooking, aluminum shields protect parts of the food that tend to overcook, such as poultry wing tips, drumsticks, and corners of products in square pans.

Metal twist ties on plastic bags should be replaced with string or a plastic strip, since the wire tie reflects energy that could cause the plastic bag to melt. Foil-lined covers and lids on frozen products or metal tops on cans of frozen fruit or juice must be removed to permit microwave penetration.

Thermometer/Temperature Probe

Microwaves can damage conventional meat and candy thermometers, making them inaccurate. Thermometers designed for microwave ovens are available, but they may not be suitable for conventional use.

Thermometers and **probes** aid in judging doneness by temperature. A dial thermometer and a silicone-in-glass thermometer have been developed for use with microwaved meats. Probes are standard equipment on many microwave ovens. The probe is inserted into the center of the food being heated and then is connected to the oven controls. When foods reach a preset internal temperature, the probe turns the oven off or automatically switches to a keep-warm setting. The use of a probe eliminates the need for a separate thermometer and relieves uncertainty about doneness of the food.

PRINCIPLES AND USES OF MICROWAVE COOKERY

Conventional cookery is concerned with time and temperature while microwave cookery is concerned with time and power level. The microwaves are absorbed by food and penetrate it, causing molecular activity and a generation of heat within. As previously noted, microwaves penetrate ¾ to 1½ inches through all food surfaces. At this depth they are absorbed by water, sugar, and fat molecules, which begin to generate heat. The heat is then conducted into the center and out to the surface. Further distribution of heat toward the center of a large food mass is by conduction. Microwave cooking is faster for most foods, but the surface remains moist.

Uses

Microwaves are used to cook, reheat, and defrost foods. Microwaves produce almost instant heat within foods to the depth they are able to penetrate. However, the microwaves may penetrate only a part of the food owing to its size and **density,** and the remainder is then heated by transfer of heat through conduction.

Cooking. Microwave cooked foods change in flavor, texture, consistency, and appearance. The desired degree of doneness is easily achieved in quick-cooking foods; however, with long-cooking foods it may be difficult to control the rate of cooking to achieve the desired results. In some cases, an alternate source of heat, which is easier to control, may yield a more satisfactory product.

Reheating. Microwaves do not change the texture or appearance of previously cooked foods during the time required to reheat them to serving temperature. Microwaves easily penetrate porous foods, and they heat through very quickly. Dense foods heat slowly and may require stirring, rearranging, or intermittent heating periods for heat to penetrate to the center without overcooking the edges.

The density of a food and its fat and sugar content primarily influence the reheating time required. Dense foods require a longer reheating period than porous foods and those high in fat or sugar, which heat very quickly. Table 24–2 gives directions for reheating some foods.

Generally each cup of dense food requires one to two minutes to reheat,

Table 24–2   Microwave Heating/Reheating of Selected Foods

Food	Quantity	Instruction	Setting	Time
Butter (melt)	1 tablespoon		High (10)	20 sec
Casserole	1 cup	Cover with waxed paper or vented plastic wrap	High (10)	1½–3 min
Chicken, cooked	2 pieces	Cover with plastic wrap or waxed paper	High (10)	1–2 min
Chocolate	1 square or 1 ounce	Melt in wrap or microwave-safe container	Medium (5)	1½–3 min
Chops, cooked	2 chops	Cover with paper or plastic wrap	High (10)	2½–4 min
Coffee, tea	1 cup		High (10)	1–1½ min
Dinner: meat, potato, and vegetable	1 plate	Cover with plastic wrap or waxed paper	High (10)	1½–2 min
Frankfurter in bun	1 sandwich	Wrap in waxed paper or plastic wrap	High (10)	20–30 sec
Meat patty, cooked	4 ounces		High (10)	30–40 sec
Milk	1 cup		Medium-high or (8)	1½–2 min
Roast, thinly sliced	4 ounces	Cover with waxed paper, plastic wrap, or gravy	Medium (5)	45–60 sec
Roll, dinner	1 roll	Cover with waxed paper	High (10)	15–20 sec
Soup	1 cup		High (10)	2 min
Water—hot	1 cup		High (10)	1–2 min
—boil	1 cup		High (10)	2–3 min

while each cup of porous food requires about one-half minute. The time is decreased slightly if the food has a high fat or sugar content. An increased quantity of food reheated requires a proportional increase in microwave-oven time. Individual items heat more quickly than the same total quantity heated in one container.

Foods reheat evenly when pieces are uniform in size and thickness and are arranged so that the thicker, more dense pieces are toward the outside. When possible, foods should be stirred and rearranged and dense foods should be covered for fast and uniform heating.

Meats and large quantities of main-dish casseroles that cannot be stirred should be reheated at 50 percent power or medium setting. The food is sufficiently reheated when it is hot enough to warm the center of the container or dish. Most foods are reheated from a refrigerated state; some have been prepared an hour or two before serving time. Foods at room temperature require less reheating time than refrigerated foods.

Defrosting. The defrosting process converts ice to water. This conversion should occur gradually so that some areas of the food will not begin to cook before other areas are defrosted. Microwave ovens with variable power levels have a defrost setting, which ranges from 30 to 50 percent of power. Table 24-3 gives directions for defrosting some foods.

An automatic defrost cycle turns the oven on and off to permit microwave and standing periods. The timer is usually set for the total microwave and standing times, although microwave heating is taking place only part of the time. The automatic defrost is convenient for dense foods, which require **standing-time** periods for a uniform distribution of heat. A large piece of meat may require a few additional standing periods as well as an occasional turning of position in the oven. Porous foods defrost quickly and do not require periods of standing time.

Table 24-3 Microwave Defrosting of Selected Foods

Frozen Food	Quantity	Instruction	Time on Defrost, Low, or 3 Setting	Hold Time
Bread:				
Bread	1 loaf	Loosen end of wrap, defrost.	3–4 min	
Bread dough	1 loaf	Defrost in plastic wrap or loosely wrap in waxed paper.	4–6 min	
Sweet rolls	2 rolls	Place on plastic or paper, cover unfrosted with paper.	2–2½ min	

Table 24-3 Microwave Defrosting of Selected Foods (*cont.*)

Frozen Food	Quantity	Instruction	Time on Defrost, Low, or 3 Setting	Hold Time
Fish:				
Fillets	1 lb	Open package. Turn over halfway through cook time.	8–12 min	8–12 min
Shrimp	12 oz	Cut 1-in slit in package; turn halfway through time.	7–9 min	7–9 min
Meat:				
Bacon	1 lb	Place on absorbent paper or slotted, plastic rack.	3–5 min	
Beef, ground	1 lb	Remove from wrap. Remove outside meat as it defrosts; break apart with fork.	10–13 min	
Patties	1 lb	Arrange in circle.	7–10 min	
Roasts	2–3 lb	Place in microwave-safe dish, cover with plastic wrap. Turn halfway through time.	10 min/lb	10 min/lb
	3–6 lb		8 min/lb	8 min/lb
	over 6 lb		12 min/lb	12 min/lb
Steaks	1 lb	Place in microwave-safe dish.	5–9 min	
Poultry:				
Fried	1 lb	Place large pieces near edge, small pieces near center of container.	4½ min	4½ min
Whole or pieces	2–5 lb	Place in microwave-safe dish, cover with plastic wrap. Use 2 defrost periods: 1st	5½ min/lb	
		2nd	5 min/lb	
		Turn halfway through defrost time.		
Desserts:				
Fruit	10 oz	Place in 1-qt casserole, cover with plastic wrap.	3½–4½ min	
	20 oz	Place in 1½-qt casserole, cover with plastic wrap or lid.	8–10 min	
Cake	12–14 oz	Place on plastic or paper plates, cover if not frosted.	2–3 min	
Pie	8 in (20–30 oz)	Place in microwave-safe pan.	12–15 min	12–15 min
Cookies	1 doz	Place on plastic or paper plate, cover with paper towel if not frosted.	1½–2½ min	

When a defrost cycle is not designated, follow the directions in the microwave oven manual. Usually the oven is turned on and off manually and the food allowed to stand a few minutes. The microwave and standing periods are of equal length. Alternate microwave and standing periods are continued to complete defrosting.

Foods packaged in paper or plastic may be defrosted in the oven without unwrapping. Waxed paper placed over unwrapped foods promotes defrosting by retaining heat.

Stirring, turning, and separation of food also promotes uniform thawing. After the first one-third to one-half of the defrosting time, pieces may be separated and large items turned for even thawing. Warm areas of large pieces should be shielded so that they will not begin to cook, and thawed portions should be removed. Thawed food feels cool and can be pierced to the center with a skewer.

FACTORS INFLUENCING COOKING TIME

Microwave cooking time is influenced by composition of food, density, size and shape, volume, and starting temperature.

Food Composition

The temperature of fat in the presence of microwaves rises twice as rapidly as that of water with the same quantity of energy. Foods containing a high proportion of fat or sugar heat very rapidly.

Density

Microwaves slowly penetrate dense or solid foods, such as potato, but readily penetrate light, porous foods, such as cake and bread, and agitate the water molecules to produce heat. Microwaves penetrate only the outer portions of dense foods and agitate these molecules. The inner portion of the food cooks as the heat is transferred by conduction to the center. When the heat takes longer to reach the center, it is necessary to use a lower power setting or a standing time, to permit the heat to reach the center of the food without overcooking the outer edges.

The density factor makes it difficult to state a definite cooking time for a specific measure of food. In determining cooking time, one must consider density and recognize that density varies among the different food types and within the same food type. Therefore recipes identify a range in cooking time, such as one to two minutes for one cup of dense food, or one-fourth to one-half minute for one cup of less-dense or porous food. Food density affects cooking time as well as reheating and defrosting time.

Size and Shape

In both microwave and conventional cooking, small pieces cook faster than large ones. Pieces that are similar in size and shape cook more evenly than those of various sizes and shapes. Thin areas of a food cook faster than the thick ones. Uneven cooking due to size and shape of food can be minimized in microwaving when thick pieces are placed to the outside edge and thin pieces toward the center of the oven.

Volume

The time required to cook, reheat, or defrost foods becomes longer as the size or amount of food becomes larger. The cooking time increases in proportion to volume or size of food mass and the number of items. The microwave oven is a time-saving method of cooking for one or two people but tends to be less time conserving when food is prepared for several persons.

All of the microwaves are available for cooking the food placed in the oven cavity. All the waves will concentrate on a small quantity of food and heat it rapidly. When large amounts of food or several items are present, and microwaves are spread over the large surface area or are shared among the items, increasing the cooking time. For example, one cup of water requires about one minute to become hot, while two cups require nearly two minutes.

The increase in cooking time also varies according to the nature of the food. Some foods are cooked as quickly as they are heated and require a time increase proportional to their volume. Other foods must remain at the heated temperature for a period of time before they are cooked to the desired doneness. These foods usually require a time increase of one-half to three-fourths the increase in quantity.

Starting Temperature

Foods at refrigerator or freezer temperatures require a longer time to cook than the same foods at room temperature. The colder the food, the longer it will take to cook.

MICROWAVING TECHNIQUES AND SPEED OF COOKING

Some cooking techniques are unique to microwaving, and others are also applicable to conventional methods. All of the following techniques equalize the flow of heat to help the food cook evenly and speed cooking. The outer areas absorb more energy than the center because microwaves penetrate the surfaces of food. Some parts of the cavity receive more energy than others in many microwave ovens. The use of the one or more of the following techniques equalizes the heat so that all parts of the food are done at the same time.

Covering

Microwaving is a moist method of cooking. Although most microwaved foods do not dry out, using a cover retains steam and helps food cook faster. A cover is used to control moisture loss, hold in heat, and prevent spattering or overcooking. For some foods the cover should permit moisture to escape; for others the cover should fit tightly.

Lids of casseroles or pans, an inverted plate on a baking dish, and plastic wrap provide tight-fitting covers. Plastic wrap is used only if it will not be touching the food since hot foods may melt or soften the plastic.

When foods are steamed, simmered, or just being kept moist during reheating, tight-fitting covers are used. The plastic may be slit to permit escape of steam. Tight-fitting covers should be removed carefully to avoid burns from escaping steam.

Semitight covers hold in steam. Waxed paper provides a semitight covering and is readily available. A semitight covering is used when food comes in contact with the cover for a prolonged period.

Paper towels and napkins are conveniently available loose-fitting covers. Because of their absorbency they are also used to avoid spattering of food in the oven and to absorb fat when meat or bacon is cooked. They allow moisture to pass through and are often used with breads and baked products.

Aluminum foil can be used to prevent overcooking of less dense or thinner areas of a food because it reflects microwaves. Thin portions of a roast or drumsticks and wings of poultry can be protected from overcooking with a small piece of foil. Care must be taken to avoid contact between the foil and oven walls; such contact causes arcing.

Stirring

Stirring food from the outside of the container toward the center redistributes heat. Food requires less stirring when microwaved than when conventionally cooked. Unless the oven has a very uneven heating pattern, several stirrings during cooking are usually sufficient. Stirring helps to distribute the heat more uniformly when reheating or defrosting foods and helps to achieve a uniformly cooked product.

Arrangement

Appropriate arrangement of food in the microwave oven or in the container speeds cooking and equalizes heat to help foods cook evenly. A single food item is naturally placed in the center of the oven. When several items or pieces are cooked at the same time, they are arranged to form a ring with spaces between each item so energy can penetrate from all sides. The center position is eliminated. The hole in the center of the ring creates more outside edges and speeds cooking.

Individual items, such as potatoes or cupcakes, should have spaces between each other, thus creating more outside edges. When these kinds of items are grouped together, dense centers are created that are difficult to cook.

Since the outer portion of the food comes in contact with microwaves first, the dense, thicker areas of the food are placed near the edge, and the thinner or more porous items or areas, near the center of the oven.

Foods should be arranged on a plate so that the larger and thicker parts of the food are toward the outside edge of the dish and the thinner and smaller parts of the food are toward the center where they will not overcook.

Turning

Since parts of the microwave oven cavity receive less energy than others, turning over large items, such as meat pieces and whole vegetables, moves them into a new energy pattern and permits all parts to cook evenly.

Rotating

Foods such as cakes, breads, or lasagne cannot be stirred during cooking to redistribute heat. Instead, the dish is rotated a quarter or half turn to bring the food into a new energy pattern and to facilitate even heating.

Shielding

Shielding protects areas that absorb the most energy from overcooking while the rest of the food continues to cook. Strips of foil are most commonly used to shield the tops of large roasts, wing tips of poultry, or the ends of a loaf dish. Sauces to cover vegetables, meats, or cheese are another form of shielding.

Standing Time

Standing time occurs after cooking and is an important technique to permit distribution of heat to the center of a food. Standing time allows the heat already in the food to be conducted more uniformly throughout the mass. Standing time may also be used intermittently during the microwave cooking of large cuts of meat and other rather large food masses that cannot be stirred to aid in distributing the heat more uniformly. Foods removed from a microwave oven continue to cook, just as they do from a conventional range, but it is far more noticeable with microwaved foods.

FOOD COMPONENTS AND MICROWAVES

Microwave food preparation requires very little, if any additional water so there is little loss of water-soluble nutrients. Although nutrients are well retained, as with proper conventional methods, overcooking leads to their needless loss.

Water

The presence of water in food and its ability to absorb microwaves permit the generation of heat within foods.

Sugar

Heat generated by microwaves or conventional cookery methods induce sugar caramelization. Sugar burns with intense heat and rapid loss of water. The temperature rises quickly when sugar-containing mixtures are heated in a microwave oven.

Starch

Starch granules gelatinize in the presence of water and heat as they do in conventional cookery. A greater thickening is promoted with rapid microwave heating than with the slow conventional heating and yields high-quality thickened products, such as gravies, sauces, and puddings. Because starch granules contain many hydrogen bonds, which can be broken by heat, excessive water can be drawn into starch granules heated beyond the optimum length of time. Then a thinning occurs in starch-thickened products as the overheated starch granules explode.

Fat

Fats promote a rapid temperature rise in food mixtures heated by both microwaves and conventional methods. Because of the capacity of fat to absorb energy from microwaves, fats can become dangerously hot in a microwave oven. For this reason and because of the hazard presented by the potential spattering when water-containing foods are placed in very hot, deep fat, deep-fat frying in a microwave oven is not recommended.

A direct relationship appears to exist between the chemical structure of a fat or a fatty acid and its ability to absorb microwaves. The temperature of unsaturated fats tends to rise more rapidly than the temperature of saturated fats. For example, a hollandaise sauce made with butter requires a longer microwaving time than one prepared with margarine because of the difference in fatty acid content.

Protein

Microwave and conventional methods can irreversibly denature proteins. An excessive denaturation of protein leads to toughness. Proteins and protein-containing foods must be heated carefully to avoid overcooking and toughening, which occur with too long a cooking time or too high a power level. The rapidly induced heating by microwaves promotes overcooking and coagulation.

Vitamins

The rapid heating of foods by microwaves favors the retention of ascorbic acid. Many microwaved foods are cooked without added water, minimizing the loss of water-soluble nutrients. Microwaved foods are believed to retain a high level of the vitamins in food.

Enzymes

Most undesirable oxidizing enzymes are quickly inactivated by the rapid heating of foods by microwaves. Microwaves quickly destroy the enzymes that convert sugar to starch, thus enabling vegetables such as peas and corn to retain their sweet flavor.

MICROWAVE-COOKERY APPLICATIONS

Foods are prepared for cooking in the same manner as for conventional cookery. Some foods are especially suitable for microwaving; others are not.

Breads

Quick breads rise well but do not develop a brown crust as in conventional baking. Procedures for microwaved yeast breads require further development. A satisfactory product is produced when yeast breads are risen at low power setting that allows yeast to remain active long enough to make breads light.

Cereals and Starch-Thickened Products

Ready-to-cook cereals cook quickly and satisfactorily in serving bowls. Although most casseroles can be cooked by microwaves, at times the flavors may be less well blended than with slow, conventional cookery.

Microwave-cooked gravies, sauces, and starch puddings are highly acceptable. Flour- and starch-thickened products are stirred well once during cooking, and with the final stirring there is sufficient movement to avoid lumping. The heat must be carefully controlled to avoid overcooking starch and possible reversion or thinning.

Fruits and Vegetables

Fruits cook rapidly in their own juice when microwaved and retain their fresh flavor, texture, and nutrients. Microwaved vegetables retain their vitamins and fresh color, flavor, texture, and are very acceptable. Overcooking must be avoided to retain the bright color and fork-tender crispness of vegetables. Cut-up or whole vegetables may be microwaved. Whole potatoes should be punctured and placed on paper towels and, when cooking more than one, rearranged once. Stem vegetables, such as asparagus, may need about two tablespoons of added water. Table 24–4 gives directions for microwave cooking of some vegetables.

Meats

Carefully cooked by microwaves and protected from overcooking, tender cuts of meat retain their moisture and good flavor. The problem of poor surface browning normally found in microwaved meats can be overcome with a ceramic browning platter.

Bones interfere with heat distribution and should be removed. Small, tender, uniform-shaped boneless roasts are best suited for microwaving. Roasts are rotated to avoid the development of hot spots. The red color of meat is changed to brown during heating. This color change occurs more readily in the interior and in certain hot spots than on the surface. Because overcooking toughens meats, it is wise to undercook and test; and also to avoid toughening, meats are salted after microwaving.

Microwaving does not tenderize less-tender meat cuts. For those cuts it is better to us conventional methods—long, slow cooking in moist heat during which collagen is converted to gelatin.

Bacon and ham microwave satisfactorily and may be cooked on paper toweling. A waxed paper cover prevents spattering.

Poultry

All poultry cooks well with microwaves unless it requires long, slow cooking, such as stewing chicken. Whole birds should be cooked on a nonmetal trivet to keep them out of the juices. Wing tips and drumsticks may be shielded with aluminum foil to prevent overcooking. Poultry pieces should be rearranged during cooking to prevent overheating.

Fish

Shell-and finfish microwave satisfactorily. They are cooked only until they become opaque or flake easily. Microwaved seafoods remain moist and are tender.

Table 24–4 How to Microwave Vegetables

Vegetable	Quantity	Preparation/Method	Full Power Cook Time Minutes
Fresh			
Asparagus	1 lb	Wash, trim, cut. Place in 1–½-qt casserole with ¼ cup water; cover tightly.	6
Beans, green	3 cups	Wash, cut. Place in 1–½-qt casserole with ¼ cup water; cover tightly.	10–12
Broccoli	1½ lb	Wash, cut into uniform spears. Place in 3-qt casserole with ¼ cup water; cover tightly.	10–11
Carrots	2 cups	Wash, scrape, cut into ½-in-thick slices. Place in 2-qt casserole with ¼ cup water; cover tightly.	6–8
Cauliflower	2 cups	Wash, separate into flowerets. Place in 1–½-qt casserole with 2 tablespoons water; cover tightly.	6–8
Peas, green	2 cups	Wash, shell. Place in 1–½-qt casserole with 2 tablespoons water; cover tightly.	6
Potatoes, baked	2 medium	Wash, prick. Place in oven on paper towel. Rearrange halfway through cook time.	5–6
boiled	4 large	Wash, peel. Place in 2-qt casserole with ¼ cup water. Cover tightly.	10–12
Frozen			
Asparagus, cut	10 oz	Place in covered 1-qt casserole with 2 tablespoons water. Stir halfway through cooking time.	5–6
Beans, green, cut	10 oz	Place in covered 1-qt casserole with 2 tablespoons water. Stir halfway through cooking time.	5–7
Broccoli, spears	8 oz	Place in covered 1-qt casserole with 2 tablespoons water. Stir halfway through cooking time.	5–7
Carrots	10 oz	Place in covered 1-qt casserole with 1 tablespoon water. Stir halfway through cooking time.	5–7
Cauliflower	10 oz	Place in covered 1-qt casserole with 2 tablespoons water. Stir halfway through cooking time.	4–5
Mixed vegetables	10 oz	Place in covered 1-qt casserole with 2 tablespoons water. Stir halfway through cooking time.	4–5½
Peas, green	10 oz	Place in covered 1-qt casserole with 2 tablespoons water. Stir halfway through cooking time.	5–6

Beverages

Microwaved instant beverages have an acceptable flavor. Individual cups of previously brewed coffee or tea reheat successfully in a microwave oven. Cocoa, chocolate, and hot fruit beverages are easily prepared in large glass containers or individual cups and are very acceptable.

Cakes and Cookies

Microwaved cakes cook quickly but do not develop a brown crust. Shortened cakes have a greater volume and moistness than conventionally baked cakes. Angel cakes are only satisfactory when the heat is very well controlled. Overcooking toughens cakes as well as all other baked products. Microwaved cakes are done when a wooden pick inserted off center comes out clean. The few moist spots on the surface will disappear on standing.

Low-fat, low-moisture doughs and bar cookies yield satisfactory microwaved products. A pale crust is camouflaged when brown sugar, molasses, chocolate, or other colorful ingredients or frostings are used.

Pastry

Pie and pastry shells bake adequately and become flaky, but do not brown. Crumb crusts may be more pleasing to the eye. Sogginess can be avoided by precooking the pastry before the filling is added. Stirring of the filling and rotation may be required.

Candies and Frostings

Candies and frostings are quickly and successfully prepared. Sugar melts quickly and caramelizes (owing to loss of water), to become brown in color. Microwaved candies require less stirring and do not scorch on the bottom of the pan.

MICROWAVING AND AESTHETIC CHARACTERISTICS

Appearance

Microwaved foods often lack the brown crust and pleasing appearance of conventionally cooked foods. Condiments, sauces, coloring, frosting, powders, and other additions contribute eye appeal and act as a substitute for the browning. These additions will also absorb any surface moisture.

Color

Chlorophyll is the plant pigment most vulnerable to microwave and conventional cooking. Green vegetables are very easily overcooked and require very careful timing. Overcooking changes the bright green color to a drab olive green.

Meat pigments change from the bright red of oxymyoglobin to the characteristic brown color of denatured globin hemichrome of well-done meats during both microwave and conventional cookery. The iron present in the color pigment is changed from the reddish ferrous to a brownish ferric form. This change occurs more readily inside microwaved meat than on the surface.

Aroma and Flavor

The aroma of microwaved food is generally pleasing but different from that of conventionally cooked food. The cooking vapors from microwaved foods pass more readily into the surrounding atmosphere, and that may be responsible for the difference in aromas. Cooking may enhance, reduce, or cause no change in, the aroma or flavor of food.

Overcooking must be avoided during conventional and microwave cookery to develop and retain the desirable flavors of food. Flavor components develop differently during various conditions of cookery. Some flavor components may be lost in cooking vapors, and others may be decomposed to form less-acceptable flavors.

Texture

Textural qualities of all cooked foods are influenced by the ingredients used, the mixing and cookery techniques, and the control of the techniques used. In microwave cooking, textural quality can be controlled by using variable power levels and careful timing.

Fruits and vegetables soften when cooked owing to changes in pectic substances. Some vegetables cooked in microwave ovens require the addition of a small quantity of water, apparently to aid in their softening. Microwaved overcooked carrots shrivel and lose color. Most vegetables can be microwaved successfully, and some are superior to those conventionally cooked.

The porous texture of cakes is due to the rapid heating of microwaves. The denaturation and toughening of protein-rich foods can be controlled or avoided during microwaving with lower power levels, shielding or covering, and careful timing.

COMPLEMENTARY MICROWAVE COOKERY

Complementary sequences can be developed for the use of microwave and conventional cookery. The rapidity of microwave cookery necessitates a change in the order in which foods are prepared, and the sequence may be very different from that followed when only conventional methods are used.

It is essential to use the instruction manual provided with the microwave oven. There may be differences in terms and operations among microwave ovens. Mastery of microwave cooking begins with the simple foods that cook or heat in familiar ways, such as beverages, sauces, or vegetables. Then the next step is to prepare foods that involve some change in techniques, but yield familiar results.

With experience, you will know which foods are better in the microwave and which ones should be cooked by conventional methods. Preferences may be based on convenience, speed, texture, flavor, or color. These preferences can be the basis of a plan for meal preparation in which complementary microwave and conventional methods are used.

It may be more practical to microwave individual foods than to combine several different foods as for conventional cookery. When the oven load is increased by cooking several foods at once or by cooking larger quantities of the same food, microwave cooking time must be increased proportionally.

MENU PLANNING FOR MICROWAVING

As with conventional cooking, plan meals so that all the foods will not require last-minute attention. The microwaving of some foods may be interrupted without harm to the food while the cooking of other foods is begun. A recipe that requires standing time can be microwaved first and another food cooked while the first stands. Dishes prepared in advance may be reheated quickly to serving temperature.

Generally, meats and main-dish casseroles are microwaved first. A standing time of four to six minutes is recommended for frozen and most fresh vegetables. During this time beverages and breads may be microwaved. Many desserts may be microwaved well in advance of serving time. Other desserts, such as defrosted frozen cakes or pastries and warm fruit desserts, may be microwaved while dishes from the main course are cleared from the table.

CONVERSION OF CONVENTIONAL RECIPES FOR MICROWAVE

Some conventional recipes may be adapted for microwave cooking. First determine whether a recipe is for a dish that will microwave well. Identify cookery techniques that are similar to microwaving techniques, such as covering, cooking in liquid, or steaming. Foods that require a dry surface or crispness are usually preferred when cooked in a conventional oven. A converted recipe may yield a product somewhat different from that cooked conventionally, but results can be acceptable and pleasing.

If the recipe is judged to be suitable for microwaving, refer to similar recipes for microwaved food in order to determine power level and timing. Recipes for moist, rich cakes, candies, and moist meat loaves do not require any changes. Because liquid does not evaporate rapidly when microwaved, it is desirable to reduce the quantity of liquid or increase the amount of thickening in sauces and gravies. Because the lack of evaporation intensifies flavors the quantity of seasonings may be reduced. Any ingredient that takes longer to microwave than others in the recipe can be replaced with a precooked or quick-cooking form, for example, minute rice for regular rice. When the adapted recipe works out satisfactorily, record all necessary changes, or rewrite the recipe for microwaving and save it for future use.

SUMMARY

The magnetron tube produces microwaves from electricity in the microwave oven. Microwave ovens use electromagnetic radiation to excite water molecules in food. Friction between molecules produce heat in the food, causing it to cook. Microwaves penetrate to a depth of three-fourths to one and one-half inches on all sides. They generate heat in the areas they penetrate but do not produce chemical changes in food. Speed is the major advantage of the microwave oven.

Containers made of glass, paper, china, and most plastics are recommended for microwaving. Metals reflect microwaves and should not be used in a microwave oven. Microwaves are used to cook, reheat, and defrost foods.

Microwave cooking is concerned with time and is influenced by density, size and shape, volume, starting temperature, and fat and sugar content of food. Techniques employed in cooking influence cooking time and include covering, stirring, arranging, turning, rotating, and shielding; standing time must also be considered.

The use of very little additional water and rapid heating favor the retention of nutrients by microwaved foods. Logical complementary microwave and conventional cookery sequences are easily developed on the basis of time involved in preparing, cooking, and serving the meal.

SELF-STUDY GUIDE

1. In what ways does microwave cookery differ from conventional cooking?
2. Describe the nature of microwaves.
3. Identify four types of appropriate utensils for microwaving.
4. How do the following factors influence microwave cooking: time, density, volume, starting temperature, fat and sugar content?
5. How do the following techniques influence microwave cooking time: arrangement of food, covering, stirring, standing time? Why?
6. Which three techniques of cookery can be successfully carried out in a microwave oven?
7. Which products are not likely to be successfully prepared in a microwave oven? Give four examples.
8. How are conventional and microwave cookery techniques integrated? Give two examples.
9. Discuss the influence of microwaves on protein and vitamins.

SUGGESTED READINGS

Better Homes and Gardens. *More from your microwave.* Des Moines: Meredith Corporation, 1981.

BODRERO, K. O.; PEARSON, A. M.; and MAGEE, W. T. Optimum cooking times for flavor development and evaluation of flavor quality of beef cooked by microwaves and conventional methods. *Journal of Food Science* 45:613, 1980.

BRITTIN, H. C., and TREVINO, J. E. Acceptabilty of microwave and conventionally baked potatoes. *Journal of Food Science* 45:1425, 1980.

CHUNG, S. Y.; MORR, C. V.; and JEN, J. J. Effect of microwaves and conventional cooking on the nutritive value of colossus peas (vigna uniguiculata). *Journal of Food Science* 46:272, 1981.

CURNUTTE, B. Principles of microwave radiation. *Journal of Food Protection* 43:618, 1980.

DAHL, C. A. and MATTHEWS, M. E. Cook/chill food service system with microwave oven, thiamin content in portions of beef loaf after microwave-heating. *Journal of Food Science* 45:608, 1980.

———. Effects of microwave heating in cook/chill food service systems. *Journal of the American Dietetic Association* 77:289, 1980.

HALL, K. N. Effect of cooking rates in electric or microwave oven on cooking losses and retention of thiamin in broilers. *Journal of Food Science* 46:1292, 1981.

HILL, M., and REAGAN, S. P. Effect of microwave and conventional baking on yellow cakes. *Journal of the American Dietetic Association* 80:52, 1982.

JOHNSTON, M. B., and BALDWIN, R. E. Influence of microwave reheating on selected quality factors of roast beef. *Journal of Food Science* 45:1460, 1980.

KHAN, A. R., et al. Degradation of starch polymers by microwave energy. *Cereal Chemistry* 56:303, 1979.

KLEIN, B. P.; KUO, C. H. Y.; and BOYD, G. Folacin and ascorbic acid retention in fresh raw microwave and conventionally cooked spinach. *Journal of Food Science* 46:640, 1981.

KLEIN, L. B., and MONDY, N. I. Comparison of microwave, conventional baking potatoes in relation to nitrogenous constituents and mineral composition. *Journal of Food Science* 46:1874, 1981.

MAI, J.; TSAI, C. H.; ARMBRUSTER, G.; CHO, P.; and KINSELLA, J. E. Effect of microwave cooking on food fatty acids; no evidence of chemical alteration or isomerization. *Journal of Food Science* 45:1753, 1980.

MOORE, L. J.; HARRISON, D. L.; and DAYTON, A. D. Differences among top round steaks cooked by dry and moist heat in a conventional or microwave oven. *Journal of Food Science* 45:777, 1980.

MUDGETT, R. E. Electrical properties of foods in microwave processing. *Food Technology* 36:109, 1982.

POUR-EL, A.; NELSON, S. O.; PECK, E. E.; TJHIO, B.; and STETSON, L. E. Biological properties of VHF and microwave heated soybeans. *Journal of Food Science* 46:880, 1981.

SHAPIRO, R. G., and BAYNER, J. F. Microwave heating in glass containers. *Food Technology* 36:46, 1982.

Standards sought for cookware used in microwave ovens. *Plastics World* 38:14, 1980.

TSEN, C. C. Microwave energy for bread baking and its effect on the nutritive value of bread. *Journal of Food Protection* 43:638, 1980.

WROLSTAD, R. E., et al. Effect of microwave blanching on the color and composition of strawberry concentrate. *Journal of Food Science* 45:1573, 1980.

ZIMMERMAN, W. J. An approach to safe microwave cooking of pork roasts containing Trichinella spiralis. *Journal of Food Science* 48:1715, 1983.

GLOSSARY

Acrolein: Irritating compound formed when glycerol is heated to a high temperature.

Actin: A globular protein in thin filaments in muscle fibers.

Aerated: Contains trapped bubbles of air or gas to lighten a mixture.

Agglomerate: To clump or gather a very fine substance into coarse granules for ease of blending.

Albumen: The white portion of the egg.

Amphoteric: Refers to substances such as amino acids or proteins that carry both negative (carboxyl group) and positive charges (amino group). Depending on the specific substances, at some level of acidity it becomes neutral and usually precipitates from solution.

Amylase: A straight chain fragment of starch.

Amylopectin: A branched chain fragment of starch.

Analog: Product processed in various forms from soy protein to resemble specific meat products.

Anthocyanins: Red, purple, and blue pigments in vegetables and fruits. They are water soluble and sensitive to acid.

Anthoxanthins: White, colorless pigment in vegetables and fruits, which change to creamy white/yellow in alkali.

Antioxidant: A compound that retards oxidative rancidity in fats.

Art: A skill in performance. Use of skill, taste, and creative imagination in the production of aesthetic objects and works.

Assessment: Systematic procedure to determine degree of perfection or quality present in terms of established standards.

Astringent: A puckery, dry sensation created in the mouth by some components in foods. Examples: in some brewed beverages, unripe fruits.

Bake: To cook in an oven, in a covered or uncovered pan.

Baste: To moisten a food while cooking, with melted fat, meat drippings, sauce, or other liquid to add flavor and prevent drying of surface.

Bavarian Cream: A dessert consisting of whipped gelatin combined with whipped cream.

Beat: To smooth a mixture or to introduce air

into it by using a brisk, regular motion that lifts the mixture over and over.

Blend: To mix two or more ingredients until thoroughly dispersed or evenly mixed.

Body: A characteristic of frozen desserts related to firmness or resistance to rapid melting.

Boil: To cook in water or other liquid in which bubbles rise continually and break on the surface. The temperature of boiling water at sea level is 212° F (100° C).

Broil: To cook by placing food beneath a direct source of heat.

Bromelin: An enzyme in fresh pineapple that degrades protein.

Caffeine: A stimulant, which contributes some bitterness and acts as a diuretic.

Capon: A fleshy, unsexed male chicken.

Caramelization: The heating of sugar or sugar-containing food until a brown color and characteristic flavor develop.

Carotenoids: Yellow-to-orange, some pink-to-red pigments in vegetables and fruits.

Carrier: An individual who does not develop the disease or illness but carries a disease organism and thus promotes contamination and spread of a disease.

Casein: The principal protein of milk.

Charlotte: Whipped gelatin and whipped cream combined and molded on lady fingers or sponge cake served as dessert.

Cheese: A food prepared from milk curds that are heated, drained, salted, pressed, and ripened.

Chemical: A substance produced by, or used in, a chemical process.

Chlorophyll: Green pigment in plant tissue.

Coagulate: Refers to an often irreversible change in protein that leads to curdling, clotting, or precipitation; may be due to mechanical action or heat.

Collagen: The insoluble protein of connective tissues, bones, tendons, and skins of animals converted to soluble gelatin by moist heat, dilute acids, or alkalies.

Colloid: Refers to a subdivision of particles that are microscopic in size and do not dissolve but remain uniformly distributed in another medium, which can be a solid, a liquid or a gas.

Colloidal: Refers to dispersion of very small particles in a second medium—a solid, a liquid, or a gas. Colloidal particles are an intermediate between very small particles found in true solutions and large particles in a suspension.

Compote: Fruit stewed in a syrup, served as dessert.

Controlled Atmosphere: Long-term storage conditions designed to provide optimal temperature and humidity and in which carbon dioxide replaces air to retard respiration. Used to store fruits commercially for relatively long periods.

Converted Rice: Rice that is parboiled to draw nutrients from the bran layers into the endosperm before the bran layers are removed.

Cream: To incorporate air into fat by beating to form a light, fluffy mass.

Crisping: The process of restoring crispness to limp plant products by rinsing with cold water and then refrigerating in covered container or plastic bag.

Crystallization: The process of forming grains, granules, or crystals of regular shape, such as ice or sugar crystals.

Cultured: Introduction of specific microorganisms to milk products to develop desired acidic flavor.

Curd: The coagulated or thickened part of milk that contains protein and which is induced by acid, enzymes, salts, and heat.

Curdle: Refers to the change from a smooth liquid or gel to one in which clots separate in a watery medium.

Curing: A process during which nitrite reacts with myoglobin pigment of meat to produce a bright pink color stable to cooking.

Cut In: To finely divide solid fat into a flour mixture.

Denaturation: A change in protein shape caused by factors of heat, agitation, acid, or enzyme.

Denatured Protein: An alteration in the structure of the original protein molecule due to an unfolding of the chain that usually leads to a change in molecular shape and/or solubility. The alteration may be due to heat, agitation, freezing, high pressure, salts, or acids.

Density: Closeness or compactness of a substance; ratio of mass to volume.

Dextrin: Polysaccharide formed during the partial hydrolysis of starch molecules by heat, acid, or enyzme.

Dextrinization: Breaking down of starch molecules to dextrins by dry heat.

Disperse: To distribute or scatter a component in some other substance.

Dispersion: Consists of dispersed particles in

another medium. Example, gelatin scattered in a cold liquid.

Elastin: Insoluble protein holding muscle fibers in meat; is not changed during cooking.

Emulsifier: A substance such as lecithin that aids the uniform dispersion of a substance, such as oil in water. Used to promote the development and stability of emulsions in salad dressing.

Emulsify: To disperse one liquid in another liquid to form an emulsion.

Emulsion: A dispersion of one liquid in another with which it does not usually blend.

Enriched Cereal: Refined cereals to which thiamin, riboflavin, niacin, and iron have been added at levels specified by federal regulations.

Enzymes: Substances found in plant and animal cells where they function as organic catalysts in chemical reactions, controlling speed of the reactions.

Ester: The compound formed when an organic acid and an alcohol interact. For example, glycerol (an alcohol) and fatty acid (organic acid) join to form an ester.

Fat: A compound composed of three molecules of fatty acid combined with one molecule of glycerol.

Ferment: To convert a complex organic substance into smaller molecules by action of microorganisms. Example: developing flavor and color components in cacao, tea leaves, coffee beans.

Fermentation: Breakdown of organic substances into smaller molecules by yeast and bacteria. Example: yeast ferments sugar to carbon dioxide and alcohol.

Fillet: A flat, boneless slice or piece of meat or fish. A lengthwise slice of fish cut parallel to the backbone.

Flakiness: Describes the texture and appearance of thin layers of baked dough separated by open spaces, which form flakes when cut or broken.

Flavonoids: Phenolic compounds. A heterogeneous group of water-soluble pigments that include anthocyanins and the flavones, flavonols, and flavanones. The last three compounds grouped are known as anthoxanthins.

Foam: Air or a gas dispersed in a liquid.

Fold: Applies to incorporation of a foam into another mixture by cutting vertically through mixture with a spoon or whisk and then turning over and sliding implement across bottom of bowl and up the side, across top, repeating motion until mixture is evenly distributed.

Foodborne Poisoning: A commonly used term for foodborne illness caused by microbial toxins.

Food Illness: An illness caused by microorganisms such as bacteria, mold, virus, or toxins present in food consumed.

Food Safety: Procedures/actions that retain wholesomeness and quality of food; that reduce or eliminate contamination with harmful substances and retain the nutritional and overall eating quality of food.

Fortification: Addition of nutrients to a food but not necessarily the nutrients that were originally present. Larger amounts of nutrients may be added than were naturally present in the food.

Fowl: A general term for a matured bird either male or female.

Fricassee: Usually applied to cooking pieces of fowl, veal, or rabbit by braising.

Gel: To thicken, become firm, retain shape. A colloidal system that is like a solid, yet retains shape of the container.

Gelatinization: The swelling and thickening of starch granules when heated in water.

Gelation: The formation of a gel.

Glaze: To coat with a thin layer of sugar syrup cooked to the crack stage. Example: glazed fruit.

Gluten: A substance with an elastic characteristic formed from insoluble wheat proteins when dough is manipulated.

Holding: The length of time a microcooked food will stay hot if properly covered or wrapped.

Homogenize: To break up into small particles, such as fat globules in milk, which do not separate.

Hydrate: The absorption of water, often accompanied by swelling due to intake or absorption of water.

Hydration: Absorption of water by another compound.

Hydrogenation: A process in which unsaturated fatty acids combine chemically with hydrogen to produce a fat with a higher melting point than the original oil.

Hydrolysis: Splitting of a substance into smaller units by reaction with water.

Hygroscopic: Tendency of a substance to absorb water rapidly.

Ice: Frozen dessert prepared with fruit juice or pulp, water, and sugar; may include some gelatin or egg white.

Immiscible: Describes a substance that cannot be blended or mixed but instead separates.

Infection: Occurs when disease-producing microorganisms are present in food consumed.

Intoxication: Occurs when poisonous substances (toxins) are present in food consumed.

Inversion: Chemical change during which sucrose is split into its monosaccharide components of glucose and fructose. This change may be induced by the enzyme invertase or by heating sucrose in presence of acid.

Isoelectric: To have the same electric charge; a net charge of zero or neutral.

Knead: To manipulate dough with a pushing, stretching, and folding motion to develop gluten and redistribute ingredients.

Lactose: Enzyme that degrades milk sugar (lactose) to glucose and galactose.

Leavener: A substance that contributes a gas, such as carbon dioxide, to lighten a mixture.

Legumes: Plants that can fix nitrogen and yield seeds in pods. Examples: beans, peas, soybeans.

Limiting Amino Acid: Essential amino acid not present in a food or lacking in quantity to meet human needs.

Lipid: Group of organic compounds soluble in fat solvents (ether, carbon tetrachloride, etc.) but insoluble in water.

Lycopene: A red pigment in vegetables and fruits such as tomato, red grapefruit, and watermelon; classed as a carotenoid.

Maillard Reaction: A browning reaction due to the interaction of an aldehyde group from sugar and an amino group from a protein, which form many complex substances.

Marinade: A mixture of oil, acid, and seasoning in which foods are placed for flavor enhancement or tenderizing.

Marinate: To let food remain in a marinade to impart flavor or to tenderize.

Meat Alternates: Food with a protein content similar to that of meat; can replace meat in the diet.

Meat Extender: Food with a bland flavor that extends pleasing flavors and number of servings of food of animal origin, relatively inexpensive.

Microbial: Refers to action/activity of microorganisms such as bacteria, mold, yeast.

Microbiological: Deals with microscopic forms of life such as bacteria.

Microwaves: Nonionizing electromagnetic waves of short wave length and high frequency; produced by a magnetron tube, which converts electrical energy into microwave radiation.

Microwaving: Cooking foods with microwaves enclosed in a metal box (oven).

Mold: To shape into a desired form.

Monounsaturates: Fatty acids with one double bond.

Mousse: A cream thickened with gelatin and combined with whipped cream. A rich dessert.

Myoglobin: An iron-protein complex responsible for the color of muscle.

Myosin: A muscle protein found in fibrils; makes up more than half the total muscle protein. It combines with actin to form actomyosin, which is responsible for the contractile property of muscle.

Natural Cheese: Made of curds prepared from milk, whey, or a mixture of these; may be ripened to develop desired flavor, body, and texture.

Objective: Something observable, perceptible to persons, verifiable; exists independent of mind.

Organic: A compound with carbon in the molecule.

Organic Acids: Acids that contain carbon. Examples: citric and tartaric in fruits.

Oven Spring: Refers to rapid increase in yeast dough or batter volume during first few minutes of baking due to the expansion of carbon dioxide produced by yeast.

Overrun: The increase in volume of ice cream products due to air incorporated during the freezing process.

Pan-broil: To cook uncovered in a hot skillet or fry pan.

Pan-fry: To cook in a small amount of fat.

Papain: Enzyme that degrades protein, found in juice of papaya (a tropical plant); used to tenderize meat.

Parboil: To boil until partly cooked for further cooking or processing.

Pare: To cut outside covering, as the skin of an apple.

Parfait: A dessert made of custard, syrup, and

whipped cream and frozen without agitation. Also a dessert made with layers of ice cream, fruit, syrup, and whipped cream.

Pasta: Extruded (spaghetti, macaroni) or rolled (noodles) flour products made from semolina (durum wheat flour).

Pasteurize: To preserve by heating a liquid (milk, fruit juice) to a specific temperature for a specified time to destroy harmful microorganisms.

Peel: To strip or pull off the outer covering, as the skin of a banana.

pH: Refers to the level of acidity or alkalinity of a substance on a numerical scale ranging from 1 for very acid to 14 for very alkaline; a pH value of 7 for neutral (neither acid nor alkaline).

Phosphate: A salt of phosphoric acid.

Physical: Relates to material things or natural laws, characterized or produced by forces.

Poach: To cook in a hot liquid, using precautions to retain shape.

Polyphenols: Organic compounds implicated in certain types of oxidative enzymatic browning in foods that include an unsaturated ring with more than one hydroxyl group on it.

Polyunsaturated Fatty Acid: A fatty acid having two or more double bonds.

Pot Roast: Large piece of meat cooked (braised) slowly in a covered utensil in a small amount of liquid or steam.

Power Level: Refers to amount of power utilized on a specific setting. Most microwave ovens have power settings ranging from high (fast cooking) to low power (slow cooking).

Precipitate: The solid part of a solution; separates from the liquid. To separate in a solid form from a state of solution.

Probe: Special piece of equipment to measure internal temperature of food and turn microwave off or switch over to keep warm setting automatically when food reaches the preset temperature.

Process Cheese: A blend of shredded fresh and aged natural cheeses to yield a cheese with desired characteristics.

Processing: Techniques such as milling, flaking, granulating, enriching, and precooking applied to the original product in its preparation for the market.

Proofing: Generally refers to rising of yeast dough or batter to increase volume, usually until doubled, in preparation for baking.

Proteolytic Enzymes: Enzymes capable of splitting protein into smaller units.

Rancidity: A chemical change in fats and oils that causes a disagreeable odor and taste.

Reheating: Warming foods prepared in advance to serving temperature.

Rehydrate: To restore moisture lost during drying by soaking in water or cooking slowly.

Rennet: An extract containing the enzyme rennin, obtained from stomach of calf.

Restored: Addition of optional nutrients, along with the enrichment nutrients (thiamin, riboflavin, niacin, iron), such as calcium, vitamin D, and ascorbic acid, to restore some of the milling losses.

Retrogradation: A process of gel formation or precipitation. Amylase becomes less soluble and recrystallizes.

Reversion: An oxidative deterioration, which causes an undesirable flavor change in fats.

Rheology: Science dealing with deformation and flow of matter.

Rigor Mortis: The stiffening and rigidity of muscles that occurs in the animal carcass shortly after slaughter.

Ripening: A holding process during which desired flavor, aroma, and texture develop due to the action of microorganisms, enzymes, or a combination of these, which initiate chemical and physical changes in the food.

Rise: Allowing yeast dough to rest in a warm place while carbon dioxide is produced by yeast (during fermentation) to increase dough volume.

Rotating: In microwaving, giving the container of food a quarter or half turn to bring the food into a new energy pattern and help it heat evenly.

Roux: A blend of flour and fat heated but not browned, used as a thickening agent in sauces and gravies.

Sample: Representative part from a larger whole or group.

Sanitation: Procedure/action that promotes and protects health and prevents the spread of disease agents—microorganisms and harmful substances.

Saturated Fatty Acid: A fatty acid with all the carbon atoms of the molecule linked by simple bonds.

Scallop: To bake pieces or cut-up foods in a

sauce or a liquid. The sauce may be blended with the food, or layers of food and sauce may be alternated in a baking dish. There may be a crumb topping.

Science: A systematic knowledge of a subject attained through study. Knowledge and general truths based on scientific principles.

Sensory: Relates to sensation or the senses.

Sherbet: Frozen dessert made of fruit ice with milk, egg white, or gelatin.

Shielding: Protecting areas of a food that cook quickly with pieces of foil to prevent overcooking so rest of the food may complete cooking.

Sift: To use a sieve or flour sifter to mix flour or other dry ingredients in order to aerate or to separate coarse particles from the fine.

Simmer: To cook in liquid maintained at just below the boiling point (185–210° F, 84–99° C).

Sol: A colloidal system with water or liquid as the dispersing medium.

Solute: A dissolved substance, such as salt or sugar, distributed evenly through a solution.

Solution: Contains dissolved particles that do not settle out or filter. A solution consists of two or more substances—one substance dissolves the others.

Solvent: The substance that contains the dissolved particles in a solution. In cookery the solvent is usually water.

Soufflé: A light, spongy baked dish made with beaten egg whites, thick cream sauce, and other ingredients to contribute desired flavor.

Spanish Cream: Stirred egg custard containing hydrated gelatin served as a dessert.

Standing Time: The time during which microwaved foods stand covered to permit completion of cooking and to develop flavor.

Steak: A slice of meat. Cross-section slice of a large fish.

Steam: To cook in steam, usually on a rack or in a perforated pan over boiling water, with or without pressure.

Stew: To simmer a food in a small quantity of liquid.

Stir: To mix foods or mixtures with a circular motion to blend.

Subjective: Based upon one's own feelings.

Superglycerinated: Fats with 2 or 3 percent added monoglycerides to improve the emulsification property of the shortening.

Supersaturated: Describes solution containing more of a substance than will normally dissolve.

Syneresis: The separation of liquid from a gel.

Tartrate: A salt of tartaric acid.

Technology: The means used to provide goods and materials needed for human maintenance and comfort. Science of industrial arts and manufactures.

Texture: Refers to the structure or feel of food and includes properties such as creaminess, graininess, crumbliness, firmness, crispness, softness, roughness, smoothness.

Textured Vegetable Protein: Prepared from high-protein-flour mixture spun or extruded to develop desired texture and processed into meat extenders and imitation meat products, or analogs.

Theobromine: Chief stimulant in cocoa, chocolate.

Tofu: A cheeselike curd prepared from fermented soy milk.

Toxin: A harmful substance produced by living organisms such as bacteria.

Translucent: Appears partly transparent and with a shine or gloss.

Truss: To tie or skewer the legs and wings of fowl to the body to prevent drying or overcooking during roasting.

Vegan: An individual who excludes all foods of animal origin from diet, consumes only foods of plant origin.

Vegetarianism: A dietary in which plant foods rather than foods of animal origin are consumed.

Viscosity: A property of liquids that determines whether they flow readily (degree or resistance to flow).

Viscous: Sufficiently thick to resist flow.

Volatile: A substance that easily yields a gas or a vapor.

Whey: The liquid portion of milk that remains after the curd (chiefly protein, casein) precipitates.

Whip: To incorporate air by beating to increase volume.

Winterize: A process during which vegetable oils are chilled and fat components that solidify at refrigerator temperature are removed.

INDEX